CN00729620

Your home from home

In many areas of the country B&Bs are a way of life and a vital part of the local economy. For visitors, it's a great way to get to know Scotland – and meet friendly, hospitable people who just love to welcome visitors into their own home.

From big cities to remote Highland glens, there are all sorts of places with comfortable rooms and tasty home-made food. It's an economical way to travel too and is ideal if you want the flexibility to stay a few days in one place and then move on to explore another.

Touring holidays will also be enhanced enormously by the local knowledge of your hosts. There's nothing better than starting the day with a hearty Scottish breakfast and a good planning session round the table, peppered with lots of tips and suggestions from folk who live in the local community.

A warm wel

When you've
forward to a
renowned fc
time like the
New Year with a wee dram, swirling your partner at a ceilidh or enjoying a sumptuous dinner for two in an exclusive restaurant with a stunning view, unforgettable experiences are never far away.

There's always the likelihood too that you'll meet some great folk – locals and visitors alike – some of whom could well become friends for life. That's all just part of a visit to Scotland.

As they say in the Gaelic tongue, *ceud mille failte* – 'a hundred thousand welcomes'. Come and enjoy our beautiful country.

ANGUS COUNCIL
CULTURAL SERVICES
WITHDRAWN
FROM STOCK

Plockton, looking across Loch Carron towards Applecross, Highlands

Join the Homecoming Scotland celebrations throughout 2009

HOMECOMING 2009

Join us in 2009 when Scotland will host its first ever Homecoming year which has been created and timed to mark the 250th anniversary of the birth of Scotland's national poet, the international cultural icon Robert Burns. From Burns Night to St Andrew's Day 2009 a country-wide programme of exciting and inspirational Homecoming events and activities will celebrate some of Scotland's great contributions to the world: Burns himself, Whisky, Golf, Great Scottish Minds and Innovations and our rich culture and heritage which lives on at home and through our global family. The best small country in the world.

From Orkney to Aberdeen, from Oban to the Scottish Borders, there will be a packed calendar of over 200 events and activities to choose from.

Here's a taste of what's on next year:

January 2009

Heralded by Scotland's internationally renowned Hogmanay Celebrations, the Homecoming Scotland 2009 programme will officially kick off on the weekend of Robert Burns' 250th anniversary (24-25 January) with a programme of high profile Burns events planned in key locations across Scotland.

Spring 2009

May is Whisky Month with an invitation extended to come to the Home of Whisky to explore and appreciate the expertise of the stillsmen and master blenders whose diligence has created one of Scotland's biggest exports and extensions of its culture. Kicking off at the biggest ever Spirit of Speyside Whisky Festival (1-10 May), the distilleries open their doors to visitors and locals alike. From a tasting session at The Scotch Whisky Experience in Edinburgh to a 3 day whisky course in Fife, there are a range of ways to sample Scotland's national tipple. New for 2009, The Spirit of the West event (16-17 May) in the beautiful surroundings of Inveraray Castle will provide a showcase for the 16 distilleries that make up the Whisky Coast. The month concludes with Feis Ile, Islay's Annual Malt and Music Festival.

Summer 2009

Over the summer months, Homecoming Scotland 2009 will present some brand new and enhanced major international events: The Gathering 2009 in Edinburgh (25-26 July) has been created especially for the Homecoming year to celebrate the contribution that Scottish clans have made to the history and culture of the world, whilst some of Scotland's stellar international events including The Edinburgh International Festival, The Edinburgh Military Tattoo, The Edinburgh International Book Festival and The Open Golf Championship will be celebrating the year with special Homecoming activity.

Autumn 2009

In October the Highlands will present a fortnight long festival (15-30 October, provisional dates) celebrating the best of traditional Highland Culture. Built around a major international conference exploring Scotland's Global Impact, regional and fringe events will take place across the region.

Closing Celebrations

In November around St Andrew's Day and as a sensational finale to the year, Homecoming Scotland will present a major celebration of Scottish Music (28-30 November, across Scotland). From traditional Scottish folk heroes to the cutting edge of contemporary Scottish bands currently making their mark internationally, expect a truly unique St Andrews Day celebration.

2009 is a special year for Scots and for those who love Scotland.

Look out for Homecoming events throughout this guide.

Go to homecomingscotland2009.com to find out more about all the different events.

homecomingscotland2009.com

Enjoy a dram in May, Homecoming Scotland's Whisky month

Top left: Two Hillwalkers take in the view from Sgurr A Ghreadaidh on the Black Cuillin Ridge towards Loch Curuisk, Isle of Skye. Top right: A puffin perches on a cliff edge, the Treshnish Isles, Inner Hebrides. Above: Sandy beach near Durness, Sutherland.

DON'T MISS

Walking

From the rolling hills in the south to the mountainous north, Scotland is perfect for walkers - whether it's a gentle stroll with the kids or a serious trek through the wilderness.

Beaches

Scotland's beaches are something special whether it's for a romantic stroll, or to try some surfing. Explore Fife's Blue Flag beaches or the breathtaking stretches of sand in the Outer Hebrides.

Wildlife

From dolphins in the Moray Firth to capercaillie in the Highlands and seals and puffins on the coastline, you never know what you might spot.

Culture & Heritage

From the mysterious standing stones in Orkney and the Outer Hebrides to Burns Cottage and Rosslyn Chapel, Scotland's fascinating history can be encountered throughout the country.

Rosslyn Chapel, Roslin, Midlothian

Adventure

From rock climbing to sea kayaking, you can do it all. Try Perthshire for unusual adventure activities or the south of Scotland for some serious mountain biking.

Kayaking around the island of Vatersay, Outer Hebrides

Shopping

From designer stores to unique boutiques, from Glasgow's stylish city centre to Edinburgh's eclectic Old Town, Scotland is a shopper's paradise with lots of hidden gems to uncover.

Victoria Street, Edinburgh.

Golf

The country that gave the world the game of golf is still the best place to play it. With more than 500 courses in Scotland, take advantage of one of the regional golf passes on offer.

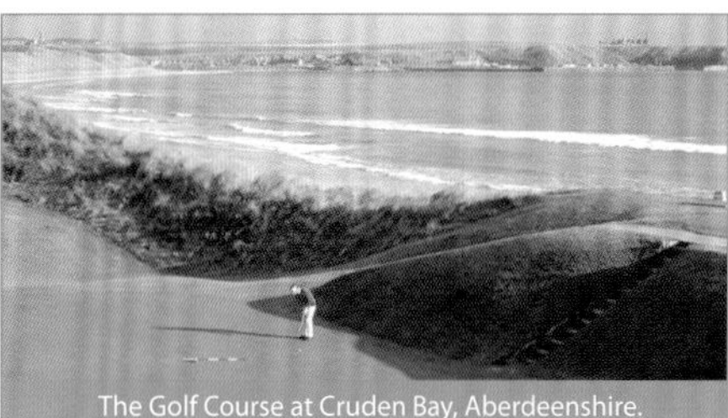

The Golf Course at Cruden Bay, Aberdeenshire.

Castles

Wherever you are in Scotland you are never far from a great Scottish icon, whether it's an impressive ruin or an imposing fortress, a fairytale castle or country estate.

Eilean Donan Castle, Loch Duich, Highlands.

Highland Games

From the famous Braemar Gathering in Aberdeenshire to the spectacular Cowal Highland Gathering in Argyll, hot foot it to some Highland Games action for pipe bands, dancers, and tossing the caber.

The sword dance at the Cowal Highland Gathering, Dunoon.

Events & Festivals

In Scotland there's so much going on with fabulous events and festivals throughout the year, especially this year of Homecoming Scotland 2009, from the biggest names to the quirky and traditional.

The Royal Mile during the Festival, Edinburgh

If you love food, get a taste of Scotland. Scotland's natural larder offers some of the best produce in the world. Scotland's coastal waters are home to an abundance of lobster, prawns, oysters and more, whilst the land produces world famous beef, lamb and game.

There's high quality food and drink on menus all over the country often cooked up by award-winning chefs in restaurants where the view is second to none. You'll find home cooking, fine dining, takeaways and tearooms. Whether you're looking for a family-friendly pub or a romantic Highland restaurant there's the perfect place to dine. And there's no better time to indulge than when you're on holiday!

Live it. Visit Scotland.
eatscotland.com 0845 22 55 121

Traditional fare

Haggis and whisky might be recognised as traditional Scottish fare but why not add cullen skink, clapshot, cranachan, and clootie dumpling to the list…discover the tastes that match such ancient names. Sample some local hospitality along with regional specialities such as the Selkirk Bannock or Arbroath Smokies. Or experience the freedom of eating fish and chips straight from the wrapper while breathing in the clear evening air. Visit **eatscotland.com** and see our 'Food & Drink' section to find out more.

Farmers' markets

Scotland is a land renowned for producing ingredients of the highest quality. You can handpick fresh local produce at farmers' markets in towns and cities across the country. Create your own culinary delights or learn from the masters at the world famous Nick Nairn Cook School in Stirling. Savour the aroma, excite your taste buds and experience the buzz of a farmers' market. To find out more visit the Farmers Market information on the **eatscotland.com** website that can be found in the 'Food & Drink' section.

EATING AND DRINKING

Events

Scotland serves up a full calendar of food and drink festivals. Events like Taste of Edinburgh and Highland Feast are a must for foodies. Whisky fans can share their passion at the Islay Malt Whisky Festival, the Highland Whisky Festival, or the Spirit of Speyside Whisky Festival. Visit **eatscotland.com** to find out more about the events and festivals that are on in the 'What's on' section.

Tours and trails

If you're a lover of seafood spend some time exploring the rugged, unspoilt coastline of mid-Argyll following The Seafood Trail. Or if you fancy a wee dram visit the eight distilleries and cooperage on the world's only Malt Whisky Trail in Speyside. Visit visitscotland.com/cafedays to find out more about some great cafés that our visitors have discovered and enjoy a cup of something lovely surrounded by amazing scenery.

EatScotland Quality Assurance Scheme

EatScotland is a nationwide Quality Assurance Scheme from VisitScotland. The scheme includes all sectors of the catering industry from chip shops, pubs and takeaways to restaurants.

A trained team of assessors carry out an incognito visit to assess quality, standards and ambience. Only those operators who meet the EatScotland quality standards are accredited to the scheme so look out for the logo to ensure you visit Scotland's best quality establishments.

The newly launched EatScotland Silver and Gold Award Scheme recognises outstanding standards, reflecting that an establishment offers an excellent eating out experience in Scotland.

To find great EatScotland places to dine throughout the country visit **eatscotland.com**

Beach at Elie in Fife

GREEN TOURISM

Scotland is a stunning destination and we want to make sure it stays that way. That's why we encourage all tourism operators including accommodation providers to take part in our Green Tourism Business Scheme. It means you're assured of a great quality stay at an establishment that's trying to minimise its impact on the environment.

VisitScotland rigorously assesses accommodation providers against measures as diverse as energy use, using local produce on menus, or promoting local wildlife walks or cycle hire. Environmentally responsible businesses can achieve Bronze, Silver or Gold awards, to acknowledge how much they are doing to help conserve the quality of Scotland's beautiful environment.

Look out for the Bronze, Silver and Gold Green Tourism logos throughout this guide to help you decide where to stay and do your bit to help protect our environment.

For a quick reference see our directory at the back of the book which highlights all quality assured accommodation that has been awarded the Gold, Silver or Bronze award.

green-business.co.uk

Bronze Green Tourism Award

Silver Green Tourism Award

Gold Green Tourism Award

Friendly faces... a wealth of helpful advice... loads of local knowledge... get the most out of your stay...

Visitor Information Centres are staffed by people 'in the know', offering friendly advice, helping to make your stay in Scotland the most enjoyable ever... whatever your needs!

LOCAL KNOWLEDGE • WHERE TO STAY • ACCOMMODATION BOOKING PLACES TO VISIT THINGS TO DO • MAPS AND GUIDES TRAVEL ADVICE • ROUTE PLANNING • WHERE TO SHOP AND EAT LOCAL CRAFTS AND PRODUCE • EVENT INFORMATION • TICKETS

VisitScotland, under the Scottish Tourist Board brand, administers the 5-star grading schemes which assess the quality and standards of all types of visitor accommodation and attractions from castles and historic houses to garden centres and arts venues. We grade around 80 per cent of the accommodation in Scotland and 90 per cent of the visitor attractions – so wherever you want to stay or visit, we've got it covered. The schemes are monitored all year round and each establishment is reviewed once a year. We do the hard work so you can relax and enjoy your holiday.

The promise of the stars:

★

It is clean, tidy and an acceptable, if basic, standard

★★

It is a good, all round standard

★★★

It is a very good standard, with attention to detail in every area

★★★★

It is excellent – using high quality materials, good food (except self-catering) and friendly, professional service

★★★★★

An exceptional standard where presentation, ambience, food (except self-catering) and service are hard to fault.

IT'S WRITTEN IN THE STARS...

How does the system work?

Our advisors visit and assess establishments on up to 50 areas from quality, comfort and cleanliness to welcome, ambience and service. If an establishment scores less than 60 per cent it will not be graded. The same star scheme now runs in England and Wales, so you can follow the stars wherever you go.

Graded visitor attractions

Visitor attractions from castles and museums to leisure centres and tours are graded with 1-5 stars depending on their level of customer care. The focus is on the standard of hospitality and service as well as presentation, quality of shop or café (if there is one) and toilet facilities.

We want you to feel welcome

Walkers Welcome and Cyclists Welcome. Establishments that carry the symbols below pay particular attention to the specific needs of walkers and cyclists.

 Cyclists Welcome

 Walkers Welcome

There are similar schemes for Anglers, Bikers, Classic Cars, Golfers, Children and Ancestral Tourism. Check with establishment when booking.

Access all areas

The following symbols will help visitors with physical disabilities to decide whether accommodation is suitable. The directory at the back of this book will highlight all quality assured establishments that have suitable accommodation.

 Unassisted wheelchair access

 Assisted wheelchair access

 Access for visitors with mobility difficulties

Further information:

Quality Assurance (at VisitScotland)
Tel: 01463 244111
Fax: 01463 244181
Email: qainfo@visitscotland.com

We welcome your comments on star-awarded properties
Tel: 01463 244122
Fax: 01463 244181
Email: qa@visitscotland.com

FOR A FULL LIST OF ALL OTHER SYMBOLS, PLEASE REFER TO THE BACK FOLD-OUT PAGE

The Glenfinnan Viaduct, near Fort William, Highlands

TRAVEL TO SCOTLAND

It's really easy to get to Scotland whether you choose to travel by car, train, plane, coach or ferry. And once you get here travel is easy as Scotland is a compact country.

By Air

Flying to Scotland couldn't be simpler with flight times from London, Dublin and Belfast only around one hour. There are airports at Edinburgh, Glasgow, Glasgow Prestwick, Aberdeen, Dundee and Inverness. The following airlines operate flights to Scotland (although not all airports) from within the UK and Ireland:

bmi
Tel: 0870 60 70 555
From Ireland: 1332 64 8181
flybmi.com

bmi baby
Tel: 0871 224 0224
From Ireland: 1 890 340 122
bmibaby.com

British Airways
Tel: 0844 493 0787
From Ireland: 1890 626 747
ba.com

Eastern Airways
Tel: 08703 669 100
easternairways.com

easyJet
Tel: 0905 821 0905
From Ireland: 1890 923 922
easyjet.com

Flybe
Tel: 0871 700 2000
From Ireland: 1392 268 529
flybe.com

Ryanair
Tel: 0871 246 0000
From Ireland: 0818 30 30 30
ryanair.com

Air France
Tel: 0870 142 4343
airfrance.co.uk

Aer Arann
Tel: 0870 876 76 76
From Ireland: 0818 210 210
aerarann.com

Jet2
Tel: 0871 226 1737
From Ireland: 0818 200017
jet2.com

AirBerlin
Tel: 0871 5000 737
airberlin.com

Aer Lingus
Tel: 0870 876 5000
From Ireland: 0818 365 000
aerlingus.com

By Rail

Scotland has major rail stations in Aberdeen, Edinburgh Waverley and Edinburgh Haymarket, Glasgow Queen Street and Glasgow Central, Perth, Stirling, Dundee and Inverness. There are regular cross border railway services from England and Wales, and good city links. You could even travel on the First ScotRail Caledonian Sleeper overnight train service from London and wake up to the sights and sounds of Scotland.

First ScotRail
Tel: 08457 55 00 33
scotrail.co.uk

Virgin Trains
Tel: 08457 222 333
virgintrains.co.uk

National Express East Coast
Tel: 08457 225 225
nationalexpresseastcoast.com

National Rail
Tel: 08457 484950
nationalrail.co.uk

By Road

Scotland has an excellent road network from motorways and dual carriageway linking cities and major towns, to remote single-track roads with passing places to let others by. Whether you are coming in your own car from home or hiring a car once you get here, getting away from traffic jams and out onto Scotland's quiet roads can really put the fun back into driving. Branches of the following companies can be found throughout Scotland:

Arnold Clark
Tel: 0845 607 4500
arnoldclarkrental.com

Avis Rent A Car
Tel: 08445 818 181
avis.co.uk

Budget
Tel: 0845 581 9998
budget.co.uk

easyCar
Tel: 08710 500444
easycar.com

Enterprise Rent-A-Car
Tel: 0870 350 3000
enterprise.co.uk

Europcar
Tel: 0870 607 5000
europcarscotland.co.uk

Hertz
Tel: 08708 44 88 44
hertz.co.uk

National Car Rental
Tel: 0870 400 4560
nationalcar.com

Sixt rent a car
Tel: 0844 499 3399
sixt.co.uk

By Ferry

Scotland has over 130 inhabited islands so ferries are important. And whether you are coming from Ireland or trying to get to the outer islands, you might be in need of a ferry crossing. Ferries to and around the islands are regular and reliable and most carry vehicles. These companies all operate ferry services around Scotland:

Stena Line
Tel: 08705 204 204
stenaline.co.uk

P&O Irish Sea
Tel: 0870 24 24 777
poirishsea.com

Caledonian MacBrayne
Tel: 08000 665000
calmac.co.uk

Western Ferries
Tel: 01369 704 452
western-ferries.co.uk

Northlink Ferries
Tel: 08456 000 449
northlinkferries.co.uk

By Coach

Coach connections include express services to Scotland from all over the UK, and there is a good network of coach services once you get here too. You could even travel on the Postbus – a special feature of the Scottish mail service which carries fare-paying passengers along with the mail in rural areas where there is no other form of transport, bringing a new dimension to travel.

National Express
Tel: 08705 80 80 80
nationalexpress.com

City Link
Tel: 08705 50 50 50
citylink.co.uk

Postbus
Tel: 08457 740 740
royalmail.com/postbus

DRIVING DISTANCES

	Aberdeen	Birmingham	Cardiff	Dover	Dumfries	Dundee	Edinburgh	Fort William	Glasgow	Harwich	Hawick	Hull	Inverness	Kyle of Lochalsh	London	Manchester	Newcastle	Oban	Perth	Prestwick	Rosyth	Stirling	Stranraer	Thurso	Troon	Ullapool
Birmingham	421 687																									
Cardiff	529 851	113 182																								
Dover	617 993	200 322	224 361																							
Dumfries	214 344	234 376	335 539	436 700																						
Dundee	71 114	357 575	465 749	553 890	149 240																					
Edinburgh	131 210	290 467	398 641	486 782	80 128	62 99																				
Fort William	161 258	396 637	504 811	592 952	179 288	123 197	138 221																			
Glasgow	152 243	286 461	394 634	482 776	76 122	84 134	45 72	108 173																		
Harwich	604 972	187 300	242 390	130 210	370 595	540 869	473 761	578 931	469 754																	
Hawick	178 287	243 391	344 554	417 671	53 86	113 182	50 81	185 298	85 137	370 596																
Hull	387 619	137 221	251 405	255 411	205 330	318 509	255 408	384 614	275 440	214 346	206 331															
Inverness	118 189	446 717	553 890	641 1032	239 385	134 214	162 259	69 110	178 285	628 1011	209 337	444 710														
Kyle of Lochalsh	200 320	469 755	577 929	665 1070	253 407	179 286	207 331	76 122	184 294	652 1049	254 408	459 734	82 131													
London	549 878	118 190	150 242	75 122	349 561	481 770	412 659	514 822	406 650	78 126	358 576	216 346	573 917	590 944												
Manchester	345 556	93 150	201 324	281 453	157 252	281 453	214 345	320 515	210 338	268 431	166 267	95 154	370 595	393 633	201 322											
Newcastle	244 390	208 336	323 519	350 563	91 147	175 280	112 179	267 427	159 254	309 498	64 102	148 237	274 438	343 549	288 461	147 237										
Oban	190 304	385 620	493 794	581 935	168 270	121 194	125 200	50 80	96 154	568 914	175 281	371 594	112 180	125 200	502 803	309 498	310 496									
Perth	86 139	348 560	449 723	550 884	128 205	21 34	43 69	104 166	64 104	484 778	96 155	319 513	114 183	158 254	463 744	271 436	152 245	94 151								
Prestwick	177 285	304 489	411 662	500 804	61 98	113 182	79 127	131 210	32 52	486 783	105 168	279 449	201 324	204 329	418 673	228 366	168 271	120 193	96 155							
Rosyth	115 185	324 522	425 684	477 768	104 170	48 77	14 23	124 200	47 76	430 692	67 108	265 426	145 233	189 304	437 703	247 398	123 198	114 183	31 49	79 127						
Stirling	120 193	313 503	414 666	514 823	92 149	55 89	38 61	97 157	29 47	448 722	87 141	284 456	145 234	172 277	427 688	236 379	143 231	87 140	37 60	61 99	26 42					
Stranraer	241 386	297 478	404 651	489 787	71 115	172 275	133 213	196 314	89 142	475 765	125 202	284 454	265 424	272 435	415 664	224 358	161 259	172 277	149 240	54 87	131 211	114 611				
Thurso	234 374	555 893	663 1066	750 1208	348 560	250 400	278 445	183 293	293 469	737 1186	319 513	559 894	112 180	177 283	690 1104	499 798	391 626	233 373	221 311	355 500	254 409	252 406	382 183			
Troon	183 295	314 505	415 668	516 830	64 104	119 191	82 132	126 203	35 56	450 724	106 171	285 459	209 336	200 322	429 690	237 381	171 276	116 186	101 162	5 8	80 129	63 101	60 96	316 508		
Ullapool	179 286	499 803	607 976	695 1118	293 472	194 310	222 355	119 190	238 381	681 1097	263 424	504 806	63 101	91 146	635 1016	444 710	335 536	169 270	168 270	255 411	199 320	199 320	128 205	327 523	263 423	
York	343 552	132 212	246 396	273 439	151 243	279 449	191 308	318 511	208 335	233 374	152 245	41 65	367 591	391 630	208 335	70 113	90 146	307 495	237 382	226 363	212 341	230 370	477 767	218 352	231 372	421 678

M KM

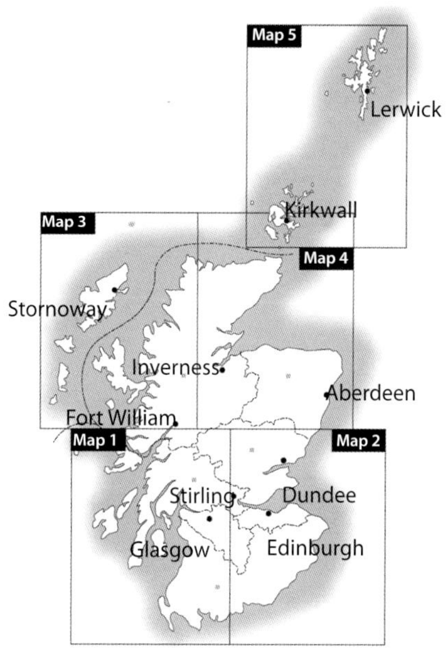
Map 5
Lerwick
Kirkwall
Map 3
Map 4
Stornoway
Inverness
Aberdeen
Fort William
Map 1
Map 2
Stirling
Dundee
Glasgow
Edinburgh

MAPS

MAP 1

Locations shown indicate establishmnets that are advertised in our three Where to Stay guides, including Hotels & Guest Houses and Self Catering/Caravan & Camping. Please use a current road atlas for route planning and touring.

MAP 2

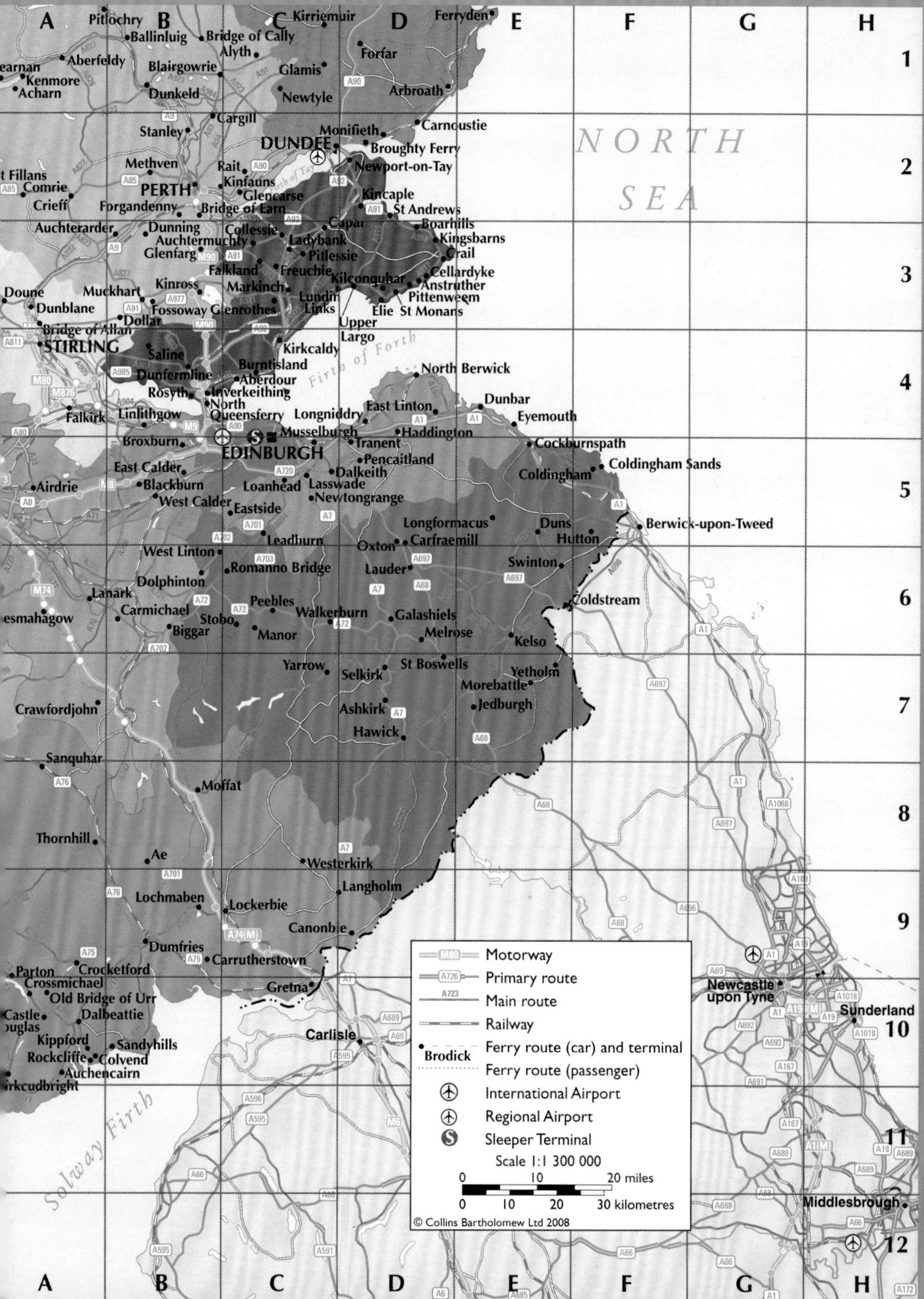

NORTH SEA
Firth of Forth
Solway Firth
Pitlochry
Kirriemuir
Ferryden
Ballinluig
Bridge of Cally
Alyth
Forfar
Aberfeldy
Kenmore
Acharn
Blairgowrie
Glamis
Dunkeld
Newtyle
Arbroath
Cargill
Carnoustie
Stanley
Monifieth
DUNDEE
Broughty Ferry
Methven
Rait
Newport-on-Tay
St Fillans
Comrie
Kinfauns
PERTH
Glencarse
Kincaple
Crieff
Forgandenny
Bridge of Earn
St Andrews
Auchterarder
Dunning
Collessie
Cupar
Boarhills
Auchtermuchty
Ladybank
Kingsbarns
Glenfarg
Pitlessie
Crail
Falkland
Freuchie
Kilconquhar
Cellardyke
Doune
Muckhart
Kinross
Markinch
Anstruther
Pittenweem
Dunblane
Fossoway
Glenrothes
Lundin Links
Elie
St Monans
Dollar
Upper Largo
Bridge of Allan
STIRLING
Saline
Kirkcaldy
Burntisland
North Berwick
Dunfermline
Aberdour
Rosyth
Inverkeithing
Dunbar
North Queensferry
East Linton
Falkirk
Linlithgow
Longniddry
Eyemouth
Musselburgh
Haddington
Broxburn
Tranent
Cockburnspath
EDINBURGH
Pencaitland
Coldingham Sands
East Calder
Dalkeith
Coldingham
Airdrie
Blackburn
Loanhead
Lasswade
Newtongrange
West Calder
Eastside
Longformacus
Duns
Berwick-upon-Tweed
Hutton
Leadburn
Oxton
Carfraemill
West Linton
Swinton
Romanno Bridge
Lauder
Dolphinton
Lanark
Coldstream
Peebles
Carmichael
Walkerburn
Galashiels
Lesmahagow
Stobo
Melrose
Biggar
Manor
Kelso
St Boswells
Yarrow
Selkirk
Yetholm
Morebattle
Crawfordjohn
Ashkirk
Jedburgh
Hawick
Sanquhar
Moffat
Thornhill
Ae
Westerkirk
Langholm
Lochmaben
Lockerbie
Canonbie
Dumfries
Parton
Crocketford
Carrutherstown
Crossmichael
Gretna
Old Bridge of Urr
Castle Douglas
Dalbeattie
Carlisle
Kippford
Sandyhills
Rockcliffe
Colvend
Auchencairn
Kirkcudbright
Newcastle upon Tyne
Sunderland
Middlesbrough
Motorway
Primary route
Main route
Railway
Ferry route (car) and terminal
Brodick
Ferry route (passenger)
International Airport
Regional Airport
Sleeper Terminal
Scale 1:1 300 000
0 10 20 miles
0 10 20 30 kilometres
© Collins Bartholomew Ltd 2008

MAP 3

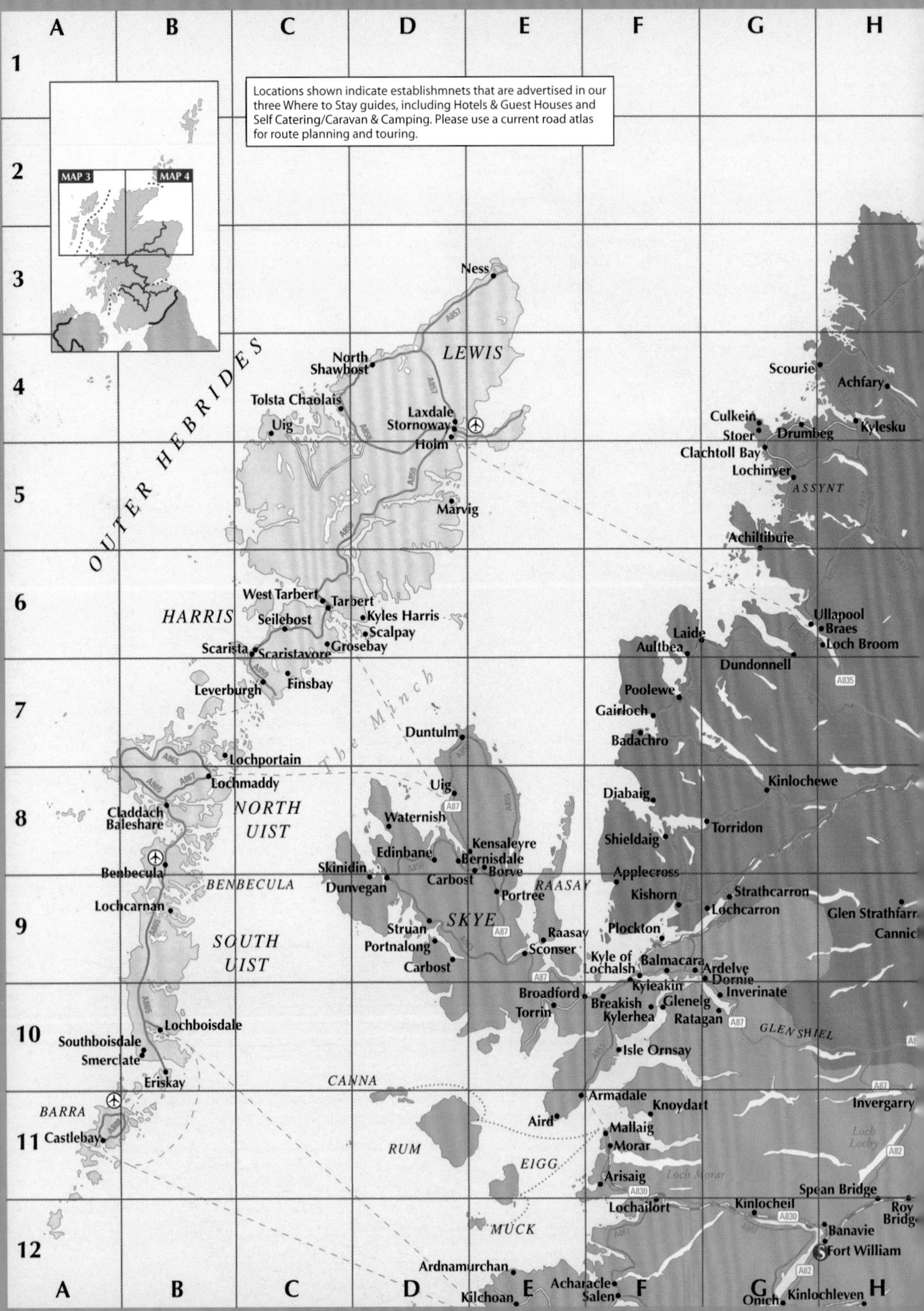

Locations shown indicate establishmnets that are advertised in our three Where to Stay guides, including Hotels & Guest Houses and Self Catering/Caravan & Camping. Please use a current road atlas for route planning and touring.
MAP 3
MAP 4
OUTER HEBRIDES
LEWIS
HARRIS
NORTH UIST
BENBECULA
SOUTH UIST
BARRA
SKYE
RAASAY
CANNA
RUM
EIGG
MUCK
ASSYNT
GLEN SHIEL
The Minch
Ness
North Shawbost
Tolsta Chaolais
Uig
Laxdale
Stornoway
Holm
Marvig
West Tarbert
Tarbert
Kyles Harris
Seilebost
Scalpay
Scarista
Scaristavore
Grosebay
Leverburgh
Finsbay
Lochportain
Lochmaddy
Claddach Baleshare
Benbecula
Lochcarnan
Lochboisdale
Southboisdale
Smerclate
Eriskay
Castlebay
Duntulm
Uig
Waternish
Kensaleyre
Edinbane
Bernisdale
Skinidin
Borve
Dunvegan
Carbost
Portree
Struan
Portnalong
Carbost
Raasay
Sconser
Broadford
Torrin
Isle Ornsay
Armadale
Aird
Knoydart
Mallaig
Morar
Arisaig
Lochailort
Ardnamurchan
Kilchoan
Acharacle
Salen
Scourie
Achfary
Culkein
Stoer
Drumbeg
Kylesku
Clachtoll Bay
Lochinver
Achiltibuie
Ullapool
Braes
Loch Broom
Laide
Aultbea
Dundonnell
Poolewe
Gairloch
Badachro
Kinlochewe
Diabaig
Torridon
Shieldaig
Applecross
Kishorn
Strathcarron
Lochcarron
Glen Strathfarr
Cannic
Plockton
Kyle of Lochalsh
Balmacara
Ardelve
Dornie
Kyleakin
Inverinate
Breakish
Glenelg
Kylerhea
Ratagan
Invergarry
Loch Lochy
Loch Morar
Spean Bridge
Kinlocheil
Roy Bridg
Banavie
Fort William
Onich
Kinlochleven
A857
A858
A859
A865
A867
A888
A87
A850
A855
A851
A830
A82
A835
A861

MAP 4

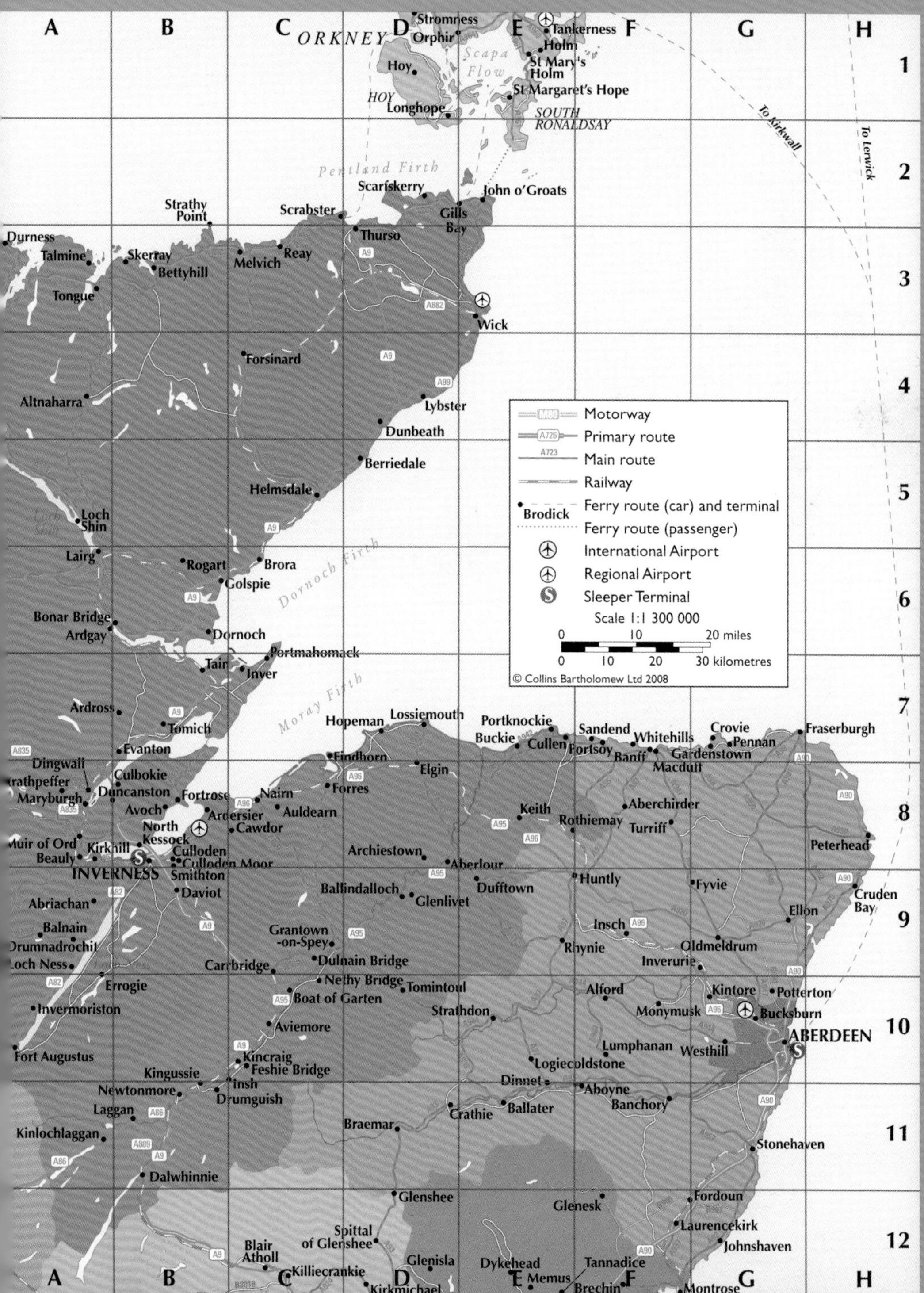

A
B
C
D
E
F
G
H
1
2
3
4
5
6
7
8
9
10
11
12
ORKNEY
Stromness
Orphir
Tankerness
Holm
St Mary's Holm
Hoy
Scapa Flow
HOY
Longhope
St Margaret's Hope
SOUTH RONALDSAY
To Kirkwall
To Lerwick
Pentland Firth
Scarfskerry
John o'Groats
Strathy Point
Scrabster
Gills Bay
Durness
Talmine
Skerray
Bettyhill
Melvich
Reay
Thurso
Tongue
Wick
Forsinard
Altnaharra
Lybster
Dunbeath
Berriedale
Helmsdale
Loch Shin
Lairg
Rogart
Brora
Golspie
Dornoch Firth
Bonar Bridge
Ardgay
Dornoch
Portmahomack
Tain
Inver
Moray Firth
Ardross
Tomich
Evanton
Dingwall
Strathpeffer
Culbokie
Maryburgh
Duncanston
Fortrose
Avoch
North Kessock
Muir of Ord
Kirkhill
Beauly
INVERNESS
Culloden
Culloden Moor
Smithton
Daviot
Abriachan
Balnain
Drumnadrochit
Loch Ness
Errogie
Invermoriston
Fort Augustus
Hopeman
Lossiemouth
Findhorn
Elgin
Forres
Nairn
Ardersier
Auldearn
Cawdor
Archiestown
Aberlour
Dufftown
Ballindalloch
Glenlivet
Grantown-on-Spey
Dulnain Bridge
Carrbridge
Nethy Bridge
Tomintoul
Boat of Garten
Aviemore
Kincraig
Feshie Bridge
Kingussie
Insh
Newtonmore
Drumguish
Laggan
Kinlochlaggan
Dalwhinnie
Portknockie
Buckie
Cullen
Sandend
Portsoy
Whitehills
Banff
Macduff
Crovie
Pennan
Gardenstown
Fraserburgh
Keith
Rothiemay
Aberchirder
Turriff
Peterhead
Huntly
Fyvie
Cruden Bay
Ellon
Insch
Rhynie
Oldmeldrum
Inverurie
Alford
Kintore
Potterton
Monymusk
Bucksburn
ABERDEEN
Westhill
Lumphanan
Strathdon
Logiecoldstone
Dinnet
Aboyne
Banchory
Crathie
Ballater
Braemar
Stonehaven
Glenshee
Glenesk
Fordoun
Laurencekirk
Johnshaven
Spittal of Glenshee
Blair Atholl
Killiecrankie
Glenisla
Dykehead
Tannadice
Memus
Brechin
Montrose
Kirkmichael
A9
A882
A99
A835
A96
A95
A82
A86
A889
A90
A93
Motorway
Primary route
Main route
Railway
Ferry route (car) and terminal
Brodick
Ferry route (passenger)
International Airport
Regional Airport
Sleeper Terminal
Scale 1:1 300 000
0 10 20 miles
0 10 20 30 kilometres
© Collins Bartholomew Ltd 2008

MAP 5

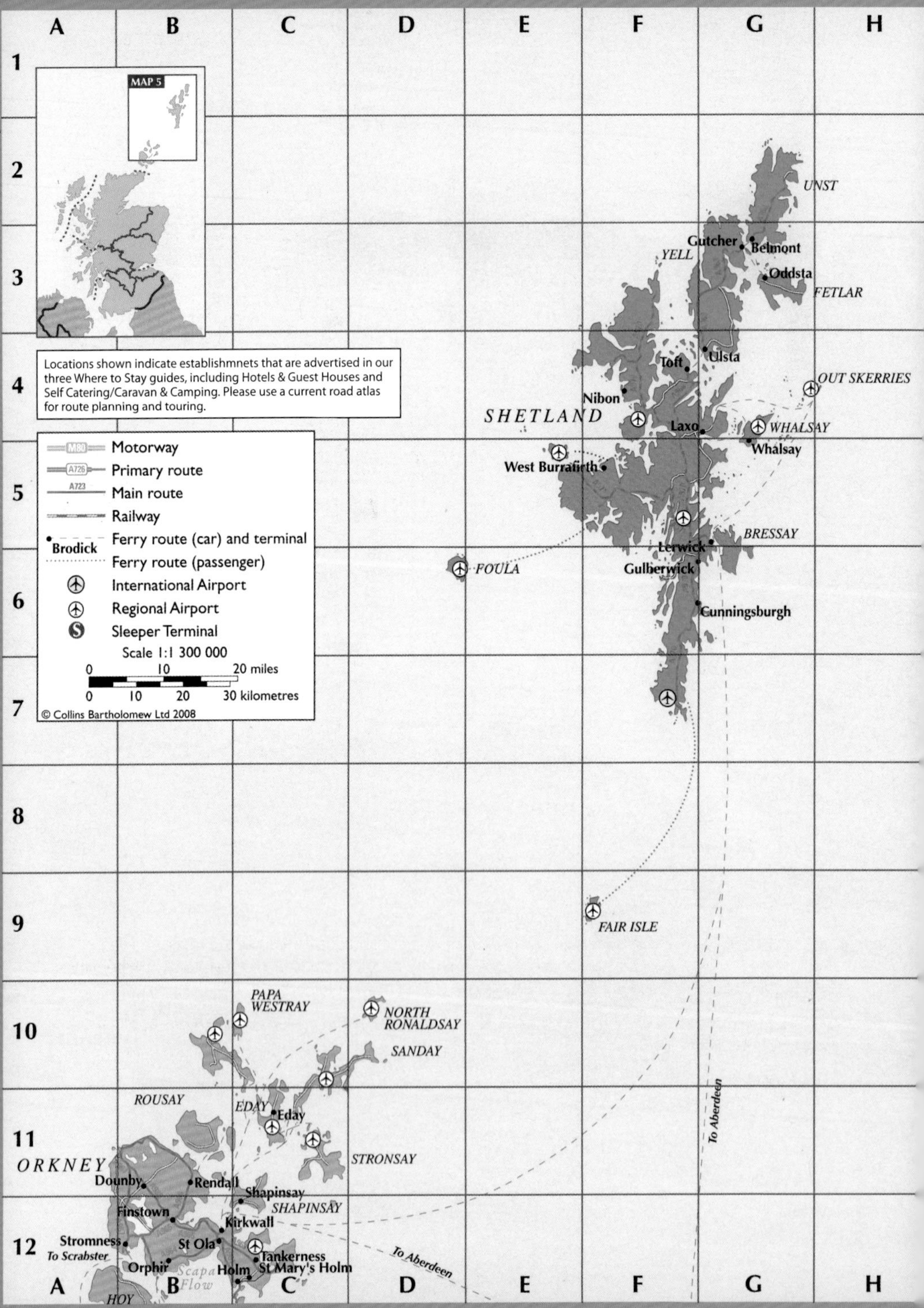

A B C D E F G H
1 2 3 4 5 6 7 8 9 10 11 12
MAP 5
Locations shown indicate establishmnets that are advertised in our three Where to Stay guides, including Hotels & Guest Houses and Self Catering/Caravan & Camping. Please use a current road atlas for route planning and touring.
Motorway
Primary route
Main route
Railway
Ferry route (car) and terminal
Brodick
Ferry route (passenger)
International Airport
Regional Airport
Sleeper Terminal
Scale 1:1 300 000
0 10 20 miles
0 10 20 30 kilometres
© Collins Bartholomew Ltd 2008
UNST
Gutcher
Belmont
YELL
Oddsta
FETLAR
Ulsta
Toft
OUT SKERRIES
Nibon
SHETLAND
Laxo
WHALSAY
Whalsay
West Burrafirth
BRESSAY
Lerwick
Gulberwick
FOULA
Cunningsburgh
FAIR ISLE
PAPA WESTRAY
NORTH RONALDSAY
SANDAY
ROUSAY
EDAY
Eday
To Aberdeen
STRONSAY
ORKNEY
Dounby
Rendall
Shapinsay
SHAPINSAY
Finstown
Kirkwall
Stromness
To Scrabster
St Ola
Tankerness
To Aberdeen
Orphir
Scapa Flow
Holm
St Mary's Holm
HOY

Glengorm Castle, Mull, Inner Hebrides

ACCOMMODATION LISTINGS

- Bed and breakfast **accommodation listings** for all of Scotland.
- Establishments are listed **by location** in alphabetical order.
- At the back of this book there is a directory showing all VisitScotland quality assured **Serviced Accommodation**. This directory shows **Accessible Accommodation** for visitors with mobility difficulties and also lets you know what **Green Award** has been obtained.
- You will also find an **Index by location** which will tell you where to look if you already know where you want to go.
- Inside the back cover flap you will find a **key to the symbols**.

The town of Melrose, showing Abbey and River Tweed, Scottish Borders

SOUTH OF SCOTLAND

Ayrshire & Arran, Dumfries & Galloway, Scottish Borders

No matter how many times you holiday in the Scottish Borders, Ayrshire & Arran or Dumfries & Galloway, you'll always find something new and interesting to do.

The proud heritage, distinct traditions and enthralling history of Scotland's most southerly places are sure to capture your imagination.

Explore the region's imposing castles and ruined abbeys and follow the trail of an often bloody and turbulent past. It's a story of battles and skirmishes - from all out war to cattle rustling cross-border raids.

Living history

Though you'd be hard pushed to find a more peaceful part of the country these days, the legacy of these more unsettled times can still be experienced in many a Scottish Borders town during the Common Ridings. Throughout the summer months hundreds of colourful riders on horseback commemorate the days when their ancestors risked their lives patrolling town boundaries and neighbouring villages.

The South is alive with history. Traquair House, near Innerleithen, is Scotland's oldest continuously inhabited house, dating back to 1107. In Selkirk the whole town is transformed in early December as locals step back to the days when Sir Walter Scott presided over the local courtroom, by partaking in the Scott's Selkirk celebrations.

Beautiful beaches

Southern Scotland isn't just about rolling hills and lush farmland, both coasts are well worth a visit. To the east you can see the rocky cliffs and picturesque harbours at St Abbs Head and Eyemouth, while over on the west, there are the beautiful Ayrshire beaches and more than 200 miles of the lovely Solway Coast to explore.

To find out more, call 0845 22 55 121 or go to visitscotland.com

And off the Ayrshire coast is the Isle of Arran – one of Scotland's finest islands and everything a holidaymaker could want.

Whatever your interests, you'll be spoiled for choice in southern Scotland. If you love angling, there's world-class salmon fishing on the River Tweed. If golf's your game, Turnberry, Prestwick and Royal Troon are up with the best.

If you're a mountain biker, you won't find better than Glentress or Kirroughtree, two of the 7stanes mountain bike routes. Enjoy reading? Head for Wigtown, Scotland's National Book Town and home to more than 20 bookshops. Ice cream? Who can resist Cream o' Galloway at Gatehouse of Fleet?

If you're a gardener, you'll be inspired all year round by the flourishing collection of rare plants at the Logan Botanic Garden near Stranraer and Dawyck Botanic Gardens near Peebles.

What's more, 2009 is a big year for Scotland – we're celebrating the 250th anniversary of the birth of Robert Burns. There's over 200 special events taking place throughout the year, all over Scotland. Go to homecomingscotland2009.com to find out about events in this area.

That's the South of Scotland. Bursting with brilliant places, waiting with a hearty Scottish welcome and ready to captivate you with a holiday experience you will never forget.

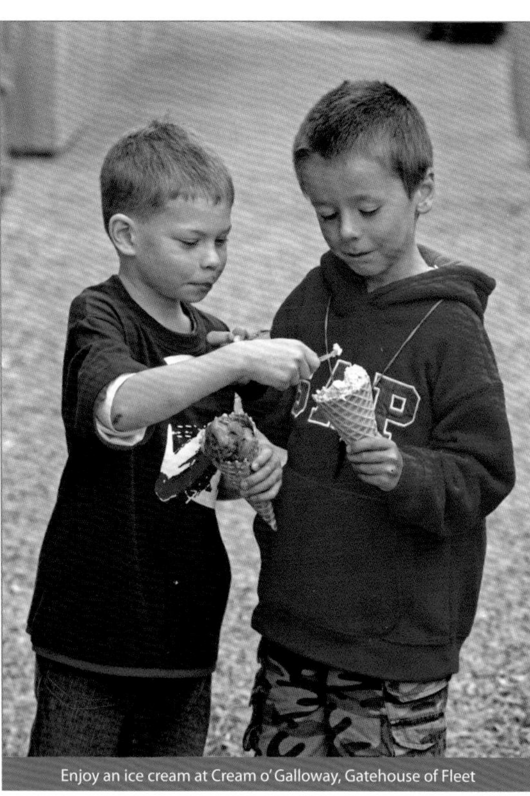

Enjoy an ice cream at Cream o' Galloway, Gatehouse of Fleet

What's On?

Burns Light
25 January 2009
Homecoming on your Doorstep.

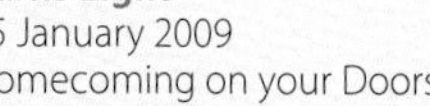

Melrose 7's Rugby Tournament
11 April 2009
The Greenyards, Melrose, April 2009
Melrose is the home of rugby 7's and this popular and expanding tournament is certain to be a big crowd puller!
melrose7s.com

Spring Fling
May Bank Holiday weekend 2009
Arts and crafts open studio event.
spring-fling.co.uk

Burns an 'a' That! Festival

16 – 24 May 2009
Celebrate the 250th anniversary of Rabbie Burns' birth: more than 100 events across Ayrshire will bring together the biggest names in music, comedy and the arts.
burnsfestival.com

Ayr Flower Show
2 – 9 August 2009
Scotland's answer to the Chelsea Flower Show, the Ayr Flower Show takes place in the beautiful grounds of Rozelle Park.
ayrflowershow.org

Return To The Ridings: Border Common Ridings
7 -30 August 2009
across the Scottish Borders

Marymass
13 - 24 August 2009
A local Queen is crowned and the oldest horse racing event in the world takes place on the moor.
marymass.org

In the Footsteps of the Reivers
5 – 12 September 2009
Throughout Jedburdh and Hawick.

Wigtown Book Festival
25 Sept – 4 Oct 2009
Meet famous writers and broadcasters in the idyllic Galloway countryside.
wigtownbookfetstival.com

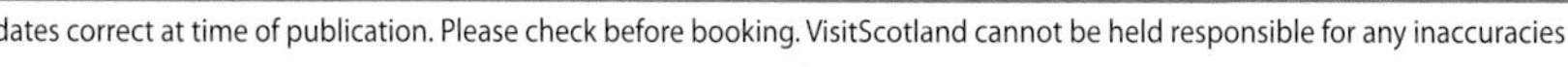

All dates correct at time of publication. Please check before booking. VisitScotland cannot be held responsible for any inaccuracies

MAP

©Collins Bartholomew Ltd 2008

VISITOR INFORMATION CENTRES

Visitor Information Centres are staffed by people 'in the know' offering friendly advice, helping to make your stay in Scotland the most enjoyable ever . . . whatever your needs!

Ayrshire & Arran

Ayr	22 Sandgate, Ayr, KA7 1BW	Tel: 01292 290300
Brodick	The Pier, Brodick, Isle of Arran, KA27 8AU	Tel: 01770 303774/776

Dumfries & Galloway

Dumfries	64 Whitesands, Dumfries DG1 2RS	Tel: 01387 253862
Gretna	Unit 38, Gretna Gateway Outlet Village, Glasgow Road, Gretna, DG16 5GG	Tel: 01461 337834
Kirkcudbright	Harbour Square, Kirkcudbright DG6 4HY	Tel: 01557 330494
Southwaite	M6 Service Area, Southwaite, CA4 0NS	Tel: 01697 473445
Stranraer	Burns House, 28 Harbour Street, Stranraer, Dumfries DG9 7RA	Tel: 01776 702595

Scottish Borders

Hawick	Tower Mill, Heart of Hawick Campus, Kirkstile, Hawick, TD9 0AE	Tel: 01450 373993
Jedburgh	Murray's Green, Jedburgh, TD8 6BE	Tel: 01835 863171/864099
Kelso	Town House, The Square, Kelso, TD5 7HF	Tel: 01573 228055
Melrose	Abbey House, Abbey Street, TD6 9LGR	Tel: 01896 822283
Peebles	23 High Street, Peebles, EH45 8AG	Tel: 01721 723159

LOCAL KNOWLEDGE • WHERE TO STAY • ACCOMMODATION BOOKING • PLACES TO VISIT • THINGS TO DO • MAPS AND GUIDES • TRAVEL ADVICE • ROUTE PLANNING • WHERE TO SHOP AND EAT • LOCAL CRAFTS AND PRODUCE • EVENT INFORMATION • TICKETS

For information and ideas about exploring Scotland in advance of your trip, call our booking and information service **0845 22 55 121** or go to **visitscotland.com**

If calling from outside the UK and Ireland **+44 1506 832 121** From Ireland **1800 932 510**

A £4 booking fee applies for accommodation bookings made via a Visitor Information Centre and through our booking and information service.

Live it. Visit Scotland.
visitscotland.com/wheretofindus

Canyoning in North Glen Sannox on the Isle of Arran

Ayrshire & Arran

Ayrshire is home to 80 miles of unspoiled coastline and rolling green hills. Southwest of Glasgow, the area is steeped in history from Bronze Age standing stones to Medieval Viking battles and the majestic splendour of some of the best-preserved castles in the UK.

Not forgetting it is also the birthplace of world-renowned poet Robert Burns, to whom homage is paid on January 25th throughout the world. Why not experience Burns night surrounded by the scenery and culture that inspired the Bard himself.

Arran offers everything that is good about Scotland in one small and easily accessible island. It has mountains and lochs in the north, and rolling hills and meadows in the south. With fantastic walks, seven golf courses, breathtaking scenery and delicious food and drink, Arran has something for everyone.

Brodick Highland Games

DON'T MISS

1 See what happens when you bring 4 of the world's best graffiti artists to Scotland and provide them with a castle as a canvas. This is exactly what the owners of **Kelburn Castle** did. Kelburn is the ancient home of the Earls of Glasgow and dates back to the 13th century. The **graffiti project** on the castle is a spectacular piece of artwork, surrounded by a beautiful country estate and wooden glen. There is plenty to interest all the family.

2 The island of **Great Cumbrae**, accessible via a 10-minute ferry crossing from Largs, has an undeniable charm and a fabulous setting on the Clyde with views towards Arran. The capital, Millport, is every inch the model Victorian resort, with its own museum and aquarium, as well as the Cathedral of the Isles, Europe's smallest cathedral. The sportscotland National Centre Cumbrae is perfect for thrill seekers, while Country & Western fans will enjoy the week-long festival in late summer.

3 Opened in 1995, the **Isle of Arran Distillery** at Lochranza enjoys a spectacular location and is among the most recent to begin production in Scotland. The distillery has a visitor centre that offers fully guided tours, and the opportunity to pour your own bottle. Peat and artificial colourings aren't used in Arran whisky, which the distillers proudly claim offers 'the true spirit of nature'.

4 **Dean Castle** lies in Kilmarnock, East Ayrshire. Known for its astounding collection of medieval instruments and armoury, the castle sits in a glorious country park. Dean Castle is a family favourite, with a pet corner, an adventure playground and many different woodland walks and cycle routes. Contact the castle ahead of your visit to confirm seasonal opening hours for the Castle and its facilities.

5 For some crazy outdoor fun, head to **Loudoun Castle**, in Galston, Ayrshire. Loudoun Castle is a terrific day out for younger kids with swashbuckling fun in the Pirates' Cove, and pony treks and tractor rides at McDougal's Farm.

6 One of the finest collections of Bronze Age **standing stones** in Scotland can be found at scenic Machrie Moor on Arran. Around seven separate rings of stones have been discovered on the moor, with many still laying undiscovered beneath the peat which now grows in the vicinity. Visit during the summer solstice for a truly atmospheric experience.

1

3

6

FOOD AND DRINK

eatscotland.com

7 With excellent local produce such as cheese, ale, honey, ice cream and chocolate made to the highest standard, the Ayrshire & Arran kitchen will delight the palate and ignite culinary creativity.

8 Being on the west coast, seafood is delicious and could not be fresher. Take advantage of the opportunity to visit an up-market fish and chip shop or order the seafood at one of the excellent restaurants.

9 With such a range of natural & local ingredients to inspire, it is no wonder that Ayrshire & Arran has such fabulous restaurants. From Michelin Star and AA rosette winning restaurants to the best that gastro pubs have to offer, Ayrshire & Arran will satisfy the biggest gourmet's appetite.

8

10

GOLF

visitscotland.com/golf

10 Scotland is not only the Home of Golf, it is the home of links golf, the original form of the game that had its beginnings in Scotland over 600 years ago. Ayrshire & Arran have some of the finest and most famous links golf courses in the world; Western Gailes, Glasgow Gailes, West Kilbride, Royal Troon, Prestwick, Prestwick St Nicholas, Turnberry Alisa (pictured) and Shiskine on the Isle of Arran are all part of the Great Scottish Links collection.

11 However, it is not just the championship courses that Ayrshire is famous for. It is the good value and spectacular play of some of the lesser renowned courses. The charm and challenge of hidden gems like Belleisle, Brodick, Prestwick St. Cuthbert, Routenburn, Lochgreen and Largs, to name just a few, offer brilliant golf at a very reasonable price.

12 Ayrshire & Arran offer 3 different golf passes which are great value for money. By spending less on the course, you will have more to spend at the 19th hole. Visit ayrshire-arran.com for more information.

13 The Open returns to Ayrshire in 2009. It will see the world's best professional golfers flock to the legendry links of Turnberry to take on the greatest challenge in professional golf. If previous years are anything to go by, the competition will be fierce and the sun will be shining.

WALKS

visitscotland.com/walking

14 Going through forest, along the beach and across fields, the Kings Cave Forest Walk offers beautiful views across the sea to Kintyre. You also get the chance to explore the cave where reputedly Robert the Bruce hid from the English and was inspired by a spider to try, try and try again.

15 If you are looking for a short and pleasant walk with a combination of forest and open hills Dinmurchie Trail is ideal. Look out for local wildlife including deer, foxes, hares, kestrels and buzzards.

16 The Isle of Arran Coastal Way allows you to walk around the island. It is 75 miles long, but can be broken down into 7 more manageable sections. This route offers spectacular scenery and enjoyable challenges. Guide books are available at Brodick Visitor Information Centre.

17 The River Ayr Way is the first source to sea path network, which follows the river (66km) from its source at Glenbuck to the sea at Ayr. With beautiful scenery and abundant wildlife it is enjoyable to walk all or part of this route.

19

HISTORY

18 Robert Adam's fairytale Culzean Castle, perched on a clifftop overlooking Ailsa Craig and the Firth of Clyde, is a study in extravagance. A favourite of President Eisenhower, he was given his own apartment here by its previous owner, the Kennedy's. Fans of military history should explore the Armoury, filled with antique pistols and swords. 565 acres of country park surround the castle, with woodland walks, a walled garden and even a beach.

19 On 25th January 1759, Scotland's National Bard was born in the picturesque village of Alloway, a must for admirers of the man and his work. Here, you can visit Burns Cottage and a museum containing prized artefacts such as an original manuscript of Auld Lang Syne. Numerous surrounding sites, including the Brig O'Doon and Kirk Alloway, are familiar from Burns' epic poem Tam O'Shanter, which even has an entire visitor attraction dedicated to it.

20 The Isle of Arran Heritage Museum can be found on the main road at Rosaburn, just north of Brodick. The present group of buildings was once a working croft and smiddy, and include a farmhouse, cottage, bothy, milk house, laundry, stable, coach house and harness room. The fascinating exhibits reflect the social history, archaeology and geology of the island.

21 To visit Dalgarven Mill, and the Museum of Ayrshire Country life and Costume, is to step back in time. The comprehensive exhibition of tools, machinery, horse and harness, churns, fire irons and furnishings, evokes a powerful sense of the past, which cannot fail to leave an impression. The costume collection is constantly changing, and demonstrates how fashion has changed from 1780. The grind and splash of the wooden mill ensures the museum has an authentic ambience.

22 Dumfries House, the Georgian masterpiece designed by the renowned Scottish architect Robert Adam, opened to the public on 6th June 2008. The house, which sits in 2000 acres of East Ayrshire countryside, is opening its doors for the first time in 250 years. The former home of the Marquises of Bute, it was saved for the nation at the eleventh hour by a consortium of organisations and individuals brought together by HRH The Duke of Rothesay.

Brodick, Isle of Arran

Ormidale Hotel

Map Ref: 1F6

48704

Open: April-October

Brodick, Isle of Arran KA27 8BY

T: 01770 302293

E: reception@ormidale-hotel.co.uk

W: ormidale-hotel.co.uk

Total number of rooms: 7

Prices from:

Single:	**£39.00**	Double:	**£39.00**
Twin:	**£39.00**	Family room:	**£39.00**

Whiting Bay, Isle of Arran

Ellangowan

Map Ref: 1F7

24796

Open: All year

Middle Road, Whiting Bay, Isle of Arran KA27 8QH

T: 01770 700784

E: mary.robinson1@virgin.net

W: arranwelcome.co.uk

A warm welcome awaits you at our spacious comfortable home with superb sea views. Home baking on arrival and substantial breakfast made with Arran produce. Five minutes walk from eating places, shops and shore. Cyclists, walkers, golfers welcome with facilities for drying clothes and boots. Secure undercover protection. Sorry no pets.

Total number of rooms: 3

Prices from:

Single:	**£30.00**	Double:	**£25.00**
Twin:	**£25.00**		

Ayr

Daviot House

Map Ref: 1G7

74293

Open: All year excl Xmas and New Year

12 Queens Terrace, Ayr KA7 1DU

T: 01292 269678

E: daviothouse@hotmail.com

W: daviothouse.co.uk

Situated close to the beach and town centre, Daviot Guest House is ideal for visitors. Accommodation is extremely comfortable with all rooms decorated to a high standard. Breakfast is of good quality with a varied choice. Relaxed and friendly atmosphere brings guests back time and time again. See for yourself!

Total number of rooms: 5

Prices from:

Single:	**£40.00**	Double:	**£30.00**
Twin:	**£30.00**	Family room:	**£80.00pr**

ADVENTURE SCOTLAND

For everything you need to know about Adventure Breaks in Scotland and for an Adventure Brochure and an Adventure Pass call

0845 22 55 121

or log on to **visitscotland.com/adventurepass**

Important: Prices stated are estimates and may be subject to amendments.

Ayr

The Dunn Thing

Map Ref: 1G7

Open: All year 23775

13 Park Circus, Ayr KA7 2DJ
T: 01292 284531
E: sheiladunn13@aol.com
W: thedunnthing.co.uk

Welcoming cup of tea on arrival in our residents lounge. Extensive breakfast menu available. Tea and coffee available between 9.30 pm and 10.00 pm. Free pick up from Prestwick Airport, bus station, train station.

Total number of rooms: 3

Prices from:

Single:	**£33.00**	Double:	**£29.00**
Twin:	**£29.00**	Family room:	**£65.00pr**

Ayr

Eglinton Guest House

Map Ref: 1G7

Open: All year 24621

23 Eglinton Terrace, Ayr, Ayrshire KA7 1JJ
T: 01292 264623
E: eglintonguesthouse@yahoo.co.uk
W: eglintonguesthouse.com

Victorian terraced house in residential area overlooking tennis courts. A short walk from the sea, yet convenient for town centre and swimming pool. Ensuite rooms available.

Total number of rooms: 6

Prices per room from:

Single:	**£26.00**	Double:	**£50.00**
Twin:	**£50.00**	Family room:	**£70.00**

Ayr

Garth Madryn

Map Ref: 1G7

Open: All year 27335

71 Maybole Road, Alloway, Ayr KA7 4TB
T: 01292 443346
E: mackie294@btinternet.com
W: garthmadryn.co.uk

Total number of rooms: 3

Prices from:

Single:	**£24.00**	Double:	**£22.50**
Twin:	**£22.50**		

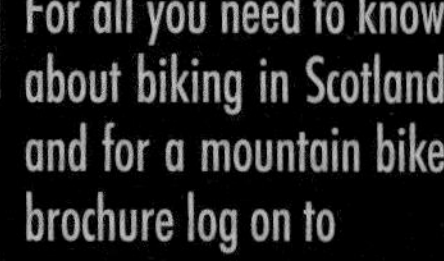

For all you need to know about biking in Scotland and for a mountain bike brochure log on to
visitscotland.com/cycling

Ayr

Leslie Anne Guest House

Map Ref: 1G7

Open: All year excl Xmas

35320

13 Castlehill Road, Ayr KA7 2HX
T: 01292 265646
E: leslieanne2@btinternet.com
W: leslieanne.org.uk

A warm welcome and comfortable accommodation awaits you at our family run Victorian guest house. Close to Ayr railway station and town centre. Prestwick Airport is five miles. Ideally situated for golf courses, Ayr Race Course, Burns country, Culzean Castle and the Ayrshire coast. Private parking. Two ground floor rooms.

Total number of rooms: 3

Prices from:

Single: **£25.00** Double: **£25.00**
Twin: **£25.00**

Ayr

Sunnyside Bed & Breakfast

Map Ref: 1G7

Open: All year

57253

26 Dunure Road, Alloway, Ayr KA7 4HR
T: 01292 441234
E: helen@ayrbandb.co.uk
W: ayrbandb.co.uk

Be spoiled at Sunnyside next to Alloway, birth place of Robert Burns. Scottish breakfast includes haggis, smoked salmon and hen or duck eggs from local farm. Spacious, well furnished double, twin or family rooms. Eight minutes walk to beautiful beach. We are praised for our high standard of personal service.

Total number of rooms: 3

Prices from:

Single: **£35.00** Double: **£27.50**
Twin: **£29.50** Family room: **£25.00**

Barmill, Beith

Shotts Farm B&B

Map Ref: 1G6

Open: All year

54622

Barmill,Beith, Ayrshire KA15 1LB
T: 01505 502273
E: shotts.farm@btinternet.com

Set in beautiful countryside with stunning views from dining room window. Shotts Farm is ideally situated for various visitor attractions such as Isle of Arran, Loch Lomond, Burns District, Bird Sanctuary at Lochwinnoch and including all this enjoy a hearty breakfast with home made bread and free range eggs.

Total number of rooms: 3

Prices from:

Single: **£25.00** Double: **£20.00**
Family room: **£50.00pr**

Important: Prices stated are estimates and may be subject to amendments.

Millport, Isle of Cumbrae

The Cathedral of the Isles

Map Ref: 1F6

Open: March 15th-December 30th

20016

The College of the Holy Spirit,
College Street, Millport, Isle of Cumbrae KA28 0HE
T: 01475 530353
E: tccumbrae@argyll.anglican.org
W: island-retreats.org

Unique opportunity to stay in this recently refurbished Grade A listed building next to Britain's smallest Cathedral. Several ensuite rooms available. There are eight acres of grounds and the site is five minutes from the sea. Classical music concerts are held every Sunday through the summer.

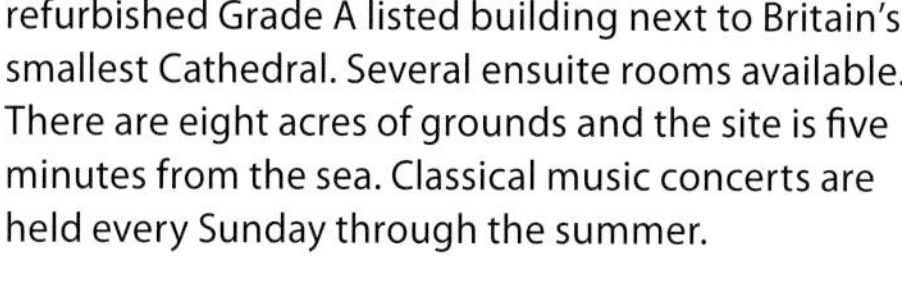

Total number of rooms: 16

Prices per room from:

Single:	**£38.00**	Double:	**£75.00**
Twin:	**£75.00**	Family room:	**£95.00**

Kilmarnock, Ayrshire

West Tannacrieff B&B

Map Ref: 1G6

Open: All year excl Xmas

63738

Fenwick, Kilmarnock KA3 6AZ
T: 01560 600258/07773226332
E: westtannacrieff@btopenworld.com
W: smoothhound.co.uk/hotels/westtannacrieff.html

Total number of rooms: 3

Prices from:

Single:	**£30.00**	Double:	**£27.50**
Twin:	**£27.50**	Family room:	**£27.50**

Kilwinning, Ayrshire

Blairholme

Map Ref: 1G6

Open: All year excl Xmas and New Year

15409

45 Byres Road, Kilwinning, Ayrshire KA13 6JU
T: 01294 552023

Total number of rooms: 2

Prices from:

Single:	**£30.00**	Double:	**£25.00**
Twin:	**£25.00**	Family room:	**£55.00pr**

Arbroath Smokies
at Portsoy Festival
EatScotland.com
Discover Scotland's
superb produce and
great places to dine.

Carsphairn View, Dumfries and Galloway

Dumfries & Galloway

Dumfries & Galloway is a naturally inspiring place, where landscapes, people and atmosphere conspire to make this a holiday experience you'll never forget.

Poets and artists have found inspiration here, capturing the look and feel of this beautiful region where 200 miles of coastline meet the tide and impressive hills rise up to greet the vast clear sky.

Remember to visit Kirkcudbright Artists' Town with its thriving artistic community, studios and galleries. From the Galloway Forest Park to the Solway Coast, there are so many picturesque places to explore and an abundance of wildlife habitats.

Look out for red deer, rare red kites, wild goats and even ospreys at Wigtown, Scotland's Book Town.

For those looking for adventure, there's world class mountain biking, challenging golf courses and many activity centres waiting to offer an adrenaline rush.

Whatever you choose to do, you'll find Dumfries & Galloway the perfect setting for a great holiday adventure.

Picnic, Priorwood Gardens, Melrose

DON'T MISS

1 As you travel through Dumfries & Galloway taking in the breathtaking scenery, you will come face to face with some amazing **environmental artworks** set in the landscape: head carvings in a sheep pen in the Galloway Forest Park, sculpture within Creetown town square, Andy Goldsworthy's Striding Arches near Moniaive. You never know what intriguing works you'll discover around the next corner!

2 Set in the pretty village of New Abbey, you'll find the origin of the word sweetheart at the splendid remains of this Cistercian Abbey, **Sweetheart Abbey**, established by Lady Devorgilla in memory of her husband John Balliol. Lady Devorgilla's love for her departed husband extended to carrying his embalmed heart around with her in an ivory box. Devorgilla and the heart are now buried together before the high altar. Be sure to pop in to the welcoming Abbey Cottage tearoom after your visit.

3 **Logan Botanic Garden**, under the care of the Royal Botanic Garden, Edinburgh is Scotland's most exotic garden where a fabulous array of bizarre and exotic plants and trees flourish outdoors. Warmed by the Gulf Stream, the climate provides ideal growing conditions for many plants from the southern hemisphere including a number of palm trees, which means you may forget where you are!

4 Built in the 17th century as a home for the first Duke of Queensberry, surrounded by the 120,000 acre Queensberry Estate, Country Park and grand Victorian Gardens, **Drumlanrig Castle** houses one of the finest private art collections in the UK. Join a Castle tour, a Land Rover Tour of the Estate, stroll through beautiful gardens and woodland walks enjoying the wildlife or take to your bike on a mountain bike trail. Kids are sure to enjoy the adventure playground, and the only museum in Scotland devoted to the history of cycling.

5 Set in a beautiful woodland location at Shambellie House, New Abbey, **The National Museum of Costume** opens the door on fashion and society from the 1850s to 1950s using lifelike room settings, in conjunction with a programme of special exhibitions, workshops and children's events.

6 Painters, artists and craftsmen have flocked to this area for centuries, no place more so than **Kirkcudbright** with its pastel coloured houses and traditional working harbour, now known as the Artists' Town for its historic artistic heritage. During the summer of 2009, the annual art exhibition, in the Town Hall, provides another chance to view the successful exhibition of 2000, **'The Homecoming'**, featuring works by many of the artists who made Kirkcudbright famous as an artists' town.

3

4

HERITAGE

historic-scotland.gov.uk

7 **Caerlaverock Castle** is everyone's idea of a medieval fortress, with its moat, twin towered gatehouse and imposing battlements. Britain's only triangular castle, close to Dumfries, has a turbulent history which is brought back to life with a medieval re-enactment each summer.

8 An amazing exhibition at Eastriggs tells the story of the greatest munitions factory on earth. **Devil's Porridge** was the highly explosive mixture of nitro-glycerine and nitro-cotton, hand mixed in HM Factory Gretna during World War 1. The exhibition tells the story of over 30,000 brave men and women who worked in the factory. Get an insight into their work and social life through sight and sound. Why not follow in the footsteps of runaway couples and visit nearby romantic Gretna Green?

9 **Homecoming Scotland 2009** is inspired by the 250th anniversary of the birth of Scotland's National Bard, **Robert Burns**. Pay a visit to **Ellisland Farm**, just north of Dumfries, where he wrote the famous song Auld Lang Syne, sung all over the world at New Year celebrations, **Robert Burns House**, in Dumfries where he spent the last years of his life, **The Globe Inn** his favourite "howff" (pub) and his final resting place, The Mausoleum in **St Michael's Churchyard**.

10 Dating back to about 2000 BC, the impressive remains of 2 chambered cairns at **Cairnholy** are surrounded by hills on three sides, but open to the sea to the south. With glorious views across Wigtown Bay to the Machars and the Isle of Man, just relax and enjoy the tranquillity of this historic setting.

WALKS

visitscotland.com/walking

11 Scotland's longest waymarked walking route, the **Southern Upland Way**, runs 212 miles from Portpatrick in the west to Cockburnspath on the east coast, traversing some beautiful hill scenery. If this is too challenging, there are several sections which can be enjoyed as part of shorter walks. The coastal section from Portpatrick to Killantringan Lighthouse is a great place to start or why not try the 7½ mile section between Wanlockhead and Sanquhar for a completely different experience of the Way.

12 There are many great walks around **Moffat**, Scotland's first "Walkers are Welcome" town, where a warm welcome is guaranteed. **The Grey Mare's Tail**, in the care of the National Trust for Scotland, just a short drive from Moffat along the Selkirk Road, provides a glorious walk up the side of this impressive 61m waterfall. At the top of the falls you will reach its source, Loch Skene, whose clear waters are populated by vendace, Britain's rarest freshwater fish. Join an experienced walk leader to discover more great walks during the **Moffat Walking Festival**, held in October each year.

13 The **River Annan** walk, takes you along one side of the river from Battery Park, Annan to the village of Brydekirk, some 3 miles away, and returns along the opposite bank. This calm and peaceful walk never takes you far from the river. Should you require a shorter walk, there are 2 additional bridges over the river, allowing shorter walks of 1½ and 3 miles.

14 Enjoy a leisurely stroll along the **Jubilee Path**, linking the picturesque coastal villages of Kippford and Rockcliffe. This 2 mile walk can be made from either village as you return by the same route, although some detours can be made on other minor paths. All the walks within this section have been taken from **"Dumfries & Galloway 12 Walks"** guide which can be requested via visitdumfriesandgalloway.co.uk/walking.

WILDLIFE

visitscotland.com/wildlife

15 The graceful red kite has been successfully reintroduced to Galloway, in an area around Loch Ken. The **Galloway Red Kite Trail** takes a circular route through some impressive scenery, designed to take you closer to this elusive raptor with observation points and interpretation boards. Visit the feeding station at Bellymack Farm, near Laurieston where up to 30 have been seen at once - feeding time, 2pm.

16 **Ospreys** are back in Galloway after a break of over 100 years. Visit the County Buildings in Wigtown where you can watch live CCTV coverage of the ospreys, or edited highlights once the birds have left for Africa. Nesting ospreys can also be seen via a live video link at WWT Caerlaverock. Get an unparalleled view of ospreys sitting on their eggs and bringing up their young, the male coming back with fish to share with the female and taking over nesting duties while she eats.

17 Dumfries & Galloway is home to 20% of the Scottish population of **red squirrel**, making them easier to spot here than anywhere else. Red squirrels are well adapted to the woodland habitat in which they live, and you can even follow a waymarked Red Squirrel Walk within Dalbeattie Forest for a good chance of seeing these endearing mammals.

18 Thousands of **barnacle geese** return every year from Norway to winter on the wetlands of the Solway Firth. Dumfries & Galloway is an ornithologist's paradise, and places such as **WWT Caerlaverock** and **Mersehead Nature Reserve** make it easy to get up close. Why not join an expert on a guided walk to find out more about the birds and wildlife? Events take place from Mull of Galloway to Wanlockhead – pick up your free Countryside Events booklet at Visitor Information Centres.

ACTIVITIES

19 Scotland's Biking Heaven – world class mountain biking at the **7stanes** centres across southern Scotland offering mile upon mile of exhilarating fast flowing single track. The highlight at **Kirroughtree** is 'McMoab' with its huge slabs and ridges of exposed granite linked by boulder causeways. **Dalbeattie's** most talked about section is 'The Slab', sheer granite lying at an extreme angle. Are you brave enough to tackle 'The Dark Side', expert level northshore at **Mabie** or the 'Omega Man' descent at **Ae**, do you have the stamina to tackle the 58km 'Big Country Ride' at **Glentrool?** If this all sounds too much, don't worry, as these centres offer trails for beginners up to the most expert riders, and coupled with some stunning scenery you'll want to return again and again.

20 Explore Dumfries & Galloway using our extensive network of quiet B Roads. Take your time to discover the hidden treasures along the **Solway Coast Heritage Trail**, the **Border Reiver Trail** or **The Burns Heritage Trail**. For an extra special tour, hire a vintage car from Motorparty, near Dumfries and take to these quiet routes in style. Kirkpatrick McMillan invented the bicycle in Dumfries & Galloway and there's still no better place to travel on two wheels with over 400 miles of **signposted cycle routes**.

21 Dumfries' new state of the art leisure centre, **DG One** has a three separate swimming pool areas, one with a moveable floor, leisure water and flumes. The 80 station fitness suite is furnished with state-of-the-art equipment, and the sports hall is the biggest in Dumfries & Galloway. With a 1200 seating capacity, DG One is the ideal venue with a great programme of events and arts and entertainment performances.

22 Enjoy a fun packed break with attractions that are **great for all the family**. Show your artistic side by painting a pot at **Dalton Pottery Art Café** near Lockerbie, shoot down the astroslide at **Mabie Farm Park**, near New Abbey, take a trip on the flying fox followed by some delicious ice cream at **Cream o' Galloway**, Gatehouse of Fleet or take to the zip slide at **Dalscone Farm** on the outskirts of Dumfries. You will be spoiled for choice!

Canonbie, Dumfriesshire

Byreburnfoot Country House B&B Map Ref: 2D9

77658

Open: All year excl Xmas and New Year

Byreburnfoot, Canonbie,
Dumfries and Galloway DG14 0XB
T: 01387 371209
E: info@byreburnfoot.co.uk
W: byreburnfoot.co.uk

Set in an idyllic location on the Border Esk this beautiful Victorian sandstone house, dating from 1850, is peacefully situated in it's own well stocked and secluded gardens. Supremely comfortable, with ensuite facilities, luxurious Egyptian cotton bedding and period furnishings. Byreburnfoot is the perfect location for a relaxing break.

Total number of rooms: 3

Prices from:
Single: **£45.00** Double: **£35.00**
Twin: **£35.00**

Canonbie, Dumfriesshire

Ms G Matthews (Four Oaks B&B) Map Ref: 2D9

26661

Open: All year excl Xmas and New Year

Four Oaks, Canonbie, Dumfriesshire DG14 0TF
T: 01387 371329
E: gwen@mmatthews.fsbusiness.co.uk
W: fouroaks.biz or 4-oaks.co.uk

Bed and Breakfast accommodation in comfortable, peaceful family home, with open views of lovely rolling countryside and farmland. Near the village of Canonbie, off the A7, just north of Carlisle, providing an excellent base for touring the beautiful Borderlands, with good fishing on the River Esk.

Total number of rooms: 2

Prices from:
Single: **£26.00** Double: **£26.00**
Twin: **£26.00**

Castle Douglas, Kirkcudbrightshire

Airds Farmhouse Map Ref: 2A10

11280

Open: All year excl Xmas and New Year

Airds Farm, Crossmichael, Castle Douglas DG7 3BG
T: 01556 670418
E: tricia@airds.com
W: airds.com

Airds farmhouse offers comfortable accommodation in a scenic location overlooking Loch Ken and the picturesque village and church of Crossmichael. Airds is ideal for a restful or active stay to enjoy the benefits of the Galloway region, including golf, fishing, bird-watching, walking or water sports.

Total number of rooms: 3

Prices from:
Single: **£35.00** Double: **£25.00-31.00**
Twin: **£29.00-31.00** Family room: **£23.00-31.00**

Important: Prices stated are estimates and may be subject to amendments.

Dalbeattie, Dumfriesshire

Heritage Guest House

Map Ref: 2A10

80371

★★★★ B&B

Open: All year

273 High Street, Dalbeattie,
Dumfries and Galloway DG5 4DW
T: 01556 610817
E: reception@heritage-house.info
W: heritage-house.info

Located close to the town boundary, about five minutes from Dalbeattie Forest, eight minutes drive to Colvend Coast. Convenient for 7 Stanes mountain bike routes; also walking, golfing, fishing and bird-watching. Rooms are very comfortable, all are ensuite. Spacious lounge with wide screen Sky television. Evening meals by arrangement.

Total number of rooms: 3

Prices from:

Double: **£30.00** Family room: **£90.00pr**

Dumfries

Burnett House

Map Ref: 2B9

21927

★★★ B&B

Open: All year

4 Lover's Walk, Dumfries DG1 1LP
T: 01387 263164
E: burnetthousebb@aol.com
W: burnetthouse.co.uk

Total number of rooms: 4

Prices from:

Single:	£27.00	Double:	£32.50
Twin:	£32.50	Family room:	£32.50

Dumfries

Hamilton House

Map Ref: 2B9

78420

★★★★ GUEST HOUSE

Open: All year excl Xmas and New Year

12 Moffat Road, Dumfries, Dumfries and Galloway DG1 1NJ
T: 01387 266606
E: bookings@hamiltonhousedumfries.co.uk
W: hamiltonhousedumfries.co.uk

A family run guest house in a central location Hamilton House is ideal for touring the area. Recently refurbished throughout, accommodation is comfortable and spacious. Tastefully decorated with soft colours and complimented with mahogany furniture. Private parking is to the rear of the property. Free WiFi connection throughout.

Total number of rooms: 6

Prices per room from:

Single:	£35.00	Double:	£56.00
Twin:	£56.00	Family room:	£65.00

Fish
IN SCOTLAND
Experience world-class fishing

For information on fishing breaks in Scotland and for a brochure call

0845 22 55 121

visitscotland.com/fish

Dumfries

Inverallochy Bed and Breakfast Map Ref: 2B9

31906

Open: All year

15 Lockerbie Road, Dumfries DG1 3AP

T: 01387 267298
E: shona@inverallochy.com
W: inverallochy.com

Total number of rooms: 4

Prices from:

Single:	£26.00-35.00	Double:	£26.00-28.00
Twin:	£26.00-27.00		

Dumfries

Low Kirkbride Farmhouse B&B Map Ref: 2B9

36483

Open: All year

Mrs Zan Kirk, Dunscore, Dumfries DG2 0SP

T/F: 01387 820258
E: lowkirkbride@btinternet.com
W: lowkirkbridefarm.com

Warm comfortable farmhouse set amid beautiful countryside, lovely views from every room. Friendly atmosphere with superb breakfasts and tasty Aga home baking and cooking. Conservatory looking onto attractive garden. Our own walking leaflet. Working beef and sheep farm with pedigree herd of Belted Galloways. Games room. Free bikes. Ten miles north of Dumfries.

Total number of rooms: 3

Prices from:

Single:	£30.00	Double:	£22.00-25.00
Twin:	£22.00-25.00	D,B&B:	£39.00-42.00

Dumfries

Wallamhill House Bed and Breakfast Map Ref: 2B9

63283

Open: All year excl Xmas and New Year

Kirkton, Dumfries DG1 1SL

T: 01387 248249
E: wallamhill@aol.com
W: wallamhill.co.uk

Spacious house in quiet countryside, beautiful views of Nith Valley. Two miles from Dumfries town centre, safe parking. All rooms ground floor level, spacious, with ensuite shower rooms. Ideal and luxurious base to explore Dumfries and Galloway. Small health suite with steam shower and sauna.

Total number of rooms: 3

Prices from:

Single:	£38.00	Double:	£30.00
Twin:	£30.00	Family room:	£30.00

Scotland. The Home of Golf

For everything you need to know about golfing in Scotland and for a brochure call: 0845 22 55 121

Important: Prices stated are estimates and may be subject to amendments.

Gretna Green, Dumfriesshire
Barrasgate House

Map Ref: 2C10

14379

★★★ B&B

Open: All year

Millhill, Gretna, Dumfriesshire DG16 5HU
T: 01461 337577
E: info@barrasgate.co.uk
W: barrasgate.co.uk

Situated on the old coaching route South, one mile from the motorway junction, it is the ideal resting place for travellers crossing the border. Highly Commended AA ★★★ certification. The old farm croft is tastefully modernised ensuite accommodation on the ground and first floors. Comfortable beds and local food. Free parking.

Total number of rooms: 5

Prices per room from:

Single:	**£32.50**	Double:	**£60.00**
Twin:	**£56.00**	Family room:	**£90.00**

Kirkcudbright, Kirkcudbrightshire
Fludha Guest House

Map Ref: 2A10

28210

★★★★ GUEST HOUSE

Open: All year

Fludha, Tongland Road,
Kirkcudbright, Dumfries and Galloway DG6 4UU
T: 01557 331443
E: steve@fludha.com
W: fludha.com

Fludha (the ONLY five star Guest House in Dumfries and Galloway), is a prestige property set in two acres of elevated grounds facing south and overlooking the river with commanding views of Kirkcudbright and the Galloway hills beyond. This feature rich home has six double /twin rooms all with top quality furnishing, fixtures and fittings, and all have beautiful ensuites. As well as award winning breakfast we are also happy to provide evening meals. Our wine list features classic wines so you can enjoy a glass of quality wine to accompany good food while watching the sun go down over the river!

Total number of rooms: 6

Prices from:

Single:	**£70.00-75.00**	Double:	**£46.50-50.00**
Twin:	**£46.50-50.00**		

Sail in Scotland

For everything you need to know about sailing in Scotland and for a brochure call

0845 22 55 121

Kirkcudbright, Kirkcudbrightshire

Sassoon House Bed and Breakfast Map Ref: 2A10

Open: All year 80011

3 High Street, Kirkcudbright,
Dumfries & Galloway DG6 4JZ
T: 01557 330390
E: info@sassoonhouse.co.uk
W: sassoonhouse.co.uk

A beautiful Georgian Townhouse on the historical High Street. We offer quality dinner, bed and breakfast within charming surroundings. Located opposite Broughton House and 50 metres walk from Scotland's only blue flag marina. Relax and enjoy gourmet food coupled with home comforts.

Total number of rooms: 3

Prices per room from:

Single: **£40.00** Double: **£65.00**
Twin: **£64.00**

Moffat, Dumfriesshire

Blairdrummond House Map Ref: 2B8

Open: All year 15391

School Lane, Moffat, Dumfriesshire DG10 9AX
T: 01683 221240
E: geoff.kelland@whsmithnet.co.uk
W: blairdrummondhouse.co.uk

A warm welcome at this family run Bed & Breakfast which offers high standards throughout. Very comfortable and well appointed rooms, quiet location yet only minutes from town centre. Breakfast is our speciality, a whole range of home produce, jams, preserves, muffins, breads. No smoking house. Private parking.

Total number of rooms: 3

Prices from:

Single: **£36.00** Double: **£32.50**
Twin: **£32.50**

Moffat, Dumfriesshire

Hartfell House & The Limetree Restaurant Map Ref: 2B8

Open: All year excl Xmas 29655

Hartfell Crescent, Moffat, Dumfriesshire DG10 9AL
T: 01683 220153
E: enquiries@hartfellhouse.co.uk
W: hartfellhouse.co.uk

Set in an 'outstanding conservation area' Hartfell House is a listed building famous for it's fine interior woodwork. Boasting breathtaking views of the surrounding hills, it is only a four minute walk from the town centre. Visit the award winning Limetree Restaurant at Hartfell House for a memorable dining experience.

Total number of rooms: 7

Prices from:

Single: **£40.00** Double: **£35.00**
Twin: **£35.00** Family room: **£35.00**

Important: Prices stated are estimates and may be subject to amendments.

Moffat, Dumfriesshire

Limetree House

Map Ref: 2B8

35499

Open: All year excl Xmas and New Year

Eastgate, Moffat, Dumfriesshire DG10 9AE
T: 01683 220001
E: info@limetreehouse.co.uk
W: limetreehouse.co.uk

Limetree House is a Georgian townhouse in a secluded street in Moffat, offering high standards and extra services. An ideal base to explore the Borders, Edinburgh and Glasgow. Famed breakfasts with specialities like pancakes and scrambled eggs with smoked salmon! Secure storage for bikes and motorbikes. Please check out our website.

Total number of rooms: 7

Prices from:

Single:	**£42.50**	Double:	**£32.50**
Twin:	**£32.50**	Family room:	**£32.50**

Moffat, Dumfriesshire

Queensberry House

Map Ref: 2B8

76984

Open: All year

Beechgrove, Moffat, Dumfries & Galloway DG10 9RS
T: 01683 220538
E: info@queensberryhouse.com
W: queensberryhouse.com

A warm welcome and generous hospitality awaits you at this well appointed, listed house. Quiet rooms, all ensuite, comfortable beds and lounge and dining room, all ground floor. Locally sourced produce and delicious homemade bread. Drying room. Ample parking.

Total number of rooms: 3

Prices from:

Single:	**£45.00**	Double:	**£35.00**

Old Bridge of Urr, Castle Douglas

Croys House

Map Ref: 2A10

21515

★★★★ B&B

Open: All year excl Xmas and New Year

Old Bridge of Urr, Castle Douglas DG7 3EX
T: 01556 650237
E: alanwithall@aol.com
W: croys-house.co.uk

A warm welcome awaits you at this Georgian House set in 35 acres of parkland and gardens. It boasts a walled garden and topiary. Home grown produce is used for breakfast and evening meals, guests can relax in reception rooms with open fires. Ample parking. Delicious food and comfort. Outside kennels available.

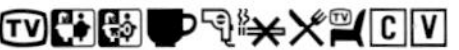

Total number of rooms: 3

Prices from:

Twin:	**£35.00**	Double:	**£35.00**
Dinner:	**£17.50**		

Sanquhar, Dumfriesshire

Newark Famhouse B&B

Map Ref: 2A8

47216

Open: All year excl Xmas and New Year

Newark, Sanquhar, Dumfriesshire DG4 6HN
T: 01659 50263
E: info@newarkfarm.com
W: newarkfarm.com

Traditional family run working beef and sheep farm in beautiful southern uplands with magnificent views of the River Nith Valley. Characteristic, spacious rooms. Whether you want to go fishing, walking, cycling, exploring or simply enjoy the views and wildlife, Newark farm is an ideal location. WiFi. Salmon and trout fishing can be arranged.

Total number of rooms: 3

Prices from:

Single: **£25.00-29.00** Double: **£21.50-27.50**
Twin: **£21.50-27.50** Family room: **POA**

Stranraer, Wigtownshire

The Ivy House & Ferry Link

Map Ref: 1F10

32384

Open: All year

London Road, Stranraer, Wigtownshire DG9 8ER
T: 01776 704176
E: ivyplace3@hotmail.com
W: ivyplace.worldonline.co.uk

A friendly welcome awaits you at this family run B&B situated close to town centre and Irish Ferry Terminals. Convenient base for visiting Castle Kennedy, Ardwell and Logan Botanic Gardens. Parking available at all times.

Total number of rooms: 4

Prices from:

Single: **£24.00-30.00** Double: **£24.00-26.00**
Twin: **£24.00-26.00** Family room: **£24.00-26.00**

nr Stranraer, Wigtownshire

East Challoch Farmhouse

Map Ref: 1F10

24096

Open: All year

Dunragit, Stranraer, Wigtownshire DG9 8PY
T: 01581 400391

Situated seven miles from Stranraer with spectacular views over Luce Bay, our farmhouse offers a warm and friendly welcome with excellent spacious quality accommodation. All bedrooms ensuite, colour TV, tea/coffee facilities and central heating. Dinner available on request. Ideal for walking, fishing, cycling and touring the S.W. Scottish coast. Gardens nearby.

Total number of rooms: 3

Prices from:

Single: **£29.00** Double: **£24.00**
Twin: **£24.00**

Important: Prices stated are estimates and may be subject to amendments.

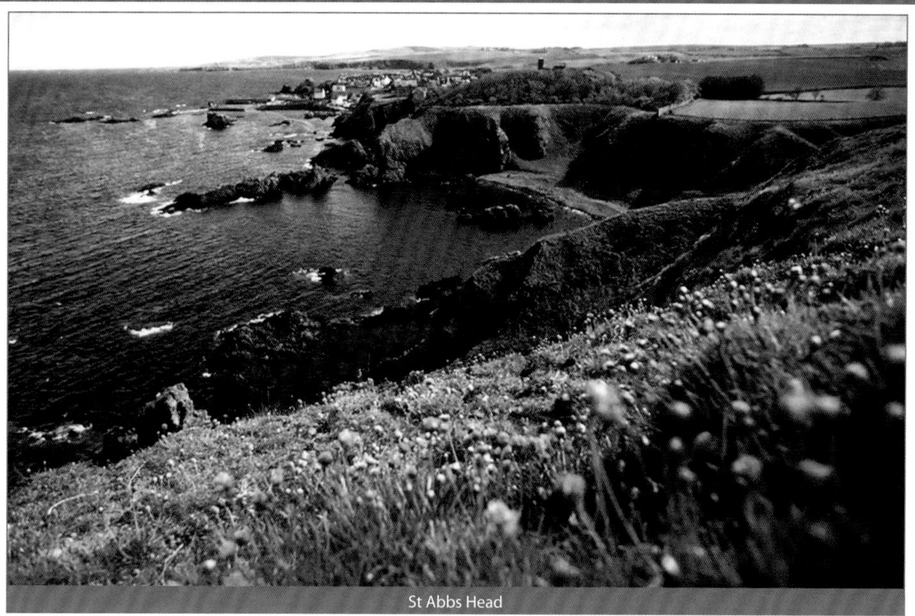
St Abbs Head

Scottish Borders

The Scottish Borders stretches from rolling hills and moorland in the west, through gentler valleys to the high agricultural plains of the east, and on to the rocky Berwickshire coastline with its secluded coves and picturesque fishing villages.

In the bright spring months, fresh new growth fills the valleys and forests of the Scottish Borders. Enjoy the lure of long summer days or relax in more mellow shades of autumn when mauves and purples tint the moors. The Scottish Borders is truly 'A Destination for all seasons'.

There are many lovely towns to visit in the Scottish Borders and a huge amount to see. Take the four great Borders abbeys of Dryburgh, Kelso, Jedburgh and Melrose. They were founded by King David I in the 12th century and though each is in ruins, a strong impression of their former glory remains.

Hawick is the centre of the local textile industry and you can still pick up bargain knitwear, tartans and tweeds at the many outlets and mills in the area.

Abbotsford, the former home of Sir Walter Scott, is now a visitor attraction just west of Melrose and you can also visit his old courtroom in Selkirk, preserved as it was in the 1800s when he presided over trials.

There's some great walking in the Scottish Borders with over 1500 miles of designated walking routes. The St Cuthbert's Way stretches 62 miles from Melrose to Lindisfarne; the Southern Upland Way is a 212 mile coast to coast trek taking in forest, farmland and hills while the Borders Abbeys Way is a very pleasant 65 mile circular route visiting all four historic abbeys.

DON'T MISS

1 Take the B6404 St Boswells to Kelso road and turn onto the B6356, signposted Dryburgh Abbey. About 1 mile along this road there is a junction signposting **Scott's View** to the right. Follow this road for about 2 miles for panoramic views of the Eildon Hills and the Scottish Borders countryside stretched out before you. Great spot for a picnic.

2 **Traquair House**, near Innerleithen, dates back to the 12th century and is said to be the oldest continuously inhibited house in Scotland. Discover the Traquair Maze, one of the largest hedged mazes in Scotland. Watch out for the Medieval Fayre in May and the Summer Fair in August.

3 The **Berwickshire Coastal Path** combines great natural beauty, with magnificent birdlife. There are spectacular views with sandstone cliffs, small coves, sandy beaches and natural harbours. The 15 mile (24km) route is way-marked and strong walkers may manage it in one day. Most people prefer to break it down into shorter stretches and stop off at the pretty villages along the way. Eyemouth is the largest town on this route – enjoy fresh fish and chips from Giacopazzi's by the harbour and watch out for the family of seals in the harbour!

4 The four great **Borders Abbeys** of Kelso, Melrose, Jedburgh and Dryburgh are a must see for any visitor to the area. Melrose Abbey is said to be the resting place of the casket containing the heart of King Robert the Bruce. Dryburgh is the burial place of Field Marshall Earl Haig and Sir Walter Scott. All of the Abbeys are under the care of Historic Scotland. Kelso is the most incomplete and has free access. For access to Melrose, Jedburgh and Dryburgh an admission charge applies.

5 **Floors Castle** in Kelso is the largest inhabited castle in Scotland and home to the Roxburghe family. The house has 365 windows, one for every day of the year. The castle, grounds, gardens and restaurant are open from Easter to October with The Terrace Restaurant, walled gardens, playground and garden centre open all year. The castle hosts an extensive events calendar throughout the year.

RETAIL, CRAFTS & TEXTILES

visitscottishborders.com

6 There are still **independent artists and craftsmen** working in wool in the Borders - spinners, weavers, knitwear designers and tapestry makers - but they have also been joined by workers in other crafts, potters, glass makers, workers in stone and wood and many more, who are more than willing to welcome the visitor into their workshop and demonstrate their skills. Many sell direct to the public. A visit to the Scottish Borders will allow you to enjoy the beautiful scenery of rolling hills, meandering rivers and romantic landscapes, which provide a source of inspiration to the artists.

7 In many towns throughout the Scottish Borders, high streets are a vibrant mix of independent specialists and boutiques. Bakers carrying on the tradition of the Selkirk Bannock, a fruited tea bread; butchers winning plaudits for their haggis recipes; confectioners satisfying the Scottish sweet tooth for Soor Plooms and Hawick Balls; each add to the pleasure of shopping here. Of particular note is **Peebles**, recently voted the **'Top Independent Retailing Town in Scotland'** for its quality range of individual shops.

8 The Scottish Borders knitwear business is world famous, take a look at the catwalks each season and it is clear that top designers around the world are increasingly turning to Scotland for inspiration and materials. **Tartan, tweed, wool and cashmere**; all strut their stuff down the runway. The Scottish Borders is at the very hub of the world's woollen industry, creating colours and garments for the ever changing and exacting fashion houses. **Lochcarron of Scotland** has recently opened a new retail outlet in Selkirk and **Hawick Cashmere, Peter Scott** and **Pringle of Scotland** are all found in Hawick.

6

7

8

WALKS

visitscottishborders.com

9 The life and progress of St Cuthbert provided the inspiration for the **St Cuthbert's Way** walking route. Starting in Melrose and ending on Holy Island (Lindisfarne) it passes through rolling farmland, river valleys, sheltered woods, hills and moorland culminating in The Holy Island Causeway, passable only at low tide. The full route is 100km / 60 miles in length but this can be broken down into shorter stages.

10 The **Borders Abbeys Way** is a circular route linking the four great ruined Border Abbeys in Kelso, Jedburgh, Dryburgh and Melrose. The full route is 105km / 65 miles in length and can easily be broken down into stages.

11 The **Southern Upland Way** is Britain's first official coast to coast long distance footpath. It runs 212 miles (340km) from Portpatrick in the west to Cockburnspath on the Berwickshire coast. This route takes in some of the finest scenery in Southern Scotland and, of the total route, 130km / 82 miles is in the Scottish Borders. The Way goes through many remote uplands areas, providing a real challenge for the experienced walker, while some parts lie within easy reach of towns and villages and are more suitable for families and the less ambitious.

12 The **John Buchan Way** is named after the writer and diplomat who had many associations with the Scottish Borders. The 22km / 13 mile route takes you from Peebles to Broughton and ends at the John Buchan centre, which houses a collection of photographs, books and other memorabilia.

ACTIVITIES

13 **Glentress** and **Innerleithen** in the Tweed Valley and **Newcastleton** to the south have a massive reputation for some of the best **mountain biking** in the UK and beyond. Glentress is probably the best biking centre in Britain, with brilliant trails of all grades, a top-notch cafe, a bike shop with bike hire, changing and showering facilities, and a great atmosphere. Innerleithen, situated just a few miles south east of Glentress, is quite different from its better-known sister. It's a venue for the more experienced rider and home to the Traquair XC Black run – not for the faint-hearted! All three centres are part of the **7Stanes** – 7 mountain biking centres of excellence across the South of Scotland.

14 **'Freedom of the Fairways'** is Scotland's best selling **golf** pass. This pass offers access to 21 superb courses ranging from the coastal course at Eyemouth to the winner of the 'most friendly' 9-hole course, St Boswells to the championship The Roxburghe and Cardrona. The Freedom of the Fairways scheme runs between April and October and offers both senior and junior passes, available to book online at visitscottishborders.com

15 Along with mountain biking the Scottish Borders offers some superb road **cycle** routes through the peaceful Borders countryside. The **Borderloop** is a magnificent 250 mile way-marked circular route linking Peebles in the west with the Berwickshire coast at Eyemouth. The **Tweed Cycleway** starts 650 feet above sea level near Biggar and runs close by to the River Tweed through the Scottish Borders to the finish at Berwick upon Tweed. This 89 mile way-marked route can be broken down into sections and it takes in some of the key Borders towns en-route, including Peebles, Melrose, Kelso and Coldstream.

16 The Scottish Borders has everything for the angler. From the internationally famous salmon **fishing** on the **River Tweed** to the excellent sea trout fishing on its tributaries; from the rainbow trout in the local lochs to wild brown trout in the rivers; and from the course fishing of the lower Tweed to the sea fishing off the Berwickshire coast; there is plenty to choose from.

17

18

WILDLIFE

visitscotland.com/wildlife

17 The elusive, native **red squirrel** can still be found in pockets throughout the Scottish Borders. Try Paxton House, nr Berwick, Tweed Valley Forest Park and Floors Castle Estate. Anywhere with plenty of trees and peace and quiet, be sure to keep your eyes peeled!

18 The **Tweed Valley Osprey Watch** has two centres; Glentress and Kailzie Gardens. Both are open from Easter until mid-August and September respectively. Enjoy live camera action from an osprey nest within The Tweed Valley Forest Park. Follow the progress of the family, from nest building in spring to chicks hatching in May, to fledglings in August. Both centres have a variety of interpretative materials and volunteer guides. A small admission charge applies.

19 On the Berwickshire Coast, **St Abbs Head** is a National Nature Reserve. It is a landmark site for birdwatchers and wildlife enthusiasts. Thousands of breeding seabirds can be seen between April and August and migrating birds in October. The scenery is stunning with wide-sweeping views from the lighthouse on 'The Head' north towards Edinburgh and the Fife coast and south towards Holy Island, Bamburgh and the Farne Islands. There are a number of way-marked trails around the reserve which all start from the car park and information centre.

Coldingham Sands, Berwickshire

Dunlaverock House

Map Ref: 2F5

★★★★ GUEST HOUSE

23747

Open: All year excl Xmas

Coldingham Bay, Coldingham,
Eyemouth, Berwickshire TD14 5PA

T: 018907 71450

E: info@dunlaverock.com

W: dunlaverock.com

Dunlaverock House occupies an elevated position overlooking Coldingham Bay. Peaceful gardens with path to beach, spectacular views. Sumptuous dinner menu including locally obtained sea food. Dog friendly. Special two night dinner, bed and breakfast breaks from £46 pppn. Wheelchair accessible.

Total number of rooms: 6

Prices from:

Single: **£40.00** Double: **£35.00**

Twin: **£35.00** Family room: **£102.00pr**

Galashiels, Selkirkshire

Ettrickvale

Map Ref: 2D6

★★★ B&B

45019

Open: All year excl Xmas and New Year

33 Abbotsford Road, Galashiels, Selkirkshire TD1 3HW

T: 01896 755224

E: ettrickvale@aol.com

W: ettrickvalebandb.co.uk

Total number of rooms: 3

Prices from:

Double: **£22.50** Twin: **£25.00**

Melrose, Roxburghshire

Dunfermline House

Map Ref: 2D6

★★★ GUEST HOUSE

23707

Open: All year

Buccleuch Street, Melrose, Roxburghshire TD6 9LB

T: 01896 822411

E: dunfermline.house@virgin.net

W: dunfermlinehouse.co.uk

Total number of rooms: 5

Prices from:

Single: **£35.00** Double: **£30.00**

Twin: **£30.00**

Melrose, Roxburghshire

Fauhope House

Map Ref: 2D6

★★★★ B&B

25704

Open: All year

Fauhope, Gattonside, Melrose, Roxburghshire TD6 9LU

T: 01869 823184

E: info@fauhopehouse.com

A charming and secluded Country house built in 1897, set in it's own spacious grounds with views to the River Tweed, Melrose Abbey and the Eildon Hills, 20 minutes scenic walk into Melrose. Non smoking.

AA 2008 B&B Awards – Fauhope House – Guest Accommodation of the Year, Scotland

Total number of rooms: 3

Prices from:

Single: **£60.00** Double: **£40.00**

Twin: **£40.00**

Peebles

Drochil Castle Bed and Breakfast

Map Ref: 2C6

23203

Open: All year excl Xmas and New Year

Drochil Castle Farm,
Romanno Bridge, Peebles, Peeblesshire EH46 7DD

T: 01721 752249
E: black.drochil@talk21.com
W: drochilcastle.co.uk

A warm welcome awaits you at this traditional working beef and sheep farm. Set amongst rolling Borders hills with fine views down the Lyne and Tweed Valley. Located beside the ruins of the 16th century Drochil Castle.

Total number of rooms: 5

Prices from:

Single:	**£25.00-£30.00**	Double:	**£30.00**
Twin:	**£25.00-£30.00**	Family room:	**£30.00**

Peebles

Lyne Farmhouse

Map Ref: 2C6

36638

Open: All year

Lyne Farm, Peebles, Peeblesshire EH45 8NR

T: 01721 740255
E: lynefarmhouse@btinternet.com
W: lynefarm.co.uk

Total number of rooms: 3

Prices from:

Single:	**£30.00**	Double:	**£50.00**
Twin:	**£50.00**		

St. Boswells, Roxburghshire

Mrs A. Lee

Map Ref: 2D7

42404

Open: All year

Mainhill, St. Boswells, Melrose, Roxburghshire TD6 0HG

T: 01835 823788
E: annmainhill@hotmail.co.uk

Total number of rooms: 2

Prices from:

Single:	**£35.00**	Twin:	**£30.00**

Selkirk

The Firs

Map Ref: 2D7

78609

Open: March-October

Manorhill Road, Philiphaugh, Selkirk TD7 5LS

T: 01750 20409 F: 01750 22325
E: marybathgate@hotmail.com
W: the-firs-selkirk.com

Very comfortable accommodation in this fine country house situated on the outskirts of Selkirk. Ideal for touring this beautiful area of Scotland. The Southern Upland Way can be accessed nearby and cycling is available at Glentress Forest. Within easy reach of Melrose and Galashiels.

Total number of rooms: 2

Prices from:

Single:	**£45.00**	Double:	**£40.00**
Twin:	**£40.00**		

Important: Prices stated are estimates and may be subject to amendments.

Selkirk

Sunnybrae House

Map Ref: 2D7

Open: All year excl Xmas and New Year

12349

75 Tower Street, Selkirk, Selkirkshire TD7 4LS
T: 01750 21156
E: bookings@sunnybraehouse.fsnet.co.uk

A warm welcome awaits you at Sunnybrae which has two suites, both with sitting room and ensuite bathroom. Bedrooms have views over the town to the hills beyond. Breakfast using local produce. Private parking.

Total number of rooms: 2

Prices from:
Single: **£40.00** Double: **£28.00**
Twin: **£28.00** Family room: **£28.00**
Children: **£12.00**

West Linton, Peeblesshire

Jerviswood B&B

Map Ref: 2B6

Open: All year excl Xmas and New Year

43942

Linton Bank Drive, West Linton, Peeblesshire EH46 7DT
T/F: 01968 660429

Total number of rooms: 3

Prices from:
Single: **£25.00** Double: **£20.00**
Twin: **£20.00**

West Linton, Peeblesshire

The Meadows B&B

Map Ref: 2B6

Open: All year

59651

4 Robinsland Drive, West Linton, Peeblesshire EH46 7JD
T: 01968 661798
E: mwthain@btinternet.com
W: themeadowsbandb.co.uk

West Linton is a pretty conservation village 11 miles from Edinburgh bypass on the A702. West Linton lies at the foot of the Pentland Hills. The Meadows is a 5 minute walk from the village centre where there is a good pub and restaurant. Accommodation is private but friendly with very comfortable beds.

Total number of rooms: 3

Prices from:
Single: **£25.00** Double: **£24.00**
Twin: **£24.00**

For everything you need to know about skiing and snowsports in Scotland call 0845 22 55 121

ski-scotland.com

The Old Town skyline at dusk, Edinburgh

EDINBURGH AND THE LOTHIANS

Each year, more than three and a half million visitors arrive in Scotland's capital and discover one of the finest cities in the world.

Whether you're partying at the biggest Hogmanay celebrations on Earth or taking your seat in the audience at the planet's largest arts festival, Edinburgh always offers more than you could ever hope to take on in one visit.

Streets steeped in history

No trip to Edinburgh is complete without a visit to the world famous Castle. Over a million people take to its ramparts every year. Many then set off down the Esplanade and onto the Royal Mile, touching history with every step. During the Festival weeks, hundreds of performers take to the Mile in an explosion of colour and sound, creating an exciting mêlée that changes every day.

Although the trappings of modern life are never far away in the shops, cafés and bars, the Old Town's fascinating history is impossible to ignore. Edinburgh's ghosts whisper in the closes: grave robbers and thieves rubbing shoulders with poets, philosophers, kings and queens – each conjured up and colourfully interpreted in the museums, exhibitions and visitor attractions you'll pass along the way.

A city of beauty

The city's rich history is matched by its beauty. Architecturally, Edinburgh is a stunning city. That beauty extends to its parks, gardens and wild places. Don't miss the Royal Botanic Garden, the view from the top of majestic Arthur's Seat or the Water of Leith walkway, which brings a touch of the countryside right into the city.

Edinburgh is also a city by the sea with a rapidly changing seafront. The busy port of Leith has been transformed in recent years and it boasts a wonderful selection of bars and restaurants.

Get out of town

Further out of town, there's much to explore. Take a trip down the coast to places like Aberlady, Gullane, Longniddry, Dirleton, North Berwick and Dunbar. Play golf on top class courses, watch the seabirds on beautiful sandy beaches or take a boat trip around the Bass Rock.

You could cycle for miles along the Union Canal towpath, visit Roslin Glen and the mysterious Rosslyn Chapel, head for Linlithgow and its ruined Palace or enjoy a thrilling day out at the Musselburgh races.

What's more, 2009 is a big year for Scotland – we're celebrating the 250th anniversary of the birth of Robert Burns. There's over 200 special events taking place throughout the year, all over Scotland. Go to homecomingscotland2009.com to find out about events in this area.

So what is it you'd like to do on your visit to Edinburgh and the Lothians? And where would you like to stay? There's a spectacular selection of B&B accommodation, from small hotels and guesthouses to family-run establishments with a handful of individual rooms, you've got so much to choose from in an area that will continue to inspire you and leave you longing for more.

Ceilidh Culture

What's On?

Ceilidh Culture
27 March – 19 April 2009
A vibrant celebration of traditional Scottish arts.
ceilidhculture.co.uk

Edinburgh International Science Festival

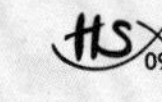

6 – 18 April 2009
Stir the curiosity of inquiring minds.
sciencefestival.co.uk

Mary King's Ghost Fest
8 - 18 May 2009 (dates provisional)
Explore Edinburgh's haunted places.
edinburghghostfest.com

Edinburgh International Film Festival

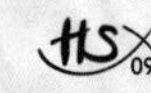

17- 28 June 2009
The festival where the films are the stars.
edfilmfest.org.uk

The Gathering 2009

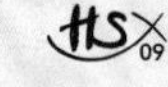

25 – 26 July 2009
Edinburgh will witness one of the largest clan gatherings in history as part of the Homecoming 2009 celebrations.
clangathering.org

Edinburgh Military Tattoo
7 – 29 August 2009
This military extravaganza is an international favourite.
edinburgh-tattoo.co.uk

Edinburgh Festival Fringe
7 – 31 August 2009
The largest arts festival on the planet.
edfringe.com

Edinburgh International Festival
7 – 30 August 2009
The very best of opera, theatre, music and dance.
eif.org.uk

East Lothian Food & Drink Festival
25 – 27 September 2009
Food and entertainment for all ages.
foodanddrinkeastlothian.com

Edinburgh's Christmas
24 November – 25 December 2009
Edinburgh becomes a winter wonderland.
edinburghschristmas.com

Edinburgh's Hogmanay
29 December – 1 January 2010
The world's favourite place to celebrate Hogmanay.
edinburghshogmanay.com

All dates correct at time of publication. Please check before booking. VisitScotland cannot be held responsible for any inaccuracies

DON'T MISS

1 Stroll down the **Royal Mile**, so-called because it boasts Edinburgh Castle at the top and the Palace of Holyroodhouse at the bottom. Browse through the wide range of quirky, independent gift shops and stop off in one of the many tea rooms or cafés along the way. Upon reaching the Canongate, you will find the new Scottish Parliament, famed for its striking contemporary architecture.

2 Never a month passes without a major event or **festival** in Edinburgh, the International Science Festival in April, the Heineken Cup, the Rugby Sevens World Series and Children's Theatre in May, International Film Festival in June, Jazz and Blues in July, Christmas or Hogmanay. And of course, there's the world's largest international arts festival in August, taking in the Fringe, the Tattoo, the Book and International Festivals.

3 **The National Galleries of Scotland** exhibit work by some of the world's most influential artists in five galleries across Edinburgh. From Rembrandt and Monet, to Picasso and Bacon, not to mention major touring exhibitions.

4 **Linlithgow Palace**, once an important royal residence and birthplace of Mary, Queen of Scots, is now a magnificent ruin. Set beside a loch, with a huge number of rooms, passages and stairways, you can imagine what life must have been like in this vast palace.

5 Within minutes of Edinburgh, you can stroll along the white sands of **East Lothian**, with only the sound of water lapping on the shore. Head for Gullane, Yellowcraig or North Berwick. The sheer expanse of each beach is truly breathtaking.

6 Set amidst the beauty of Roslin Glen, the mysterious **Rosslyn Chapel** is undoubtedly Scotland's most outstanding Gothic church. According to Dan Brown's The Da Vinci Code, this chapel is on the trail of the Holy Grail, which only adds to the intrigue.

2

3

4

6

FOOD AND DRINK

eatscotland.com

7 **Farmers' markets** are great ways to get the freshest quality, local produce. Held on every Saturday morning on Castle Terrace and the last Saturday of each month in Haddington (except December) in East Lothian, be sure to pop along early to pick up the very best supplies.

8 For the story of whisky, try either the **Scotch Whisky Experience** in Edinburgh or **Glenkinchie Distillery**, by Pencaitland. The former tells how the amber nectar is made and how best to enjoy it, while the latter is ideal for warming you up on your return from walking the East Lothian beaches.

9 For restaurants with the best views in Edinburgh, visit **Oloroso** on Castle Street or the **Forth Floor Restaurant** at Harvey Nichols in Edinburgh. Combine fine dining with panoramic cityscapes. Don't forget your camera!

10 **East Lothian** holds its annual **Food and Drink Festival** in late September each year, giving you ample opportunity to savour the best of the region's produce and hospitality.

9

12

13

HISTORY AND HERITAGE

11 **The Scottish Mining Museum** is located at the former Lady Victoria Colliery at Newtongrange in Midlothian. The five-star attraction has turned the story of Scotland's coal into a fascinating tour and exhibition. With every guide an ex-miner, you'll see and hear the authentic stories of a working mine.

12 **The Royal Yacht *Britannia***, former floating home of the monarchy, offers a superb visitor experience that will guide you through 40 years of royal life, including private quarters, the sick bay and the laundry!

13 Edinburgh is one of Europe's most haunted cities, surrounded by myth and legend. Take a journey back in time and experience the narrow underground closes at **Real Mary King's Close** or try one of the many walking ghost tours, if you dare!

14 With fantastic views over the Firth of Forth, the imposing 15th century **Blackness Castle** looks almost poised to set sail. Explore its darkened corridors, which still capture the atmosphere of a garrison fortress and state prison.

SHOPPING

15 **Multrees Walk** is located at the heart of the city and is headed by Scotland's flagship Harvey Nichols. Known locally as The Walk, shops include Louis Vuitton, Links of London, Azendi, Calvin Klein Underwear and Reiss. The focal point for luxury shopping, this is a must-see for all shoppers.

16 Surrounding the city centre, Edinburgh has a number of urban villages where you'll find **specialist shops**, from up-and-coming designers to crafts, jewellery, food and gifts. In the centre, try the West End, Victoria Street and Royal Mile, while Bruntsfield and Stockbridge are a little further from the city centre.

17 Only a short bus ride from the city centre, take a refreshing stroll along the waterfront in **Leith**, where you'll find independent shops and galleries, alongside contemporary bars and cafes.

ACTIVITIES AND ATTRACTIONS

18 Edinburgh and the Lothians is a superb base for **golf**, whether you choose to play some of the city's fine courses or go east to the coast. Stay in the city for the challenges of Bruntsfield Links, Prestonfield or Duddingston. Or head to the Lothians for the perfect mixture of parkland and links courses. You can enjoy inspirational views across to Fife from some courses in East Lothian.

19 There is a fantastic range of **walks and trails** throughout the scenic and historic countryside of Edinburgh and the Lothians. Through the heart of the city runs the Water of Leith where a peaceful path offers a handy escape from the vibrant centre. In East Lothian the stretch of beach from Gullane to Yellowcraig is perfect for a walk or a picnic, whilst Roslin Glen in Midlothian and Avon River in West Lothian are exhilarating walks to make best use of an afternoon.

20 The area is home to some of Scotland's most impressive visitor attractions. From interactive exhibits to wonders of the natural world, there is something for everyone. Head to the **Scottish Seabird Centre** in North Berwick or **Edinburgh Zoo** to see wildlife up close, travel back in time at **Our Dynamic Earth** or try rock climbing at the **Edinburgh International Climbing Arena**.

21 With free entry to over 30 top attractions, free return airport and city centre bus transport, a free comprehensive guidebook as well as many exclusive offers, the **Edinburgh Pass** is the best way to discover all that Edinburgh has to offer. Buy a 1, 2 or 3 day Pass from edinburghpass.com or from one of the Visitor Information Centres in Edinburgh (see next page).

MAP

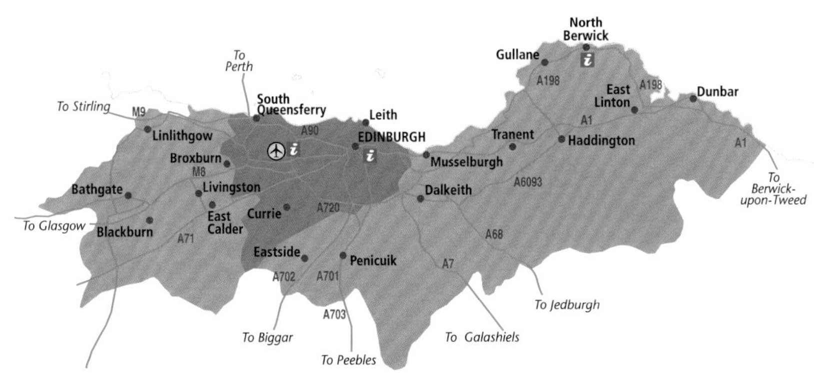

©Collins Bartholomew Ltd 2008

VISITOR INFORMATION CENTRES

Visitor Information Centres are staffed by people 'in the know' offering friendly advice, helping to make your stay in Scotland the most enjoyable ever . . . whatever your needs!

Edinburgh and Lothians		
Edinburgh	3 Princes Street, Edinburgh, EH2 2QP	Tel: 0131 473 3820
Edinburgh Airport	Main Concourse, Edinburgh International Airport, EH12 9DN	Tel: 0131 344 3120
North Berwick	1 Quality Street, North Berwick, EH39 4HJ	Tel: 01620 892197

LOCAL KNOWLEDGE • WHERE TO STAY • ACCOMMODATION BOOKING • PLACES TO VISIT • THINGS TO DO • MAPS AND GUIDES • TRAVEL ADVICE • ROUTE PLANNING • WHERE TO SHOP AND EAT • LOCAL CRAFTS AND PRODUCE • EVENT INFORMATION • TICKETS

For information and ideas about exploring Scotland in advance of your trip, call our booking and information service **0845 22 55 121** or go to **visitscotland.com**

If calling from outside the UK and Ireland **+44 1506 832 121** From Ireland **1800 932 510**

A £4 booking fee applies for accommodation bookings made via a Visitor Information Centre and through our booking and information service.

Blackburn, by Bathgate

Cruachan Bed & Breakfast

Map Ref: 2B5

Open: All year excl Xmas and New Year

21531

78 East Main Street, Blackburn, Bathgate, West Lothian EH47 7QS

T: 01506 655221
E: enquiries@cruachan.co.uk
W: cruachan.co.uk

Cruachan's central location provides a perfect base from which to explore central Scotland. Edinburgh is very easy to reach either by train or by Park and Ride bus. Owners Kenneth and Jacqueline ensure their guests are provided with meticulously presented accommodation, caring service and a hearty Scottish breakfast.

Total number of rooms: 4

Prices per room from:

Single:	**£40.00**	Double:	**£60.00**
Twin:	**£60.00**	Family room:	**£80.00**

Broxburn, West Lothian

Bankhead Farm

Map Ref: 2B5

Open: All year excl Xmas

14205

Dechmont, Broxburn, West Lothian EH52 6NB

T: 01506 811209
E: bankheadbb@aol.com
W: bankheadfarm.com

Total number of rooms: 7

Prices from:

Single:	**£40.00**	Double:	**£35.00**
Twin:	**£35.00**	Family room:	**£35.00**

Dunbar, East Lothian

Springfield Guest House

Map Ref: 2E4

Open: January-November

55620

Belhaven Road, Dunbar, East Lothian EH42 1NH

T: 01368 862502
E: smeed@tesco.net

Total number of rooms: 5

Prices per room from:

Single:	**£30.00**	Double:	**£50.00**
Twin:	**£50.00**	Family room:	**£60.00**

Edinburgh

A-Haven Townhouse Hotel

Map Ref: 2C5

Open: All year

10443

180 Ferry Road, Edinburgh EH6 4NS

T: 0131 554 6559
E: reservations@a-haven.co.uk
W: a-haven.co.uk

Total number of rooms: 14

Prices from:

Single:	**£35.00**	Double:	**£25.00**
Twin:	**£25.00**	Family room:	**£20.00**

Get the most out of your stay...

Visitor Information Centres are staffed by people 'in the know', offering friendly advice, helping to make your stay in Scotland the most enjoyable ever... whatever your needs!

Live it. Visit Scotland.
visitscotland.com/wheretofindus

Important: Prices stated are estimates and may be subject to amendments.

Edinburgh
Ailsa Craig Hotel
Map Ref: 2C5

★★★ METRO HOTEL

11232

Open: All year

24 Royal Terrace, Edinburgh EH7 5AH
T: 0131 556 6055
E: ailsacraighotel@ednet.co.uk
W: townhousehotels.co.uk

Newly refurbished elegant Georgian Townhouse hotel. Ideal city centre location within walking distance to Waverley Station, Princes Street, Edinburgh Castle and Playhouse Theatre. Combining traditional features with modern facilities, the hotel offers superb views, private gardens and friendly atmosphere providing the perfect blend of history and hospitality. Free WiFi internet access.

Total number of rooms: 16

Prices from:

Single:	**£25.00**	Double:	**£25.00**
Twin:	**£25.00**	Family room:	**£25.00**

Edinburgh
Albyn Townhouse
Map Ref: 2C5

★★★ GUEST HOUSE

79278

Open: All Year excl Xmas

16 Hartington Gardens,
Edinburgh, Midlothian EH10 4LD

T: 0131 229 6459
E: info@albyntownhouse.co.uk
W: albyntownhouse.co.uk

Albyn is a newly redecorated 3 star guest house, with 10 ensuite beautiful and comfortable bedrooms, free WiFi, Freeview TV and 3 free parking spaces, bookable in advance only. Very quiet, 15 minutes walk from the centre, Castle and restaurants. From £30.00 to £50.00 pppn including full Scottish breakfast.

Total number of rooms: 10

Prices from:

Single:	**£45.00**	Double:	**£30.00**
Twin:	**£30.00**	Family room:	**£85.00pr**

Edinburgh
Mrs Linda J. Allan
Map Ref: 2C5

★★ B&B

44146

Open: May-October
10 Baberton Mains Rise, Edinburgh EH14 3HG
T: 0131 442 3619
E: lja_bandb_edin@hotmail.com

Total number of rooms: 1

Prices from:

Double: **£17.00**

Edinburgh
Allison House
Map Ref: 2C5

★★★★ GUEST HOUSE

11676

Open: All year
17 Mayfield Gardens, Edinburgh EH9 2AX
T: 0131 667 8049
E: info@allisonhousehotel.com
W: allisonhousehotel.com

Total number of rooms: 11

Prices from:

Single:	**£42.50**	Double:	**£32.50**
Twin:	**£32.50**	Family room:	**POA**

Edinburgh

Alpha Guest House

Map Ref: 2C5

★★★ GUEST HOUSE

16323

Open: All year

19 Old Dalkeith Road, Edinburgh EH16 4TE

T: 0131 258 0810

E: webenquiries@briggend.com

W: briggend.com

Newly refurbished family run guest house. Minutes from City centre and City Bypass. Close to Edinburgh Royal Infirmary. On main bus route. Full Scottish breakfast. Sky TV/Wi-Fi. Private parking.

Total number of rooms: 6

Prices per person per night from:

Single:	**£25.00**	Double:	**£20.00**
Twin:	**£20.00**	Family room:	**£20.00**

Edinburgh

Ardgarth Guest House

Map Ref: 2C5

★★★ GUEST HOUSE

12567

Open: All year excl Xmas

1 St. Mary's Place, Portobello, Edinburgh EH15 2QF

T: 0131 669 3021

E: stay@ardgarth.com

W: ardgarth.com

Total number of rooms: 9

Prices per room from:

Single:	**£20.00**	Double:	**£40.00**
Twin:	**£40.00**	Family room:	**£40.00**

Edinburgh

Averon Guest House

Map Ref: 2C5

★ GUEST HOUSE

13577

Open: All year

44 Gilmore Place, Edinburgh EH3 9NQ

T: 0131 229 9932

E: info@averon.co.uk

W: averon.co.uk

Built in 1770 as a farmhouse, charming, centrally situated Georgian period house offers a high standard of accommodation at favourable terms.

★ Full cooked breakfast

★ All credit cards accepted

★ 10 minutes walk to Princes Street and Castle

★ AA listed

★ Private Car Park

Total number of rooms: 10

Prices from:

Single:	**£28.00**	Double:	**£26.00**
Twin:	**£26.00**	Family room:	**£21.00**

Important: Prices stated are estimates and may be subject to amendments.

Edinburgh
Balmore House
Map Ref: 2C5

67929

Open: All year

34 Gilmore Place, Edinburgh EH3 9NQ
T: 0131 221 1331
E: balmore@classicfm.net
balmore34@btinternet.com
W: balmore-holidays.co.uk

Balmore is very convenient for all Edinburgh's attractions and we are on a great bus route for attractions outside the city. We offer clean accommodation and good food. We can also provide credit card facilities and free WiFi. Our staff will do their best to ensure a comfortable stay in Edinburgh.

Total number of rooms: 14

Prices from:
Single: **£45.00** Double: **£35.00**
Twin: **£35.00** Family room: **£30.00**

Edinburgh
Bield Bed and Beakfast
Map Ref: 2C5

15091

Open: All year

3 Orchard Brae West, Edinburgh EH4 2EW
T: 0131 332 5119
E: bieldltd@hotmail.com
W: bieldbedandbreakfast.com

Ideally situated less than a mile from the city centre with local buses passing nearby. Ample off street parking for our guests. Our comfortable premises are tastefully decorated to a high standard and you are guaranteed a friendly welcome and relaxing stay in our family run bed and breakfast.

Total number of rooms: 3

Prices from:
Single: **£45.00** Double: **£30.00**
Twin: **£30.00** Family room: **POA**

Edinburgh
Blinkbonny House
Map Ref: 2C5

15464

Open: All year

23 Blinkbonny Gardens, Edinburgh EH4 3HG
T: 0131 467 1232
E: info@blinkbonnyhouse.co.uk
W: blinkbonnyhouse.co.uk

Beautiful detached bungalow in residential area on west side of city in quiet location. Within walking distance of Princes Street, Botanic Gardens and Art Gallery. Close to airport and A90 with easy access to the Forth Road Bridge and the North. Private parking available. Two ground floor rooms with ensuite.

Total number of rooms: 3

Prices from:
Single: **£30.00-50.00** Double: **£25.00-50.00**
Twin: **£25.00-50.00**

Edinburgh and the Lothians

Edinburgh

Bonnington Guest House

Map Ref: 2C5

Open: All year excl Xmas 15672

202 Ferry Road, Edinburgh EH6 4NW
T: 0131 554 7610
E: booking@thebonningtonguesthouse.com
W: thebonningtonguesthouse.com

Situated 10 minutes from Edinburgh city centre, The Bonnington Guest House is the ideal base to enjoy Edinburgh and the surrounding area. The guest house, a listed building, has seven spacious family, triple/twin, and double rooms available and is non-smoking. Private off-road car park.

Total number of rooms: 7

Prices from:

Single: **£48.00** Double: **£30.00**
Twin: **£30.00**

Edinburgh

Burns Guest House

Map Ref: 2C5

Open: All year 16942

67 Gilmore Place, Edinburgh EH3 9NU
T: 0131 229 1669
F: 0131 229 9225
E: burnsbandb@talk21.com
W: burnsguesthouse.co.uk

Charming pre-Victorian terraced house personally run by Mrs Burns. Close to city centre tourist attractions, Kings Theatre, E.I.C.C, local pubs and restaurants nearby. Parking to front and secure parking to rear. Double and twin rooms are all ensuite.

Total number of rooms: 4

Prices from:

Single: **£25.00** Double: **£25.00**
Twin: **£25.00**

Edinburgh

Castle Park Guest House

Map Ref: 2C5

Open: All year excl Xmas 18452

75 Gilmore Place, Edinburgh EH3 9NU
T: 0131 229 1215
E: castlepark@btconnect.com
W: castleparkguesthouse.co.uk

Family run guest house close to Edinburgh's city centre and main attractions. This cosy Victorian town house is not only well located but also great value for money. With Edinburgh Castle only 20 minutes walk and rooms ranging from £20.00 per person, the Castle Park Guest House should be on everyone's itinerary.

Total number of rooms: 8

Prices from:

Single: **£25.00-35.00** Double: **£25.00-35.00**
Twin: **£25.00-35.00** Family room: **£25.00-35.00**

Important: Prices stated are estimates and may be subject to amendments.

Edinburgh
Crioch Guest House
Map Ref: 2C5

★★★ GUEST HOUSE

21312

Open: All year

23 East Hermitage Place, Leith Links
Edinburgh EH6 8AD
T: 0131 554 5494
E: welcome@crioch.com
W: crioch.com

Enjoy Dora's famous full cooked, continental or vegetarian breakfast. All rooms have ensuite shower or private bathroom, and are comfortable and very clean. Crioch looks onto Leith Links park, near Leith's fine cafes , bars and restaurants. Free parking and internet (WiFi). Buses every 10 minutes to the city centre.

Total number of rooms: 6

Prices from:

Single:	**£30.00**	Double:	**£27.00**
Twin:	**£28.50**	Family room:	**£25.00**

Edinburgh
Dene Guest House
Map Ref: 2C5

★★★ GUEST HOUSE

22466

Open: All year
7 Eyre Place, Off Dundas Street, Edinburgh EH3 5ES
T: 0131 556 2700
E: deneguesthouse@yahoo.co.uk
W: deneguesthouse.com

Total number of rooms: 11

Prices per room from:

Single:	**£25.00**	Double:	**£49.00**
Twin	**£49.00**	Family room:	**£79.00**

Edinburgh
Doocote House
Map Ref: 2C5

★★★ B&B

22925

Open: All year excl Xmas

15 Moat Street, Edinburgh EH14 1PE
T: 0131 443 5455

Well established traditional B&B 2 miles from city centre on main bus route, direct bus from airport, free unrestricted on street parking available. Accommodation includes ensuite facilities, guests' kitchen and guests' sitting room/breakfast room.

Total number of rooms: 3

Prices from:

Twin:	**£28.00**	Double:	**£28.00**
Family room:	**£28.00**		

visitscotland.com/walking

For everything you need to know about walking in Scotland and for a brochure Call 0845 22 55 121
Scotland. Created for Walking

Edinburgh
Doris Crook Bed and Breakfast
Map Ref: 2C5

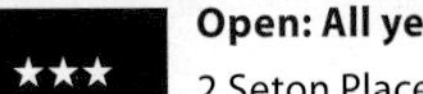

42995

Open: All year

2 Seton Place, Edinburgh EH9 2JT
T: 0131 667 6430
E: mail@dcrook.co.uk
W: dcrook.co.uk

Upper flatted Victorian house in quiet residential area. Private parking. Easy access to town centre on good bus route. Special diets catered.

Total number of rooms: 2

Prices from:
Single: **£35.00** Double: **£28.00**
Twin: **£28.00**

Edinburgh
Emerald House
Map Ref: 2C5

24910

Open: All year excl Xmas

3 Drum Street, Edinburgh EH17 8QQ
T: 0131 664 5918
E: emeraldedinburgh@msn.com

Victorian Villa on main bus route into city centre. Minutes from city bypass. Near Royal Infirmary. Good quality accommodation, excellent choice of breakfast menu.

Total number of rooms: 6

Prices from:
Single: **£25.00** Double: **£25.00**
Twin: **£25.00**

Edinburgh
Falcon Crest Guest House
Map Ref: 2C5

25545

Open: All year excl Xmas

70 South Trinity Road, Edinburgh EH5 3NX
T/F: 0131 552 5294
E: manager@falconcrest.co.uk
W: falconcrest.co.uk

A friendly welcome awaits at our family home in a Victorian Terrace. Convenient for Leith, the Royal Botanic Gardens, Newhaven Harbour and Granton Marina yet only ten minutes by frequent bus from Edinburgh city centre. Free on-street parking. Most rooms ensuite. Special diets by prior request. Room only rates available.

Total number of rooms: 5

Prices from:
Single: **£20.00** Double: **£24.00**
Twin: **£20.00** Family room: **£20.00**

Important: Prices stated are estimates and may be subject to amendments.

Edinburgh
Gildun Guest House
Map Ref: 2C5

Open: All year
9 Spence Street, Edinburgh EH16 5AG
T: 0131 667 1368
E: gildun.edin@btinternet.com
W: gildun.co.uk

27612

Total number of rooms: 8

Prices from:

Single:	**£30.00**	Double:	**£30.00**
Twin:	**£30.00**	Family room:	**£30.00**

Edinburgh
Glendevon Bed and Breakfast
Map Ref: 2C5

Open: April-October
50 Glasgow Road, Edinburgh EH12 8HN
T: 0131 539 0491
E: simpson-glendevon@fsmail.net
W: simpson-glendevon.co.uk

1930's family bungalow on major bus route to city centre and 3 miles from the airport. Private parking. Some ground floor accommodation. Non smoking.

28098

Total number of rooms: 3

Prices from:

Single:	**£25.00-35.00**	Double:	**£25.00-35.00**
Twin:	**£25.00-35.00**		

Edinburgh
Harvest Guest House
Map Ref: 2C5

Open: All year
33 Straiton Place, The Promenade, Portobello, Edinburgh EH15 2BA
T: 0131 657 3160
E: sadol@blueyonder.co.uk
W: edinburgh-bb.com

29722

Total number of rooms: 7

Prices per room from:

Single:	**£25.00-30.00pp**	Double:	**£40.00-60.00**
Twin:	**£40.00-60.00**		
Family room:	**£60.00-150.00**		

Edinburgh
Ingleneuk
Map Ref: 2C5

★★★ B&B

Open: All year excl Xmas
31 Drum Brae North, Edinburgh EH4 8AT
T: 0131 317 1743
E: ingleneukbnb@btinternet.com
W: ingleneukbandb.co.uk

Ideally located only 3 miles from Edinburgh Airport, 4 miles from city centre. All rooms are ensuite with private entrance. One room has a private conservatory overlooking lovely landscaped garden. Room served breakfasts make for a relaxed start to the day. Free off-street parking. Good bus service to city centre.

31623

Total number of rooms: 3

Prices from:

Single:	**£35.00**	Double:	**£30.00**
Twin:	**£30.00**	Family room:	**£30.00**

Edinburgh and the Lothians

Edinburgh

Kabayan

Map Ref: 2C5

★★ B&B

Open: February-November 79235

31 Craigs Gardens, Edinburgh EH12 8HA

T: 07907 326879

E: aidahunter@hotmail.com

Total number of rooms: 2			
Prices from:			
Double:	**£25.00 - 30.00**	Twin:	**£25.00 - 30.00**

Edinburgh, Lothians

No. 4 Hill Street

Map Ref: 2C5

★★★★ GUEST HOUSE

Open: All year 75747

4 Hill Street, Edinburgh, Lothian EH2 3JZ

T: 0131 225 8884

E: rooms@fourhillstreet.com

W: fourhillstreet.com

Set in the centre of Edinburgh's prestigious new town, this charming and elegant townhouse provides an ideal base to explore the attractions of this beautiful city. Enjoy period surroundings combined with 21st century luxury, a warm welcome and a delicious Scottish breakfast. You'll find nothing else like it!

Total number of rooms: 5			
Prices per room from:			
Double:	**£100.00**	Twin:	**£100.00**

Edinburgh

Panda Villa

Map Ref: 2C5

★★★ B&B

Open: All year 49076

12 Kilmaurs Road, Edinburgh EH16 5DA

T: 0131 667 5057

E: sichel@dircon.co.uk

W: pandavilla.co.uk

Victorian B&B in quiet surroundings in the heart of the city. Warm welcome, comfortable rooms, fabulous breakfasts and gardens open in the summer. Wi-Fi connection throughout. Off-road parking, excellent bus connections. All bedrooms contain freeview TV/DVD and access to DVD library. Complementary medicine offered, Tibetan meditation, hypnotherapy, colourpuncture, nutrition. Spanish spoken.

Total number of rooms: 2			
Prices from:			
Single: **£39.50**		Double:	**£33.50**
Twin: **£24.50**		Family room:	**£27.50**

Edinburgh

Priestville Guest House

Map Ref: 2C5

★★★ GUEST HOUSE

Open: All year 50456

10 Priestfield Road, Edinburgh EH16 5HJ

T: 0131 667 2435

E: bookings@priestville.com

W: priestville.com

Total number of rooms: 6			
Prices from:			
Single:	**£35.00**	Double:	**£25.00**
Twin:	**£26.00**	Family room:	**£25.00**

Important: Prices stated are estimates and may be subject to amendments.

Edinburgh

Ravensdown Guest House

Map Ref: 2C5

73495

Open: All year

248 Ferry Road, Edinburgh EH5 3AN
T: 0131 552 5438
E: david@ravensdownhouse.com
W: ravensdownhouse.com

Ravensdown is a friendly and stylish guest house, run by David and Yoke (she is Dutch) which provides excellent value high quality bed and breakfast accommodation in central Edinburgh. A spacious Edwardian house built in the early 1900's, Ravensdown has spectacular views of the city skyline, Edinburgh Castle and Arthur's Seat.

Total number of rooms: 7

Prices per room from:

Single:	**£45.00**	Double:	**£70.00**
Twin:	**£70.00**	Family room:	**£85.00**

Edinburgh

Sandeman House

Map Ref: 2C5

52950

Open: All year

33 Colinton Road, Edinburgh EH10 5DR
T: 0131 447 8080
E: joycesandeman@freezone.co.uk
W: sandemanhouse.co.uk

Victorian, non-smoking, listed house, centrally situated. All comforts thoughtfully presented with wonderful breakfasts, extensive choice. Wide range of individual shops and eating places within short walking distance. Wireless internet access available.

Total number of rooms: 3

Prices from:

Single:	**£45.00**	Double:	**£40.00**
Twin:	**£40.00**		

Edinburgh

St. Margaret's

Map Ref: 2C5

55941

Open: All year excl Xmas

13 Corstorphine High Street, Edinburgh EH12 7SU
T: 0131 334 7317
E: christine861@aol.com

Comfortable ground floor accommodation with ensuite facilities. Well-appointed bedroom with TV/DVD player. Experience the atmosphere of the old 17th century village of Corstorphine. Situated equal distance from Edinburgh Airport and City Centre (both 3 miles away). Non-smoking.

Total number of rooms: 1

Prices from:

Single:	**£30.00**	Double:	**£25.00**

Edinburgh
Tania Guest House

Map Ref: 2C5

57628

Open: All year excl Xmas
19 Minto Street, Edinburgh EH9 1RQ
T: 0131 667 4144
E: taniaguesthouse@yahoo.co.uk

Total number of rooms: 6

Prices from:

Single:	**£25.00-35.00**	Double:	**£25.00-35.00**
Twin:	**£25.00-35.00**	Family room:	**£25.00-35.00**

Haddington, East Lothian
Eaglescairnie Mains

Map Ref: 2D4

★★★★ FARMHOUSE

24029

Open: All year excl Xmas
By Gifford, Haddington, East Lothian EH41 4HN
T: 01620 810491
E: williams.eagles@btinternet.com
W: eaglescairnie.com

Beautifully furnished Georgian farmhouse in stunning countryside on working mixed farm. Tranquillity with wonderful views, yet only 30 minutes from Edinburgh, Seabird Centre, Glenkinchie Distillery, beaches and numerous golf courses. Farm walks, tennis court, log fires, wireless internet.

Total number of rooms: 3

Prices from:

Single:	**£40.00-50.00**	Double:	**£35.00-37.50**
Twin:	**£35.00 - 35.50**		

Linlithgow, West Lothian
Strawberry Bank House

Map Ref: 2B4

56994

Open: All year
13 Avon Place, Linlithgow, West Lothian EH49 6BL
T: 01506 848372
E: gillian@strawberrybank-scotland.co.uk
W: strawberrybank-scotland.co.uk

A fully modernised and comfortable B&B with all rooms ensuite. Decorated and furnished to a high standard. A non smoking establishment. Historic Linlithgow Palace is in the view of the house and the canal behind. Edinburgh is in easy driving distance.

Total number of rooms: 3

Prices per room from:

Single:	**£35.00**	Double:	**£65.00**
Twin:	**£65.00**	Family room:	**£75.00**

Inspiring places for your wedding day - Scotland knows no bounds.

For the perfect wedding visit visitscotland.com/scottishwedding

Important: Prices stated are estimates and may be subject to amendments.

Musselburgh, East Lothian

Mrs Elizabeth Aitken

Map Ref: 2C5

43190

★★ B&B

Open: All year

18 Woodside Gardens, Musselburgh
East Lothian EH21 7LJ

T: 0131 665 3170/3344

Detached bungalow in quiet residential area, close to Musselburgh Racecourse and golf course. Private parking. 7-8 miles from Princes Street, Edinburgh. Close to sandy beaches and river walks.

Total number of rooms: 3

Prices from:

Single:	**£25.00**	Double:	**£20.00**
Twin:	**£20.00**	Family room:	**£20.00**

Tranent, East Lothian

Schiehallion

Map Ref: 2D5

53175

★★★★ B&B

Open: All year

1 Edinburgh Road, Tranent, East Lothian EH33 1BA

T: 01875 611224

E: catherine@schiehallion.fsbusiness.co.uk

W: schiehallionguesthouse.co.uk

Total number of rooms: 2

Prices from:

Single:	**£35.00**	Double:	**£28.00**
Twin:	**£28.00**		

Edinburgh from Calton Hill

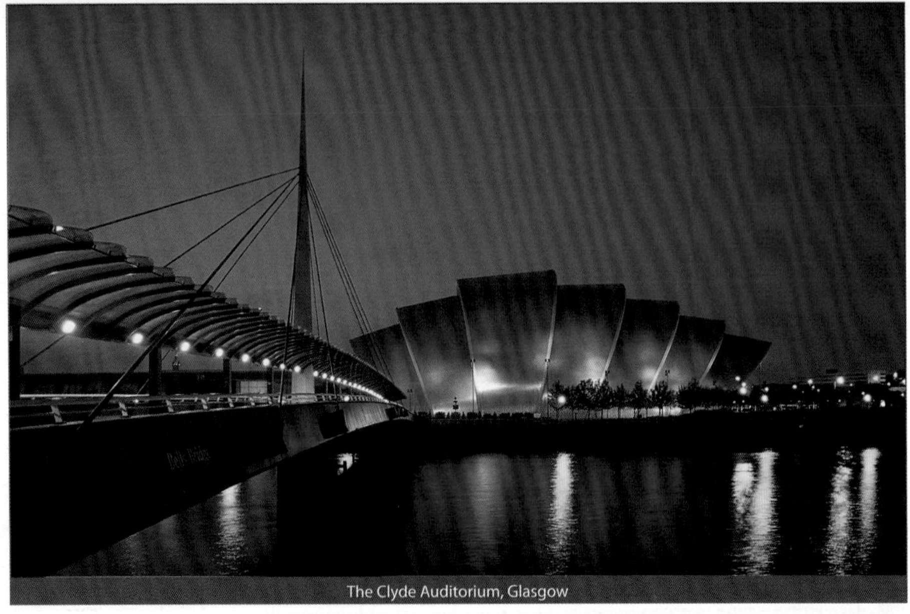

The Clyde Auditorium, Glasgow

GREATER GLASGOW AND CLYDE VALLEY

Glasgow is one of Europe's most exciting destinations, with all the energy and sophistication of a great international city.

There's so much choice it's difficult to know where to start and even harder to know when to stop.

And wherever you go in Scotland's largest city, you'll be overwhelmed by the irresistible friendliness of its inhabitants.

Shop 'til you drop

It's easy to get caught up in Glasgow's fast-moving social whirl – especially if you like shopping. Outside of London, there isn't a UK city that can touch Glasgow for quantity and quality.

If you're in need of retail therapy you'll revel in the elegance of Princes Square, the diversity of the Buchanan Galleries and the classy opulence of the Italian Centre in the chic Merchant City.

Glasgow is easily Scotland's most fashion-conscious city and its passion for all things stylish brings an exciting edge to its boutiques and malls.

That passion spills over into the cafés and bars, boutique hotels, restaurants, nightclubs, theatres and music venues. Glasgow nightlife is always exhilarating whether you're checking out the next hit band at King Tut's, watching groundbreaking theatre at Oran Mor or just sipping a pint in Ashton Lane.

The Glasgow Platter

Glasgow has one of the best restaurant scenes in the UK. From traditional afternoon tea at One Devonshire Gardens or the Willow Tearooms to every major culinary style in the world, Glasgow's restaurants have a rapidly growing international reputation.

For a selection of eating establishments available in and around Glasgow go to eatscotland.com

An Art Lover's Paradise

Glasgow is an outstanding city to step out in. The impressive legacy of its most eminent architectural sons, Charles Rennie Mackintosh and Alexander 'Greek' Thomson, can be seen in the city's streets, while its galleries and museums host one of Europe's biggest collections of civic art.

The Kelvingrove Art Gallery and Museum, restored in 2006 at a cost of £27.9 million, is a must see. This popular visitor attraction is free to enter and hosts some 8,000 exhibits.

Don't spend so long there that you miss the Burrell Collection in Pollok Country Park or the University of Glasgow's Hunterian Museum & Art Gallery.

The Great Outdoors

Despite the endless hustle and bustle, peace and tranquillity are never far away. Glasgow is known as the 'dear green place' and there are over 70 parks and gardens in the city where you can escape for a while.

Beyond the city limits, you can trace the river through the Clyde Valley all the way to the picturesque Falls of Clyde in Lanarkshire, just beside the immaculately preserved village of New Lanark which is a World Heritage Site.

On the Clyde coast you can take a trip 'doon the watter' in the P.S. Waverley, the world's last sea-going paddle steamer. At Strathclyde Country Park in Motherwell and Mugdock Country Park near Milngavie you'll enjoy a wide range of outdoor activities including walking, cycling, horse riding and much more.

Glasgow's maritime history can be explored at The Scottish Maritime Museum in Braehead and in Paisley you'll find an impressive Abbey dating back to 1163. Both places are just a short journey away from the city of Glasgow.

What's more, 2009 is a big year for Scotland – we're celebrating the 250th anniversary of the birth of Robert Burns. There's over 200 special events taking place throughout the year, all over Scotland. Go to homecomingscotland2009.com to find out about events in this area.

Whatever you choose to do, wherever you stay – either uptown in the city, in the suburbs or in the surrounding countryside – a visit to Glasgow and Clyde Valley will be a revelation and you'll be very glad you came.

Christmas lights are turned on, George Square, Glasgow

What's On?

Celtic Connections
15 January – 1 February 2009
Recognised as the principal Celtic Festival in the UK, this event is a must for any traditional music lover.
celticconnections.com

Glasgow Film Festival
12 – 22 February 2009
Premiers and previews galore as Glasgow celebrates its 5th festival celebrating the city's love of the movies.
glasgowfilmfestival.org.uk

Glasgow Art Fair
23 – 26 April 2009
With over 50 galleries and art organisations in one place, the 14th national fair is THE place to view, buy and sell art in Scotland.
glasgowartfair.com

Paisley Beer Festival
29 April – 2 May 2009
Scotland's largest real ale festival, with well over 100 real ales on tap.
paisleybeerfestival.org.uk

Glasgow River Festival
Mid July 2009
A weekend of land and water-based entertainment for the whole family on the banks of the River Clyde.
glasgowriverfestival.co.uk

Gourmet Glasgow
August 2009
A month-long festival of food and drink.
graonline.co.uk

Kirkintilloch Canal Festival
29 – 30 August 2009
Two days of fun in the 'Canal Capital of Scotland'.
kirkintillochcanalfestival.org.uk

World Pipe Band Championships
15 August 2009
Piping Live: International Piping Festival, August 10 - 16 2009
A piping spectacular, with Music of the Clans – a special series of Homecoming events dedicated to Scottish heritage and piping.
pipinglive.co.uk

Merchant City Festival, Glasgow
24 – 27 September 2009
Festival celebrating the cultural richness of the city's old commercial quarter.
merchantcityfestival.com

Glasgow's Hogmanay
31 December 2009 – 1 January 2010
Bring in the New Year with live bands.
winterfestglasgow.com

DON'T MISS

1 **Kelvingrove Art Gallery and Museum** - Scotland's most visited museum re-opened in 2006 following a three-year, £27.9 million restoration project. It now has a collection of 8,000 objects on display over three floors – 4,000 more than ever before. Old favourites and exciting new arrivals are waiting to welcome you. Forget everything you think you know about museums, Kelvingrove is different.

2 Located within the World Heritage Site of **New Lanark**, the Falls of Clyde Wildlife Reserve covers 59 hectares, has woodland along the River Clyde gorge and 4 spectacular waterfalls. Breeding peregrine falcons, tawny owls and sparrowhawks rule the air while badgers, foxes and roe deer can also be seen. The river is home to otters, dippers, herons and kingfishers. The recently refurbished visitor centre includes interactive interpretation highlighting these key species.

3 It's all about fun when you're on holidays but what if at the same time you could sneak in a bit of learning? **Glasgow Science Centre** has the answer. Easily accessible from Glasgow city centre by car, subway, train or bus, the Centre stands tall and instantly recognisable on the River Clyde. The interactive exhibits can keep not only the children entertained but the adults too and that's before you hit the IMAX cinema and the ScottishPower Planetarium.

4 Glasgow University's **Hunterian Art Gallery & Museum** hosts an extensive art collection of superb quality, with outstanding works by Rembrandt, Whistler, Chardin, Stubbs, the Scottish Colourists and many more. See the most significant collection of original Charles Rennie Mackintosh works in the world and visit the Mackintosh House – his Glasgow home.

5 One of Scotland's most magnificent medieval buildings, **Glasgow Cathedral**, is one of the few Scottish medieval churches to survive the reformation of 1560 intact.The tomb of St. Mungo, Glasgow's patron saint and founder, is located within the church. Beside the Cathedral is Glasgow Necropolis, the "City of the Dead". This Victorian garden cemetery is a real hidden gem and offers a unique insight into Glasgow's social and economic heritage.

6 The **Gallery of Modern Art** opened in 1996 and is housed in an elegant, neo-classical building in the heart of the city centre. The building was refurbished to house the city's contemporary art collection, and is an appealing combination of old and new architecture. GoMA is now the second most visited contemporary gallery outside London, offering an outstanding programme of temporary exhibitions and workshops.

FOOD AND DRINK

eatscotland.com

7 In the Merchant City, **Rogano** (11 Exchange Place) is a must. Since 1935 Rogano has been preparing the finest Scottish seafood and serving it in its unique Art Deco surroundings with the wonderful flair of that bygone era. Rogano is a Glasgow institution.

8 With a motto like "Think global, eat local" it is not surprising that the menu at **Stravaigin** (28 Gibson St) has been built from diverse world influences while focusing on the best of Scottish ingredients. The result is a collection of eclectic and globe trotting dishes. Stravaigin is an excellent example of West End dining.

9 Special occasions will go off nicely at **Brian Maule at Chardon d'Or** (176 West Regent St). Brian Maul was head chef at Le Gavroche for 7 years. He combines his French culinary skill with Scottish produce to create a taste sensation! Since opening, the restaurant has been extended to include private dining rooms and a bar in the basement.

10 If Indian food is your thing, try **The Dhabba**, (44 Candleriggs) which specialises in authentic North Indian cuisine, or the Dakhin, (First Floor, 89 Candleriggs) where the focus is on South Indian cuisine. Both restaurants are situated in the fashionable Merchant City area, and both use only the freshest ingredients to create many unusual regional dishes. Perfect for the seasoned Indian food fan and novice alike.

ACTIVITIES

11 Just north of Glasgow, near Loch Lomond, is **Glengoyne Distillery**. The distillery is open all year round and offers the most in-depth range of tours in the industry, from the Masterblender Tour, where guests create their very own blended whisky, to the Cask Tasting Tour, specially designed for guests who enjoy tasting, and learning about, cask strength whisky.

12 Enjoy a seaplane flight from Glasgow to Oban Bay on Scotland's west coast with **Loch Lomond Seaplanes**. The journey, which takes approximately 25 minutes, will take you over areas of outstanding natural beauty. Once in Oban, there's time for a bite to eat and a spot of sightseeing before the return journey. Or if you prefer, extend your stay and return at a later date.

13 As you enter through the main doors of **Xscape** you can watch brave souls hanging from the ceiling as they have a go on the state of the art aerial adventure course. The Centre houses numerous outdoor shops, restaurants, bars, bowling, rock climbing, a cinema and much more. However, without a doubt the piece-de-résistance is the incredible SNO!zone which allows you to experience indoor skiing, snowboarding or sledging on the UK's biggest indoor real snow slope.

14 Charles Rennie Mackintosh is considered the father of the 'Glasgow Style', with his motifs instantly recognisable to visitors. He was a true visionary who worked almost exclusively in the city. His legacy lives on and can be enjoyed with the help of a **Mackintosh Trail** ticket giving admission to all associated attractions in and around Glasgow including the School of Art, Scotland Street School Museum, House for an Art Lover and the Mackintosh Church. The ticket can be purchased at Glasgow Visitor Information Centres, SPT Travel Centres, all participating Mackintosh venues or online at crmsociety.com.

SHOPPING

15 **Buchanan Street** is arguably one of the classiest major shopping thoroughfares in Britain. With a tempting mix of big high street names, alternative retailers and designer outlets, it's deservedly popular. **Buchanan Galleries** at the top of the street offers a choice of over 80 shops including John Lewis. A must visit.

16 The true highlight of Buchanan Street is **Princes Square**: a speciality shopping centre in a beautifully restored listed building dating from 1841. The architects have preserved many original features whilst transforming the interior to create a venue for shopping where designer boutiques and stylish eateries are linked by escalators criss-crossing over a central courtyard.

17 Visitors in search of the city's chic and modern side should head to the **Merchant City**. Originally landscaped for the homes and warehouses of 18th century tobacco barons, it is now the city's main style quarter. Wander around its innovative boutiques in search of that must-have item.

18 With strong Italian heritage, it's only fitting that there should be somewhere to purchase the latest fashions from Milan. With designer boutiques such as Versace Collections and Emporio Armani the **Italian Centre** may be easier on the eye than on the pocket, but it's ideal for a treat.

19 Glasgow is often complimented for its European flavour, and nowhere is this more in evidence than on **Byres Road**, with its fruit and veg stalls, butchers, fishmongers, flanking hip record stores and clothing retailers. Head to the West End for some wonderful eateries in the mews lanes off Byres Road.

20 Out of town there's **Braehead Shopping Centre** near Glasgow Airport, Silverburn Shopping Centre in Pollock, which opened its doors in late 2007, and Glasgow Fort located east of the city at junction 10 on the M8.

HERITAGE AND CULTURE

21 Take in a **football** match for 90 minutes you'll never forget. It would be an understatement to say that Glaswegians have a passion for the beautiful game, and Glasgow is the only city in the UK to support three 50,000+ capacity football stadiums. Situated within the national stadium of Hampden, the Scottish Football Museum is an essential attraction for all football fans.

22 From Celtic Connections each January to the Magners International Comedy Festival in March and Piping Live! in August, the Glasgow calendar is filled with live performances, **events and festivals** and entertainment throughout the year.

23 Situated within beautiful Bellahouston Park, **House for an Art Lover** was inspired by Charles Rennie Mackintosh designs from 1901. Its restaurant houses changing art exhibitions and visitors are entertained throughout the year with a programme of dinner concerts and afternoon music recitals.

24 Built in 1898 for the people of Glasgow's East End, the **People's Palace** and **Winter Gardens** tells the story of Glasgow from 1750 to the present day. Outside the museum stands the spectacular Doulton Fountain – the largest terracotta fountain in the world. Gifted to Glasgow by Henry Doulton, it has recently been restored.

MAP

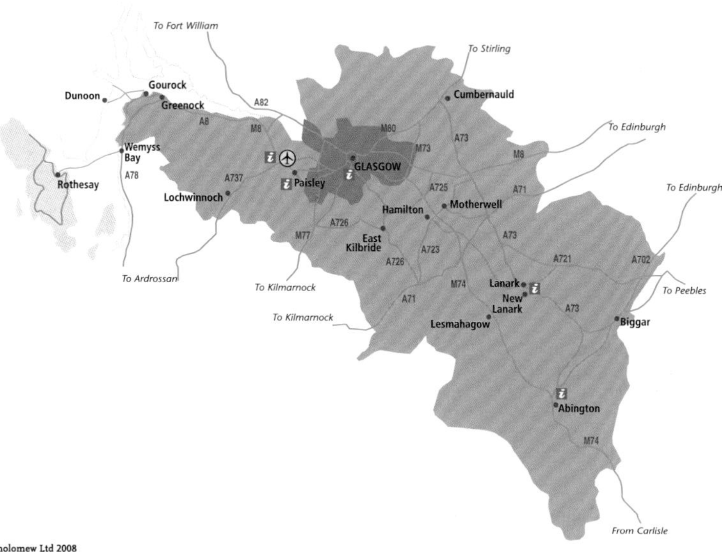

©Collins Bartholomew Ltd 2008

VISITOR INFORMATION CENTRES

Visitor Information Centres are staffed by people 'in the know' offering friendly advice, helping to make your stay in Scotland the most enjoyable ever . . . whatever your needs!

Greater Glasgow & Clyde Valley		
Abington	Welcome Break, Motorway Service Area, Junction 13, M74 Abington, ML12 6RG	Tel: 01864 502436
Glasgow	11 George Square, Glasgow G2 1DY	Tel: 0141 204 4400
Glasgow Airport	International Arrivals Hall, Glasgow International Airport, PA3 2ST	Tel: 0141 848 4440
Lanark	Horsemarket, Ladyacre Road, Lanark, ML11 7QD	Tel: 01555 661661
Paisley	9A Gilmour Street, Paisley, PA1 1DD	Tel: 0141 889 0711

LOCAL KNOWLEDGE • WHERE TO STAY • ACCOMMODATION BOOKING • PLACES TO VISIT • THINGS TO DO • MAPS AND GUIDES • TRAVEL ADVICE • ROUTE PLANNING • WHERE TO SHOP AND EAT • LOCAL CRAFTS AND PRODUCE • EVENT INFORMATION • TICKETS

For information and ideas about exploring Scotland in advance of your trip, call our booking and information service **0845 22 55 121** or go to **visitscotland.com**

If calling from outside the UK and Ireland **+44 1506 832 121** From Ireland **1800 932 510**

A £4 booking fee applies for accommodation bookings made via a Visitor Information Centre and through our booking and information service.

By Biggar, Lanarkshire

Walston Mansion Farmhouse

Map Ref: 2B6

★★★ B&B

63297

Open: All year
Walston Village, Carnwath, Lanark ML11 8NF
T: 01899 810338/ 01899 810334
E: kirby-walstonmansion@talk21.com
W: walstonmansion.co.uk

Total number of rooms: 3			
Prices from:			
Single:	**£26.00**	Double:	**£23.00**
Twin:	**£21.00**	Family room:	**£23.00**

Glasgow

Alison Guest House

Map Ref: 1H5

★★ GUEST HOUSE

57441

Open: All year
28 Circus Drive, Westercraigs, Glasgow G3 2JH
T: 0141 556 1431
E: circusdrive@aol.com
W: alisonguesthouse.co.uk

Alison Guest House is a large Victorian house. A 2-Star ex-Church Manse situated in new Merchant City at Westercraigs. Area steeped in history, minutes from Royal Infirmary, Cathedral, St. Mungo's Museum, Oldest house, Provan's Lordship, Necropolis and Universities.15 minutes walk to city centre. A warm welcome is always offered.

Total number of rooms: 5			
Prices from:			
Single:	**£25.00**	Double:	**£23.00**
Family room:	**£25.00**		

Glasgow

Craigielea House Bed & Breakfast

Map Ref: 1H5

★★ B&B

20972

Open: All year
35 Westercraigs, Glasgow G31 2HY
T: 0141 554 3446
E: craigieleahouse@yahoo.co.uk
W: visitscotland.com

Total number of rooms: 3			
Prices from:			
Single:	**£25.00**	Double:	**£22.00**
Twin:	**£22.00**		

Glasgow

University of Glasgow

Map Ref: 1H5

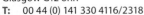

★UP TO ★★ CAMPUS

65588

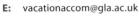

Open: All year
Residential Services, 73 Great George Street
Glasgow G12 8RR
T: 00 44 (0) 141 330 4116/2318
E: vacationaccom@gla.ac.uk
W: glasgow.ac.uk/cvso

The University of Glasgow's accommodation is the perfect base for your visit to our wonderful city! For us low prices don't mean low standards. Our accommodation is comfortable, welcoming and ideally located to explore not only the city itself but also surrounding areas such as Loch Lomond and the Trossachs.

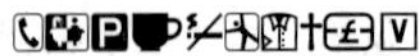

Total number of rooms: 240			
Prices per room from:			
Single:	**£25.00**	Twin:	**£30.00**

Important: Prices stated are estimates and may be subject to amendments.

Glasgow
University of Strathclyde
Map Ref: 1H5

★ CAMPUS

62602

Open: June-September

Residence & Catering Services,
50 Richmond Street, Glasgow G1 1XP
T: 0141 553 4148
E: accommodationglasgow@strath.ac.uk
W: rescat.strath.ac.uk

Total number of rooms: 300
Prices from:
Single: **£29.00**

Lesmahagow, Lanarkshire
Mrs Isobel McInally
Map Ref: 2A6

★★ FARMHOUSE

32330

Open: All year

Dykecroft Farm, Boghead,
Lesmahagow, Lanark ML11 0JQ
T: 01555 892226
E: dykecroft.bandb@tiscali.co.uk
W: dykecroftfarm.co.uk

Total number of rooms: 3	
Prices from:	
Single: **£27.00**	Double: **£23.00**
Twin: **£23.00**	

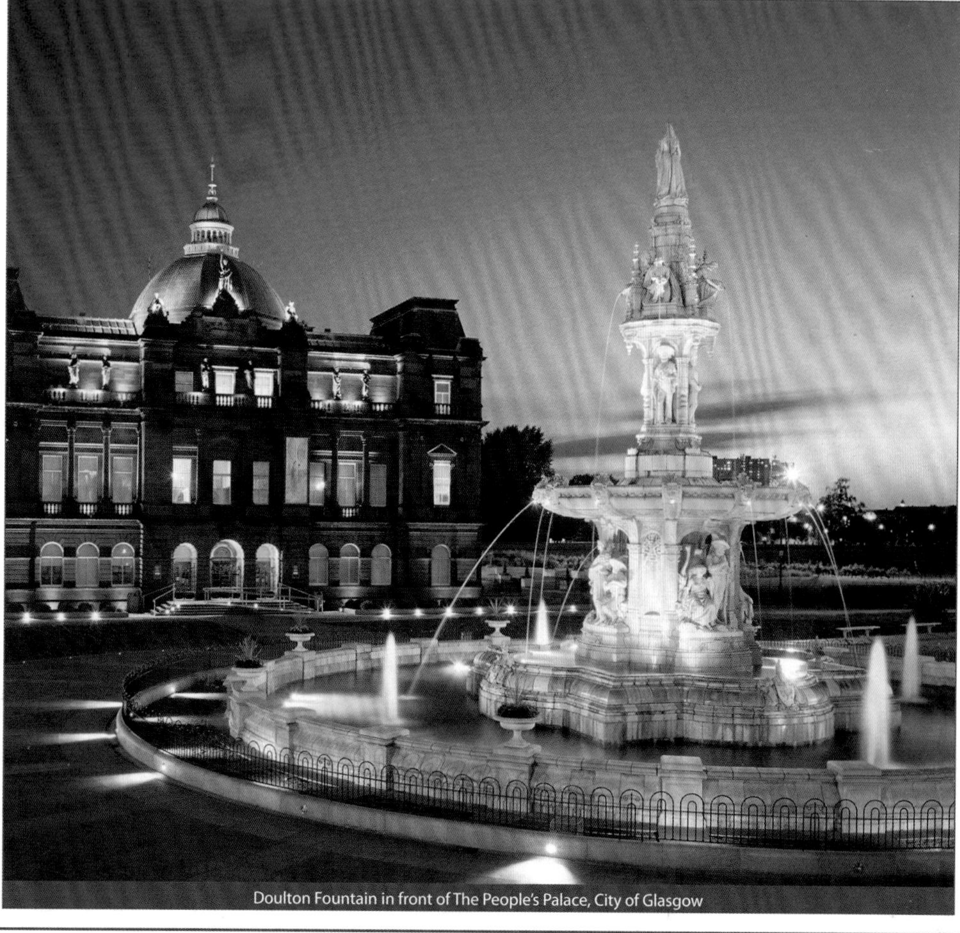

Doulton Fountain in front of The People's Palace, City of Glasgow

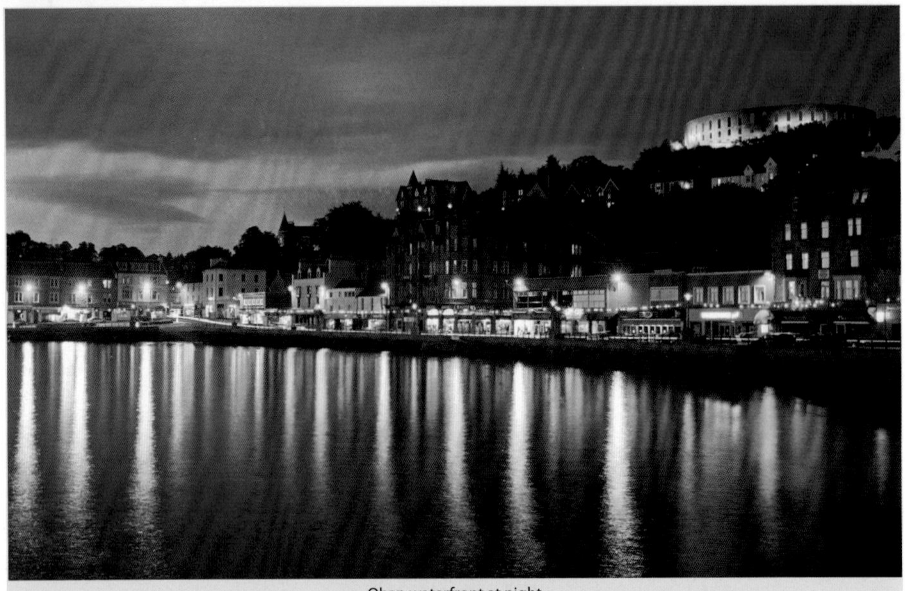

Oban waterfront at night

WEST HIGHLANDS AND ISLANDS, LOCH LOMOND, STIRLING AND TROSSACHS

Contrast is the word that best sums up an area that spans Scotland from the shores of the Forth in the east to the very tip of Tiree in the west. Here the Highlands meet the Lowlands and geography and cultures diverge.

For the visitor, the endlessly changing landscape means a rich and varied holiday experience.

There are rugged high mountains, spectacular freshwater lochs, fascinating islands and dramatic seascapes. You'll find pretty villages, mill towns, not to mention one of Scotland's newest cities, Stirling.

Discover the birthplace of the Scots nation and visit places that witnessed some of the most dramatic scenes in Scotland's history.

On the eastern side of the country the flat plain of the Forth Valley stretches up from the River Forth towards the little towns of the Hillfoots, which enjoy the spectacular backdrop of the Ochil Hills.

Elsewhere in the Forth Valley, you can visit Scotland's smallest county, Clackmannanshire, or the Wee County as it is known. Head for Dollar Glen and the magnificent Castle Campbell, once the Lowland stronghold of the Clan Campbell.

Moving to the Hillfoot towns you'll be tracing the roots of Scotland's textile industry which has thrived here for many years. Learn the history of the local woollen industry at the Mill Trail Visitor Centre in Alva.

New city, ancient history

Beyond Alva to the west lies Stirling – a city since 2002 and one of the most important places in Scottish history thanks to its strategically important location as the gateway to the Highlands.

Once, whoever controlled Stirling, controlled Scotland. Its impressive castle stands guard over all it surveys and was the capital for the Stewart Kings. It's a relatively quiet spot these days but no fewer than seven battle sites can be seen from the Castle ramparts – including Stirling Bridge, a scene of triumph for William Wallace and Bannockburn where Robert the Bruce led the Scots to victory in 1314.

A National Park on your doorstep

Scotland's first national park Loch Lomond and the Trossachs National Park, takes advantage of the natural treasures of this area and that means 20 Munros (mountains over 3,000ft) to climb, 50 rivers to fish, 22 lochs to sail and thousands of miles of road and track to cycle. When you've had your fill of activities, head for Loch Lomond Shores for a cultural and retail experience.

You can also cruise on Loch Lomond. It's Britain's biggest freshwater expanse and there's no better way to see the surrounding countryside than from the water.

Heading west the Whisky Coast round Islay and Jura are waiting to be explored – Islay alone has eight working distilleries!

A place in history

Further west still, The Cowal Peninsula with its sea lochs and deep forests is beautiful and relaxing. To get there, just jump aboard the ferry at Gourock and sail for Dunoon. While you're there, don't miss the nearby Benmore Botanic Gardens.

Explore Lochgilphead and beyond to Kilmartin where you can trace the very roots of the nation where the Scots arrived from Ireland in the 6th century.

What's more, 2009 is a big year for Scotland – we're celebrating the 250th anniversary of the birth of Robert Burns. There's over 200 special events taking place throughout the year, all over Scotland. Go to homecomingscotland2009.com to find out about events in this area.

Choosing a holiday destination in an area as diverse as this will always be difficult but the variety of high quality establishments offering bed and breakfast accommodation will help. There's a great selection of quaint cottages, working farms, little guesthouses, historical inns and modern homes that really know how to entertain their guests so you're sure to find somewhere that will tempt you to stay forever.

The Mishnish Hotel, Tobermory, Isle of Mull

What's On?

Big in Falkirk
2 – 3 May 2009
Scotland's largest streets arts festival features music, outdoor theatre and art in Callendar Park. A two-day extravaganza not to be missed!
biginfalkirk.co.uk

The Loch Lomond Food & Drink Festival
30 – 31 May 2009
A showcase for local food and great chefs, giving the visitor a chance to sample the delicious servings amongst the stunning backdrop of Loch Lomond.
lochlomondfoodanddrinkfestival.com

Scottish Pipe Band Championship
May 2009
For one day in May, Dumbarton will be alive to the skirl of pipes. A world-class competition with competitors from all over the globe.
rspba.org

World Fly Fishing Championships
5 – 12 June 2009
Welcoming anglers from over 25 countries over 7 days of competition, showcasing the fishing sites and surrounding landscapes of Stirling & Perthshire to an international audience.
worldflyfishingchampionships2009.com

Helensburgh and Loch Lomond Highland Games
14 June 2009
Come experience the Highland Games with traditional events such as tossing the caber, putting the stone, throwing the hammer and many more making this a fun-filled day out.
helensburghandlomondgames.co.uk

Cowal Highland Gathering
27 – 29 August 2009
Dating back to 1894, the Gathering is described as 'the largest and most spectacular Highland Games in the world'
cowalgathering.com

Connect Festival, Inveraray
28 – 30 August 2009
Pack your campervan and head for connect at Inveraray Castle. It's simply one of the best summer rock festivals in the UK.
connectmusicfestival.com

Off the Page – The Stirling Book Festival
13 – 20 September 2009
A celebration of writing in its various forms for adults, children and families. Lots of exciting events throughout the area in the library-organised festival that celebrates its fourth year.
stirling.gov.uk/offthepage

Cowalfest
9 – 18 October 2009
Scotland's largest walking festival with cycling, wildlife, the arts, film, music and drama thrown in.

MAP

To Lochboisdale
To Castlebay
COLL
Kilchoan
Arinagour
Tobermory
Dervaig
Calgary
A849
Salen
A884
Lochaline
A828
Appin
To Fort William
TIREE
MULL
Craignure
Lochdon
Benderloch
Connel
Oban
Taynuilt
Tyndrum
A82
A85
Killin
Lochearnhead
To Aberfeldy
Bunessan
A849
Lerags
Kilninver
Kilmore
Kilmelford
A816
Dalmally
Kilchrenan
Loch Awe
A819
A83
Inveraray
Cairndow
St Catherine's
Crianlarich
Ardlui
Strathyre
Brig O'Turk
Callander
To Perth
A9
A84
Doune
Alva
Tillicoutry
Craobh Haven
Tarbet
Arrochar
Aberfoyle
Port of Menteith
STIRLING
Kilmartin
Crinan
Minard
Strachur
A815
Loch Lomond
Luss
Gartocharn
Inchmurrin
Drymen
A811
Balfron
M80
COLONSAY
Carrick Castle
A814
A886
Glendaruel
Lochgilphead
Arden
Helensburgh
Balloch
Cardross
Dumbarton
Cove
Rhu
Kilmun
Bo'ness
Falkirk
A80
M9
To Edinburgh
JURA
Tayvallich
A83
A846
Colintraive
Dunoon
A8
To Glasgow
Sanaigmore
Ballygrant
Tarbert
Wemyss Bay
Kennacraig
Rothesay
BUTE
Bruichladdich
Port Charlotte
A847
A846
Bowmore
ISLAY
GIGHA
Claonaig
Winter Only
A78
Lochranza
Port Ellen
Kilnaughton Bay
Tayinloan
To Ayr
A83
ARRAN
Carradale
Machrihanish
Campbeltown
©Collins Bartholomew Ltd 2008

VISITOR INFORMATION CENTRES

Visitor Information Centres are staffed by people 'in the know' offering friendly advice, helping to make your stay in Scotland the most enjoyable ever . . . whatever your needs!

West Highlands		
Bowmore	The Square, Bowmore, Isle of Islay, PA43 7JP	Tel: 01496 810254
Campbeltown	Mackinnon House, The Pier, Campbeltown, PA28 6EF	Tel: 01586 552056
Craignure	The Pier, Craignure, Isle of Mull, PA65 6AY	Tel: 01680 812377
Dunoon	7 Alexander Place, Dunoon, PA23 8AB	Tel: 01369 703785
Inveraray	Front Street, Inveraray, PA32 8UY	Tel: 01499 302063
Oban	Argyll Square, Oban, PA34 4AR	Tel: 01631 563122
Rothesay	Winter Gardens, Rothesay, Isle of Bute, PA20 0AJ	Tel: 01700 502151

Loch Lomond		
Aberfoyle	Trossachs Discovery Centre, Main Street, Aberfoyle, FK8 3UQ	Tel: 01877 382352
Callander	Ancaster Square, Callander, FK17 8ED	Tel: 01877 330342
Tyndrum	Main Street, Tyndrum, FK20 8RY	Tel: 01838 400324

Stirling & Trossachs		
Falkirk	The Falkirk Wheel, Lime Road, Tamfourhill, Falkirk, FK1 4RS	Tel: 01324 620244
Stirling (Dumbarton Rd)	41 Dumbarton Road, Stirling, FK8 2LQ	Tel: 01786 475019
Stirling (Pirnhall)	Motorway Service Area, Junction 9, M9	Tel: 01786 814111
Tillicoultry	Unit 22, Sterling Mills Outlet Village, Devondale, Tillicoultry, Clackmannanshire, FK13 6HQ	Tel: 01259 769696

LOCAL KNOWLEDGE • WHERE TO STAY • ACCOMMODATION BOOKING • PLACES TO VISIT • THINGS TO DO • MAPS AND GUIDES • TRAVEL ADVICE • ROUTE PLANNING • WHERE TO SHOP AND EAT • LOCAL CRAFTS AND PRODUCE • EVENT INFORMATION • TICKETS

For information and ideas about exploring Scotland in advance of your trip, call our booking and information service **0845 22 55 121** or go to **visitscotland.com**

If calling from outside the UK and Ireland **+44 1506 832 121** From Ireland **1800 932 510**

A £4 booking fee applies for accommodation bookings made via a Visitor Information Centre and through our booking and information service.

Live it. Visit Scotland.
visitscotland.com/wheretofindus

Island of Tiree, Inner Hebrides

West Highlands and Islands

Savour the atmosphere of the rugged west coast and take a journey around some of Scotland's most magical isles and peninsulas. The pace of island life is a powerful draw for visitors and, while there are parts of the mainland around Kintyre which feel more like island than mainland, if you're looking for the genuine island experience, you'll be spoiled for choice.

The many islands to explore include Gigha, Jura, Islay and Colonsay. And no trip to these parts would be complete without visiting Oban, the gateway to the isles, from where boats make their way to and from the likes of Mull, Coll, Tiree and Colonsay.

They all have their own special allure. Visit Islay for the whisky, deeply spiritual Iona, and Mull, where you can see colourful Tobermory (or Balamory as families with young children will recognise it). On your way to the isles stop off in Oban, its harbour is always bustling and the area around the port has a great selection of shops, bars and restaurants.

Sambayabamba at the Connect Music Festival, inveraray

DON'T MISS

1 Wherever you travel in this area, you're never far from one of the **whisky distilleries**. Islay alone is home to eight working distilleries, producing world-famous whiskies such as Laphroaig and Bowmore, renowned for their peaty qualities. Here, you'll also find Kilchoman, a recently opened farm distillery. The neighbouring Isle of Jura manufactures its own popular malt, while Campbeltown on Kintyre now boasts two local whiskies, Springbank and Glengyle, the latter dating from only 2004. Facilities and opening hours vary.

2 **Island Exploring** is a must in the West Highlands and with such a diversity of locations all linked by ferry, it's a popular choice. Iona Abbey is considered the origin for the spread of Christianity throughout Scotland and is a must-visit on Iona. Explore Fingal's Cave on Staffa, the surfing on Tiree and the whiskies of Islay. White beaches, tasty organic food and spectacular scenery welcome you and urge your return.

3 Any trip which takes in the breathtaking Argyll coastline or Argyll's Atlantic Islands, known as **Scotland's Sea Kingdom**, promises a memorable experience. Negotiate the Gulf of Corryvreckan with its famous whirlpool and travel round Scarba while looking out for whales, dolphins, deer and eagles, or venture further to the remote Garvellachs. You can sail from Ardfern with Craignish Cruises, from Craobh Haven with Farsain Cruises, from Crinan with Gemini Cruises or from Easdale with Seafari Adventures or Sealife Adventures.

4 **Mount Stuart** on the Isle of Bute was the ancestral home of the Marquess of Bute. Today it is a high quality, award-winning, four-star attraction featuring magnificent Victorian Gothic architecture and design together with contemporary craftsmanship. Mount Stuart is surrounded by 300 acres of gloriously maintained grounds and gardens.

5 **Kilmartin Glen** is home to a myriad of Neolithic and Bronze Age monuments, coupled with early Christian carved stones and ruined castles. South of Oban, this site was capital of the ancient Celtic kingdom of Dalriada, as evidenced at Dunadd Fort, where a footprint in the stone is thought to have featured in royal inauguration ceremonies.

6 The common characteristic of the **Glorious Gardens of Argyll & Bute** is their individuality. Each garden has a variety of terrain; many are mainly level with smooth paths, while some are steep and rocky. The gardens range from informal woodland gardens to beautiful classic examples of 18th century design.

2

5

6

FOOD AND DRINK

eatscotland.com

7 The original **Loch Fyne Oyster Bar** and shop started in a small shed in the lay-by at the head of Loch Fyne in the early 1980s. In 1985 it moved into the old cow byre at Clachan Farm. It has been listed in the Good Food Guide every year since then.

8 Among the many fine restaurants across the West Highlands, **Coast** in Oban stands out with its clean, calming feel and contemporary approach to food. Both light bite and a la carte menus are brimming with the fresh seafood synonymous in the area. You can let your food go down while watching the sunset across Oban Bay.

9 **The Seafood Trail** takes you through some of the most spectacular coastal scenery Scotland has to offer, and enables seafood lovers to sample, share and enjoy seafood and shellfish from a wide variety of waterfront establishments.

10 The **Whisky Coast** blends incredible Scottish scenery with arguably the best sixteen single malt whiskies for a truly memorable experience. Getting to and around the Whisky Coast is surprisingly easy for the independent traveller in search of stunning landscapes and the finest whiskies, as the area is well served by road, rail, air and ferry.

7

12

WILDLIFE

visitscotland.com/wildlife

11 There are numerous operators that offer **sea trip safaris** around **Oban** and **Mull** where you can spot majestic wildlife against a backdrop of spectacular scenery. The wildlife in this area is magnificent and you may well spot the majestic sea eagle, golden eagle, or a range of seabirds along with seals, dolphins, porpoises and the occasional minke whale.

12 The extensive **Argyll Forest Park** offers a perfect introduction to Loch Lomond & The Trossachs National Park. Start at the Ardgartan Visitor Centre on the A83 at the north of Loch Long, where the Boathouse and Riverside walks provide options for pushchairs. You'll also find cycle paths, a play area and refreshments. With its spectacular mountains, glens, lochs and woodlands, many claim that Britain's first forest park is also the finest.

13 The islands of **Islay and Jura** are something of a mecca for **wildlife** lovers. With well over a hundred breeding bird species in summer, and some of Europe's largest populations of wintering wildfowl, they are a year round destination for ornithologists. Add to this some exceptional marine wildlife, including minke whales, common and bottlenose dolphins, basking sharks and literally thousands of seals, alongside some of Britain's best opportunities to spy otters, red deer and golden eagles, and you have a natural paradise. A particular highlight is the arrival of around 50,000 barnacle and white-fronted geese from the Arctic Circle each autumn.

14 **Wildlife and bird watching safaris** offer the chance to explore the remote areas of Mull with experienced guides to help you spot and learn about the wildlife which inhabits the island. This is your chance to see golden eagles, otters, harriers and merlin to name a few.

WALKS

visitscotland.com/walking

15 **Lismore** is a lovely location to get away from it all and is easy to reach by boat from Oban. The island is just 12 miles long and 1.5 miles at its widest point, and offers many interesting walks with spectacular views of the sea and mountains. Kerrera is a beautiful island where it is also possible to walk round the entire island although this walk is about 10 miles and will take some time.

16 The wonderfully unexplored Kintyre Peninsula boasts hidden coves, deserted beaches, tiny fishing communities, gentle hills, fabulous local produce and welcoming friendly people. Stretching from Tarbert to Southend, the waymarked **Kintyre Way** criss-crosses the peninsula, connecting communities and landscape, people and produce. At 89 miles long (142 kms), and with 4 to 7 days worth of walking, there's serious hiking and gentle rambles, all of which bring home the beautiful reality that is Kintyre.

17 The **West Island Way**, which opened in September 2000, is the first long distance way-marked path on a Scottish island. It encompasses some of the best walking that the Isle of Bute has to offer, runs the length of the island and embraces a variety of landscapes.

18 **The Cowal Way** follows a route running the length of Argyll's Cowal peninsula. It starts in the south-west at Portavadie beside Loch Fyne, and finishes in the north-east at Ardgartan by Loch Long, and involves walking on roads and on lochside, hill and woodland terrains. The way-marked route is 75 kms/47 miles in length and is divided into six shorter, more manageable sections.

19

21

ACTIVITIES

19 Tiny Port Askaig on Islay is something of a ferry hub, serving Colonsay, the mainland and Jura. Its proximity to the last makes it an ideal location to view the **Paps of Jura**, three rounded mountains rising out of the sea to over 730m. Relax with a drink outside the Port Askaig Hotel and soak up the view.

20 The village of Carradale on the eastern side of Kintyre makes an excellent base from which to explore the peninsula. The delightful beach and harbour area offer stunning views over the Kilbrannan Sound to the dramatic hills of **Arran**.

21 One of Scotland's most romanticised stretches of water, the narrow straits known as the **Kyles of Bute**, more than live up to their reputation. The Kyles are best admired from the viewpoint on the A886 above Colintraive, where the view to their namesake island is truly awe-inspiring. Remember to bring along your picnic so you can really make the most of this view and open space.

22 The steep 10-minute climb from the centre of Oban to **McCaig's Tower** is well worth it for the view of Oban Bay, Kerrera and the Isle of Mull. The Tower was built by a local banker in the late 19th century in an effort to replicate Rome's Colosseum. The view of the town and the islands to the west is breathtaking.

West Highlands and Islands

Benderloch, by Oban

Hawthorn

Map Ref: 1E2

Open: All year excl Xmas 29746

Keil Croft, Benderloch,
Ledaig, Oban, Argyll PA37 1QS
T: 01631 720452
E: june@hawthorncottages.com
W: hawthorncottages.com

Peaceful ground floor bedrooms furnished to a high standard. Eight miles from Oban, ideal base. Home cooking a speciality, dinner available. TV in rooms, hairdryer, tea/coffee. Bedroom with small lounge attached, also guest lounge with Sky TV. Set in 20 acres of farm land. Beach nearby. Special offer three nights or more.

Total number of rooms: 3

Prices from:

Single:	**£35.00**	Double:	**£28.50**
Twin:	**£28.50**	Family room:	**£27.50**

Rothesay, Isle of Bute

Ivybank Villa

Map Ref: 1F5

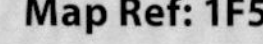

Open: All year 74725

Westlands Road, Rothesay, Isle of Bute PA20 0HQ
T/F: 01700 505064 **M:** 07774 598129
E: thomasrodger@btinternet.com
W: ivybankvilla.co.uk or ivybankvilla.com

- Beautiful 'B' listed Georgian villa, with direct historical links to Lord Bute.
- Spectacular mountain and sea views of the Cowal peninsula and mainland.
- Exotically planted two acre wildlife friendly gardens which are 'home' to a wide variety of animals – deer, bats, herons, hedgehogs, owls as well as a variety of birds.
- Close to all local amenities yet totally private.
- Safe off-road parking within grounds.
- Fabulous suite available with four-poster bed and private sitting and dressing areas, for a truly luxurious stay (by special request).
- Please contact Tom for a truly relaxing and hospitable stay at Ivybank.

Total number of rooms: 4

Prices from:

Single:	**£40.00**	Double:	**£35.00**

Rothesay, Isle of Bute

The Moorings

Map Ref: 1F5

Open: All year 59706

7 Mountstuart Road, Rothesay,
Isle of Bute PA20 9DY
T: 01700 502277 **E:** fjhbute@aol.com
W: themoorings-bute.co.uk

Total number of rooms: 5

Prices per room from:

Single:	**£35.00**	Double:	**£60.00**
Twin:	**£60.00**	Family room:	**£75.00**

Important: Prices stated are estimates and may be subject to amendments.

Campbeltown, Argyll

Dalnaspidal Guest House

Map Ref: 1D7

69974

★★★★★ GUEST HOUSE

Open: All year excl January

Dalnaspidal, Tangy,
Kilkenzie, Campbeltown PA28 6QD

T: 01568 820466
E: relax@dalnaspidal-guesthouse.com
W: dalnaspidal-guesthouse.com

Located in a spectacular rural setting just 10 minutes from Campbeltown, Dalnaspidal is a haven of peace and tranquility offering luxurious accommodation, magnificent sea and countryside views, superior service, excellent cuisine, and a warm friendly welcome. Licensed Restaurant - Small Weddings - Special Occasions - Corporate Events - Gift Vouchers.

Total number of rooms: 4

Prices from:

Single:	**£60.00**	Double:	**£42.50**
Twin:	**£42.50**	Family room:	**£36.00**

Dalmally, Argyll

Craigroyston

Map Ref: 1F2

20861

★★★ B&B

Open: All year excl Xmas and New Year

Monument Road, Dalmally, Argyll PA33 1AA

T: 01838 200234
E: bandb@craigroyston.com
W: craigroyston.com

Total number of rooms: 3

Prices from:

Single:	**£22.00**	Double:	**£24.00**
Twin:	**£22.00**		

Dunoon, Argyll

Eileagan

Map Ref: 1F5

77828

★★★★ B&B

Open: All year

47 Kilbride Road, Dunoon, Argyll and Bute PA23 7LN

T: 01369 707047
E: agnes@eileagan.co.uk
W: eileagan.co.uk

Eileagan is a large Victorian Villa situated on an elevated site overlooking Dunoon town with spectacular views of the River Clyde. We have three comfortable rooms , two with large ensuite bath/shower rooms and one private bathroom. Only fifteen minutes walk from Dunoon and adjacent to the famous Bishops Glen Forest Walks.

Total number of rooms: 3

Prices from:

Single:	**£40.00**	Double:	**£35.00**
Twin:	**£30.00**		

WILDLIFE
SCOTLAND
To find out about watching wildlife in Europe's leading wildlife destination log on to
visitscotland.com/wildlife

West Highlands and Islands

Glendaruel, Argyll

The Watermill

Map Ref: 1F4

79232

★★★★ B&B

Open: All year excl February

Glendaruel, Argyll & Bute PA22 3AB

T: 01369 820203

E: michael.webster18@btinternet.com

The apartments are well fitted out to meet the needs of anyone staying. Set on the Cowal Way Walk and in five acres of woodland, peace and quiet are the keywords. Some easy walking and some of the most stunning scenery Scotland has to offer. A good chill out stay to be had.

Total number of rooms: 5

Prices per room from:

Single: **£35.00** Double: **£55.00**

Twin: **£70.00** Family room: **£60.00**

Inverary, Argyll

Argyll Court Bed and Breakfast

Map Ref: 1F3

39651

★★★ B&B

Open: All year excl Xmas

10 Argyll Court, Inverary, Argyll PA32 8UT

T: 01499 302273

E: anne.macpherson1@btinternet.com

W: inveraryaccommodation.co.uk

Total number of rooms: 2

Prices from:

Single: **£35.00** Double: **£27.50**

Twin: **£27.50**

Kilnaughton Bay, by Port Ellen, Isle of Islay

Samhchair

Map Ref: 1C6

81290

★★★★ B&B

Open: All year excl Xmas and New Year

Samhchair, Kilnaughton Bay, Isle of Islay PA42 7AX

T: 01496 302596

E: info@samhchair.co.uk

W: samhchair.co.uk

Samhchair (Gaelic for "tranquility") is a newly-built bungalow in the style of a Hebridean long house overlooking the safe, sandy beach of the beautiful Kilnaughton Bay, within walking distance of Port Ellen on the lovely Hebridean Island of Islay-the Whisky Isle!

Total number of rooms: 2

Prices from:

Single: **£40.00** Double: **£35.00**

Twin: **£30.00**

ADVENTURE SCOTLAND

For everything you need to know about Adventure Breaks in Scotland and for an Adventure Brochure and an Adventure Pass call

0845 22 55 121

or log on to **visitscotland.com/adventurepass**

Important: Prices stated are estimates and may be subject to amendments.

Lochgilphead, Argyll
The Corran
Map Ref: 1E4

58613

Open: March-November

Poltalloch Street, Lochgilphead, Argyll PA31 8LR
T: 01546 603866
E: lamonthoy@tiscali.co.uk
W: lamonthoy.co.uk

Dating from circa 1860, this former doctor's surgery sits on the edge of Lochgilphead and offers a warm and friendly welcome. Comfortable and spacious accommodation, magnificent views over Loch Gilp towards the mountains of Aaran. The ideal base from which to explore Scotland's magnificent West Coast.

Total number of rooms: 3

Prices per room from:
Single: **£40.00** Double: **£60.00**
Twin: **£60.00** Family room: **£60.00**

Bunessan, Isle of Mull
Ardness House
Map Ref: 1C3

12641

Open: All year

Tiraghoil, Bunessan, Isle of Mull, Argyll PA67 6DU
T: 01681 700260
E: enquiries@isleofmullholidays.com
W: isleofmullholidays.com

A well appointed modern bungalow with all bedrooms ensuite. Guests lounge with panoramic views of Loch Caol and dramatic cliffs beyond. Three and a half miles from Iona ferry.

Total number of rooms: 3

Prices from:
Double: **£28.00-33.00** Twin: **£28.00-33.00**

Dervaig, Isle of Mull
Cuin Lodge
Map Ref: 1C1

76765

Open: All year excl Xmas and New Year

Dervaig, Isle of Mull, Argyll PA75 6QL
T: 01688 400346 **F:** 01688 400346
E: philippa@cuinlodgemull.co.uk
W: cuinlodgemull.co.uk

Sympathetically restored, 200 year old, former farmhouse on the banks of Loch Cuin, one mile North of the village of Dervaig, with stunning views of the loch and the mountains beyond. The accommodation is very comfortable and decorated to a high standard and attention to detail.

Total number of rooms: 2

Prices from:
Twin: **£30.00** Double: **£30.00**
Family room: **£30.00**

Dervaig, Isle of Mull

Druimnacroish

Map Ref: 1C1

Open: March-October

Dervaig, Isle of Mull, Argyll PA75 6QW

T: 01688 400274
E: stay@druimnacroish.co.uk
W: druimnacroish.co.uk

23237

Set on a hillside in the north west of the island near the village of Dervaig, with superb views from every room. Spacious, relaxed atmosphere, homemade bread, WiFi, no TV. Private guest lounges and large conservatory. Well situated for Mull's many attractions, including boat trips, walking and wildlife. Licensed.

Total number of rooms: 6

Prices from:

Double: **£32.00** Twin: **£32.00**

Tobermory, Isle of Mull

Carnaburg Guest House

Map Ref: 1C1

Open: All year

55 Main Street, Tobermory, Isle of Mull PA75 6NT

T: 01688 302479
E: vivien@carnaburg-tobermory.co.uk
W: carnaburg-tobermory.co.uk

74718

Total number of rooms: 8

Prices from:

Single: **£35.00** Double: **£27.50**
Twin: **£27.50** Family room: **£45.00**

Tobermory, Isle of Mull

West Wing Suite Raraig House

Map Ref: 1C1

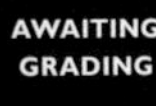

Open: All year

Raeric Road, Tobermory, Isle of Mull PA75 6PU

T: 01688 302390
E: scotshopbiz@aol.com
W: silverswift.co.uk

51132

Total number of rooms: 2

Prices per suite from:

Double: **£50.00**

Oban, Argyll

Aros Ard B&B

Map Ref: 1E2

Open: February-December

Croft Road, Oban, Argyll PA34 5JN

T: 01631 565 500
E: maclean@arosard.freeserve.co.uk
W: arosard.co.uk

12933

Total number of rooms: 2

Prices from:

Single: **£64.00** Double: **£37.00**
Twin: **£37.00**

Scotland

For all you need to know about biking in Scotland and for a mountain bike brochure log on to

visitscotland.com/cycling

Important: Prices stated are estimates and may be subject to amendments.

Oban, Argyll

Clohass

Map Ref: 1E2

★★★ B&B

39405

Open: March-October

Connel Road, Oban, Argyll PA34 5TX
T: 01631 563647
E: obanclohass@aol.com
W: clohass.com

Ideal base for day trips by ferry to Mull, Iona and beyond. Fort William and Glencoe are also an easy drive. A pleasant 10 minute walk into town where there is a wide selection of restaurants for dining.

Total number of rooms: 3

Prices from:
Double: **£27.50** Twin: **£27.50**
Family room: **£27.50**

Oban, Argyll

Don-Muir

Map Ref: 1E2

★★★★ B&B

22913

Open: All year excl Xmas

Pulpit Hill, Oban, Argyll PA34 4LX
T: 01631 564536
E: dina.donmuir@tesco.net
W: donmuir.co.uk

Quiet residential area of town 10 minutes walk to ferry terminals and 2 minutes walk to town's viewpoint, 2 minutes drive to town centre. Very comfortable accommodation with excellent Highland hospitality and good hearty breakfasts.

Total number of rooms: 3

Prices from:
Double: **£30.00** Twin: **£30.00**
Family room: **£30.00**

Oban, Argyll

Lagganbeg Guest House

Map Ref:1E2

★★★ GUEST HOUSE

34731

Open: All year excl Dec/Xmas

4 Victoria Place, Dunollie Road, Oban
Argyll PA34 5PH
T: 01631 563151
E: g.flemingmcnaughton@btinternet.com
W: lagganbegguesthouse.com

Lagganbeg Guest House is a real home from home guest house set in the heart of Oban. We are located minutes from the town centre, sea front and all amenities; ferry, train and bus terminals are ten minutes walk away. All breakfasts are freshly prepared.

Total number of rooms: 6

Prices from:
Double: **£25.00-35.00** Twin: **£25.00-35.00**

West Highlands and Islands

Oban, Argyll

Lorne View

Map Ref: 1E2

74337

Open: All year

Ardconnel Road, Oban, Argyll PA34 5DW

T: 01631 566841

E: lorneview@btinternet.com

W: lorneview.co.uk

Lorne View is a traditional town house situated high above Oban and enjoys stunning views across the harbour and bay to the Isles of Kerrera and Mull. We have two tastefully decorated ensuite double rooms with flat screen LCD TV with DVD and CD players, hairdryer, hospitality tray and other personal touches.

Total number of rooms: 3

Prices from:

Single: **£50.00** Double: **£30.00**

Twin: **£27.50**

Tarbert, Argyll

Barr Na Criche Bed and Breakfast

Map Ref: 1E5

76913

Open: All year

Tarbert, Argyll PA29 6YA

T: 01880 820833

E: barrnacriche@aol.com

W: barrnacriche.com

Total number of rooms: 1

Prices from:

Single: **£30.00** Double: **£30.00**

Twin: **£30.00** Family room: **£30.00**

Tarbert Bay, Loch Fyne, Argyll

Important: Prices stated are estimates and may be subject to amendments.

Canoeing on Loch Lomond, Argyll

Loch Lomond and The Trossachs

Whatever road you take to the bonny banks of Loch Lomond, you'll arrive at one of the most picturesque places in all of Scotland. This vast National Park is, indeed, one of the most beautiful places in the world.

Towns like Callander, Balloch, Killin and Aberfoyle make a great base to explore different corners of the park. And once you're there, you'll find so much to do, from watersports to mountain climbing, angling to gentle strolls in the stunning countryside.

You can even integrate the sedate with the active – catch the SS Sir Walter Scott from the Trossachs Pier and cruise Loch Katrine to Stronachlachar, then enjoy the 12-mile shore hike back.

Falls of Dochart, Killin

DON'T MISS

1 **Loch Lomond and The Trossachs National Park** has its Gateway Centre on the southern shore of the loch in Balloch. From here and elsewhere on the loch, boat trips offer visitors the chance to explore the largest body of freshwater in Britain. To the west, Argyll Forest Park provides secluded waymarked trails, while the Trossachs to the east have provided inspiration for poets and novelists throughout the centuries.

2 The main visitor centre of the **Queen Elizabeth Forest Park** is on the A821 north of Aberfoyle. An integral part of the National Park, it offers a host of walking, wildlife and photography opportunities from the foot of Loch Lomond to Strathyre Forest, north of Loch Lubnaig. Here, you'll find a multitude of waymarked paths, a forest shop, wildlife viewing station and Liz MacGregor's Coffee Shop.

3 The dramatic scenery of the Trossachs is said to be the inspiration behind Sir Walter Scott's The Lady of the Lake. It is fitting then that the historic steamship which regularly sets sail on Loch Katrine is named after him. The **SS Sir Walter Scott** cruises up to Stronachlachar and will return you to the Trossachs Pier.

4 At **Go Ape!** in Aberfoyle, you can take to the trees and experience a new, exhilarating course of rope bridges, tarzan swings and zip slides (including the longest in the UK) up to 37 metres above the forest floor. Approximately three hours of fun and adventure await.

5 For a fun family day out, visit the **Scottish Wool Centre** in Aberfoyle, where you can enjoy a light-hearted look at 2,000 years of Scottish history portrayed by human and animal actors, plus spinning and weaving demonstrations. The live animal show features sheepdogs rounding up both sheep and Indian Runner Ducks, whilst younger visitors can enjoy the lambs and baby goats in springtime.

2

3

4

5

FOOD AND DRINK

eatscotland.com

6 Whilst touring around Loch Lomond, be sure to stop at the **Coach House Coffee Shop** in the conservation village of Luss. Accompany a bumper homemade scone with a Lomond Latte or a Clyde Cappuccino!

7 The **Village Inn** at Arrochar is a charming country inn on the edge of Loch Long. Offering traditional Scottish home-cooking, it proves to be a great favourite with walkers exploring the adjacent 'Arrochar Alps'.

8 The family friendly **Forth Inn** at Aberfoyle is known for its good food and atmosphere. Its award-winning bar and restaurant are favourites with locals and visitors alike.

9 **The Kilted Skirlie** is a modern Scottish restaurant with a sense of theatre that caters for every taste and pocket at Loch Lomond Shores. Rain or shine, the view of Loch Lomond and the towering Ben Lomond is the perfect setting to enjoy a delicious meal.

9

11

HISTORY AND HERITAGE

10 The **islands of Loch Lomond** are home to many ancient ruins including a 7th-century monastery and the remains of a former Victorian whisky distilleries.

11 The Lake of Menteith is the only 'lake' in Scotland, all others being known as lochs. Sail from the Port of Menteith, off the A81 south of Callander, to the island that is home to **Inchmahome Priory**, an 18th century Augustinian monastery.

12 The historic village of Killin, with the spectacular Falls of Dochart, is the setting for the **Breadalbane Forklore Centre** which is housed in a beautifully restored mill with a working waterwheel. Dedicated to exploring the rich myths and legends prevalent in these parts, you can follow the stories of the local clans and learn about St Fillan and the arrival of Christianity in Scotland. Open April to October.

VIEWS

13 The beauty of **Loch Lomond** is undisputed but the finest vantage point is more open to debate. Everyone has their favourite spot and no doubt you will too. Take a cruise on the loch itself from Luss, Balloch or Tarbet or head to Inversnaid on the west bank for more rugged views.

14 'The Dumpling' is the nickname for **Duncryne Hill**, a volcanic plug, situated just off the A811 at the east end of Gartocharn. At about 465ft high and accessible by a short steep path, it is an astounding vantage point overlooking Loch Lomond's islands.

15 **Conic Hill** is located just north of Balmaha on the B837. A 358m ascent, it offers superb views of Loch Lomond and its islands. From here, you can also see the dramatic changes to the landscape caused by the Highland Boundary Fault.

16 From the Stronachlachar junction on the Inversnaid road (B829), the wild landscape of **Loch Arklet** leads down towards Loch Lomond and its surrounding hills.

14

16

19

WALKS

visitscotland.com/walking

17 To walk along the shore of **Loch Katrine**, start at the Trossachs Pier (A821 west of Callander). Here you can choose to walk the 12 mile route to Stronachlachar and get the steamer back or you can walk as far as you like and then re-trace your steps. Cycle hire is also available here.

18 The village hall in Balquhidder is your starting point for one of Breadalbane's most glorious views. Head along the Kirkton Burn and upwards onto a forest road. Soon you'll reach **Creag an Tuirc** where you can absorb the beauty of Balquhidder Glen, Loch Voil and little Loch Doine. Including a short climb, this 2½ mile walk should take you about 2 hours.

19 **Rowardennan** (B837 from Drymen) on the eastern edge of Loch Lomond is a wonderful starting and finishing point for a gentle walk along the shores, following part of the famous West Highland Way.

Arrochar, Argyll

Ben Bheula

Map Ref: 1G3

78697

★★★ B&B

Open: All year

Succoth, Arrochar, Dunbartonshire G83 7AL

T: 01301 702184
E: bookings@benbheula.co.uk
W: benbheula.co.uk

Total number of rooms: 3

Prices per room from:

Double: **£55.00** Twin: **£60.00**

Arrochar, Argyll

Dalkusha House

Map Ref: 1G3

49705

★★★★ B&B

Open: All year

Dalkusha House, Arrochar, Argyll & Bute G83 7AA

T: 01301 702234
E: dalkusha@aol.com

Total number of rooms: 3

Prices from:

Single: **£45.00** Double: **£35.00**
Twin: **£35.00** Family room: **£35.00**

Arrochar, Argyll

Fascadail Country Guest House

Map Ref: 1G3

77918

★★★ GUEST HOUSE

Open: All year excl January

Shore Road, Arrochar, Argyll and Bute G83 7AB

T: 01301 702344
E: enquiries@fascadail.com
W: fascadail.com

Two miles from Loch Lomond, Fascadail is a listed building situated in 1.5 acres of picturesque gardens on the shores of Loch Long, overlooking the 'Arrochar Alps'. This is the perfect retreat to explore the surrounding National Park, historic buildings and gardens. Excellent restaurants and pubs within walking distance.

Total number of rooms: 6

Prices per room from:

Single: **£40.00** Double: **£29.00**
Twin: **£29.00** Family room: **£34.00**

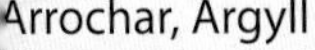

Arrochar, Argyll

Rowantree Cottage

Map Ref: 1G3

52358

★★★ B&B

Open: 1st March-30th November

Arrochar, Argyll & Bute G83 7AA

T: 01301 702882
E: bookings@rowantreecottage.com
W: rowantreecottage.com

Relax in this welcoming family run bed and breakfast, with bedrooms overlooking Loch Long with views across the loch to the Arrochar Alps beyond. Ideal centre for hill walking, climbing, mountain biking and exploring the Loch Lomond and Trossachs National Park and Argyll and Bute.

Total number of rooms: 2

Prices from:

Single: **£45.00** Double: **£30.00**
Twin: **£30.00**

Balloch, Loch Lomond

Aird House

Map Ref: 1G4

Open: All year excl Xmas and New Year

1 Ben Lomond Walk, Balloch,
West Dunbartonshire G83 8RJ

T: 01389 754464/07814 730176

11261

Total number of rooms: 2

Prices from:

Single: **£30.00-35.00** Double: **£25.00-30.00**

Twin: **£23.00-25.00**

Balloch, Loch Lomond

Gowanlea Guest House

Map Ref: 1G4

★★★★
B&B

Open: All year

Drymen Road, Balloch, West Dunbartonshire G83 8HS

T: 01389 752456

E: gowanlea@blueyonder.co.uk

W: lochlomondbandb.co.uk

79026

Loch Lomond is only a short stroll from the Gowanlea Guest House. Andrea and John welcome you as the new owners of this well established 4 star Bed and Breakfast. Balloch itself is central for visiting the mountains or enjoying the shopping in Glasgow just a short train ride away.

Total number of rooms: 4

Prices from:

Single: **£35.00-50.00** Double: **£25.00-35.00**

Twin: **£25.00-35.00** Family room: **£25.00-35.00**

Balloch, Loch Lomond

Oakvale

Map Ref: 1G4

★★★
B&B

Open: All year

Drymen Road, Balloch, West Dunbartonshire G83 8JY

T: 01389 751615

E: oakvalebb@blueyonder.co.uk

48029

Enjoy a relaxing break in charming comfortable accommodation less than 5 minutes walk to country park and Loch shore. Ideal base for exploring the magnificent countryside nearby helped by Derek and Jacqueline's local knowledge. Walking distance to Balloch's pubs and restaurants. Individually and tastefully decorated rooms await you. Warm welcome assured.

Total number of rooms: 3

Prices per room from:

Twin: **£55.00** Double: **£55.00**

Eat*Scotland*.com

Discover Scotland's superb produce and great places to dine.

Important: Prices stated are estimates and may be subject to amendments.

Balloch, Loch Lomond

The Reivers

Map Ref: 1G4 51413

Open: All year

62 Drymen Road, Balloch, West Dunbartonshire G83 8HS
T: 01389 720430/07736152512
E: the.reivers@blueyonder.co.uk
W: thereivers.co.uk

Set in a quiet part of Balloch a warm welcome awaits, nearby are country walks, Loch cruises, pubs, restaurants and local shops. We are also an ideal base for touring the Trossachs, Argyll and Bute, we offer a full breakfast menu, we are also dog friendly.

Total number of rooms: 3

Prices per room from:

Single: **£30.00** Double: **£22.50**
Twin: **£22.50** Family room: **£22.50**

Balloch, Loch Lomond

St Blanes

Map Ref: 1G4 55765

★★★ B&B

Open: All year

Drymen Road, Balloch, Dunbartonshire G83 8HR
T: 01389 729661
E: stblanes@tiscali.co.uk
W: accommodationlochlomond.com

Total number of rooms: 3

Prices per room from:

Single: **£30.00** Double: **£55.00**
Twin: **£55.00** Family room: **£85.00**

by Balloch, Loch Lomond

Braeburn Cottage

Map Ref:1G4 15982

★★★ B&B

Open: All year excl Xmas and New Year

West Auchencarroch Farm, Auchencarroch Road, by Balloch, West Dunbartonshire G83 9LU
T: 01389 710998
E: braeburn@bigfoot.com
W: braeburncottage.co.uk

Modern bungalow on our family run beef and sheep farm. Panoramic views of Loch Lomond Hills, ten minutes from the loch and Balloch. Peaceful landscaped gardens where you can rest and enjoy the views. Traditional Scottish breakfast with free range eggs from our own hens. A warm welcome awaits you.

Total number of rooms: 2

Prices from:

Single: **£35.00** Double: **£25.00**
Twin: **£25.00** Family room **£25.00**

For information on fishing breaks in Scotland and for a brochure call

0845 22 55 121

visitscotland.com/fish

Loch Lomond and the Trossachs

Callander, Perthshire

Annfield Guest House

Map Ref: 1H3

74811

Open: All year excl Xmas

18 North Church Street, Callander FK17 8EG
T: 01877 330204
E: reservations@annfieldguesthouse.co.uk
W: annfieldguesthouse.co.uk

Situated quietly yet just a minutes walk to Callander's bustling centre, shops and restaurants. Annfield is a lovely Victorian guest house recently renovated to a high standard and now providing first class accommodation with award winning breakfasts. Annfield provides a superb base to explore the beautiful Loch Lomond and Trossachs National Park.

Total number of rooms: 7

Prices from:

Single: **£35.00** Double: **£27.50**
Twin: **£27.50** Family room: **£25.00**

Callander, Perthshire

Riverview Guest House

Map Ref: 1H3

13496

Open: March-November

Riverview, Leny Road, Callander, Perthshire FK17 8AL
T: 01877 330635
E: drew@visitcallander.co.uk
W: visitcallander.co.uk

Victorian Villa set in its own gardens with private parking. Close to town centre, leisure complex and restaurants. Ideal location for motoring, walking and cycling holidays. Callander is the main town in the beautiful Loch Lomond and Trossachs National Park.

Total number of rooms: 5

Prices from:

Single: **£30.00** Double: **£30.00**
Twin: **£30.00**

Cardross, Argyll

Ben Rhydding

Map Ref: 1G4

★★★
B&B

69928

Open: All year excl Xmas

3 Ritchie Avenue, Cardross, Argyll & Bute G82 5LL
T: 01389 841659
E: benrhydding@hotmail.co.uk
W: benrhyddingbandb.co.uk

Both ensuite bedrooms have stunning river views, ideally placed for visiting Glasgow, Loch Lomond National Park, Stirling. Warm welcome and a hearty Scottish breakfast.

Total number of rooms: 2

Prices from:

Single: **£40.00** Double: **£30.00**
Family room: **£25.00**

Important: Prices stated are estimates and may be subject to amendments.

Doune, Perthshire

Glenardoch House

Map Ref: 2A3

Open: May-September (winter by arrangement) 27981

Glenardoch, Castle Road, Doune, Perthshire FK16 6EA

T: 01786 841489

E: stay@glenardochhouse.com

W: glenardochhouse.com

Total number of rooms: 2

Prices from:

Double: **£35.00**

Drymen, Loch Lomond

Elmbank

Map Ref: 1H4

★★ B&B

Open: All year 24839

10 Stirling Road, Drymen, Loch Lomond G63 0BN

T: 01360 661016/ 07977756226

E: enquiries@elmbank-drymen.co.uk

W: elmbank-drymen.co.uk

Next to Drymen's main square, in the heart of Loch Lomond and the Trossachs National Park, you'll love Elmbank's unique character and location. Cosy restaurants and taverns, leisure club, stunning countryside, golfing, fishing, boat trips, horse riding and much more just on the doorstep. Edinburgh, Glasgow, Stirling and Perth close by.

Total number of rooms: 4

Prices from:

Single: **£22.00** Double: **£22.00**

Twin: **£22.00** Family rooms **£54.00pr**

Dumbarton

Glenmar B&B

Map Ref: 1G5

WAITING GRADING

Open: All year excl Xmas and New Year 28258

27 Round Riding Road, Dumbarton G82 2HB

T: 01389 731842

E: donnaaustin@fsmail.net

Victorian mansion completely refurbished to high standard. Six minutes drive to stunning Loch Lomond, five minute walk to good quality restaurants, swimming pool three minutes away. Speciality family room with outside barbecue area exclusively for family room.

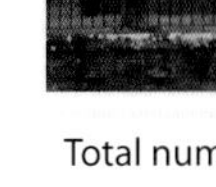

Total number of rooms: 4

Prices from:

Single: **£45.00-60.00** Double: **£30.00-40.00**

Twin: **£30.00-40.00** Family room: **£70.00-110.00**

Gartocharn, Dunbartonshire

The Old School House

Map Ref: 1G4

★★★★ B&B

Open: All year 59909

Gartocharn G83 8SB

T: 01389 830373

E: reservations@the-old-school-house.co.uk

W: the-old-school-house.co.uk

Total number of rooms: 4

Prices from:

Single: **£37.00** Double: **£37.00**

Twin: **£37.00**

For a full listing of Quality Assured accommodation, please see directory at back of this guide.

Loch Lomond and the Trossachs

Helensburgh, Argyll
Bellfield
Map Ref: 1G4

70170

Open: All year

199 East Clyde Street, Helensburgh G84 7AJ
T: 01436 673361
E: r.callaghan@virgin.net
W: scotland2000.com/bellfield

Bellfield Guest House provides the very best accommodation and bed and breakfast for those visiting the lovely locations of Helensburgh, Loch Lomond, Trossachs, Stirling, Glasgow or Edinburgh. Our guest house is centrally located within Helensburgh, only a few minutes walk away from all the towns major amenities.

Total number of rooms: 3

Prices per room from:

Single: **£35.00** Double: **£60.00**
Twin: **£60.00**

Helensburgh, Argyll
Sinclair House
Map Ref: 1G4

★★★★ GUEST HOUSE

26217

Open: All year

91/93 Sinclair Street, Helensburgh G84 8TR
T: 01436 676301
E: enquiries@sinclairhouse.com
W: sinclairhouse.com

Iain and Ishbel welcome you to our superior guesthouse, located only two minutes walk to the town centre and ten minutes drive to the National Park. Immaculate rooms with many extras including memory foam matresses, fridges, laptops with free internet access, new LCD TV's and DVD players.

Total number of rooms: 4

Prices per room from:

Single: Double: **£67.00**
Twin: **£73.00** Family room: **£73.00**

Killin, Perthshire
Ardlochay Lodge
Map Ref: 1H2

★★★ B&B

12602

Open: All year

Maragowan, Killin FK21 8TN
T: 01567 820962
E: lodge@ardlochaylodge.co.uk
W: ardlochaylodge.co.uk

Total number of rooms: 3

Prices from:

Single: **£30.00-35.00** Double: **£28.00-30.00**
Twin: **£28.00-30.00** Family room: **£26.00-30.00**

Scotland. The Home of Golf

For everything you need to know about golfing in Scotland and for a brochure call: **0845 22 55 121**

Important: Prices stated are estimates and may be subject to amendments.

Killin, Perthshire

Dall Lodge Country House

Map Ref: 1H2 22048

Open: Easter-October

Main Street, Killin, Perthshire FK21 8TN

T: 01567 820217

E: connor@dalllodge.co.uk

W: dalllodge.co.uk

Country house in picturesque village of Killin with own moorings and spectacular views of the mountains. Friendly atmosphere, perfect base for relaxing, touring or outdoor pursuits. Visit our website for more information.

Total number of rooms: 9

Prices per room from:

Single: **£32.00** Double: **£54.00**

Twin: **£60.00** Family room: **£76.00**

Lochearnhead, Perthshire

Mansewood Country House

Map Ref: 1H2 75801

★★★★ GUEST HOUSE

Open: All year

Lochearnhead, Perthshire, FK19 8NS

T: 01567 830213

E: stay@mansewoodcountryhouse.co.uk

W: mansewoodcountryhouse.co.uk

Total number of rooms: 6

Prices from:

Single: **£43.00-45.00** Double: **£33.00-35.00**

Twin: **£33.00-35.00**

Luss, Argyll

Shantron Farm Bed and Breakfast

Map Ref: 1G4 54403

Open: April to end of October

Shantron Farm, Luss, Argyll and Bute G83 8RH

T: 01389 850231

E: anne@farmstay-lochlomond.co.uk

W: farmstay-lochlomond.co.uk

Total number of rooms: 3

Prices from:

Single: **£40.00** Double: **£30.00**

Twin: **£30.00**

Rhu, Argyll

Floral Cottage Guest House

Map Ref: 1G4 26338

★★★ B&B

Open: All year

Church Road, Rhu, Helensburgh

Argyll and Bute G84 8RW

T: 01436 820687

We are located in the heart of the village, adjacent to Rhu Parish Church, and only a short walking distance from the village amenities and marina. Rhu is located on the shores of the Gareloch within a 40 minute drive of Glasgow and only 15 minutes from scenic Loch Lomond.

Total number of rooms: 3

Prices from:

Single: **£23.00-27.00** Double: **£23.00-27.00**

Twin: **£23.00-27.00** Family room: **£60.00pr**

For a full listing of Quality Assured accommodation, please see directory at back of this guide.

Rosneath, nr Helensburgh

Easter Garth Guest House

Map Ref: 1G4

★★★ GUEST HOUSE

Open: All year 24243

The Clachan, Rosneath, Argyll and Bute G84 0RF

T: 01436 831007

E: richard.w.fryer@btopenworld.com

W: lochlomondguesthouse.com

Beautiful house built 1838 Grade C listed. A touch of class at affordable prices. Family run, friendly atmosphere. Set in a conservation area with private gardens. Loch Lomond, The National Park, Coastal Route to the west, all close by. Children welcome. Evening meals by arrangement. Family suite available. Long stay discounts.

Total number of rooms: 3

Prices from:

Single: **£30.00** Double: **£25.00**

Twin: **£25.00** Family room: **£65.00pr**

Tarbet, by Arrochar

Ballyhennan Toll House

Map Ref: 1G3

★★★ B&B

Open: All year excl Xmas and New Year 14014

Ballyhennan Toll House, Tarbet,
by Arrochar, Argyll and Bute, G83 7DA

T: 01301 702203

E: jim@rawle1.freeserve.co.uk

W: oldtollhouse.co.uk

The Old Toll House is open all year round to walkers and tourists where a warm Scottish welcome awaits you. Set amongst outstanding scenery with many walks nearby we are situated on the A83 between Tarbet and Arrochar, between Loch Lomond and Loch Long, with an excellent view of Ben Lomond.

Total number of rooms: 3

Prices from:

Single: **£30.00** Double: **£25.00**

Twin: **£25.00** Family room: **£25.00**

Tarbet, by Arrochar

Stewart House Bed and Breakfast

Map Ref: 1G3

★★★ B&B

Open: All year 77285

Stewart House, Bemersyde, Tarbet, Loch Lomond
Argyll & Bute G83 7DE

T: 01301 702230

E: stewart_house@btinternet.com

W: accommodationlochlomond.co.uk

Stewart House offers an informal, friendly, home from home atmosphere where you can relax and enjoy the magnificent and peaceful setting. Located in the tranquil village of Tarbet which is situated on the Bonnie Banks of Loch Lomond which offers world famous scenery and a plethora of recreation and leisure facilities.

Total number of rooms: 3

Prices from:

Double: **£30.00** Family room: **£30.00**

Important: Prices stated are estimates and may be subject to amendments.

Stirling Castle at Dusk

Stirling and Forth Valley

Stirling and the Forth Valley offer a huge range of visitor attractions but a recent addition to the list is proving extremely popular. Built to celebrate the new Millennium and opened in 2002, The Falkirk Wheel is a triumph of engineering. It's the world's only rotating boatlift and, standing an impressive 24 metres high, it has reconnected the Forth & Clyde Canal with the Union Canal.

Scotland's industrial heritage is well represented locally at the Bo'ness and Kinneil Steam Railway, Birkhill Fireclay Mine and Callendar House, while you can see traces of Scotland's woollen industry on the shores of the Forth in Clackmannan.

History is everywhere around Stirling. Don't miss Stirling Castle and the National Wallace Monument but remember to leave enough time to take a walk round the town and enjoy a spot of shopping too.

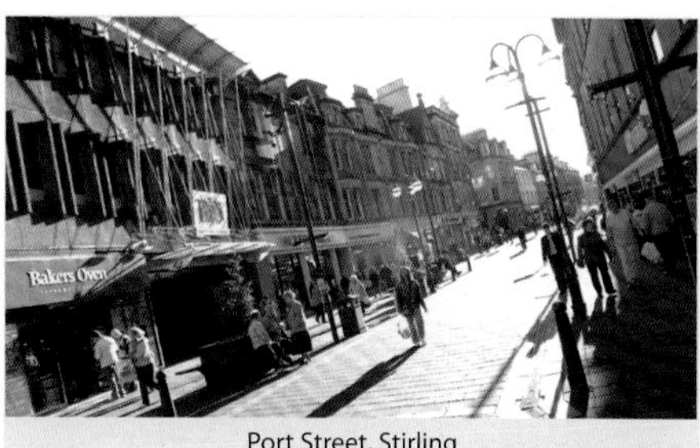

Port Street, Stirling

DON'T MISS

1 **Stirling Castle**, undoubtedly one of the finest in Scotland, sits high on its volcanic rock towering over the stunning countryside known as 'Braveheart Country'. A favourite royal residence over the centuries and a key military stronghold, visit the Great Hall, the Chapel Royal, and the Renaissance Palace. From the castle esplanade the sites of no less than seven historic battles can be seen, as can the majestic **National Wallace Monument** built in tribute to William Wallace.

2 The world's only rotating boatlift, **The Falkirk Wheel**, was constructed in 2002 to link the Forth & Clyde and Union canals. It is now possible for boats to traverse Central Scotland by canal for the first time in more than 40 years. Learn about Scotland's canal network in the visitor centre or board a vessel to take a trip on the mechanical marvel itself.

3 The **Antonine Wall** dates back to the 2nd century and once marked the northern frontier of the Roman Empire. Substantial lengths have been preserved and can still be seen at various sites around Falkirk. The site was awarded UNESCO World Heritage Status in July 2008. Follow the wall for a relaxed walk along the towpath on the north of the canal, taking you past the Falkirk Wheel to Bonnybridge.

4 Just a few miles north west of Stirling on the A84 you will find **Blair Drummond Safari Park**. Here you can drive through wild animal reserves and get close to lions and zebras, and a whole host of other animals. Or you can park and walk around the pet farm, see the only elephants in Scotland, watch a sea lion display, find out what it's like to hold a bird of prey and take a boat to Chimp Island. There is also an adventure play area, pedal boats for hire and for the more adventurous – the flying fox!

2

4

FOOD AND DRINK

eatscotland.com

5 The **Gargunnock Inn** is situated in the small village of Gargunnock on the A811 west of Stirling. A welcoming, friendly establishment, it serves freshly prepared, local produce in its restaurant and has a more informal bar adjoining for relaxing in after dinner.

6 **Harviestoun Country Hotel & Restaurant** in Tillicoultry is the perfect place to stop, whether it is for lunch, high tea or an evening meal. The restored 18th century steading, with the backdrop of the stunning Ochil Hills, is the ideal setting for relaxing with good food and fine wine.

7 The lovely Victorian spa town of Bridge of Allan is home to the **Bridge of Allan Brewery** where you can see how traditional Scottish handcrafted ales are produced and even have a free tasting session!

9

10

HISTORY AND HERITAGE

8 Built in tribute to Scotland's national hero Sir William Wallace, the **National Wallace Monument**, by Stirling, can be seen for miles around. The Monument exhibition tells of Sir Wallace's epic struggle for a free Scotland.

9 **Castle Campbell** is beautifully sited at the head of Dollar Glen, immediately north of Dollar. Sitting in lofty isolation and overlooked by the Ochil Hills, the castle became the chief lowland stronghold of the Campbell clan, upon whose members the successive titles of Earl, Marquis, and Duke of Argyll were bestowed. There are excellent walks through Dollar Glen to enjoy too.

10 On the site of the original battlefield, the **Bannockburn Heritage Centre** on the southern outskirts of Stirling, tells the story of the greatest victory of Scotland's favourite monarch King Robert the Bruce. Walk the battlefield and then enjoy the audio-visual presentation in the centre, recounting the battle. A re-enactment of the battle takes place over two days every September.

11 Open the door to **Callendar House** in Falkirk, and you open the door to 600 years of Scottish history. Journey through time from the days of the Jacobites to the advent of the railway, and don't forget to stop at the Georgian kitchens for some refreshments prepared using authentic Georgian recipes.

12 Discover what life was like for unfortunate inmates within the authentic Victorian **Stirling Old Town Jail**. You might well run into Jock Rankin, the notorious town hangman, and even witness an attempted jail break!

WALKS

visitscotland.com/walking

13 Walk around Muiravon Country Park along the River Avon and you'll pass the Avon Aqueduct, Scotland's longest and tallest, which carries the Union Canal above the river. Near Bo'Ness, the River Avon flows through the **Avon Gorge**, a well known local beauty spot where you can stroll through ancient woodlands, home to a variety of wildlife including deer and otters.

14 Not far from Dollar where the A823 meets the A977, it's worth stopping to explore the delightful **Rumbling Bridge**, so named because of the continuous rumbling sound of the falls and the river below. The unusual double bridge spans a narrow gorge and you'll find a network of platforms and paths that take you over the river and deep into the gorge with spectacular views of waterfalls and swirling pools.

15 The **Darn Walk** from Bridge of Allan to Dunblane is a beautiful walk which can be enjoyed at any time of the year. Highlights include a scenic stretch alongside the River Allan and the cave which was Robert Louis Stevenson's inspiration for Ben Gunn's cave in Treasure Island. The walk can be completed in 1½ to 2 hours.

16 At the heart of Clackmannanshire's 300-acre **Gartmorn Dam Country Park**, visitors can enjoy a short walk with gentle gradients suitable for wheelchairs or pushchairs. Gartmorn Dam is the oldest man-made reservoir still in use in Scotland, and is a nature reserve which is the winter home of thousands of migratory ducks.

17

18

19

ATTRACTIONS

17 Dating back to the 14th century, **Alloa Tower** is one of the largest surviving medieval tower houses in Scotland. The tower has been recently restored and has amazing features.

18 Situated by the banks of the River Teith, **Doune Castle** was once the ancestral home of the Earls of Moray. At one time occupied by the Jacobite troops, this castle can now be explored and makes a great picnic spot. Film lovers may also recognise the castle from scenes from 'Monty Python and the Holy Grail'.

19 Just north of Stirling, **Argaty Red Kites** is one of Scotland's red kite feeding stations. After 130 years of Scottish Natural Heritage, the RSPB has reintroduced these exciting, acrobatic birds to central Scotland. Spend a day and you can enjoy a guided walk or just watch the birds from the hide.

Dunblane, Nr Stirling
Jean MacGregor B&B
Map Ref: 2A3

19246

Open: All year

Ciar Mhor, Auchinlay Road, Dunblane
Perthshire FK15 9JS
T: 01786 823371
E: jean.macgregor@btinternet.com
W: ciar-mhor.co.uk

Modern spacious family home set on the banks of the River Allan, overlooking the park. Set in a peaceful and quiet location on the outskirts of Dunblane within close proximity of the town centre and rail station. Ideal base for touring central Scotland.

Total number of rooms: 2

Prices from:

Single:	**£30.00**	Double:	**£20.00**
Twin:	**£20.00**	Family room:	**POA**

Falkirk
Ashbank Guest House
Map Ref: 2A4

★★★★ GUEST HOUSE

13100

Open: All year excl Xmas and New Year

105 Main Street, Redding, Falkirk FK2 9UQ
T: 01324 716649
E: ashbank@guest-house.freeserve.co.uk
W: bandbfalkirk.com

Quiet comfortable B&B near main line train station and M9 motorway. Central to three cities of Stirling, Edinburgh and Glasgow. Popular with business people and tourists alike. Wonderful views over the Forth Valley to Braveheart country. Easily accessible to Falkirk Wheel, Trossachs and Loch Lomond. Courtesy pick ups at Polmont Station.

Total number of rooms: 3

Prices from:

Single:	**£50.00**	Double:	**£35.00**
Twin:	**£35.00**	Family room:	**£80.00pr**

Stirling
Mrs Elizabeth Brodie
Map Ref: 2A4

43192

Open: All year excl Xmas and New Year

Southfield, 2 Melville Terrace, Stirling FK8 2ND
T: 01786 464872
E: elizabethbrodie@tiscali.co.uk
W: brodie-stirling.co.uk

Total number of rooms: 3

Prices from:

Single:	**£35.00**	Double:	**£27.50**
Twin:	**£27.50**	Family room:	**£27.50**

For everything you need to know about skiing and snowsports in Scotland call 0845 22 55 121

ski-scotland.com

ski-scotland.com

Stirling and Forth Valley

Stirling
Garfield House
Map Ref: 2A4

★★★ GUEST HOUSE

Open: All year excl Xmas and New Year 27287

12 Victoria Square, Stirling FK8 2QZ

T: 01786 473730

Family run guest house in traditional stone built Victorian house overlooking quiet square close to town centre, castle and all local amenities. Ideal base for exploring historic Stirling, Loch Lomond and the Trossachs. Non smoking.

Total number of rooms: 7

Prices from:

Single:		Double:	**£32.00**
Twin:	**£32.00**	Family room:	**£30.00**

Stirling
Laurinda B&B
Map Ref: 2A4

★★★ B&B

Open: All year 35036

66 Ochilmount, Ochilview, Bannockburn, Stirling FK7 8PJ

T: 01786 815612

Total number of rooms: 2

Prices from:

Single:	**£25.00-30.00**	Double:	**£24.00**
Twin:	**£24.00**	Family room:	**Adult £24.00**
			Child £10.00

The Pots of Gartness, near Killearn, Stirling

The Pineapple, Falkirk

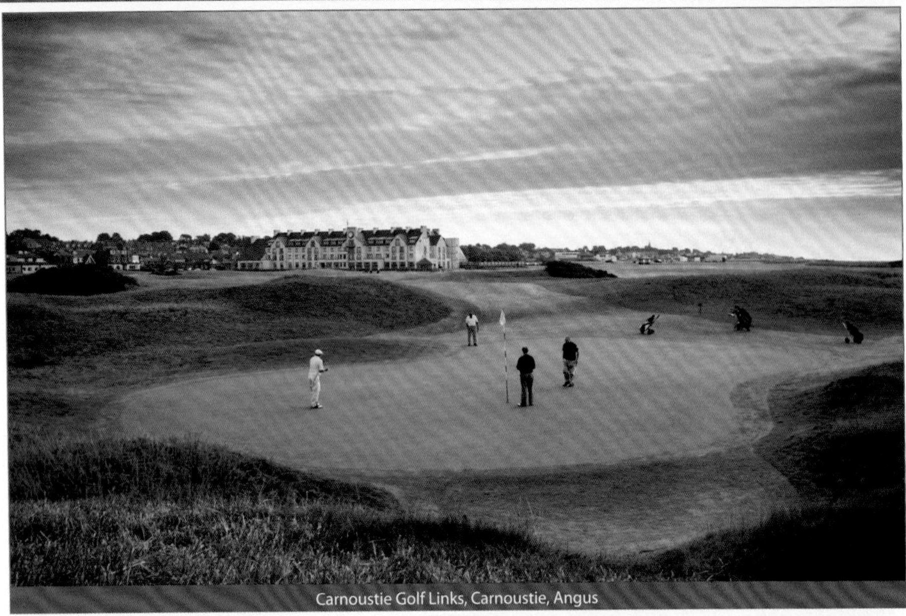

Carnoustie Golf Links, Carnoustie, Angus

PERTHSHIRE, ANGUS AND DUNDEE AND THE KINGDOM OF FIFE

Scotland's heartlands are the perfect holiday destination in many ways. There's so much to discover in this part of the world that you're sure to find something that suits you perfectly. Golfing, fishing, walking, sightseeing, there's an abundance of choice and there are some wonderful places to stay.

Bed and breakfast accommodation in this part of the world comes in all shapes and sizes. From grand Victorian mansions to former fishermen's cottages, farms, bungalows and country houses you'll find so many options in so many delightful places.

The countryside is so varied too. Fife has an enviable coastline with a number of perfect little harbour towns, Perthshire is unspoiled and magnificent, with some of Scotland's finest woodlands and stunning lochs and hills. And then there's Dundee – the area's largest city. There's always another fascinating place waiting to be explored.

This is a holiday destination that can be as active as you want it to be. For the outdoor enthusiast, there's anything from hill walking to whitewater rafting and pretty much everything in between. Anglers love the thrill of pursuing salmon and trout on some of the country's greatest river beats or heading out to sea where the catch can be bountiful.

Golfers love this area too. Some of the world's finest courses are here, from the home of golf at St Andrews to championship quality greats Gleneagles and Carnoustie.

If wildlife's your thing, the opportunities are endless. In the countryside of Perthshire and the Angus Glens there are ospreys, eagles, otters and deer. By the sea from Fife to Angus spot a wide variety of seabirds – especially around the Montrose Basin which attracts thousands of migrant species.

You don't have to be escaping civilisation to enjoy these parts, however. There are towns and cities that you'll enjoy enormously, each with their own unique attractions. Perth has specialist shops and high street retailers. St Andrews is a fine university town with a fascinating history. Dunfermline was once the seat of Scotland's Kings while Dundee, the City of Discovery, is enjoying something of a renaissance these days and is a great place for a big day out.

What's more, 2009 is a big year for Scotland – we're celebrating the 250th anniversary of the birth of Robert Burns. There's over 200 special events taking place throughout the year, all over Scotland. Go to homecomingscotland2009.com to find out about events in this area.

Fishing village of Crail overlooking the harbour, Fife

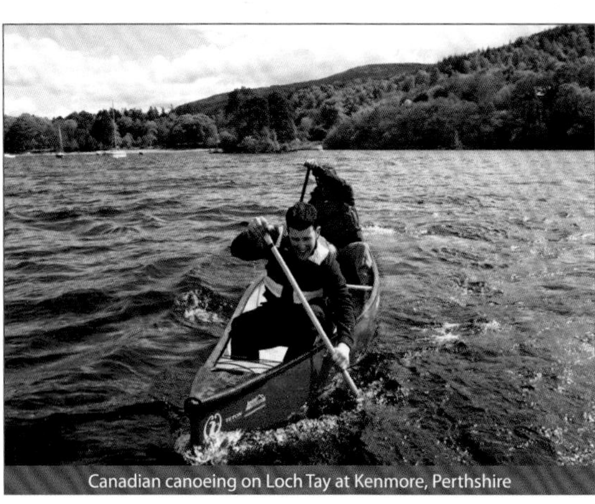

Canadian canoeing on Loch Tay at Kenmore, Perthshire

What's On?

Snowdrop Festival 2009
Feb/Mar 2009
visitscotland.com/snowdrops

StAnza 2009
Scotland's Poetry Festival
18 - 22 March 2009
stanzapoetry.org

Angus Glens Walking Festival
28 – 31 May 2009, Angus Glens
angusanddundee.co.uk/walkingfestival

Perth Festival of the Arts
21 -31 May 2009, Perth
The Festival features world-class artists.
perthfestival.co.uk

Game Conservancy Scottish Fair
3 - 5 July 2009, Scone Palace, Perth
One of the main countryside events of the year in Scotland.
www.scottishfair.com

The 34th Scottish Transport Extravaganza
11 – 12 July 2009
Glamis Castle, Angus
svvc.co.uk

Arbroath Seafest
8 –9 August 2009
Arbroath Harbour, Arbroath
angusahead.com

Culross Music & Arts Festival
August 2009
culrossfestival.com

Blair Castle International Horse Trials & Country Fair
Blair Castle, Blair Atholl
27 – 30 August 2009
Equestrian sport on an international scale!.
blairhorsetrials.co.uk

Dundee Flower and Food Festival
4 – 6 September 2009
dundeeflowerandfoodfestival.com

The Enchanted Forest
16 October – 1 November 2009
Faskally Wood, by Pitlochry
A spectacular journey of light and sound in Perthshire's Big Tree Country.
enchantedforest.org.uk

All dates correct at time of publication. Please check before booking. VisitScotland cannot be held responsible for any inaccuracies

MAP

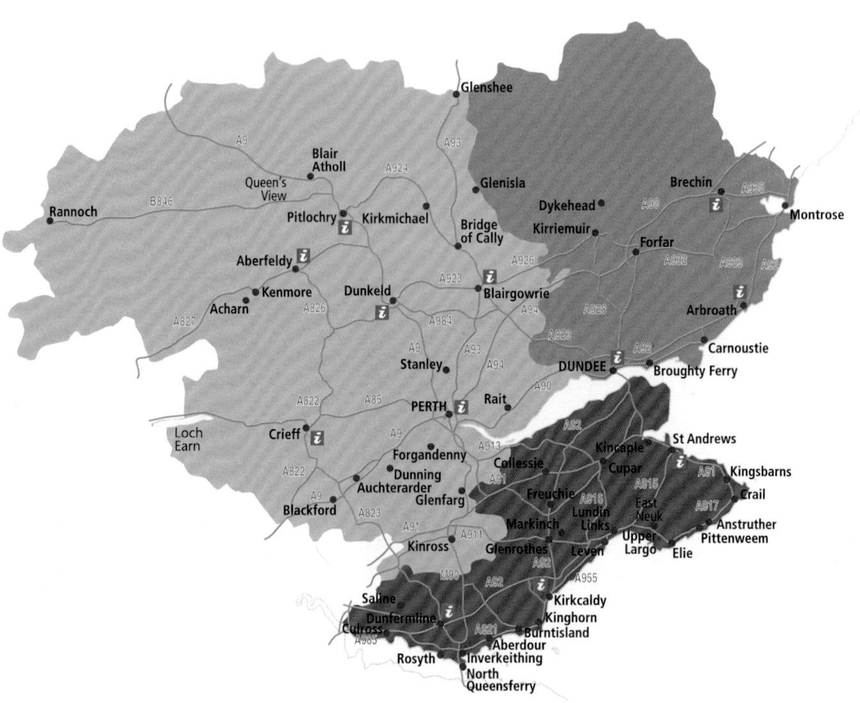

©Collins Bartholomew Ltd 2(

VISITOR INFORMATION CENTRES

Visitor Information Centres are staffed by people 'in the know' offering friendly advice, helping to make your stay in Scotland the most enjoyable ever . . . whatever your needs!

Perthshire		
Aberfeldy	The Square, Aberfeldy, PH15 2DD	Tel: 01887 820276
Blairgowrie	26 Wellmeadow, Blairgowrie PH10 6AS	Tel: 01250 872960
Crieff	High Street, Crieff, PH7 3HU	Tel: 01764 652578
Dunkeld	The Cross, Dunkeld, PH8 0AN	Tel: 01350 727688
Perth	Lower City Mills, West Mill Street, Perth, PH1 5QP	Tel: 01736 450600
Pitlochry	22 Atholl Road, Pitlochry, PH16 5BX	Tel: 01796 472215

Angus and Dundee		
Arbroath	Harbour Visitor Centre, Fishmarket Quay, Arbroath, DD11 1PS	Tel: 01241 872609
Brechin	Pictavia Centre, Haughmuir, Brechin	Tel: 01356 623050
Dundee	Discovery Point, Discovery Quay, Dundee DD1 4XA	Tel: 01382 527527

Fife		
Dunfermline	1 High Street, Dunfermline, KY12 7DL	Tel: 01383 720999
Kirkcaldy	The Merchant's House, 339 High Street, Kirkcaldy, KY1 1JL	Tel: 01592 267775
St Andrews	70 Market St St Andrews Fife FY16 9NU	Tel: 01334 472021

LOCAL KNOWLEDGE • WHERE TO STAY • ACCOMMODATION BOOKING • PLACES TO VISIT • THINGS TO DO • MAPS AND GUIDES • TRAVEL ADVICE • ROUTE PLANNING • WHERE TO SHOP AND EAT • LOCAL CRAFTS AND PRODUCE • EVENT INFORMATION • TICKETS

For information and ideas about exploring Scotland in advance of your trip, call our booking and information service **0845 22 55 121** or go to **visitscotland.com**

If calling from outside the UK and Ireland **+44 1506 832 121** From Ireland **1800 932 510**

A £4 booking fee applies for accommodation bookings made via a Visitor Information Centre and through our booking and information service.

Live it. Visit Scotland.
visitscotland.com/wheretofindus

Schiehallion and Loch Tummel from The Queen's View, by Pitlochry

Perthshire

Perthshire is one of the most strikingly picturesque parts of Scotland. It ranges from wild and mountainous to sophisticated and cultured, from the wilderness of Rannoch Moor to the lap of luxury at the 5-star Gleneagles Hotel.

You can experience everything here, from traditional activities like golf, fishing and horse riding to more recent innovations like sphereing and white water rafting. Whatever you pursue, it will be against a backdrop of spectacular scenery; high mountains, deep forests, sparkling lochs and wide rivers.

But you don't have to spend the day pushing yourself to the limits; a walk through the forests of Big Tree Country may suffice. Take a romantic stroll through the Birks o' Aberfeldy, visit one of nine great gardens, marvel at a reconstructed Iron Age crannog on Loch Tay or simply enjoy the Queen's View near Pitlochry.

Sphereing

DON'T MISS

1 The **Scottish Crannog Centre** at Kenmore on Loch Tay is an authentic recreation of an ancient loch-dwelling. Imagine a round house in the middle of a loch with a thatched roof, on stilts. You can tour the Crannog to see how life used to be 2,600 years ago. Upon your return to shore, have a go at a variety of Iron Age crafts; see if you can grind the grain, drill through stone or make fire through wood friction.

2 **Scone Palace**, near Perth, was renowned as the traditional crowning place of Scottish kings, as the capital of the Pictish kingdom and centre of the ancient Celtic Church. Nowadays, the great house and its beautiful accompanying grounds are home to the Earls of Mansfield, and offer an ideal day out.

3 **Blair Castle**, the stunningly situated ancient seat of the Dukes and Earls of Atholl, is a five-star castle experience. The unmistakeable white façade is visible from the A9 just north of Blair Atholl. Dating back 740 years, the castle has played a part in some of Scotland's most tumultuous events but today it is a relaxing and fascinating place to visit.

4 The **Famous Grouse Experience** is housed within Glenturret Distillery, Scotland's oldest malt whisky distillery. It is an interactive attraction where visitors can familiarise themselves with this renowned tipple and the brand that accompanies it! As well as a tour of the production areas, you can enjoy a unique audio-visual presentation which gives a grouse's eye view of Scotland, and delicious food.

5 Among its many other attractions, Perthshire – known as **Big Tree Country** - can boast some of the most remarkable trees and woodlands anywhere in Europe. The 250 miles of way-marked paths give you an excellent opportunity to explore the area and, if you're lucky, catch a glimpse of the many different species of wildlife which make Perthshire their home. Here you'll discover Europe's oldest tree in Fortingall Churchyard, the world's highest hedge and one of Britain's tallest trees at The Hermitage by Dunkeld.

6 You'll find some of Scotland's most beautiful parks and gardens in Perthshire, ranging from small privately owned gardens to formal sumptuous gardens, containing examples of native Scottish plants and rare and exotic species from around the world. The **Perthshire Gardens Collection** brings together 9 spectacular examples of the gardener's art such as Kinross House, Drummond Castle and Branklyn Gardens. Heather, wild woodlands and Himalayan treasures will inspire you whether you're a horticultural enthusiast or someone who simply loves beautiful gardens.

2

6

FOOD AND DRINK

eatscotland.com

7 Farmers' markets have seen a resurgence in recent years in the UK and **Perth's Farmers' Market** is arguably the best known in Scotland. Taking place throughout the year on the first Saturday of each month, it is something of a showcase for local producers and growers and is a rewarding visit in its own right. Look out for fish, meat and game, baked goods, fruit wines and liqueurs, honeys and preserves, fruit and vegetables, sweets and herbs. Sound tempting? Many stallholders also offer free tastings.

8 The area around Blairgowrie is Europe's centre for soft fruit production and a particular feature of the area are the signs at farms inviting you to 'pick your own' strawberries, raspberries, gooseberries, redcurrants, and tayberries. Sample the local produce of field and hedgerow at **Cairn O' Mohr Wines** in Errol. A family-run business it produces Scottish fruit wines made from local berries, flowers and leaves - a truly unique end product. Explore the winery through one of the on site tours before undertaking a tasting session!

9 **Edradour Distillery** – Scotland's smallest malt whisky distillery - can be found in the Highland foothills just to the east of Pitlochry. Built in the early 19th century Edradour is the only remaining 'farm' distillery in Perthshire and seems to have hardly changed in the 170 years of its existence. Visitors can enjoy a guided tour of the production areas, before relaxing with a wee dram of the amber nectar.

10 In addition to outstanding restaurant facilities, **Baxters at Blackford** offers a fantastic Scottish showcase of inspirational fine food, gifts and much, much more. Visitors are invited to taste a variety of products, from specialist chocolate in The Chocolate Parlour to tasting what Baxters is most famous for, specialty soups, in The Baxters Hub. Whether making a quick stop or for those wishing to stay a little bit longer, Baxters is ideal for the perfect day out.

7

9

13

WALKS

visitscotland.com/walking

11 A 63 mile (101 km) circular waymarked walking route through the scenic Perthshire and Angus Glens, **The Cateran Trail** follows paths used by the 15th century Caterans (cattle rustlers). Complete the whole route in a leisurely five days or enjoy a shorter section on a day's walk. Take in the soft contours of Strathardle on the Bridge of Cally to Kirkmichael section or head for the hills between Kirkmichael and the Spittal of Glenshee.

12 Revered in poetry by the national bard, Robert Burns, the **Birks of Aberfeldy** ('birks' being the old Scots for birch trees) line a short walk alongside the Moness Burn, reached from a car park on the Crieff Road. A circular path leads to a beautiful waterfall, where birds and flowers are abundant.

13 **Lady Mary's Walk** in Crieff is one of the most popular in Perthshire and provides a peaceful stroll beside the beautiful River Earn, along an avenue of mature oak, beech, lime and sweet chestnut trees. Partly accessible for wheelchairs and pushchairs, the walk is particularly photogenic in the late autumn when the beech trees are a riot of rust and gold.

14 On the A9 just north of Dunkeld, you'll find **The Hermitage**. A beautiful walk along the banks of the River Braan takes you to the focal point, Ossian's Hall set in a picturesque gorge and overlooking Black Linn Falls. Ask the local rangers for advice or read the display panels as you pass amidst the huge Douglas Firs en route.

WILDLIFE

visitscotland.com/wildlife

15 Glengoulandie Country Park is located in the beautiful shelter of Schiehallion, one of Scotland's best known and most popular mountains. The park is home to a beautiful herd of red deer and is a lovely escape for the whole family. It's also an ideal location for setting up camp with a site right next door.

16 Visit Loch of the Lowes between April and August and there's every chance you'll encounter its famous nesting ospreys. The Scottish Wildlife Trust's visitor centre provides interpretation on the birds, which migrate to Scotland from their winter homes in West Africa. There are also telescopes and binoculars on hand to give you a better view. Between October and March, the nature reserve is worth visiting for the sheer numbers of wildfowl which are present.

17 The Black Wood of Rannoch is one of the few remaining areas of the original Caledonian pine forest that covered the majority of Scotland. After being hunted to extinction, the capercaillie was reintroduced to Scotland at Drummond Hill, Kenmore in the 1830s. The Black Wood is an important site for capercaillie and Scottish Natural Heritage aims to extend it by removing the non-native trees to encourage a return to its natural state.

18 Each year between April and October an average of 5,400 salmon fight their way upstream from Atlantic feeding grounds to spawn in the upper reaches of the River Tummel. They must by-pass the Hydro-Electric dam at Pitlochry by travelling through the interconnected pools that form the Pitlochry 'fish ladder' – a very special attraction.

ADVENTURE

visitscotland.com/adventure

In this area you'll find over 35 different adventure activities! Here's a selection:

19 Perthshire is renowned for its stunning lochs and rivers, many of which are excellent for white water rafting. A truly unforgettable experience awaits you with a spectacular combination of rugged Highland scenery and the adrenaline rush of this activity - it's easy to understand why it's one of the most popular. Get some friends together and go for it!

20 Perthshire is the only place in Scotland where you can try sphereing. Like so many unique adventure activities, this one originated in New Zealand and is described as a 'truly amazing adrenaline buzz'. It involves a huge 12 ft inflatable ball which the willing participants strap themselves safely into and then take a wild and bouncy tumble down the hill.

21 Wet, wild and wonderful - canyoning is all this and more! Unleash your adrenaline streak as you swim through rapids, cliff jump into deep clear pools, abseil through waterfalls and slide down natural stone 'flumes'. This one is awesome and not to be missed!

22 If you enjoy wide-open spaces try a microlight flight for the nearest experience to flying like a bird. With the latest microlight technology, enjoy up to sixty miles of spectacular views and scenery in one hour. This is a great way to enjoy the Perthshire landscape as well as being the experience of a lifetime.

23 Not only can you enjoy river bugging in Perthshire but also the new innovation of Adventure Tubing at Nae Limits. The idea is simple. Take a specially designed reinforced inner tyre tube with handles and navigate your way through steep gorges, white-water runs, and jump off cliffs into deep pools below. It's truly pulse quickening stuff!

Balnaguard, by Pitlochry

Balbeagan

Map Ref: 2A1

Open: All year excl Xmas and New Year 12155

Balnaguard, Pitlochry, Perthshire PH9 0PY
T: 01796 482627
E: paulscroft@aol.com
W: balbeagan.com

Ann and Paul Croft welcome you to Balbeagan in quiet Balnaguard. Comfortable ensuite rooms and a range of breakfasts await you. Superbly situated for castles, gardens, walking (both hills and glens), and within easy day visit reach of east and west coasts. Stay a few days and avoid constant packing.

Total number of rooms: 3

Prices from:

Single: **£25.00** Twin: **£25.00**

Blair Atholl, Perthshire

Dalgreine Guest House

Map Ref: 4C12

Open: All year 22028

Off St Andrews Crescent,
Bridge of Tilt, Blair Atholl, Perthshire PH18 5SX
T: 01796 481276
E: info@dalgreineguesthouse.co.uk
W: dalgreineguesthouse.co.uk

Dalgreine, a luxury 4 star B&B. With guests' lounge and quiet mature garden, a real home from home. Wireless broadband available. Hospitality tray, TV/DVD in rooms. Private parking and secure bike storage. A perfect base in Highland Perthshire, walking distance to Blair Castle, restaurants and pubs.

Total number of rooms: 6

Prices from:

Single: **£30.00** Double: **£30.00**
Twin: **£30.00** Family room: **£85.00pr**

Blair Atholl, Perthshire

The Firs Bed and Breakfast

Map Ref: 4C12

Open: January-November 44075

St Andrews Crescent,
Blair Atholl, Perthshire PH18 5TA
T: 01796 481256
E: kirstie@firs-blairatholl.co.uk
W: firs-blairatholl.co.uk

Friendly, family run guesthouse in this quiet Highland village 7 miles from Pitlochry. By day, golf, fishing and miles of woodland, riverside and mountain walks and cycle trails - by night pub and restaurant eating. All rooms ensuite with TV, courtesy coffee/tea etc. Superior rooms available.

Total number of rooms: 5

Prices from:

Single: **£35.00** Double: **£27.50**
Twin: **£27.50** Family room: **£27.50**

Important: Prices stated are estimates and may be subject to amendments.

Blairgowrie, Perthshire
Garfield House
Map Ref: 2B1

27286

★★★ B&B

Open: All year excl Xmas and New Year
Perth Road, Blairgowrie, Perthshire PH10 6ED
T: 01250 872999
E: info@garfieldhouse.com
W: garfieldhouse.com

Total number of rooms: 4

Prices from:
Single: **£24.00** Double: **£25.00**
Twin: **£25.00**

Blairgowrie, Perthshire
Heathpark House
Map Ref: 2B1

29945

★★★★ B&B

Open: All year excl Xmas
Coupar Angus Road,
Rosemount, Blairgowrie, Perthshire PH10 6JT
T: 01250 870700
E: lori@forsyth12.freeserve.co.uk
W: heathparkhouse.com

Our lovely Victorian family home is set in two acres of private gardens. All bedrooms have quality furniture and bedding, are extremely spacious and are all ensuite. An ideal location from which to explore scenic Perthshire and beyond with easy access to the area's many visitor attractions.

Total number of rooms: 3

Prices from:
Single: **£40.00** Double: **£35.00**
Twin: **£35.00**

By Blairgowrie, Perthshire
Bankhead Bed and Breakfast
Map Ref: 2B1

14200

★★★ FARMHOUSE

Open: All year excl Xmas and New Year
Clunie, Blairgowrie, Perthshire PH10 6SG
T: 01250 884 281
E: hilda@hwightman.orangehome.co.uk
W: bankheadbnb.co.uk

Total number of rooms: 2

Prices from:
Single: **£30.00** Double: **£25.00**
Twin: **£25.00** Family room: **£25.00**

Crieff, Perthshire
Dunfillan
Map Ref: 2A2

82757

AWAITING GRADING

Open: All year excl Xmas
Dunfillan, Lower Flat, Gwydyr Road, Crieff PH7 4BP
T: 01764 650640 M: 07776321115
E: kscott574@googlemail.com
W: dunfillan.co.uk

Be our only guests, assured of a warm but discreet welcome in this peaceful location, away from crowds, but with tourist attractions easily accessible. Your extremely comfortable and tastefully appointed bed/sitting room with private bath/shower looks over beautiful countryside. Quality linen, bathrobes, fresh fruit, flowers and homebaking provided.

Total number of rooms: 1

Prices from:
Single: **£35.00** Double: **£30.00**

For a full listing of Quality Assured accommodation, please see directory at back of this guide.

Crieff, Perthshire

Fendoch Guest House

Map Ref: 2A2

25760

Open: All year

Sma Glen, Crieff, Perthshire PH7 3LW
T: 01764 653446/655619
E: bookings@fendoch.co.uk
W: fendoch.co.uk

Total number of rooms: 4			
Prices from:			
Single:	**£25.00**	Double:	**£25.00**
Twin:	**£25.00**	Family room:	**£25.00**

Crieff, Perthshire

Merlindale

Map Ref: 2A2

38135

Open: Mid January-mid December

Perth Road, Crieff, Perthshire PH7 3EQ
T: 01764 655205/07740873111
E: merlin.dale@virgin.net
W: merlindale.co.uk

Merlindale is a luxurious Georgian house situated close to the town centre. All bedrooms are ensuite, two with sunken bathrooms. A large library is available for you to browse in. Merlindale is Michelin rated AA red diamond and two times Glenturret tourism award winner. A sumptuous family home waits to welcome you.

Total number of rooms: 3			
Prices per room from:			
Single:	**£45.00**	Double:	**£70.00**
Twin:	**£65.00**		

Dunkeld, Perthshire

Hatton Grange

Map Ref: 2B1

67456

Open: All year

Lower Hatton, by Dunkeld, Perthshire PH8 0ET
T: 01350 727137
E: katehowie1@yahoo.co.uk
W: hattongrange.com

Hatton Grange offers an opportunity to stay in a recently built Scottish Baronial style family home in a tranquil setting. Nestling in 3 acres of stunning countryside surrounded by breathtaking hills and glens. Close to the Loch of the Lowes Nature Reserve. Ideal for fishing , shooting, walking and golf.

Total number of rooms: 3			
Prices from:			
Single:	**£35.00**	Double:	**£30.00**
Twin:	**£30.00**	Family room:	**£30.00**

Dunkeld, Perthshire

Letter Farm

Map Ref: 2B1

35352

Open: May-October

Loch of the Lowes, Dunkeld, Perthshire PH8 0HH
T: 01350 724254
E: letterfarm@btconnect.com
W: letterfarm.co.uk

Total number of rooms: 3			
Prices per person per night from:			
Single:	**£32.00**	Double:	**£30.00**
Twin:	**£30.00**		

Important: Prices stated are estimates and may be subject to amendments.

Kinross

Burnbank

Map Ref: 2B3

AWAITING GRADING

Open: All year

79 The Muirs, Kinross, Kinross-shire KY13 8AZ

T: +44 (0) 1577861931

E: bandb@burnbank-kinross.co.uk

W: burnbank-kinross.co.uk

84193

Total number of rooms:3

Prices from:

Double: **£32.00-38.00** Twin: **£32.00-38.00**

Family room: **£35.00-40.00**

Perth

Achnacarry Guest House

Map Ref: 2B2

Open: All year

3 Pitcullen Crescent, Perth PH2 7HT

T: 01738 621421

E: info@achnacarry.co.uk

W: achnacarry.co.uk

10981

Total number of rooms: 4

Prices from:

Single: **£35.00** Double: **£27.50**

Twin: **£27.50** Family room: **£65.00pr**

Perth

Ackinnoull Guest House

Map Ref: 2B2

★★★★ GUEST HOUSE

Open: All year

5 Pitcullen Cresent, Perth, Perthshire PH2 7HT

T: 01738 634165

E: ackinnoull@yahoo.com

W: ackinnoull.com

11010

Total number of rooms: 4

Prices from:

Single: **£30.00** Double: **£23.00-33.00**

Twin: **£23.00-33.00** Family room: **£20.00**

Perth

Albert Villa Guest House

Map Ref: 2B2

Open: All year excl Xmas Day

63 Dunkeld Road, Perth, Perthshire PH1 5RP

T: 01738 622730

E: caroline@albertvilla.co.uk

11436

Total number of rooms: 10

Prices from:

Single: **£27.00** Double: **£30.00**

Twin: **£27.00** Family room: **£75.00**

Perth

Beeches Guest House

Map Ref: 2B2

Open: All year

2 Comely Bank, Perth, Perthshire PH2 7HU

T: 01738 624486

E: enquiries@beeches-guest-house.co.uk

W: beeches-guest-house.co.uk

44851

Total number of rooms: 5

Prices from:

Single: **£25.00** Double: **£25.00**

Twin: **£25.00**

Get the most out of your stay...

Visitor Information Centres are staffed by people 'in the know', offering friendly advice, helping to make your stay in Scotland the most enjoyable ever... whatever your needs!

Live it. Visit Scotland.
visitscotland.com/wheretofindus

Perth

Cherrybank Guest House

Map Ref: 2B2

19048

Open: All year

217 Glasgow Road, Perth PH2 0NB
T: 01738 451982
E: m.r.cherrybank@blueyonder.co.uk
W: cherrybankguesthouse.com

Maggie and Robert welcome you to our family run Guest House with secure off road parking. Situated 1 mile from motorway network and within easy reach of city centre. We offer ensuite rooms with 4 star facilities including WiFi. Our tasteful and comfortable guest lounge is available to add to your home comforts.

Total number of rooms: 5

Prices from:

Single:	**£45.00**	Double:	**£27.00**
Twin:	**£27.00**	Family room:	**£75.00pr**

Perth

Clunie Guest House

Map Ref: 2B2

19736

Open: All year

12 Pitcullen Crescent, Perth PH2 7HT
T: 01738 623625
E: ann@clunieguesthouse.co.uk
W: clunieguesthouse.co.uk

Total number of rooms: 7

Prices from:

Single:	**£30.00**	Double:	**£27.50**
Twin:	**£27.50**	Family room:	**£70.00pr**

Perth

Comely Bank Cottage

Map Ref: 2B2

20100

Open: All year excl Xmas and New Year

19 Pitcullen Crescent, Perth, Perthshire PH2 7HT
T: 01738 631118
E: comelybankcott@hotmail.com
W: comelybankcottage.co.uk

Enjoy true Scottish hospitality in this well appointed, comfortable Victorian home, only half a mile from city centre. Attractive ensuite rooms with every facility for your comfort. An ideal base for touring. Near Scone Palace and Racecourse. St. Andrews, Glamis, Stirling and Edinburgh under an hour's drive. Substantial breakfast. Ground floor bedroom.

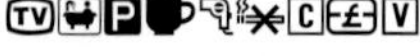

Total number of rooms: 3

Prices per room from:

Single:	**£30.00**	Double:	**£52.00**
Twin:	**£54.00**	Family room:	**£65.00**

Perth

Dalvey

Map Ref: 2B2

22130

Open: All year excl Xmas and New Year

55 Dunkeld Road, Perth, Perthshire PH1 5RP
T: 01738 621714
E: info@dalvey-perth.co.uk
W: dalvey-perth.co.uk

Total number of rooms: 3

Prices from:

Single:	**£35.00**	Double:	**£30.00**
Twin:	**£30.00**		

Important: Prices stated are estimates and may be subject to amendments.

Perth
New County Hotel
Map Ref: 2B2

Open: All year
22/30 County Place, Perth, Perthshire PH2 8EE
T: 01738 623355
E: enquiries@newcountyhotel.com
W: newcountyhotel.com

59770

Total number of rooms: 23

Prices from:

Single:	**£45.00**	Double:	**£60.00**
Twin:	**£60.00**	Family room:	**£90.00pr**

Perth
Westview Bed and Breakfast
Map Ref: 2B2

Open: All year
49 Dunkeld Road, Perth PH1 5RP
T: 01738 627787
E: angiewestview@aol.com

63893

Total number of rooms: 3

Prices from:

Single:	**£30.00**	Double:	**£26.00**
Twin:	**£26.00**	Family room:	**£60.00pr**

Pitlochry, Perthshire
Almond Lee
Map Ref: 2A1

Open: All year
2 East Moulin Road, Pitlochry PH16 5HU
T: 01796 474048
E: mary@almondlee.com

83487

Enjoy a warm welcome at Almond Lee. We have four spacious ensuite bedrooms with hospitality tray and TV. We are a non-smoking bungalow with private parking. Breakfast is an enjoyable experience, the buffet is extensive and there is a varied choice of freshly cooked options.

Total number of rooms: 4

Prices from:

Single:	**£25.00, £10.00 s/s**	Double:	**£25.00**
Twin:	**£25.00**		

Pitlochry, Perthshire
Ashbank House
Map Ref: 2A1

Open: All year
14 Tomcroy Terrace, Pitlochry, Perthshire PH16 5JA
T: 01796 472711
E: ashbankhouse@btinternet.com
W: ashbankhouse.co.uk or ashbankhouse.com

13104

Total number of rooms: 3

Prices from:

Double:	**£25.00**	Twin:	**£25.00**

visitscotland.com/walking

For everything you need to know about walking in Scotland and for a brochure Call 0845 22 55 121
Scotland. Created for Walking

For a full listing of Quality Assured accommodation, please see directory at back of this guide.

Pitlochry, Perthshire

Craigroyston House

Map Ref: 2A1

21058

Open: All year

2 Lower Oakfield, Pitlochry, Perthshire PH16 5HQ
T: 01796 472053
E: reservations@craigroyston.co.uk
W: craigroyston.co.uk

Quietly situated in mature garden grounds, with direct pedestrian access to the town centre. The Laura Ashley designed bedrooms are ensuite and together with the reception rooms with their crackling fires, reflect the Victorian ambience. Safe private parking, flat screen TVs and Wi-Fi throughout.

Recommended by:

- ★ Michelin Green Guide
- ★ Guide de Routard
- ★ The Lonely Planet
- ★ Trotters
- ★ Rick Steve
- ★ Micheal Miller-verlag
- ★ Ilvanowski-verlag . . . and many others.

An AA Highly Recommended Guest House. Glenturret Tourism Award.

Total number of rooms: 8

Prices from:
Twin: **£30.00** Double: **£30.00**

Pitlochry, Perthshire

Derrybeg Guest House

Map Ref: 2A1

22516

Open: January-November

18 Lower Oakfield, Pitlochry, Perthshire PH16 5DS
T: 01796 472070
E: marion@derrybeg.fsnet.co.uk
W: derrybeg.com

Total number of rooms: 8

Prices from:
Single **£28.00** Double: **£28.00**
Twin **£28.00**

Pitlochry, Perthshire

Easter Dunfallandy Country House B&B

Map Ref: 2A1

24239

Open: All year excl Xmas

Dunfallandy, Pitlochry, Perthshire PH16 5NA
T: 01796 474128
E: sue@dunfallandy.co.uk
W: dunfallandy.co.uk

Located in a quiet countryside location in the heart of Highland Perthshire, with castles, lochs, historical sites and distilleries nearby. A great base for touring or just relaxing. Lots of activities in the local area; golf, walking, cycling, fishing and Pitlochry Festival Theatre , all of Scotland in one County.

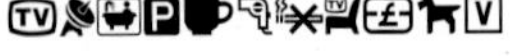

Total number of rooms: 3

Prices per room from:
Single: **£60.00** Double: **£80.00**
Twin: **£80.00**

Important: Prices stated are estimates and may be subject to amendments.

Pitlochry, Perthshire

Lavalette

Map Ref: 2A1

★★★ B&B

44940

Open: March-October

Manse Road, Moulin, Pitlochry, Perthshire PH16 5EP
T: 01796 472364
E: barrypheonix@aol.com
W: visitscotland.com

Total number of rooms: 3

Prices per room from:

Single: **£26.50** Double: **£27.50**
Twin: **£27.50**

Pitlochry, Perthshire

Pine Trees Hotel

Map Ref: 2A1

★★★★ COUNTRY HOUSE HOTEL

49840

Open: All year

Strathview Terrace, Pitlochry, Perthshire PH16 5QR
T: 01796 472121
E: info@pinetreeshotel.co.uk
W: pinetreeshotel.co.uk

Total number of rooms: 20

Prices per room from:

Single: **£45.00** Double: **£90.00**
Twin: **£90.00**

Blair Castle, north of Pitlochry, Perthshire

RRS Discovery at Discovery Point, Dundee

Angus and Dundee

The Angus and Dundee area boasts some of Scotland's best beaches – wonderful unspoiled stretches of sand which are at times windswept and dramatic, but more frequently warm and inviting, with the peace only occasionally shattered by the cries of the seabirds.

Dundee, you'll discover, has a proud maritime history. Captain Scott's polar research ship the RRS Discovery has returned to the city that built it and is now a top tourist attraction. The city's industrial past also features high on the tourist trail – don't miss the Verdant Works where you can learn about the jute trade that was once a mainstay of the city's economy. Today Dundee has a thriving cosmopolitan feel and dynamic cultural quarter.

For a complete contrast to city life, explore the Angus Glens. There are five: Glen Isla, Glen Prosen, Glen Lethnot, Glen Clova and Glen Esk. Each has its own unique features but all are exceptionally beautiful and wonderfully peaceful places to explore.

Lunan Bay, Angus

DON'T MISS

1 Perhaps Scotland's finest fairytale castle, **Glamis Castle** is famed for its Macbeth connections, as well as being the birthplace of the late Princess Margaret and childhood home of the late Queen Mother. Set against the backdrop of the Grampian Mountains, Glamis is an L-shaped castle built over 5-storeys in striking pink sandstone. The grounds host the Grand Scottish Proms in August each year, complete with spectacular fireworks display.

2 Little more than half an hour's drive north of the bustling city of Dundee, a series of picturesque valleys runs north into the heart of the Grampians. Collectively known as the **Angus Glens**, they offer the perfect escape for those seeking a walk, a spot of wildlife watching, a scenic picnic or a pub lunch. Ranging from gentle and wooded (Glen Isla) to the truly awe-inspiring (Glen Clova and neighbouring Glen Doll), there is more to discover here than you can fit into a single trip.

3 Discover Dundee's polar past at **Discovery Point**. Step aboard Captain Scott's famous ship that took Scott and Shackleton to Antarctica in 1901 and come face to face with the heroes of the ice in the award winning visitor centre.

4 Dundee is the perfect place for a city break, with great shopping, restaurants and nightlife. Spend a day at Dundee's vibrant and cool **Cultural Quarter** where you can indulge in speciality shopping at the Westport, visit Sensation, Dundee's Science Centre which explores the world of the senses, take in a film or an exhibition at Dundee Contemporary Arts, visit Dundee's acclaimed Rep Theatre, and round it all off with a meal at one of the many restaurants and a drink at one of the area's contemporary bars.

5 For the chance to see bottlenose dolphins at close proximity, why not book a trip on one of the **River Tay Dolphin Trips**. If you prefer to stay on dry land the dolphins can sometimes be seen from Broughty Ferry Beach. The best time to see them is from March-September.

6 Angus was the heartland of the Picts, a warrior people who lived in Scotland around 2,000 years ago and left behind many intriguing monuments. **Pictavia**, at Brechin, provides a fascinating insight including hands-on exhibits and a themed play area for all the family. The small hamlet of Aberlemno, 6 miles north-east of Forfar, is famous for its intricately sculptured Pictish cross-slab in the churchyard.

7 For an excellent view of the City and beyond, take a trip to the top of **The Law** – Dundee's highest point – an extinct volcano. Enjoy magnificent views over the River Tay, and to the hills of Angus and beyond on a clear day.

1

2

FOOD AND DRINK

eatscotland.com

8 The **But 'n Ben** in Auchmithie, just 5 miles north of Arbroath, is one of the best seafood restaurants in the area and serves as its speciality the 'smokie pancake'.

9 **Jute Café Bar** is situated on the ground floor of Dundee Contemporary Arts Centre. Its menu ranges widely, with the emphasis on informality, while the ambience goes from a relaxing morning coffee venue to a stylish evening hotspot. Eat, drink and enjoy yourself with freshly cooked contemporary dishes, everything from a light snack to a full meal.

10 **The Roundhouse Restaurant** at Lintrathen, by Kirriemuir, is an award-winning restaurant offering innovative modern menus using Angus and Perthshire produce in a peaceful rural setting. The chef is a former Master Chef of Great Britain, whose specialities include local Angus beef and game.

11 No visit to the area would be complete without stopping off to pick up some of the area's best local produce to take home. **Milton Haugh Farm Shop** specialises in the freshest seasonal potatoes, own reared beef and free range chickens. The Corn Kist Coffee Shop also serves up some delicious home made meals and tempting treats.

9

12

14

WALKS

visitscotland.com/walking

12 Scenic **Glen Doll** is one of the famous Angus Glens, north of Dundee. Follow one of the waymarked forest walks from the car park, or more ambitious hikers can take any of three rights of way leading over the surrounding hills into the neighbouring valleys of Glen Shee and Royal Deeside.

13 Situated five miles North West of Carnoustie, **Crombie Country Park** covers 100 hectares of mixed woodland around a picturesque reservoir. Great opportunities for wildlife watching including butterflies, water and woodland birds.

14 **Seaton Cliffs Nature Trail** is a self guided trail which goes from Arbroath into Sites of Special Scientific Interest, and the sea cliffs are spectacular. There are 15 interpretative points of interest and a wide variety of sea bird species can be seen including puffins, guillemots, razorbill and eider duck to name but a few. Allow approximately 2 hours and 30 minutes.

15 If you want to get out and about in the fresh air, see some of what Dundee has to offer, and get fit at the same time, why not try out one of the themed **Dundee city centre walks** in the Dundee Walking Guide available from the Visitor Information Centre. The trails include buildings of historical significance, examples of both 19th and 20th century architecture, plus explorations of Dundee's maritime and industrial heritage. You will also pass many of Dundee's visitor attractions where you can stop en route.

GOLF

visitscotland.com/golf

16 If you want to experience the very best in Scottish golf, a visit to the **Carnoustie Championship Course** is a must. Venue of the 2007 Open Golf Championship, the course has been deemed the 'toughest links course in the world'.

17 **Montrose Medal Golf Course**, established in 1562, is the fifth oldest golf course in the world with a traditional links layout.

18 **Downfield Golf Club** is an attractive parkland course that has played host to many golfing tournaments and has an excellent reputation as a challenging course.

19 **Kirriemuir Golf Course** is a gem of a parkland course designed by the renowned James Braid. Look out for the notorious oak tree at the 18th!

16

20

21

22

HISTORY AND HERITAGE

20 **JM Barrie's Birthplace** at Kirriemuir has been carefully restored to reflect how it might have looked in the 1860s. The exhibition next door details the life and work of this hugely talented and celebrated author, whose books include Peter Pan.

21 In 1178 William the Lion founded the now ruined Tironensian monastery that is **Arbroath Abbey**, near the harbour in Arbroath. The abbey is famously associated with the Declaration of Arbroath, signed here in 1320, which asserted Scotland's independence from England. An adjacent visitor centre tells the building's story.

22 **Edzell Castle** is an elegant 16th century residence with tower house that was home to the Lindsays. The beautiful walled garden was created by Sir David Lindsay in 1604 and features an astonishing architectural framework. The 'Pleasance' is a delightful formal garden with walls decorated with sculptured stone panels, flower boxes and niches for nesting birds.

Brechin, Angus

Blibberhill Farmhouse

Map Ref: 4F12

15458

Open: All year

Blibberhill Farm, Aberlemno, Brechin, Angus DD9 6TH
T: 01307 830323
E: wendysstewart@aol.com
W: blibberhill.co.uk

Relax in our traditionally furnished home and garden. Walk along a farm track and experience the wonderful countryside. Peacefully situated between the Glens and coast along B9134, Forfar 7 miles. Central for golf, fishing and walking. Glamis, Edzell and Dunnottar Castles nearby. Under one hour's drive from Aberdeen, St. Andrews and Perth.

Total number of rooms: 3

Prices from:

Single:	**£28.00**	Double:	**£24.00**
Twin:	**£24.00**	Family room:	**£25.00**

Carnoustie, Angus

Park House

Map Ref: 2D2

49179

Open: All year excl Xmas and New Year

12 Park Avenue, Carnoustie, Angus DD7 7JA
T: 01241 852101
E: parkhouse@bbcarnoustie.fsnet.co.uk
W: bbcarnoustie.fsnet.co.uk

Beautiful Victorian villa, 3 minutes walk from Carnoustie Championship Golf Course and with fifty golf courses available within a 60 minute drive. Spacious and comfortable bedrooms with attractive ensuite facilities. Large walled garden with private parking. Convenient for bus/rail travel. Carnoustie's only 5 star Bed and Breakfast. Relaxed and friendly atmosphere!

Total number of rooms: 3

Prices from:

Single:	**£40.00**	Double:	**£40.00**
Twin:	**£40.00**		

Inspiring places for your wedding day - Scotland knows no bounds.

For the perfect wedding visit visitscotland.com/scottishwedding

Important: Prices stated are estimates and may be subject to amendments.

Dundee, Angus

Duntrune House

Map Ref: 2C2

★★★★ B&B

Open: March-October

23864

Duntrune, Dundee DD4 0PJ
T: 01382 350239
E: info@duntrunehouse.co.uk
W: duntrunehouse.co.uk

Superior accommodation in 1820's country house offering superb views and spacious, well-maintained grounds. Situated in a quiet rural area close to the city and well located for touring the East of Scotland. Guests dine with the hosts whose interests include family history, gardening and antiques. Wireless internet access available.

Total number of rooms: 3

Prices from:

Single:	**£45.00**	Double:	**£35.00**
Twin:	**£35.00**	Family room:	**£35.00**

Forfar, Angus

Farmhouse Bed and Breakfast

Map Ref: 2D1

★★★ B&B

Open: March-October

25644

West Mains of Turin, Rescobie, Forfar, Angus DD8 2TE
T: 01307 830229
E: cjolly3@aol.com
W: turinfarmhouse.com

A working farm in an elevated position overlooking Rescobie Loch, our accommodation is of a high standard providing ensuite and private bathrooms. Relax in our spacious lounge with a wood burning fire. TV etc. Centrally located base for castles, hill walking, golfing and award winning sandy beaches.

Total number of rooms: 3

Prices from:

Single:	**£30.00**	Double:	**£25.00**
Twin:	**£25.00**	Family room:	**£60.00pr**

WILDLIFE
SCOTLAND
To find out about watching wildlife in Europe's leading wildlife destination log on to
visitscotland.com/wildlife

Kirriemuir, Angus

Purgavie Farm

Map Ref: 2C1

50669

Open: All year

Lintrathen, Kirriemuir, Angus DD8 5HZ
T: 01575 560213
E: purgavie@aol.com
W: purgavie.co.uk

Total number of rooms: 3

Prices per room from:

Single:	**£32.00**	Double:	**£29.00**
Twin:	**£29.00**	Family room:	**£29.00**

Montrose, Angus

Oaklands Guest House

Map Ref: 4F12

48017

Open: All year excl Xmas and New Year

10 Rossie Island Road, Montrose, Angus DD10 9NN
T: 01674 672018
E: oaklands1@btopenworld.com
W: nebsnow.com/oaklands

Family run guest house near the Montrose Basin, within walking distance from the town centre. All rooms ensuite with colour TV, secure parking for bicycles and motorcycles. Lounge available for all our guests with plenty of maps to plan your touring in the region. Motorcycle tours and special breaks available. Children welcome.

Total number of rooms: 7

Prices from:

Single:	**£35.00**	Double:	**£27.50**
Twin:	**£27.50**	Family room:	**£27.50**

The conservatory at the House of Pitmuies, Guthrie, by Forfar , Angus

Important: Prices stated are estimates and may be subject to amendments.

The golf course at Aberdour, Fife

Kingdom of Fife

If you're a golfer, the ancient Kingdom of Fife will be a powerful draw. Every serious golfer wants to play the Old Course at St Andrews at least once in a lifetime and, thanks to a public allocation of rounds each day, you can. There are also 45 other fabulous courses in Fife to put your game to the test.

For keen walkers, one of the great ways to explore Fife is on foot. The Fife Coastal Path takes in some truly delightful places and you'll get to relax on some of the best beaches in the country – with five Fife beaches achieving the top standard Blue Flag status in 2008.

Fife's seaside communities have their roots in fishing and the North Sea herring fleet used to land its catch in the East Neuk's ports. The harbour at Anstruther is still busy but the halcyon days of deep sea fishing have been consigned to the fascinating exhibitions in the Scottish Fisheries Museum in the town.

Harbour at Anstruther Fife, Fisheries Museum behind

DON'T MISS

1. Travel through the quaint fishing villages of the **East Neuk** of Fife and you travel back through time. This corner of Fife is filled with traditional cottages with red pantile roofs and crow-stepped gable ends which appear unchanged from a bygone age. Fishing boats lie at rest in the harbours follows the bustle of unloading their catch. Between communities lie unspoilt stretches of sandy beaches, perfect for walks and picnics. Visit Pittenweem for art, Crail for crafts or Anstruther for a trip to the Isle of May, followed by some of Britain's finest fish and chips.

2. Fife boasts some of Scotland's finest and cleanest sandy **beaches**, great for peaceful strolls or quiet contemplation. The area is home to five of Scotland's six Blue Flag award-winning strands at Aberdour, Burntisland, Elie Harbour, Leven East and St Andrews West Sands.

3. Stretching for 150 kms around much of Fife's coastline from North Queensferry to the Tay Bridge, the **Fife Coastal Path** can be experienced in short bite-sized walks or as a long distance route to bring your senses to life. Listen to the seabirds soaring above the waves, smell the salt sea air and savour the sea breezes on this wonderful stretch of coastline.

4. The **Royal Palace of Falkland** was the countryside residence of Stuart Kings and Queens when they hunted deer and wild boar in the forests of Fife, and was a favourite childhood playground of Mary, Queen of Scots. Built in the 1500s, the spacious garden houses the original Royal Tennis Court – the oldest in Britain still in use – built in 1539.

1

3

4

To find out more, call 0845 22 55 121 or go to visitscotland.com

FOOD AND DRINK

eatscotland.com

5 **Balbirnie House**, a Georgian Mansion set in its own 416 acre country estate, is recognised as one of Scotland's finest Grade A listed historic houses. Dining in either the Orangery or the Balbirnie Bistro provides a delightful way to experience the natural larder that Scotland has to offer and both have built up a deserved reputation as some of the best restaurants in Fife.

6 The renowned **Peat Inn**, 3 miles from Cupar, offers top quality modern Scottish cuisine. Only the very best of local produce is used and dishes are prepared with great skill and flair. A mouth-watering wine list is available and visitors wishing to sleep off a hearty meal can stay over in the indulgent 5-star accommodation.

7 No trip to Fife is complete without a trip to the multi-award winning **Anstruther Fish Bar & Restaurant**. Voted Scotland's Fish & Chip Shop of the Year 2006/07, they serve only the freshest prime quality seafood, offering a true taste of Scotland.

8 **The Inn at Lathones**, near St Andrews, is a coaching inn with a history spanning back 400 years. The restaurant here continues to welcome travellers with a tempting menu featuring the best of local produce transformed into à la carte, gourmet delights.

BEACHES AND GOLF

visitscotland.com/golf

9 Recognised worldwide as the Home of Golf – the **Old Course** in St Andrews is where it all began and still remains a favourite of today's champions. To play on these hallowed fairways and greens is a dream come true for the golfing fan and an experience which will not be forgotten.

10 As well as the iconic Old Course, the small peninsula of the Kingdom of Fife boasts over 45 other wonderful **golf courses** each offering something different for the visiting golfer. Try the testing challenges of the Open Qualifying courses or an enjoyable, relaxing game, links or parklands, 9 or 18 hole – golf is a way of life in the Kingdom of Fife and there is something for everyone.

11 The long stretches of golden sandy beaches at **Elie** are undoubtedly some of the best in the East Neuk. From summer cricket on the beach to long, peaceful strolls, this is an idyllic spot not to be missed.

12 The sand dunes and beach at the mouth of the Tay estuary are one of the fastest growing parts of Scotland and home to **Tentsmuir** – one of Scotland's National Nature Reserves. This dynamic coastline is important for waders and wildfowl, common and grey seals, ducks and seaduck. It is truly one of Scotland's most magical coastlines and well worth a visit.

WALKING AND WILDLIFE

visitscotland.com/walking

13 Dominating the skyline of central Fife, the **Lomond Hills** are one of the area's most popular walking destinations. The regional park, which encompasses the hills extends over 65 square miles and provides ample opportunity for all levels of walker, with spectacular vistas over the surrounding countryside.

14 The **Scottish Deer Centre**, near Cupar, allows visitors to spot nine species of deer in over 55 acres of scenic parkland as well as its very own pack of wolves. There are daily falconry displays, featuring native Scottish species, a range of shops and a cosy café.

15 For keen bird watchers, the **Fife Ness Muir Wildlife Reserve** on the outskirts of Crail is excellent for migrant and breeding birds. Over 150 species of bird have been seen from the reserve, including 7 species of warbler and migrant butterflies.

16 Culross and the immediate vicinity are rich in historical interest. **The Culross Town Walk**, starting west of the town, passes by a malthouse, tollbooth, mercat cross, abbey house and various other historical buildings. All are worth further exploration.

14

17

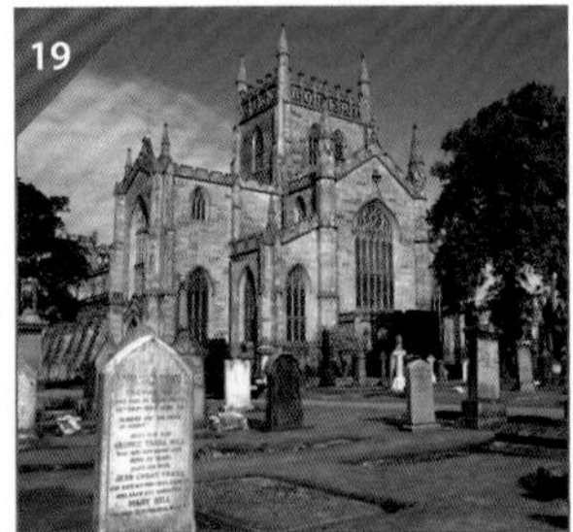
19

HERITAGE AND GARDENS

17 **Cambo Gardens** is a romantic 'Secret Garden' nestled on the coast between St Andrews and the East Neuk of Fife. Created around Cambo Burn, the garden boasts everything from spectacular snowdrops to glowing autumn borders, a wild array of woodland plants and animals, waterfalls and rose-clad wrought-iron bridges. This truly is a plantsman's paradise.

18 **Aberdour Castle** was built by the Douglas family in the 13th century and has been added to throughout the centuries, to create a wonderful mix of styles. Situated in the delightful village of Aberdour, the castle boasts fine interior painted ceilings, galleries, a doocot and a recently-uncovered walled garden.

19 **Dunfermline's** royal and monastic past dominates the town. This former capital of Scotland, birthplace of James I and Charles I, boasts a royal palace and a 12th century abbey, which is the final resting place of Robert the Bruce and the burial site of eleven other Scottish kings and queens.

Anstruther, Fife

Mrs Liz Mudie

Map Ref: 2D3

78499

Open: All year

Spalefield Lodge, Spalefield, by Anstruther
Fife KY10 3LB
T: 01333 313659
E: enquiries@spalefieldlodge.co.uk
W: spalefieldlodge.co.uk

Spacious modern bungalow set in its own spacious grounds with beautiful views of Anstruther at the front and the countryside at the back. Garden for guests use, private sitting room, ample parking and space for bicycles. Quiet location, less than two miles from Anstruther and seven miles from St. Andrews.

Total number of rooms: 2

Prices from:

Single: **£40.00** Double: **£25.00**
Twin: **£25.00**

Burntisland, Fife

Mrs Veronica Martin

Map Ref: 2C4

71353

Open: All year

60 Aberdour Road, Burntisland, Fife KY3 0EN
T: 01592 870481
M: 07944 416512

Total number of rooms: 2

Prices per room from:

Single: **£45.00** Double: **£70.00**
Twin: **£70.00** Family room: **£85 .00**

Crail, Fife

Caiplie House

Map Ref: 2D3

17390

Open: All year

53 High Street North, Crail, Fife KY10 3RA
T: 01333 450564
E: mail@caipliehouse.co.uk
W: caipliehouse.co.uk

Total number of rooms: 5

Prices from:

Single: **£35.00** Double: **£30.00**
Twin: **£30.00** Family room: **£30.00**

Dunfermline, Fife

Clarke Cottage Guest House

Map Ref: 2B4

19522

Open: All year

139 Halbeath Road, Dunfermline, Fife KY11 4LA
T: 01383 735935
E: clarkecottage@ukonline.co.uk
W: clarkecottageguesthouse.co.uk

Total number of rooms: 9

Prices from:

Single: **£33.00** Double: **£26.00**
Twin: **£26.00**

Dunfermline, Fife

Mrs Gerletti

Map Ref: 2B4

★★★★ B&B

30599

Open: All year

Hillview House, 9 Aberdour Road, Dunfermline
Fife KY11 4PB
T: 01383 726278
E: info@hillviewhousedunfermline.co.uk
W: hillviewhousebb.co.uk

Total number of rooms: 3

Prices from:

Single: **£35.00** Double: **£25.00**
Twin: **£25.00**

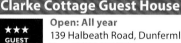

Glenrothes, Fife

Hollytree Bed and Breakfast

Map Ref: 2C3

68624

Open: All year

122 Main Street, Coaltown of Balgonie, Fife KY7 6HZ

T: 07859 313513

E: malcolm@hollytreebandb.com

W: hollytreebandb.com

Total number of rooms: 3

Prices per room from:

Single:	**£30.00**	Double:	**£60.00**
Twin:	**£60.00**	Family room:	**£85.00**

Inverkeithing, Fife

The Roods Bed and Breakfast

Map Ref: 2B4

60209

Open: All year

16 Bannerman Avenue, Inverkeithing, Fife KY11 1NG

T: 01383 415049

E: isobelmarley@hotmail.com

W: the-roods.co.uk

Quietly secluded family home close to rail station, M90 and Edinburgh with a wealth of home and business comforts. In the privacy of your own room enjoy Freeview TV, DVD's, unlimited access to the internet via your laptop and make free phonecalls at your leisure from our direct dial telephones.

Total number of rooms: 2

Prices from:

Single:	**£27.00**	Double:	**£27.00**
Twin:	**£27.00**		

Kingsbarns, St. Andrews

Sir Peter Erskine and Lady Erskine

Map Ref: 2D3

17703

Open: All year excl Xmas and New Year

Cambo House, Kingsbarns, nr St Andrews, Fife KY16 8QD

T: 01333 450313

E: cambo@camboestate.com

W: camboestate.com

Relax and unwind in the elegant splendour of this historic family home set in acres of unspoilt woodland with walks to the sea and to Kingsbarns Golf Links, yet close to St. Andrews, picturesque fishing villages, numerous castles and attractions. Guest drawing room. Evening meal by prior arrangement.

Total number of rooms: 3

Prices per person per night from:

Single:	**£57.00**	Double:	**£47.00**
Twin:	**£47.00**		

Kirkcaldy, Fife

Lynda McCuaig

Map Ref: 2C4

12223

Open: All year excl Xmas

Annie's Lan, 36 Bennochy Road, Kirkcaldy Fife KY2 5RB

T: 01592 262231

E: enquiries@roominfife.co.uk

W: roominfife.co.uk

Total number of rooms: 2

Prices per room from:

Twin:	**£50.00**	Family room:	**£55.00**

Important: Prices stated are estimates and may be subject to amendments.

Kirkcaldy, Fife
Scotties B&B
Map Ref: 2C4

53445

Open: All year

Scotties B&B, 15 Bennochy Road, Kirkcaldy
Fife KY2 5QU
T: 01592 268596
E: bhscott43@msn.com
W: scottiesbandb.co.uk

A warm welcome from Helaine and Bryan awaits you on arrival at our recently refurbished home. Individual tables in dining room. Three twin ensuite rooms have flat screen TV/DVD players, WiFi, hospitality trays, and complimentary safes. Close to town centre, rail and bus stations. Own keys, private parking.

Total number of rooms: 3

Prices per room from:
Single: **£35.00** Twin: **£56.00**

Markinch, by Glenrothes
Mrs Rita Varney
Map Ref: 2C3

60113

Open: All year excl 16th December-16th January

Priory Star, East End, Star of Markinch, Fife KY7 6LQ
T: 01592 754566
E: priorystarbb@aol.com
W: priorystar.com

Whether its a relaxing quiet break or a golfing trip to Fife's 40+ courses and you require superb accommodation combined with genuine first class hospitality please take a few minutes to visit our website. We promise all our guests that they will experience their most enjoyable stay with value for money.

Total number of rooms: 3

Prices from:
Single: **£30.00** Double: **£26.00**
Twin: **£26.00** Family room: **£25.00**

Pittenweem, Fife
Mr John Philp
Map Ref: 2D3

67482

★★★ B&B

Open: All year

4 St Abbs Crescent, Pittenweem, Fife KY10 2LT
T: 01333 311964
E: stabbshouse@aol.com
W: stabbshouse.co.uk

We are situated in a picturesque fishing village. Small, friendly B&B, close to all amenities and popular coastal walk and golf course. Superb views of sea makes a fantastic holiday choice. 9 miles from St. Andrews. Great location for golf, walking and exploring the East Neuk.

Total number of rooms: 3

Prices per room from:
Double: **£58.00** Twin: **£54.00**

St. Andrews, Fife
McIntosh Hall
Map Ref: 2D2

79439

★★ CAMPUS

Open: June-September
St Andrews, Fife KY16 9HT
T: 01334 467035
E: mchall@st-andrews.ac.uk
W: discoverstandrews.com

Total number of rooms: 30

Prices per room from:
Single: **£29.50** Twin: **£61.00**

St. Andrews, Fife
Millhouse
Map Ref: 2D2

67115

★★★★ B&B

Open: All year
2 Cauldside Farm Steading, Strathkinness
High Road, St. Andrews, Fife KY16 9TY
T: 01334 850557
E: airlie@fsmail.net
W: millhouse-standrews.com

Total number of rooms: 2

Prices from:
Double: **£35.00** Twin: **£35.00**

St. Andrews, Fife
Mrs J Mitchell
Map Ref: 2D2

48275

★★★★ B&B

Open: All year excl mid Dec-mid Jan
Old Fishergate House,
35 North Castle Street, St. Andrews, Fife KY16 9BG
T: 01334 470874
E: stay@oldfishergatehouse.co.uk
W: oldfishergatehouse.co.uk

Total number of rooms: 2

Prices from:
Twin: **£45.00**

St Andrews, Fife
Spinkstown Farmhouse
Map Ref: 2D2

55491

★★★★ B&B

Open: All year excl Xmas and New Year
Spinkstown Farmhouse, St Andrews, Fife KY16 8PN
T: 01334 473475
E: anne@spinkstown.com
W: spinkstown.com

Two miles from St Andrews on A917 to Crail this bright uniquely designed farmhouse furnished to a high standard has spacious bedrooms, ensuite bathrooms (bath and shower) comfortable lounge dining room where substantial breakfast sets you up for the day. Historic St Andrews famous Old Course, fishing villages, National Trust properties nearby.

Total number of rooms: 3

Prices from:
Single: **£35.00** Double: **£32.00**
Twin: **£32.00**

nr St. Andrews, Fife
Milton Lea B&B
Map Ref: 2D2

69777

★★★★ B&B

Open: All year
Milton Lea, by Balmullo, St. Andrews, Fife KY16 0AB
T: 05602 988 677/07851467207
E:· miltonlea@btinternet.com

Total number of rooms: 1

Prices from:
Single: **£65.00** Double: **£35.00**
Family room: **£30.00**

Important: Prices stated are estimates and may be subject to amendments.

nr St Andrews, Fife

Robin's Nest

Map Ref: 2D2

★★★★ B&B

Open: February-December excl Xmas and New Year

83281

29 Main Street, Dairsie, Fife KY15 4SR

T: 01334 871466

E: christinamowatt@btinternet.com

W: robinsnestbedandbreakfast.com

Total number of rooms: 2			
Prices from:			
Single:	**£40.00**	Double:	**£35.00**
Twin:	**£30.00**	Family room:	**£30.00**

nr St. Andrews, Fife

Mr Roy Verner

Map Ref: 2D2

★★★★ B&B

Open: All year

29764

Hawthorne House,
33 Main Street, Strathkinness, Fife KY16 9RY

T: 01334 850855

E: info@thehawthornehouse.co.uk

W: thehawthornehouse.co.uk

Total number of rooms: 3			
Prices from:			
Double:	**£25.00**	Twin:	**£25.00**

Saline, nr Dunfermline

Kirklands House

Map Ref: 2B4

★★★★ B&B

Open: All year

34325

Mrs Gill Hart, Saline, Fife KY12 9TS

T: 01383 852737

E: stay@kirklandshouseandgarden.co.uk

W: kirklandshouseandgarden.co.uk

Enjoy the luxury and comfort of Georgian country house surrounded by 2 acres of stunning gardens and 20 acres of ancient woodland - secluded yet close to Edinburgh, Dunfermline, Perth, St Andrews and Glasgow. The perfect base to tour Scotland.

Total number of rooms: 2			
Prices from:			
Single:	**£38.00**	Double:	**£30.00**
Twin:	**£30.00**	Family room:	**£30.00**

Fyvie Castle, Aberdeenshire

ABERDEEN CITY AND SHIRE

Aberdeen City and Shire is an area of contrasts. From the mountains and forests to the towering cliffs, rocky inlets, endless sandy beaches and captivating harbour towns.

Aberdeen is a thriving and cosmopolitan city with magnificent architecture and a host of cultural opportunities, from museums and art galleries to theatres and concert halls.

The 'Granite City' is also famous for its award winning floral displays. With 45 parks in the city and a celebrated Winter Garden at Duthie Park, Aberdeen is always in bloom and every season brings new floral flights of fancy.

It has a busy central shopping area yet just a short distance away there's a brilliant beach complete with an all-year funfair.

The many fascinations of the Aberdeenshire coastline extend beyond the city however. Along the coast you'll find captivating harbour towns like Stonehaven, Peterhead, Fraserburgh and Banff, as well as quaint little places like the stunning Pennan, a former smuggler's town at the foot of a cliff.

Castles and whisky galore

Aberdeen City and Shire is renowned for its castles which come in all shapes and sizes from fairytale castles to crumbling ruins and even royal holiday homes Some great trails have been laid out for visitors to follow, including the intriguing Castle Trail.

The Deeside towns of Banchory, Ballater and Braemar have all enjoyed many decades of royal patronage, the annual highlight of which is the Braemar Gathering in September.

To find out more, call 0845 22 55 121 or go to visitscotland.com

Alongside the whisky, there are other delights that will soon have you raising your glass – music, song and, of course, fine food. Beautiful Aberdeen Angus beef, sumptuous seafood, fabulous fruit and vegetables – all come fresh to the table, prepared by the finest chefs. The Taste of Grampian, held annually in June at Inverurie, is a must for foodies.

What's more, 2009 is a big year for Scotland – we're celebrating the 250th anniversary of the birth of Robert Burns. There's over 200 special events taking place throughout the year, all over Scotland. Go to homecomingscotland2009.com to find out about events in this area.

So what do you want from your holiday home from home in Aberdeen City and Shire? There's a wonderful range of places providing excellent B&B accommodation both in the city and in the surrounding countryside – many in some of the best locations in all of Scotland.

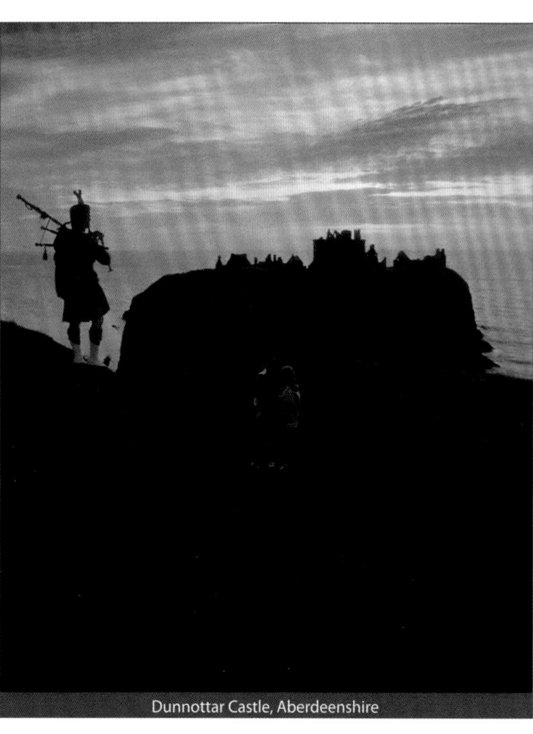
Dunnottar Castle, Aberdeenshire

What's On?

Word 09 – University of Aberdeen Writers Festival
13 – 17 May 2009
A packed programme of readings, lectures and debates as well as musical events, art exhibitions and film screenings showcasing how the Scottish word has changed the world!
abdn.ac.uk/word

Taste of Grampian, Inverurie
6 June 2009
Discover and sample a wide range of quality food and drink products.
tasteofgrampian.co.uk

The Scottish Traditional Boat Festival
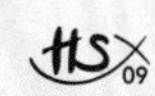
2 – 5 July 2009
A colourful celebration of Scotland's great maritime heritage, with events throughout Portsoy and Banff.
stbf.bizland.com/2009

Lonach Gathering & Highland Games
22 August 2009
lonach.org

Braemar Gathering
5 September 2009
Traditional highland games.
braemargathering.org

Stonehaven Fireball Festival
31 December 2009
A spectacular winter festival to bring in the New Year.

DON'T MISS

1 The restored Victorian **Old Royal Station**, Ballater now houses a museum focusing very much on Queen Victoria's journeys here, when heading to Balmoral, including a recreated waiting room and a replica of a carriage used by Queen Victoria when travelling from Windsor to Ballater. In its heyday, many famous people, including the Tsar of Russia, used Ballater Station.

2 **Balmoral Castle**, Scottish home of the Royal Family since the mid 19th century is set amid spectacular scenery. See why Queen Victoria described Balmoral as "my dear paradise in the Highlands". Visit the largest room in the castle, the ballroom, and learn the history of the castle through an audio-visual presentation.

3 From its days as a lively fishing port to its current status as Europe's North Sea oil capital, Aberdeen's historic relationship with the sea unfolds at the five-star **Aberdeen Maritime Museum** through exciting displays and exhibitions.

4 **Duff House**, a magnificent Baroque mansion designed by William Adam, is now a treasure house and cultural arts centre operated by a unique partnership of Historic Scotland, the National Galleries of Scotland and Aberdeenshire Council. Storytellers, musicians and artists are at home here and Duff House organises a regular artistic programme of exhibitions, music and lectures.

5 Held on the first Saturday of September, one of Scotland's oldest and biggest Highland Gatherings, **The Braemar Gathering** is notable not only for its size, but also for their unique chieftain, Her Majesty the Queen. Royalty is always in attendance, presiding over a programme of events that includes Highland dancing, tossing the caber, tug of war and piping.

6 Take a stroll along 2 miles of sandy beach at **Aberdeen's beachfront** and discover a range of attractions for all the family. The beach itself is famous for its golden sand and its long curved length between the harbour and the mouth of the River Don. The beach is a favourite for walkers, surfers and windsurfers and has a popular amusement area along the famous Beach Esplanade where there are restaurants, a cinema and the city's amusement park.

2

3

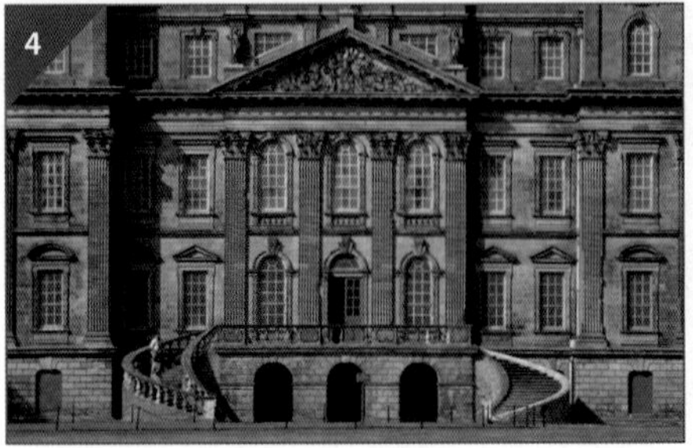
4

5

HERITAGE

7 Built in the 16th century, **Crathes Castle** is a splendid example of a tower house, retaining many original interior features, and a stunning walled garden complete with herbaceous borders and an array of unusual plants.

8 The charming **Braemar Castle**, now run by the community of Braemar, re-opened to the public in May 2008, and is undergoing an ambitious restoration programme to ensure a memorable experience for visitors.

9 Wander around the extensive buildings of **Dunnottar Castle**, set in a dramatic cliff top location with the sound of waves crashing on the rocks below and discover the significance of this impenetrable castle which holds many secrets of Scotland's colourful past.

10 With so many stunning castles in the region, it's no surprise that there is a **Castle Trail** taking in thirteen of the most unique examples, from fairytale castles, through rugged ruins to the elegant grandeur of country houses set in some of the most spectacular grounds.

7

8

11

WALKS

11 The walk around **Loch Muick**, in the shadow of Lochnagar, is mainly on fairly flat ground, following a route close to the loch side, with good views of the hills around. Look out for red deer. A short wooded section follows after reaching a Royal lodge, and then continues round the loch, passing a sandy beach, rising slightly before returning to the start point.

12 Scottish Wildlife Trust reserve at **Gight Woods**, north of Aberdeen, offers walks of up to 3 miles. The route follows the forestry track through Badiebath Woods towards the ruined Gight Castle (Byron's ancestral home) passing a number of interesting ruins, and with the opportunity to spot red squirrels.

13 The 5 mile route from **Duff House to Bridge of Alvah** is full of variety, starting through a mature deciduous wood, near the banks of the River Deveron, where you may spot kingfisher and goldeneye. The path then crosses the river, at **Bridge of Alvah**, along tracks and minor roads lined with shrubs, returning via the grounds of MacDuff Distillery back over the river, to Duff House affording great views of Banff.

14 **Ballater Royal Deeside Walking Festival** takes place each year in May, and provides a programme of walks for walkers of all capabilities from 'Munro-baggers' to those who prefer a gentle stroll, all set in magnificent walking country surrounded by breathtaking scenery.

FOOD & DRINK

15 **The Milton Restaurant & Conservatory**, situated opposite Crathes Castle on Royal Deeside, offers exquisite food in picturesque surroundings. The Milton's kitchen team of award winners, including **Grampian Chef of the Year 2008**, is renowned not only for the flavour, but also the stunning presentation of the dishes.

16 Scotch Beef can be found on the menus of top restaurants throughout Europe and the reputation of this high-class product remains undiminished. **Aberdeen Angus** is arguably the best known breed, renowned for the rich and tasty flavour of the meat.

17 On a farm near Inverurie in Aberdeenshire, **Mackie's award winning ice cream** is made using milk from their own Jersey and Holstein herds. Over 20 flavours of ice cream are created using renewable energy: the farm has three wind turbines which produce all the energy required to make this delicious ice cream.

18 **Dean's of Huntly** bake traditional Scottish all-butter shortbread, and at the visitor centre you can learn about its history and watch how the delicious shortbread is made in the viewing gallery, before visiting the café for a tasting.

19

20

ACTIVITIES

19 The fairways of Aberdeen City and Shire provide a variety of golfing experiences, from the historic links **Royal Aberdeen** with its towering dunes to the splendid inland and parkland courses which offer new challenges.

20 If you want to take part in an activity, head for **Deeside Activity Park**, where you will be amazed by the number and variety of activities on offer, from fly fishing, rock climbing, archery, kart racing, quad bike trekking to digger manoeuvres. There's a restaurant and farm shop too.

21 Aberdeen City and Shire has miles of unspoilt and often rugged coastline, so why not try **water sports** here? Yachting, canoeing, scuba diving, surfing, and water skiing are all available, but if big waves are your thing, visit Fraserburgh, former host to rounds of Scottish Wavesailing Championships. Or why not team up with Surf and Watersport Club, Banff for some expert tuition?

MAP

VISITOR INFORMATION CENTRES

Visitor Information Centres are staffed by people 'in the know' offering friendly advice, helping to make your stay in Scotland the most enjoyable ever . . . whatever your needs!

Aberdeen City and Shire		
Aberdeen	23 Union Street, Aberdeen, AB11 5BP	Tel: 01224 288828
Ballater	The Old Royal Station, Station Square, Ballater, AB35 5QB	Tel: 01339 755306
Braemar	Unti 3, The Mews, Mar Road, Braemar, AB35 5YL	Tel: 01339 741600

LOCAL KNOWLEDGE • WHERE TO STAY • ACCOMMODATION BOOKING • PLACES TO VISIT • THINGS TO DO • MAPS AND GUIDES • TRAVEL ADVICE • ROUTE PLANNING • WHERE TO SHOP AND EAT • LOCAL CRAFTS AND PRODUCE • EVENT INFORMATION • TICKETS

For information and ideas about exploring Scotland in advance of your trip, call our booking and information service **0845 22 55 121** or go to **visitscotland.com**

If calling from outside the UK and Ireland **+44 1506 832 121** From Ireland **1800 932 510**

A £4 booking fee applies for accommodation bookings made via a Visitor Information Centre and through our booking and information service.

Aberdeen

Aldridge Bed and Breakfast

Map Ref: 4G10

79183

Open: All year

60 Hilton Drive, Aberdeen AB24 4NP

T: 01224 485651

Total number of rooms: 2

Prices per room from:

Single: **£36.00** Double: **£58.00**

Aberdeen

Armadale Guest House

Map Ref: 4G10

12869

Open: All year

605 Holburn Street, Aberdeen AB10 7JN

T: 01224 580636

E: armadaleguesthouse@tiscali.co.uk

W: armadaleguesthouse.co.uk

Providing comfortable accommodation furnished to a high standard we are situated on the West bank of the River Dee. Duthie Park, Robert Gordon's University and Alten's are all close by. Easy access to the city centre, Aberdeen University, hospitals and airport. We are an ideal base for local golf courses. Wi-Fi.

Total number of rooms: 9

Prices per room from:

Single: **£30.00** Double: **£60.00**

Twin: **£60.00** Family room: **£70.00**

Aberdeen

Furain Guest House

Map Ref: 4G10

26933

Open: All year excl Xmas and New Year

92 North Deeside Road, Peterculter
Aberdeen AB14 0QN

T: 01224 732189

E: furain@btinternet.com

W: furain.co.uk

Late Victorian house built of red granite. Family run, convenient for town, Royal Deeside and Castle Trail. Private car parking. Close to River Dee, well located for fishing, golf and walking.

Total number of rooms: 8

Prices from:

Single: **£43.00** Double: **£28.00**

Twin: **£28.00** Family room: **£74.00pr**

Aberdeen

MacLeans B&B

Map Ref: 4G10

★★
B&B

36978

Open: All year

8 Boyd Orr Avenue, Aberdeen AB12 5RG

T: 01224 248726

E: j.maclean@abdn.ac.uk

W: macleansbb.com

Total number of rooms: 3

Prices per room from:

Single: **£40.00** Double: **£60.00**

Twin: **£60.00**

Important: Prices stated are estimates and may be subject to amendments.

Alford, Aberdeenshire

Bydand Bed and Breakfast

Map Ref: 4F10

★★★ B&B

Open: All year 17128

18 Balfour Road, Alford, Aberdeenshire AB33 8NF

T: 01975 563613

E: jajack@tiscali.co.uk

W: alfordaccommodation.com

Total number of rooms: 2

Prices from:

Single: **£30.00** Double: **£26.00**

Twin: **£26.00**

Ballater, Aberdeenshire

Glenernan Guest House

Map Ref: 4E11

★★★ GUEST HOUSE

Open: All year 73409

37 Braemar Road, Ballater, Aberdeenshire AB35 5RQ

T: 01339 753111

E: enquiries@glenernanguesthouse.com

W: glenernanguesthouse.com

Glenernan is an elegant Victorian grand house retaining many original features. Tastefully converted to provide homely guest house accommodation. Ideally located in the picturesque and historic village of Ballater within the Cairngorms National Park. A hearty breakfast menu is provided with fine Scottish smoked salmon being a speciality.

Total number of rooms: 7

Prices from:

Single: **£38.00** Double: **£28.00**

Twin: **£28.00** Family room: **£28.00**

Braemar, Aberdeenshire

Clunie Lodge Guest House

Map Ref: 4D11

★★★ GUEST HOUSE

Open: All year excl Xmas and New Year 19737

Cluniebank Road, Braemar, Aberdeenshire AB35 5ZP

T: 013397 41330

E: bookings@clunielodge.com

W: clunielodge.com

Total number of rooms: 5

Prices from:

Single: **£40.00** Double: **£28.00**

Twin: **£28.00** Family room: **£27.00**

Ellon, Aberdeenshire

Stevenson's Bed and Breakfast

Map Ref: 4G9

★★ B&B

Open: All year 78620

49 School Crescent, Newburgh, Ellon
Aberdeenshire, AB41 6B

T: 01358 789017

E: natnewburgh@aol.com

Total number of rooms: 2

Prices from:

Single: **£25.00** Double: **£25.00**

Twin: **£25.00** Family room: **£70.00pr**

Huntly, Aberdeenshire

Greenmount Guest House

Map Ref: 4E9

★★★ GUEST HOUSE

Open: All year excl Xmas and New Year 29032

43 Gordon Street, Huntly, Aberdeenshire AB54 8EQ

T: 01466 792482

E: greenmountguest@btconnect.com

W: deveronfishing.com

Total number of rooms: 8

Prices from:

Single: **£23.00** Double: **£25.00**

Twin: **£23.00** Family room: **£25.00**

Inverurie, Aberdeenshire

Breaslann Guest House

Map Ref: 4G9

Open: All year excl Xmas and New Year 16155

Old Chapel Road, Inverurie, Aberdeenshire AB51 4QN

T: 01467 621608

E: breaslann@btconnect.com

W: breaslann.co.uk

Comfortable rooms all with private ensuite facilities. Quiet location, off street private parking, full Scottish breakfast, free WiFi access available to your own laptop. 15 minute drive from Aberdeen Airport. Comfortable residents lounge.

Total number of rooms: 5

Prices from:

Double: **£27.50** Twin: **£27.50**

Family room: **£27.50**

By Inverurie, Aberdeenshire

Broadsea

Map Ref: 4G9

Open: All year excl Xmas and New Year 16500

Burnhervie, Inverurie, Aberdeenshire AB51 5LB

T: 01467 681386

E: broadseafarm@aol.com

Accommodation of a high standard on this family farm of 200 acres. Inverurie 5 miles, Aberdeen 20 miles. Bennachie is very close by. Ideally situated for Archaeolink, Castle and Whisky Trails. Evening meal by arrangement. A non-smoking household.

Total number of rooms: 2

Prices per room from:

Double: **£56.00** Twin: **£56.00**

Johnshaven, Aberdeenshire

Ellington B&B

Map Ref: 4G12

Open: All year excl Xmas and New Year 24816

Station Place, Johnshaven, Aberdeenshire DD10 0JD

T: 01561 362756

E: ellington13@supanet.com

W: ellingtonbandb.co.uk

Total number of rooms: 2

Prices from:

Single: **£35.00** Double: **£25.00-27.00**

Twin: **£25.00-27.00**

MacDuff, Banffshire

Monica and Martin's B&B

Map Ref: 4F7

★★★★ B&B

Open: All year 38842

21 Gellymill Street, MacDuff, Banffshire AB44 1TN

T: 01261 832336

E: gellymill@aol.com

Total number of rooms: 3

Prices from:

Single: **£25.00** Double: **£23.00**

Twin: **£23.00** Family room: **£23.00**

Important: Prices stated are estimates and may be subject to amendments.

Oldmeldrum, Aberdeenshire

Cromlet Hill Guest House

Map Ref: 4G9

21414

Open: All year

South Road, Oldmeldrum, Aberdeenshire AB51 0AB

T: 01651 872315
E: johnpage@cromlethill.co.uk
W: cromlethill.co.uk

Spacious, elegant, listed Georgian House in large secluded gardens within conservation area overlooking Bennachie and the Grampian Hills beyond. Private parking. Aberdeen city centre 30 minutes, airport 20 minutes. On the Castle Trail and close to many well known National Trust properties, including Fyvie Castle, Haddo House and Pitmedden Gardens.

Total number of rooms: 3

Prices from:

Single: **£40.00** Double: **£28.00**
Twin: **£28.00** Family room: **£70.00pr**

Peterhead, Aberdeenshire

The Buchan Braes Hotel

Map Ref: 4H8

83600

Open: All year

Buchan Braes, Boddam by Peterhead, Aberdeenshire AB42 3AR

T: 01779 871472
E: info@buchanbraes.co.uk
W: buchanbraes.co.uk

Total number of rooms: 47

Prices per room from:

Single: **£95.00** Double: **£105.00**
Twin: **£110.00** Family room: **£120.00**

Peterhead, Aberdeenshire

Carrick Guest House

Map Ref: 4H8

18278

Open: All year

16 Merchant Street, Peterhead, Aberdeenshire AB42 1DU

T: 01779 470610
E: carrickpeterhead@aol.com

Total number of rooms: 6

Prices from:

Single: **£30.00** Double: **£25.00**
Twin: **£25.00** Family room: **£70.00pr**

Peterhead, Near Fraserburgh

Rose Lodge Bed and Breakfast

Map Ref: 4H8

52070

Open: All year excl Xmas and New Year

Rose Lodge, New Leeds, Peterhead, Aberdeenshire AB42 4HX

T: 01346 531148
E: lucinda@roselodge.fsworld.co.uk
W: roselodge.fsworld.co.uk

Rose Lodge is an attractive new bungalow set in Aberdeenshire, offering friendly hospitality and comfortable accommodation furnished and decorated to a high standard. A homely welcome waits for you in a picturesque rural setting with panoramic views.

Total number of rooms: 2

Prices from:

Single: **£26.00** Double: **£25.00**
Twin: **£25.00**

Aberdeen City and Shire

Potterton, Aberdeenshire

Viewfield Bed and Breakfast

Map Ref: 4G10

62929

★★★ B&B

Open: All year excl Xmas and New Year
Panmure Gardens, Potterton, Aberdeenshire AB23 8UG
T: 01358 742605
E: john@viewfield1.f9.co.uk
W: viewfield1.f9.co.uk

Total number of rooms: 3

Prices from:
Single: **£25.00** Twin: **£25.00-30.00**

Stonehaven, Aberdeenshire

Ambleside B&B

Map Ref: 4G11

11874

★★★ B&B

Open: All year
Netherley, Stonehaven, Aberdeenshire AB39 3RB
T: 01569 731105
E: helensbb@ambleside350.fslife.co.uk
W: ambleside-bb.co.uk

Total number of rooms: 3

Prices from:
Single: **£50.00** Double: **£30.00**
Twin: **£30.00**

Stonehaven, Aberdeenshire

Cardowan

Map Ref: 4G11

78617

★★★★ B&B

Open: All year excl Xmas and New Year
31 Slug Road, Stonehaven, Aberdeenshire AB39 2DU
T: 01569 762759
E: thelmaritchie@btinternet.com
W: stonehavenaccommodation.co.uk

Total number of rooms: 2

Prices from:
Single: **£50.00** Double: **£32.50**
Twin: **£32.50**

Stonehaven, Aberdeenshire

Tewel Farmhouse B&B

Map Ref: 4G11

57963

★★ FARMHOUSE

Open: All year
Tewel, Stonehaven, Aberdeenshire AB39 3UU
T: 01569 762306
E: tewelfarmhouse@btinternet.com

Total number of rooms: 2

Prices from:
Single: **£25.00-27.00** Double: **£22.00-24.00**
Twin: **£22.00-24.00** Family room: **£70.00pr**

Important: Prices stated are estimates and may be subject to amendments.

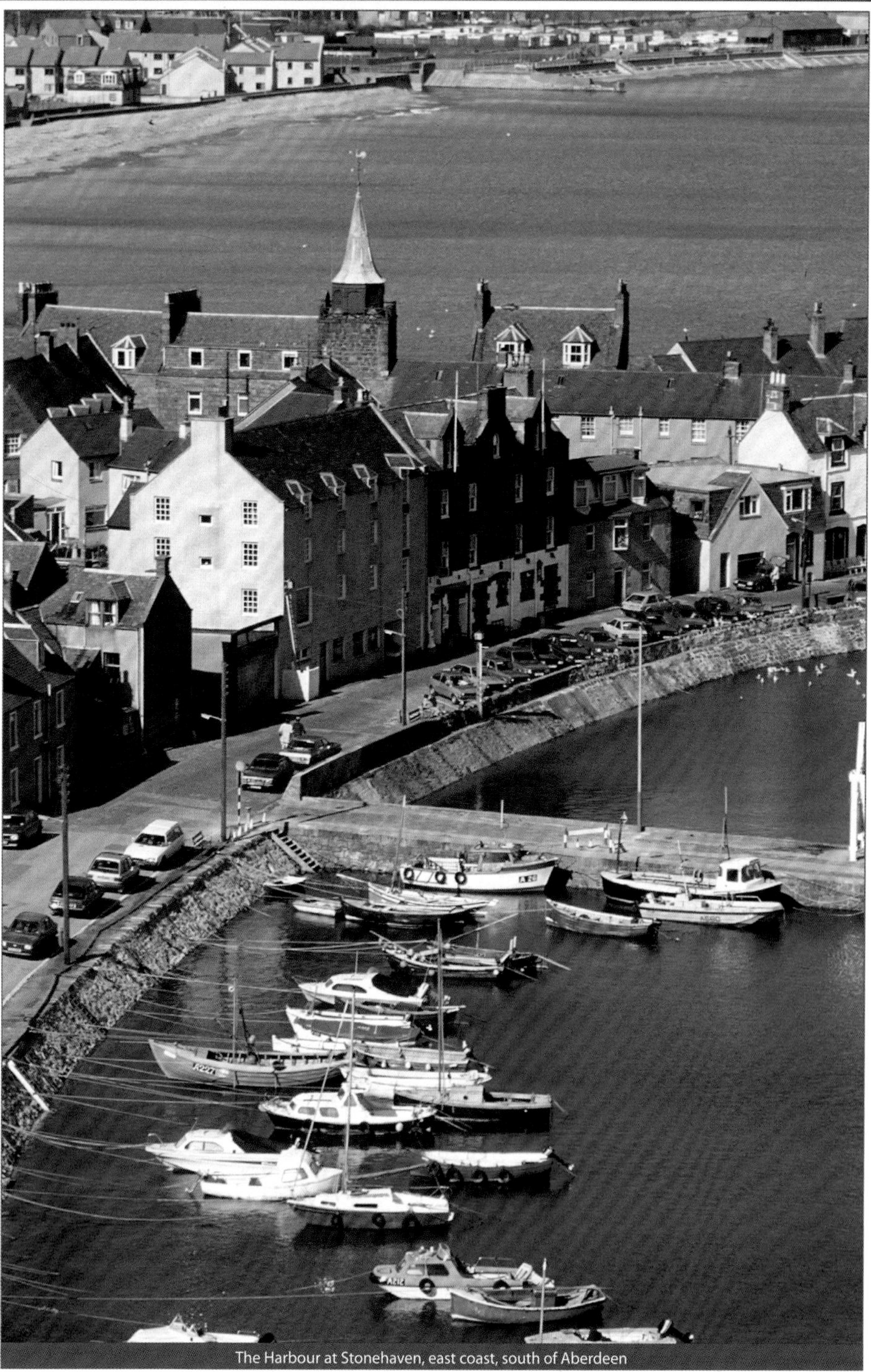

The Harbour at Stonehaven, east coast, south of Aberdeen

Glen Coe, Highlands

THE HIGHLANDS AND MORAY

If you're searching for tranquillity, you'll find that life in the Highlands moves at a refreshingly relaxed pace.

Exciting, dramatic and romantic, it's hard not to be moved by the rugged majesty of the mountainous north. It's the stuff of picture postcards, with views that will be etched in your memory forever.

Unspoiled beauty

There are so many places you have to experience: the eerie silence of Glen Coe; the arctic wilderness of the Cairngorms; the deep mysteries of Loch Ness; the wild flatlands of the Flow Country; the astonishing beauty of Glen Affric; and the golden beaches of the west and north coast where you can gaze out to the Atlantic and never meet a soul all day. In this unspoiled natural environment, wildlife flourishes. You'll see red squirrels and tiny goldcrests in the trees, otters chasing fish in fast flowing rivers, deer coming down from the hills to the forest edge, dolphins and whales off the coast, ospreys and eagles soaring overhead.

A natural playground

And this natural playground is yours to share. Climbers, walkers, mountain bikers and hunters take to the hills. Surfers, sailors, canoeists and fishermen enjoy the beaches, rivers and lochs. For the more adventurous there's skiing, canyoning and white water rafting. Whatever outdoor activity you like to pursue, you'll find experienced, professional experts on hand to ensure you enjoy it to the full.

Highland hospitality

Once you've had enough exercise and fresh air, you can be assured of some fine Highland hospitality - whether you're staying in a tiny village, a pretty town, a thriving activity centre like Aviemore or in the rapidly expanding city of Inverness. In the pubs and hotels, restaurants and other venues around the community, you'll find music and laughter. Perhaps a riotous ceilidh in full fling and unforgettable nights of eating and drinking into the wee small hours.

Back to your roots

Highlanders know how to enjoy life and they're always keen to welcome visitors – especially those who are tracing their Scottish roots. Every year people come to discover the traditional homeland of their clan, learn about their history and walk in their ancestors' footsteps over battlefields like Culloden where the Jacobite army made its last stand. You could follow Bonnie Prince Charlie over the sea to Skye, whether it's by boat or by bridge. You can even take a glass bottom boat trip around the island and watch the sea life below.

What's more, 2009 is a big year for Scotland – we're celebrating the 250th anniversary of the birth of Robert Burns. There's over 200 special events taking place throughout the year, all over Scotland. Go to homecomingscotland2009.com to find out about events in this area.

Wherever you decide to go, the Highlands, Skye and Moray will cast a spell on you and it will be a holiday you will remember for as long as you live.

Belladrum Tartan Heart Festival

What's On?

O'Neill Highland Open, Thurso
29 April – 7 May 2009
One of the most progressive events in competitive surfing.
oneilleurope.com/highlandopen

UCI Mountain Bike World Cup, Fort William
6 - 7 June 2009
Voted best event on the tour two years running.
fortwilliamworldcup.co.uk

Rock Ness, Dores, Loch Ness
13 - 14 June 2009
The only dance event with its own monster.
rockness.co.uk

Tulloch Inverness Highland Games HS 09
18 - 19 July 2009
Clan gathering and heavyweight competition in Inverness. The Highland Clans are hosting the Masters World Championships.
invernesshighlandgames.com

Inverness Highland Tattoo
21 July - 1 August 2009
Previewing artists from the Edinburgh International Tattoo.
tattooinverness.org.uk

Belladrum Tartan Heart Festival, Beauly
7 - 8 August 2009
Open air, family-friendly traditional music festival.
tartanheartfestival.co.uk

Highland Feast
September – various dates
A series of unique culinary and gastronomic events.
highlandfeast.co.uk

Blas Festival – Celebrating the Highlands HS 09
4 - 12 September 2009
A vast programme of traditional music and events, staged in some of Scotland's most spectacular and iconic landscapes.
blas-festival.com

MAP

Cape Wrath
Strathy Point
To Stromness (Orkney)
To St Margaret's Hope
Scrabster
Gills Bay
John o'Groats
Durness
Talmine
Melvich
Thurso
Reay
A836
A838
Skerray
A838
Bettyhill
A882
A99
Tongue
Wick
A9
Scourie
A99
A894
A838
A836
Altnaharra
A897
Drumbeg
To Stornoway
Clachtoll Bay
A837
Kylesku
Lochinver
A837
Loch Shin
Helmsdale
Lairg
A9
Brora
A835
A839
To Tarbert
Golspie
Ullapool
A837
Braes
Ardgay
Dornoch
Laide
Dundonnell
A836
Portmahomack
Aultbea
A832
Tain
Ardross
A9
Poolewe
A835
Lossiemouth
Gairloch
Invergordon
Cromarty
A832
To Lochmaddy
Staffin
A832
Garve
Culbokie
Elgin
A96
Kinlochewe
Dingwall
Fortrose
Uig
A855
A896
Black Isle
Forres
Waternish
Torridon
Strathpeffer
Avoch
Nairn
Keith
A87
Achnasheen
A96
Shieldaig
Muir of Ord
Culloden
A940
Aberlour
Dufftown
Carbost
Applecross
Beauly
Kirkhill
Smithton
Archiestown
To Aberdeen
Dunvegan
A850
A890
Struy
Skinidin
Glen Strathfarrar
A833
A82
INVERNESS
A95
A921
Portree
RAASAY
Struan
SKYE
Plockton
A831
Brackla
A9
Dulnain Bridge
Grantown -on-Spey
Kyle of Lochalsh
Cannich
A863
Balmacara
Drumnadrochit
Nethy Bridge
Cuillin Hills
Breakish
Dornie
Carrbridge
Boat of Garten
Inverinate
Loch Ness
Broadford
A939
Glenelg
Aviemore
Cairngorm Mountains
Kyleakin
Kylerhea
A87
A887
Fort Augustus
To Aberdeen
A851
Kincraig
CANNA
Armadale
A87
Kingussie
Insh
Knoydart
Sleat
Invergarry
Drumguish
Mallaig
A82
Laggan
Newtonmore
RUM
Spean Bridge
A889
A9
Arisaig
Dalwhinnie
EIGG
Glenfinnan
A86
Lochailort
Roybridge
A830
MUCK
A861
Fort William
A82
Acharacle
Corran
Onich
Kinlochleven
A861
Kilchoan
Ballachulish
Glencoe
To Perth
A884
To Tobermory
A828
Lochaline
A82
To Fishnish
To Oban
To Glasgow
©Collins Bartholomew Ltd 2008

VISITOR INFORMATION CENTRES

Visitor Information Centres are staffed by people 'in the know' offering friendly advice, helping to make your stay in Scotland the most enjoyable ever . . . whatever your needs!

Northern Highlands, Inverness, Loch Ness and Nairn		
Inverness	Castle Wynd, Inverness, IV2 3BJ	Tel: 01463 252401
Drumnadrochit	The Car Park, Drumnadrochit, Inverness-shire, IV63 6TX	Tel: 01456 459086

Fort William and Lochaber, Skye and Lochalsh		
Fort William	15 High Street, Fort William, PH33 6DH	Tel: 01397 701801
Portree	Bayfield Road, Portree, Isle of Skye, IV51 9EL	Tel: 01478 614906
Dunvegan	2 Lochside, Dunvegan, Isle of Skye, IV55 8WB	Tel: 01470 521878

Moray, Aviemore and the Cairngorms		
Aviemore	Grampian Road, Aviemore, PH22 1PP	Tel: 01479 810930
Elgin	17 High Street, Elgin, IV30 1EG	Tel: 01343 542666

LOCAL KNOWLEDGE • WHERE TO STAY • ACCOMMODATION BOOKING • PLACES TO VISIT • THINGS TO DO • MAPS AND GUIDES • TRAVEL ADVICE • ROUTE PLANNING • WHERE TO SHOP AND EAT • LOCAL CRAFTS AND PRODUCE • EVENT INFORMATION • TICKETS

For information and ideas about exploring Scotland in advance of your trip, call our booking and information service **0845 22 55 121** or go to **visitscotland.com**

If calling from outside the UK and Ireland **+44 1506 832 121** From Ireland **1800 932 510**

A £4 booking fee applies for accommodation bookings made via a Visitor Information Centre and through our booking and information service.

Live it. Visit *Scotland.*
visitscotland.com/wheretofindus

Looking over to the Summer Isles, Highlands

Northern Highlands, Inverness, Loch Ness and Nairn

Scotland's most northerly mainland territory is characterised by its dramatic mountains, vast wilderness and spectacular coastline.

Take in the west coast, where views of Quinag from near Kylesku are unmissable. Equally essential on the itinerary of any Highland visitor is Loch Ness, Britain's deepest and most mysterious freshwater expanse.

Don't miss the opportunity to see the Moray Firth dolphins from Chanonry Point on the Black Isle or up close from one of many wildlife cruises.

There are many fine towns and villages to visit - Ullapool, Lochcarron, Lochinver and Kinlochbervie to the west, Thurso, John O'Groats, Wick, Dornoch, Strathpeffer and Nairn on the eastern side. You should also take some time to explore the rapidly growing city of Inverness. Capital of the Highlands, it's a thriving, modern city with lots to see and do.

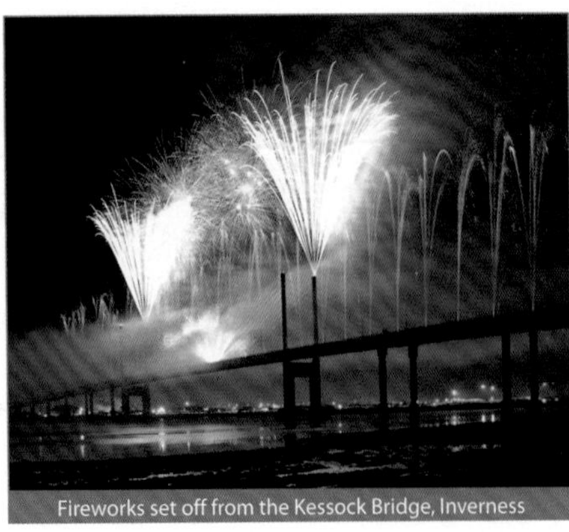
Fireworks set off from the Kessock Bridge, Inverness

DON'T MISS

1 **Assynt** is stunningly beautiful and is home to a variety of attractions. Chief among them are; the Assynt Visitor Centre, Hydroponicum at Achiltubuie and Kerracher Gardens, Highland Stoneware, Inverpolly Nature Reserve and Ardvreck Castle.

2 **Culloden Battlefield** is the site of the last major battle fought on mainland Britain in 1746. Bonnie Prince Charlie's Jacobite troops were defeated here by the Duke of Cumberland and the Hanoverian government forces. The new visitor centre – opened in 2007 – features a battle immersion cinema and handheld multi-lingual audio devices to bring the battle to life.

3 No visit to this part of Scotland would be complete without taking time to visit **John o'Groats** and the famous signpost pointing towards Lands End – a mere 874 miles away! From here there are also regular summer sailings to Orkney so you can hop on one of the John o'Groats day tours which incorporate the ferry and a coach tour of the main island.

4 Perhaps the most spectacularly scenic of all Scottish lochs, **Loch Maree** greets unsuspecting visitors travelling north-west on the A832 between Inverness and Gairloch. Bounded by the imposing masses of Beinn Eighe to the west and Slioch to the east, the loch's shores play host to a wealth of wildlife, as well as fragments of ancient Caledonian pinewood.

5 One of the largest castles in Scotland, the ruins of **Urquhart Castle** lie on the banks of Loch Ness, near Drumnadrochit. Blown up in 1692 to prevent Jacobite occupation, this 5-star visitor attraction has a fascinating interactive visitor centre which depicts the story of the castle's turbulent history. Explore the ruins of the castle, before visiting the on-site café where you will be rewarded with breathtaking views of Loch Ness.

6 At **Golspie Highland Wildcat Trails** an adrenaline filled mix of testing uphills and challenging fast downhill sections make for an exhilarating day's mountain biking on Ben Bhraggie. After you've reached the top, views west across Sutherland and south across the Dornoch Firth make the uphill all worth it.

FOOD AND DRINK

eatscotland.com

7 Only the freshest of fish straight from the daily catch make it to the table in the **Captain's Galley**. Set in a tastefully renovated old ice house in Scrabster, near Thurso, the award winning restaurant serves up to 10 different species of fish every night. Booking is recommended.

8 **Highland Feast**, an annual food and drink festival held in September, is a celebration of the fantastic produce and culinary skills present in the local area and beyond.

9 Fresh, local ingredients are combined to make the **Falls of Shin Visitor Centre** the ultimate place to stop for lunch. See salmon leap on the magnificent waterfall as you tuck in. There is also a children's playground so you can fill up while the kids are kept entertained.

10 As with many restaurants across the Highlands, **Sutor Creek** prides itself on the use of fresh, local produce, but few produce 'real pizza' like this place. Cooked in their specially built wood-fired oven this friendly bistro in Cromarty also slow-roasts the perfect Sunday meal with local meats infused with home grown herbs and garlic.

GOLF

visitscotland.com/golf

11 **Gairloch Golf Course** is superbly situated above a sandy bay beside the road into Gairloch. This 9-hole links course is one of the Highland's best kept secrets. Take your time soaking up the views towards Skye. Arrange tee times in advance to guarantee a round.

12 **Durness Golf Course**, surrounded by stunning coastal scenery, is notorious for its 9th hole, which requires players to clear the Atlantic Ocean! Check with the secretary in advance to ensure a round is possible.

13 Considered one of the finest links courses in the world, **Royal Dornoch Golf Course** is situated on public land in its namesake royal burgh, 45 miles north of Inverness. Play on the course about which Tom Watson famously remarked 'the most fun I've ever had on a golf course'.

14 A traditional Scottish links course, **Nairn West Golf Club** offers a challenge for all abilities. 20 minutes drive from Inverness, this 18-hole favourite is perfect for the discerning golfer looking to experience a course steeped in tradition.

OUTSTANDING VIEWS

15 A classic view of **Loch Ness** is to be savoured from the beach at the village of Dores (B862 from Inverness), at the quieter side of the loch to the south. Look out for Nessie, or at the very least, the resident Nessie spotter!

16 Round the bay from **Lochinver**, a minor road allows fantastic views back towards the community and the incredible sugar loaf of Suilven rising up in the background.

17 Near John o'Groats see a dramatic coastline where thousands of seabirds nest in vast colonies. A walk across the clifftop fields will reward you with a stunning view south to Thirle Door and the **Stacks of Duncansby**. The first is a rocky arch, the second a group of large jagged sea stacks. This is a spot you will want to savour, with a view that varies as you move along the clifftop path and bring into play different alignments of the stacks and arch.

18 The **Corrieshalloch Gorge** National Nature Reserve, south-east of Ullapool, comprises a box canyon dropping 200ft to the river below. Adding to the drama are the spectacular **Falls of Measach**, best seen from the viewing platform further down the footpath.

16

17

18

WALKS

visitscotland.com/walking

19 **Reelig Glen** is a short walk through spectacular old conifer and broad-leaved trees on easy paths with short gentle gradients, making it a suitable walk for almost anyone. Approximately 10 minutes from Inverness, take the A862 west towards Beauly and after 8 miles, turn left onto the minor road signposted to Reelig and Moniack and continue for 1 mile – follow the Forestry Commission of Scotland sign and look out for Britain's tallest tree named Dughall Mor.

20 Although within the city of Inverness, the **Ness Islands** walk could be a million miles from it. The islands, linked by several old bridges, offer a quiet, scenic walk through tall, native and imported trees. It offers plenty of photo opportunities and an enjoyable family walk which accommodates wheelchairs.

21 Take the minor B869 road to Stoer lighthouse, from which a 3-hour circular walk leads to a spectacular rock-stack – the **Old Man of Stoer** - surrounded by jaw-dropping cliff scenery. The path is clear throughout, and offers views to the Assynt mountains in the south, and to the islands of Lewis and Harris many miles to the west.

22 The **Caithness and Sutherland Walking Festival**, held in May, consists of themed walks led by local guides. These interesting walks explore archaeology, history and wildlife and are a great way to learn more about the surrounding area.

Ardgay, Sutherland

Corvost B&B

Map Ref: 4A6

★★ B&B

20578

Open: All year excl Xmas and New Year
Corvost, Ardgay, Sutherland IV24 3BP
T: 01863 755317
F: 01863 755317

Total number of rooms: 3			
Prices from:			
Single:	**£20.00**	Double:	**£20.00**
Twin:	**£20.00**		

Avoch, Ross-shire

Ardvreckan

Map Ref: 4B8

★★★★ B&B

73132

Open: All year excl Xmas and New Year
Knockmuir Brae, Avoch, Ross-shire IV9 8RD
T: 01381 621523
E: jennifer.patience@yahoo.co.uk
W: go-bedandbreakfast.co.uk/ardvreckan

Total number of rooms: 2			
Prices per room from:			
Single:	**£40.00**	Double:	**£60.00**
Twin:	**£60.00**		

Brora, Sutherland

Glenaveron

Map Ref: 4C6

27991

Open: All year excl Xmas and New Year
Golf Road, Brora, Sutherland KW9 6QS
T: 01408 621601
E: alistair@glenaveron.co.uk
W: glenaveron.co.uk

Glenaveron is a luxurious Edwardian house set amid extensive gardens, it is a few minutes walk to Brora Golf Course and beautiful beaches. Dunrobin Castle is close by and the Castle of Mey is only a one hour drive. Glenaveron is an ideal base for touring the Northern Highlands.

Total number of rooms: 3			
Prices from:			
Single:	**£45.00**	Double:	**£34.00-36.00**
Twin:	**£34.00-36.00**		

Culbokie, Black Isle

Ben Wyvis Views

Map Ref: 4B8

67938

Open: All year
Bydand, Culbokie, Ross-Shire IV7 8JH
T: 01349 877430
E: jane@culbokie.net
W: culbokie.net

A warm Scottish welcome awaits in this modern detached home. Set in its own beautiful grounds with stunning views and breathtaking sunsets. Memorable breakfasts enjoyed overlooking Ben Wyvis and the Cromarty Firth. Our guests return again and again, so book early. Ample parking, internet access, television lounge.

Total number of rooms: 3			
Prices from:			
Single:	**£38.00**	Double:	**£29.00**
Twin:	**£29.00**	Family room:	**£75.00pr**

Important: Prices stated are estimates and may be subject to amendments.

Culloden Moor, by Inverness

Eiland View Bed and Breakfast

Map Ref: 4B8

24639

Open: All year excl Xmas and New Year

Woodside of Culloden, Westhill, Inverness IV2 5BP

T: 01463 798900
E: info@eilandview.com
W: eilandview.com

Our wonderful Scottish hospitality ensures an enjoyable stay at our modern home situated close to the famous Culloden battlefield on the outskirts of Inverness. Excellent Scottish breakfast assured. Panoramic views over Inverness and the Moray Firth. Ideally situated for touring the Highlands. Bus service available and Inverness Airport close by.

Total number of rooms: 3

Prices from:

Single: **£30.00** Double: **£28.00**
Twin: **£28.00**

Culloden Moor, by Inverness

Westhill House

Map Ref: 4B8

63857

Open: April-October, excl Xmas and New Year

Westhill, Inverness, Inverness-shire IV2 5BP

T: 01463 793225
E: j.honnor@bigfoot.com
W: scotland-info.co.uk/westhill.htm

Total number of rooms: 3

Prices from:

Single: **£28.00** Double: **£28.00**
Twin: **£28.00** Family room: **£28.00**

Dornoch, Sutherland

Cartomie

Map Ref: 4B6

80323

Open: March-October inclusive

Edderton, Tain IV19 1LB
T: 01862 821599/07840 930415
E: wrustle@lineone.net
W: cartomie.co.uk

Cartomie is a modern bungalow in a rural setting close to Dornoch, Tain and the Dornoch Firth. We are a non smoking household with two ensuite rooms, one double and one king-size/twin. You can enjoy breakfast in the conservatory with lovely views of Struie Hill.

Total number of rooms: 2

Prices from:

Single: **£30.00** Double: **£22.00**
Twin: **£22.00**

ADVENTURE SCOTLAND

For everything you need to know about Adventure Breaks in Scotland and for an Adventure Brochure and an Adventure Pass call

0845 22 55 121

or log on to **visitscotland.com/adventurepass**

Scotland. Europe's adventure capital.

Dornoch, Sutherland

Hillview

Map Ref: 4B6

Open: All year 30587

Evelix Road, Dornoch, Sutherland IV25 3RD

T: 01862 810151
E: hillviewbb@talk21.com
W: milford.co.uk/go/hillviewbb.html

Relax in comfort in our superb 4 star accommodation with ensuite facilities, colour TV, coffee/tea, hairdryers in all rooms. Guests lounge with satellite TV, private parking. Two minutes by car from Royal Dornoch Golf Club and superb sandy beaches. Ideal area for walking, golfing, fishing and touring the Highlands.

Total number of rooms: 2

Prices from:
Double: **£30.00** Twin: **£30.00**

Drumnadrochit, Loch Ness

Kilmore Farmhouse

Map Ref: 4A9

Open: March-October 33864

Drumnadrochit, Inverness IV63 6UF
T: 01456 450524
E: kilmorefarm@supanet.com
W: visitscotland.com

Total number of rooms: 3

Prices from:
Single: **£35.00** Double: **£30.00**
Twin: **£30.00** Family room: **£30.00**

Fort Augustus, Loch Ness

Carn A' Chuilinn

Map Ref: 4A10

Open: All year 18161

Golf Course Road, Fort Augustus PH32 4BY
T: 01320 366387
E: anne@carnachuilinn.co.uk
W: carnachuilinn.co.uk

A warm Scottish welcome awaits you at our family run bed and breakfast. Carn A' Chuilinn is an ideal base for touring the Highlands and Skye. Situated close to the shores of Loch Ness in the heart of the Great Glen. Picturesque nine hole golf course two minutes from the house.

Total number of rooms: 3

Prices from:
Single: **£30.00** Double: **£28.00**
Twin: **£28.00**

Fort Augustus, Inverness-shire

Sonas B&B

Map Ref: 4A10

Open: All year excl Xmas and New Year 55180

Inverness Road, Fort Augustus PH32 4DH
T: 01320 366291
W: nessaccom.co.uk/sonas

Total number of rooms: 3

Prices from:
Single: **£30.00** Double: **£25.00**
Twin: **£25.00** Family room: **£23.00**

Important: Prices stated are estimates and may be subject to amendments.

Fort Augustus, Inverness-shire

Thistle Dubh B&B

Map Ref: 4A10

90909

Open: All year

Auchterawe Road,
Fort Augustus, Inverness-shire PH32 4BN
T: 01320 366380
E: thistledubh@supanet.com
W: visitscotland.com

Peaceful rural setting yet within walking distance of the village of Fort Augustus and Loch Ness. Situated on the Great Glen Way we provide very comfortable accommodation in ensuite rooms in large modern house. The village boasts some fine eating places, many on the side of the famous Caledonian Canal.

Total number of rooms: 3

Prices from:

Single: **£28.00** Double: **£26.00**
Twin: **£26.00**

Fortrose, Ross-shire

Waters Edge

Map Ref: 4B8

76567

Open: All year excl Xmas and New Year

Canonbury Terrace, Fortrose, Ross-shire IV10 8TT
T: 01381 621202
E: gill@watersedge.uk.com
W: watersedge.uk.com

Waters Edge is a haven of cosiness and character, the garden goes down to the sea, just fifteen minutes from Inverness. Spot dolphins at breakfast, all our bedrooms have a large terrace with spectacular views over the sea. Our warm welcome and generous hospitality makes this a special place to stay.

Total number of rooms: 3

Prices per room from:

Single: **£80.00** Double: **£90.00**

Gairloch, Ross-shire

Heatherdale

Map Ref: 3F7

29913

Open: March-November

Charleston, Gairloch, Ross-shire IV21 2AH
T/F: 01445 712388
E: brochod1@aol.com

A warm welcome awaits at Heatherdale, situated on the outskirts of Gairloch, overlooking the harbour and bay beyond. Within easy walking distance of golf course and sandy beaches. Ideal base for hill-walking. All rooms ensuite facilites, some with seaview. Excellent eating out facilities nearby. Ample parking. Residents lounge with open fire.

Total number of rooms: 3

Prices from:

Double: **£27.00** Twin: **£27.00**

Inverness

Abermar Guest House

Map Ref: 4B8

Open: All year excl Xmas and New Year 10835

25 Fairfield Road, Inverness IV3 5QD

T: 01463 239019
E: abermar@talk21.com
W: abermar.co.uk

Enjoy Scottish hospitality at its best in our comfortable family run guest house situated in a quiet residential area. Abermar is less than ten minutes walk from the city centre and all amenities. Inverness is an ideal base for touring the Highlands. Private parking and wireless internet access available.

Total number of rooms: 9

Prices from:
Single: **£30.00** Double: **£26.00**
Twin: **£26.00**

Inverness

Advie Lodge

Map Ref: 4B8

★★★★ B&B

Open: All year 11159

31 Crown Drive, Inverness IV2 3QQ

T: 01463 237247
E: advielodge@fsmail.net

Total number of rooms: 3

Prices from:
Single: **£30.00** Double: **£30.00**
Twin: **£30.00**

Inverness

Ballifeary Guest House

Map Ref: 4B8

Open: All year excl Xmas 13974

10 Ballifeary Road, Inverness IV3 5PJ

T: 01463 235572
E: info@ballifearyguesthouse.co.uk
W: ballifearyguesthouse.co.uk

Total number of rooms: 6

Prices from:
Single: **£40.00** Double: **£35.00**
Twin: **£35.00**

Inverness

Bayview

Map Ref: 4B8

Open: April-October 14476

Westhill, Inverness IV2 5BP

T: 01463 790386
E: bayview.guest@lineone.net
W: bayviewguesthouses.com

Very comfortable homely accommodation. Choice of breakfast. Lovely views, set in a beautiful garden, plenty of free parking. Central location for touring the Highlands.

Total number of rooms: 3

Prices from:
Single: **£30.00** Double: **£27.00**
Twin: **£27.00**

Important: Prices stated are estimates and may be subject to amendments.

Inverness

Castle View Guest House

Map Ref: 4B8

★★★ GUEST HOUSE

Open: All year 18524

2a Ness Walk, Inverness IV3 5NE

T: 01463 241443

E: jmunro4161@aol.com

W: castleviewinverness.co.uk

Total number of rooms: 6			
Prices from:			
Single:	**£30.00**	Double:	**£26.00**
Twin:	**£26.00**	Family room:	**£70.00pr**

Inverness

Fraser House

Map Ref: 4B8

Open: All year 26777

49 Huntly Street, Inverness IV3 5HS

T: 01463 716488

E: fraserlea@btopenworld.com

W: fraserhouse.co.uk

Family owned and run guest house superbly situated on the west bank of River Ness in the heart of the Highland capital. Bedrooms all ensuite overlooking the river. Just 5 minutes walk from city centre and main attractions. Warm welcome and big Scottish breakfast assured for all our visitors.

Total number of rooms: 5			
Prices per person from:			
Single:	**£30.00**	Double:	**£25.00**
Twin:	**£25.00**	Family room:	**£25.00**

Inverness

Glendoune B&B

Map Ref: 4B8

Open: All year excl Xmas and New Year 28111

24 Perceval Road, Inverness IV3 5QE

T: 01463 231493

E: angusnoble@aol.com

W: glendoune.co.uk

Detached Victorian house a few minutes walk to heart of Inverness city centre, Eden Court Theatre, bus and train stations. Easily accessible from all routes into Inverness. Ideal base for exploring the city and touring the Highlands.

Total number of rooms: 3			
Prices from:			
Double:	**£25.00**	Twin:	**£25.00**
Family room:	**£25.00**		

Inverness

Heathcote Bed and Breakfast

Map Ref: 4B8

★★★★ B&B

Open: All year 79508

59 Glenurquhart Road, Inverness IV3 5PB

T: 01463 243650

E: info@heathcotebandb.co.uk

W: heathcotebandb.co.uk

Total number of rooms: 3			
Prices from:			
Double:	**£25.00**	Twin:	**£25.00**
Family room:	**£25.00**		

Inverness

Inverglen Guest House

Map Ref: 4B8

31988

Open: All year

7 Abertarff Road, Inverness IV2 3NW
T: 01463 236281
E: welcome@inverglenguesthouse.com
W: inverglenguesthouse.com

Inverglen is a Victorian stone villa built in 1894 with many traditional features. We are situated in the quiet residential crown area, only five minutes walk from the centre of Inverness. Therefore the river, theatre, shops, restaurants, pubs, railway and bus stations are all very accessible by foot.

Total number of rooms: 5

Prices from:

Single:	**£37.00**	Double:	**£30.00**
Twin:	**£30.00**	Family room:	**£28.00**

Inverness

Lorne House

Map Ref: 4B8

36397

Open: All year excl Xmas and New Year

40 Crown Drive, Inverness, IV2 3QG
T: 01463 236271

Total number of rooms: 2

Prices from:

Double:	**£35.00**	Twin:	**£35.00**

Inverness

Strathmhor Guest House

Map Ref: 4B8

56940

Open: All year

99 Kenneth Street, Inverness IV3 5QQ
T: 01463 235397
E: strathmhor@btinternet.com

Total number of rooms: 5

Prices per room from:

Single:	**£25.00-35.00**	Double:	**£50.00-60.00**
Twin:	**£50.00-65.00**	Family room:	**£70.00-90.00**

Inverness

Strathness House

Map Ref: 4B8

70379

Open: All year excl Xmas and New Year

4 Ardross Terrace, Inverness IV3 5NQ
T: 01463 232765
E: info@strathnesshouse.com
W: strathnesshouse.co.uk

Total number of rooms: 12

Prices per room from:

Single:	**£50.00**	Double:	**£60.00**
Twin:	**£60.00**	Family room:	**£80.00**

Scotland

For all you need to know about biking in Scotland and for a mountain bike brochure log on to

visitscotland.com/cycling

Important: Prices stated are estimates and may be subject to amendments.

John o' Groats, Caithness
Bencorragh House
Map Ref: 4E2

14913

Open: All year excl Xmas and New Year
Upper Gills, Canisbay, by John O' Groats
Caithness KW1 4YD
T: 01955 611449
E: bartonsandy@hotmail.com
W: bencorraghhouse.com

Total number of rooms: 3

Prices per room from:

Single:	**£40.00**	Double:	**£52.00**
Twin:	**£52.00**	Family room:	**£70.00**

Lochinver, Sutherland
Ardmore House
Map Ref: 3G5

67947

Open: May-September
Torbreck, Lochinver, Sutherland IV27 4JB
T: 01571 844310

Mrs MacLeod offers warm, comfortable accommodation. Ardmore is an ideal B&B to use as a base for touring the Northern Highlands. Many excellent walks in the area and plenty of wildlife and sandy beaches.

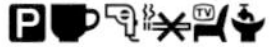

Total number of rooms: 2

Prices from:

Double:	**£25.00**	Twin:	**£25.00**

Lochinver, Sutherland
Davar B&B
Map Ref: 3G5

★★★★
B&B

22220

Open: March-November
Davar, Lochinver, Sutherland IV27 4LJ
T: 01571 844 501
E: jean@davar36.fsnet.co.uk
W: davar-lochinver.co.uk

Total number of rooms: 3

Prices per person from:

Single:	**£40.00**	Double:	**£28.00**
Twin:	**£28.00**	Family room:	**£28.00**

Poolewe, Ross-shire
Bruach Ard
Map Ref: 3F7

16641

Open: All year
7 Braes, Inverasdale, Poolewe, Ross-shire IV22 2LN
T: 01445 781765
E: dgeorge@globalnet.co.uk
W: davidgeorge.co.uk

Total number of rooms: 3

Prices from:

Double:	**£27.00**	Twin:	**£27.00**

Eat*Scotland*.com

Discover Scotland's superb produce and great places to dine.

Reay, Thurso

The Old Inn

Map Ref: 4C3

79565

Open: All year

Reay, Caithness KW14 7RE
T: 01847 811554
E: derek.theoldinn@btinternet.com
W: theoldinnatreay.co.uk

The Old Inn at Reay is a piece of Scottish history. Built in 1739 as an inn, it is still used as a private home and bed and breakfast today. If you are touring our beautiful North Coast or heading for the Orkney ferry, we can offer the perfect solution.

Total number of rooms: 2

Prices from:
Double: **£25.00** Twin: **£25.00**

Scourie, Sutherland

Scourie Lodge B&B

Map Ref: 3H4

53874

★★★★ B&B

Open: March-November

Scourie, Sutherland IV27 4TE
T: 01971 502248
E: scourielodge@aol.com
W: scourielodge.co.uk

Total number of rooms: 3

Prices from:
Single: **£50.00** Double: **£35.00**
Twin: **£35.00**

Smithton, by Inverness

Stonea

Map Ref: 4B8

56701

Open: All year excl Xmas and New Year

3a Resaurie, Smithton, Inverness IV2 7NH
T: 01463 791714
E: mbmansfield@uk2.net
W: mansfieldhighlandholidays.com

Total number of rooms: 3

Prices from:
Single: **£21.00** Double: **£23.00**
Twin: **£21.00**

Strathy Point, Sutherland

Sharvedda

Map Ref: 4B3

54321

Open: All year excl Xmas and New Year

Strathy Point, Strathy, Thurso, Sutherland KW14 7RY
T: 01641 541311
E: patsy@sharvedda.co.uk
W: sharvedda.co.uk

Sharvedda is a modern family home situated at Strathy Point on Sutherland's superb north coast. A perfect paradise for nature lovers and the outdoor enthusiasts. Enjoy delicious meals served in conservatory with panoramic views to Orkney and Dunnet Head. Ideal stopover for Orkney day trips and Castle of Mey.

Total number of rooms: 3

Prices from:
Single: **£35.00-40.00** Double: **£28.00-30.00**
Twin: **£28.00-30.00**

Important: Prices stated are estimates and may be subject to amendments.

Tain, Ross-shire

Carringtons

Map Ref: 4B7

★★★ B&B

18300

Open: All year

Morangie Road, Tain, Ross-shire IV19 1PY
T: 01862 892635
E: mollie1@btinernet.com

A warm welcome awaits you at Carrington's Victorian House facing the sea. Ensuite facilities, colour TV, tea and coffee making facilities in bedrooms, private parking. Children and pets welcome.

Total number of rooms: 4

Prices from:

Single: **£25.00** Double: **£25.00**
Twin: **£25.00** Family room: **£25.00**

Talmine, Sutherland

Cloisters

Map Ref: 4A3

★★★★ B&B

19692

Open: All year

Church Holme, Talmine, Sutherland IV27 4YP
T: 01847 601286
E: reception@cloistertal.demon.co.uk
W: cloistertal.demon.co.uk

Located four miles north of Tongue, off the A838, Cloisters built in traditional style alongside our home a converted 19th century church offers superb B&B accommodation with stunning views over inshore islands to the Orkneys beyond. Excellent licensed restaurant close by. Escape to the peace and tranquility of Scotland's outback.

Total number of rooms: 3

Prices from:

Single: **£30.00** Twin: **£25.00**

Thurso, Caithness

Annandale

Map Ref: 4D3

★★★★ B&B

12185

Open: All year excl Xmas and New Year

2 Rendel Govan Road, Thurso, Caithness KW14 7EP
T: 01847 893942
M: 07733 167085
E: thomson@annandale2.freeserve.co.uk

Total number of rooms: 3

Prices from:

Double: **£26.00** Twin: **£26.00**

Thurso, Caithness

Mrs J Oag

Map Ref: 4D3

★★★ B&B

45857

Open: All year excl Xmas and New Year

9 Couper Street, Thurso, Caithness KW14 8AR
T: 01847 894529/07789258837
E: joanoag@aol.com

Total number of rooms: 3

Prices from:

Single: **£21.00** Double: **£23.00**
Twin: **£21.00**

Tongue, Sutherland

Tigh-nan-Ubhal Guest House

Map Ref: 4A3

★★★ B&B

78926

Open: All year

Tongue, by Lairg, Sutherland IV27 4XF
T: 01847 611281
E: tigh_nan_ubhal@btinternet.com
W: spanglefish.com/tigh-nan-ubhal

Situated in the heart of the village and home to the most Northerly palm tree. An ideal base for touring the north coast of Scotland. A warm Highland welcome very comfortable accommodation and a hearty Scottish breakfast awaits you. Perfect retreat for walkers, families, anglers or a relaxing time.

Total number of rooms: 3

Prices from:

Twin: **£30.00** Family room: **£35.00**

Ullapool, Ross-shire

Ardvreck House

Map Ref: 3G6

12714

Open: March-November

North Road, Morefield, Ullapool, Ross-shire IV26 2TH
T: 01854 612028
E: ardvreck@btconnect.com
W: smoothhound.co.uk/hotels/ardvreck

Ardvreck House offers quality accommodation in a spectacular setting overlooking Ullapool and Loch Broom. Our rooms have ensuite shower rooms and over half have superb Loch views. We provide Bed and Breakfast and can recommend places to eat in the village. Quiet country location. Free wireless internet.

Total number of rooms: 10

Prices from:

Single: **£35.00** Double: **£32.50**
Twin: **£32.50** Family room: **£85.00pr**

Ullapool, Ross-shire

Broombank Bungalow

Map Ref: 3G6

★★★ B&B

16566

Open: All year

4 Castle Terrace, Ullapool, Ross-shire IV26 2XD
T: 01854 612247
E: stay@broombankullapool.com
W: broombankullapool.com

A warm welcome awaits in our cosy, modern bungalow, overlooking golf course, Loch Broom and Summer Isles. Beautiful sunsets. Ten minute walk to all amenities, restaurants, pubs, shops, harbour etc. Quiet area. Wireless internet available.

Total number of rooms: 3

Prices from:

Double: **£25.00-30.00** Twin: **£20.00-30.00**

Important: Prices stated are estimates and may be subject to amendments.

Ullapool, Ross-shire
Penny Browne

Map Ref: 3G6 13701

Open: End of March-Middle of October

3 Castle Terrace, Ullapool, Wester Ross
Ross-shire IV26 2XD
T: 01854 612409
W: freewebs.com/pennybrowne

Total number of rooms: 3

Prices from:

Single: **£26.00-28.00** Double: **£27.00-28.00**
Twin: **£26.00-27.00**

Ullapool, Ross-shire
Jackie Macrae

Map Ref: 3G6 45854

★★★★
B&B

Open: All year excl Xmas Day

3 Vyner Place, Morefield, Ullapool
Ross-shire IV26 2XR
T: 01854 612023
E: jackie.macrae@virgin.net

A modern and comfortable accommodation in a peaceful residential area within walking distance of Ullapool. Close to golf course and ferry terminal to Western Isles. Ideal base for touring the north west Highlands of Scotland.

Total number of rooms: 2

Prices from:

Double: **£27.00** Twin: **£27.00**
Family room: **£27.00** Discount 3rd person

Ullapool, Ross-shire
Point Cottage Guest House

Map Ref: 3G6 50057

★★★★
GUEST HOUSE

Open: 1 March-31 October

22 West Shore Street, Ullapool, Ross-shire IV26 2UR
T: 01854 612494
E: macrae@pointcottage.co.uk
W: pointcottage.co.uk

As featured in *Holiday Which*, a tastefully converted beautifully situated 19th century fisherman's cottage where a warm welcome and a high level of local knowledge are assured. Marvellous lochside views to mountains beyond, peaceful location. Two minutes walk to village centre. Comfortable guest lounge, wide breakfast choice with vegetarian options.

Total number of rooms: 3

Prices from:

Single: **£25.00-55.00** Double: **£24.00-34.00**
Twin: **£24.00-34.00**

For information on fishing breaks in Scotland and for a brochure call

0845 22 55 121

visitscotland.com/fish

Ullapool, Ross-shire

Torran

Map Ref: 3G6

★★★ B&B

Open: April-October 61575

Loggie, Lochbroom, Ullapool, Ross-shire IV23 2SG
T: 01854 655227/ 07753854281
E: mairi@torranloggie.co.uk
W: torranloggie.co.uk

Family home on working croft in peaceful setting overlooking the beautiful Loch Broom. Enjoy a Scottish breakfast using our own free range eggs. Iron age brochs and salmon farm close by. A relaxing and peaceful holiday location.

Total number of rooms: 2

Prices from:

Single:	**£50.00**	Double:	**£28.00-30.00**
Twin:	**£28.00-30.00**		

Wick, Caithness

The Clachan

Map Ref: 4E3

★★★★ B&B

Open: All year excl Xmas and New Year 58504

13 Randolph Place, South Road, Wick, Caithness KW1 5NJ
T: 01955 605384
E: enquiry@theclachan.co.uk
W: theclachan.co.uk

Total number of rooms: 3

Prices from:

Single:	**£40.00-45.00**	Double:	**£25.00-28.00**
Twin:	**£25.00-28.00**		

Dunbeath Bay and Dunbeath Castle, south west of Wick, Caithness

Important: Prices stated are estimates and may be subject to amendments.

Elgol, Loch Scavaig, Isle of Skye

Fort William, Lochaber, Skye and Lochalsh

Fort William is known as the 'Outdoor Capital of the UK' – and little wonder. The area annually hosts the Mountain Bike World Cup and is next door to Scotland's highest mountain, Ben Nevis. The surrounding area provides a huge range of opportunities to enjoy the great outdoors.

The local scenery is quite stunning and there are hundreds of amazing places to visit. From the dramatic beauty of Glen Coe to the breathtaking views across Loch Duich, not forgetting the wild isolation of Knoydart and Ardnamurchan Point.

Take in some of the finest coastal and hill scenery on what is considered one of the great railway journeys of the world. Travel the length of the legendary Road to the Isles on the Jacobite Steam Train from Fort William to Mallaig. Take in the iconic Neptune's Staircase, Glenfinnan Viaduct and glorious coastline of Arisaig and Morar, and when you reach Mallaig you'll be able to see the jagged peaks of the Cuillin mountains on the Isle of Skye.

The turbulent history and majestic scenery of Skye and Lochalsh make the area one of Scotland's most romantic destinations. From the delightfully situated Eilean Donan Castle and the picture-postcard village of Plockton to the soaring craggy heights of the Cuillin and the eerie pinnacles of Trotternish, the area is sure to leave an imprint on your heart.

DON'T MISS

1. One of the most picturesque – and most photographed – castles in Scotland, **Eilean Donan Castle**, sits on Loch Duich, beside the tiny village of Dornie. Stroll across the causeway that links it to the shore and explore it for yourself. For a panoramic view, follow the path from the village which leads up to the Carr Brae viewpoint.

2. Take a boat trip from Elgol (B8083 from Broadford) to isolated and inspiring **Loch Coruisk**. You will get up close to Britain's most dramatic landscapes, while your local guide will make sure you don't miss out on seeing the abundant wildlife – including the famous seal colony on the banks of the loch.

3. Accessible only by boat from Mallaig or via a very long walk from Kinlochhourn, **Knoydart** is recognised as the remotest part of mainland Britain and is perfect for adventurous families. One of the best hiking spots in the country, there are also options for wildlife watching, canoeing and fishing. The scenery is outstanding and will leave a lasting impression.

4. **Camusdarach, Traigh** and the **Silver Sands of Morar** are just a selection of exquisite beaches along the shoreline between Arisaig and Mallaig. While away a few hours picnicking with the breathtaking backdrop of the Small Isles of Eigg and Rum rising sheer out of the sea in front of you and admire the changing light on the sea catching the numerous skerries that pepper the coast.

5. To travel the whole length of the Road to the Isles, hop aboard the **Jacobite Steam Train**. This steam engine runs between Fort William and Mallaig throughout the summer months and takes in some truly impressive sites such as Neptune's Staircase, the Glenfinnan Viaduct and the glorious coastline of Arisaig and Morar. Regarded as one of the Great Railway Journeys of the World, this is a must while in the area, especially for Harry Potter fans who will recognise it from the films.

6. The biggest indoor ice climbing facility in the world, **The Ice Factor**, is situated in a former aluminium works in Kinlochleven. With rock climbing walls, a gym, sauna, and plunge pool, this is a great day out for the activity enthusiast or indeed, the whole family. As the National Centre for Indoor Ice Climbing, experts can try out new techniques whilst novices can get to grips with the basics in a safe and secure environment.

1

4

FOOD AND DRINK

eatscotland.com

7 The **Three Chimneys** restaurant on Skye is known far and wide as one of the most romantic eateries in the land. The candlelit crofter's cottage on the shores of Loch Dunvegan, voted 28th in Restaurant Magazine's 'definitive list' of the World's Top 50 Restaurants, is an idyllic setting for a proposal, a honeymoon or any special occasion. Book ahead to ensure your table.

8 Among the host of west coast seafood restaurants, the EatScotland approved **Holly Tree** in Kentallen stands out. The catch comes into their own pier on the shore of Loch Linnhe and is served up with magnificent views across to the Morven hills.

9 **Crannog** at the Waterfront in Fort William serves the very best in seafood. Be sure to give their speciality a try – the langoustine fresh from Loch Linnhe!

10 For an AA rosette dinner, seek out **Russell's Restaurant**, Smiddy House in Spean Bridge. Innovation and flair are deftly applied to a fine range of local produce.

7

12

13

WALKS

visitscotland.com/walking

11 **Glen Finnan** - From the Glenfinnan Visitor Centre car park, follow the Mallaig road across a bridge and then look out for a sign pointing towards Glenfinnan Lodge. From here continue up the glen where kids will be impressed by the famous viaduct, featured in the Harry Potter films. An easy 5½ mile route, taking in most of this scenic glen, can be completed in roughly 2 hours.

12 **Morar to Loch Morar and Mallaig** - A relatively easy walk you can enjoy without the hassle of taking the car. The starting and finishing points are both adjacent to train stations, so check out scotrail.co.uk to ensure you're onboard! Set off from Morar station and walk south, taking a left turn onto the minor road along Loch Morar's north shore. Kids should keep a look out for Nessie's cousin 'Morag' who supposedly occupies this loch. Continue along, as the road becomes a path, before arriving in Tarbet. Here, a boat departs daily at 3.30 pm throughout the summer to take you back via Loch Nevis to the connecting train at Mallaig. Allow 6 hours for the walk.

13 **Glen Coe** is one of the most popular hiking destinations in Scotland with the likes of Allt Coire for more experienced hikers and, for the less experienced walker, places like the Lost Valley to seek out. From the car parks on the A82, the path takes you across the bridge over the River Coe towards the triple buttresses known as the Three Sisters. Turn right after the bridge and follow the trail upwards. After a couple of miles you'll reach the false summit marking the edge of the hidden basin where the MacDonald clan used to hide their cattle in times of attack.

14 For a longer more challenging walk, drive 6 miles north from Portree on the Isle of Skye (A855), where you will find a car park. A path leads through woodland onto a steep climb to an area of geological formations. There are then a number of paths that can be followed to the base of the **Old Man of Storr**. Along the way you can enjoy good views across the Sound of Raasay. This walk should take in excess of 3 hours.

OUTSTANDING VIEWS

15 As you drive south on the A828, **Castle Stalker** appears before you against a beautiful backdrop. Stop at the View Café and Gift Shop for stunning vistas across Loch Linnhe to the Morvern Hills. Such a panorama has inspired many artists and here you can really appreciate their motivation.

16 From Rannoch Moor on the A82, the twin peaks of **Buachaille Etive Mor** and Buachaille Etive Beag spectacularly mark the entrance to Glen Coe. Appearing like steep-sided pyramids they stand sentinel on the moor, offering a glimpse of the wild landscape just around the corner.

17 There are many classic views of the **Cuillin Ridge**. However, for sheer drama, few views in all of Scotland compare with the sight of Sgurr Nan Gillean rearing up behind Sligachan bridge, or the full mountain range rising almost sheer from Loch Scavaig, opposite the tiny village of Elgol, west of Broadford on Skye.

18 To see the **Five Sisters of Kintail** from Ratagan Pass, take the Glenelg road from Shiel Bridge on the A87. As you rise up towards Mam Ratagan, about a mile along, take a look back over Loch Duich, framed by the majestic peaks of Kintail. Simply stunning.

15

17

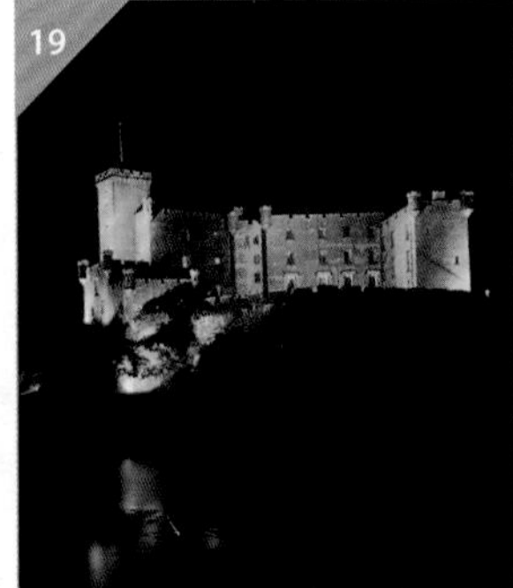
19

HERITAGE

19 **Dunvegan Castle** (follow the A850 from Portree), the stronghold of the MacLeod chiefs for nearly 800 years, remains their home today. Highland Cattle roam around the estate, making you feel that you've well and truly reached the Scottish Highlands!

20 Skye's only distillery, **Talisker Distillery**, is set on the shores of Loch Harport with dramatic views of the Cuillin hills. Enjoy a tipple of this alluring, sweet, full-bodied single malt on the distillery tour.

21 For a full interpretation of this amazing setting, head to the **Glencoe Visitor Centre** on the A82, 17 miles south of Fort William. Particularly eco-friendly, this centre provides a great viewing platform, as well as an interactive exhibit for kids of all ages where you can find out how it feels to climb on ice!

22 The **West Highland Museum** is to be found in Fort William and houses an historic collection that dates from Mesolithic times to the modern day. All elements of society are included, from crofters to soldiers and princes to clergy.

Ballachulish, Argyll

Craiglinnhe House

Map Ref: 1F1

Open: All year excl December 24th-26th incl.

73699

Lettermore, Ballachulish, Argyll PH49 4JD
T: 01855 811270
E: info@craiglinnhe.co.uk
W: craiglinnhe.co.uk

Your hosts David and Beverly Hughes welcome you to Craiglinnhe House, a lochside Victorian villa set in spectacular scenery with superb loch and mountain views. Craiglinnhe offers period charm with modern comforts, a warm, friendly atmosphere, excellent food and a varied wine selection. Ideal base for exploring the Western Highlands.

Total number of rooms: 5

Prices from:
Double: **£25.00-40.00** Twin: **£25.00-40.00**

Dornie, Ross-shire

Eilean A Cheo Guest House

Map Ref: 3G9

Open: All year

24651

Dornie, Ardelve, Kyle, Ross-shire IV40 8DY
T: 01599 555485
E: stay@scothighland.com
W: scothighland.com

Total number of rooms: 5

Prices per room from:
Single: **POA** Double: **POA**
Twin: **POA** Family room: **POA**

Fort William, Inverness-shire

Alt-An Lodge

Map Ref: 3H12

Open: All year excl Xmas and New Year

11780

Achintore Road, Fort William, Inverness-shire PH33 6RN
T: 01397 704546
E: altanlodge@googlemail.com
W: bedandbreakfastfortwilliam.co.uk

Enjoying a superb location on the banks of Loch Linnhe. Ensuite rooms with loch views. Private parking. Quality accommodation with hearty breakfast. Town centre just a pleasant one-mile stroll along the loch-side. Ideal base for walks or touring.

Total number of rooms: 3

Prices from:
Single: **£35.00** Double: **£23.00-27.00**
Twin: **£23.00-27.00**

Scotland. The Home of Golf

For everything you need to know about golfing in Scotland and for a brochure call: 0845 22 55 121

Fort William, Inverness-shire

Argyll House

Map Ref: 3H12

★★★★ B&B

82550

Open: All year excl Xmas

Hillside Estate, Fort William PH33 6RS

T: 01397 700004

E: mairi@argyllhousebandb.co.uk

W: argyllhousebandb.co.uk

Located in Fort William town centre and with views of Loch Linnhe and the Ardgour Hills, Argyll House is ideally located for hill walking and sight seeing. Conveniently placed for train and bus stations with ample private parking. All rooms very comfortable fully ensuite and finished to a high standard.

TV P V C

Total number of rooms: 2

Prices from:

Single: **£45.00** Double: **£30.00**

Twin: **£30.00**

Fort William, Inverness-shire

Ben Nevis View

Map Ref: 3H12

★★★ B&B

14886

Open: February-October

Station Road, Corpach,
Fort William, Inverness-shire PH33 7JH

T: 01397 772131

E: info@bennevisview.co.uk

W: bennevisview.co.uk

Modern house situated on the Road to The Isles near the beginning of the Caledonian Canal. Only three miles from the centre of Fort William. Beautiful view of Ben Nevis and surrounding hills. Ample private parking. Local restaurants/pubs within walking distance. Comfortable guests lounge with Sky TV.

TV P V C

Total number of rooms: 2

Prices from:

Double: **£25.00** Twin: **£25.00**

Family room: **£75.00pr**

Fort William, Inverness-shire

Ben View Guest House

Map Ref: 3H12

★★★ GUEST HOUSE

14895

Open: March-October

Belford Road, Fort William, Inverness-shire PH33 6ER

T: 01397 702966

E: benview@gowanbrae.co.uk

TV P V

Total number of rooms: 10

Prices per room from:

Double: **£50.00** Twin: **£50.00**

Sail in Scotland

For everything you need to know about sailing in Scotland and for a brochure call

0845 22 55 121

Important: Prices stated are estimates and may be subject to amendments.

Fort William, Inverness-shire

Carna B&B

Map Ref: 3H12

★★★★ B&B

Open: All year excl Xmas

83178

Carna, Achintore Road, Fort William PH33 6RQ
T: 01397 708995
E: stay@carnabandb.co.uk
W: carnabandb.co.uk

Located on the edge of Loch Linnhe with stunning views over the Loch to the Ardgour Hills. A short walk from Fort William town centre. Carna offers modern, high quality bedroom and bathroom facilities together with comfortable residents lounge. Carna is the ideal base for exploring the Highlands and Islands.

Total number of rooms: 3

Prices from:
Double: **£40.00** Twin: **£40.00**

Fort William, Inverness-shire

The Gantocks

Map Ref: 3H12

★★★★ B&B

Open: March-November

78946

Achintore Road, Fort William PH33 6RN
T: 01397 702050
E: thegantocks@hotmail.co.uk
W: scotland2000.com/thegantocks

A luxurious little gem in a stunning location. The refurbished Gantocks is an ideal base for your Highland holiday. Personally run by hosts Sandra and Allan, Highland hospitality is assured. All the rooms have power showers (some plus bath) and sumptuous super king beds. Mallaig, Isle of Skye ferry, Oban, Loch Ness, Cairngorm National Park are all only approximately one pleasant hour away. Enjoy spectacular loch views while savouring a wide variety of homemade delights for breakfast. Free off road parking, no smoking, WiFi.

Total number of Rooms: 3

Prices from:
Single: **£70.00** Double: **£40.00-50.00**

Fort William, Inverness-shire

Kildonan

Map Ref: 3H12

★★★ B&B

Open: March-October

69520

Station Road, Corpach, Fort William PH33 7JH
T: 01397 772872
E: info@fortwilliambedandbreakfast.com
W: fortwilliambedandbreakfast.com

Total number of rooms: 2

Prices from:
Double: **£24.00-26.00** Twin: **£24.00-26.00**

Fort William, Inverness-shire

The Neuk Guest House

Map Ref: 3H12

59765

Open: All year excl Xmas and New Year

Corpach, Fort William, Inverness-shire PH33 7LR
T: 01397 772244
E: norma.mccallum@theneuk.fsbusiness.co.uk
W: fortwilliamguesthouse.com

Total number of rooms: 3

Prices per room from:

Single:	**£40.00**	Double:	**£50.00**
Twin:	**£56.00**	Family room:	**£70.00**

Fort William, Inverness-shire

Quaich Cottage

Map Ref: 3H12

50709

Open: All year excl Xmas and New Year

Upper Banavie, Fort William, Inverness-shire PH33 7PB
T: 01397 772799
E: macdonaldquaichcottage@hotmail.com
W: quaichcottage.co.uk

Having perhaps the best view in Lochaber, Quaich Cottage offers a home from home. The ideal touring base for the Western Highlands. The quiet atmosphere will help re-charge the batteries, all bedrooms are ensuite and have magnificent views of Ben Nevis and Nevis Range. Good quality restaurants close by.

Total number of rooms: 3

Prices from:

Single:	**£45.00**	Double:	**£25.00**
Twin:	**£25.00**	Family room:	**£25.00**

Fort William, Inverness-shire

St Anthonys

Map Ref: 3H12

81424

Open: All year

Argyll Road, Fort William, Inverness-shire PH33 6LF
T: 01397 708496
E: welcome@stanthonysfortwilliam.co.uk
W: stanthonysfortwilliam.co.uk

Overlooking Loch Linnhe St Anthony's offers lovely views, excellent hospitality and a great base to visit Lochaber.

Total number of rooms: 4

Prices from:

Single:	**£35.00**	Double:	**£25.00**
Family room:	**£25.00**		

Fort William, Inverness-shire

Taormina

Map Ref: 3H12

42183

★
B&B

Open: April-September

Banavie, Fort William, Inverness-shire PH33 7LY
T: 01397 772217

Total number of rooms: 4

Prices from:

Single:	**£24.00**	Double:	**£23.00**
Twin:	**£23.00**	Family room:	**£23.00**

Important: Prices stated are estimates and may be subject to amendments.

Fort William, Inverness-shire

Treetops

Map Ref: 3H12

Open: All year

67968

Badabrie, Banavie, Fort William PH33 7LX
T: 01397 772496
E: p.w737@virgin.net

An ideal base for exploring the Highlands, Treetops is located in a quiet elevated position, enjoying sweeping views of Ben Nevis, the Caledonian Canal and Loch Linnhe. The spacious, tastefully decorated ensuite bedrooms offer a high standard of accommodation. Large car park.

Total number of rooms: 3

Prices from:
Double: **£30.00** Twin: **£30.00**
Family room: **£30.00**

Glencoe, Argyll

Highland View B&B

Map Ref: 1F1

Open: All year

72867

Creag Dhu House, North Ballachulish PH33 6RY
T: 01855 821555
E: highlandviewbb@btinternet.com
W: highlandviewbandb.co.uk

Enjoy luxury accommodation set amidst magnificent Scottish Highland loch and mountain scenery. Explore the Highlands and then relax and unwind in one of our spacious, individually furnished, ensuite rooms - including superking size beds, WiFi access and satellite television. Visit our website to view our outstanding facilities in more detail.

Total number of rooms: 3

Prices from:
Double: **£27.50** Twin: **£27.50**
Family room: **£27.50**

Glencoe, Argyll

Scorrybreac Guest House

Map Ref: 1F1

Open: All year excl Xmas Day

53242

Hospital Drive, Glencoe, Argyll PH49 4HT
T: 01855 811354
E: scorrybreac@btinternet.com
W: scorrybreac.co.uk

Set on the edge of Glencoe village in an elevated tranquil spot. Scorrybreac has been modernised and upgraded over the years and offers six well appointed bedrooms with ensuite facilities. A spectacular view is offered from our spacious dining room and cosy lounge across Loch Leven and the mountains beyond.

Total number of rooms: 6

Prices from:
Single: **£38.00** Double: **£25.00**
Twin: **£25.00**

Glencoe, Argyll

Strathassynt Guest House

Map Ref: 1F1

56833

Open: All year

Loan Fern, Nr Glencoe, Ballachulish, Argyll PH49 4JB
T: 01855 811261
E: info@strathassynt.com
W: strathassynt.com

Set close to the majesty of Glencoe, Ballachulish is an ideal base for exploring the Highlands. All of our rooms have ensuite facilities, controllable heating, colour TV/DVD, hairdryer and hospitality tray. Other facilities include guest lounge, mini-bar, car parking, drying room and access to a swimming pool, jacuzzi and sauna.

Total number of rooms: 6

Prices from:

Single:	**£25.00**	Double:	**£20.00**
Twin:	**£20.00**	Family room:	**£20.00**

Invergarry, Inverness-shire

Craigard Guest House

Map Ref: 3H11

82377

Open: All year

Invergarry, Inverness-shire PH35 4HG
T: 01809 501258
E: andrew_middleton@tiscali.co.uk
W: craigard.saltire.org

Set in the splendour of Glengarry, centrally located in the Highlands, Craigard House retains many original Victorian features. An ideal base for a varied holiday exploring what this area and the surrounding Highlands has to offer. We are licensed and offer home cooked evening meals, by arrangement, Wi-Fi available.

Total number of rooms: 7

Prices from:

Single:	**£27.50**	Double:	**£25.00**
Twin:	**£25.00**		

Kinlochleven, Argyll

Edencoille Guest House

Map Ref: 3H12

24382

Open: All year

Edencoille, Garbhein Road,
Kinlochleven, Argyll PH50 4SE
T: 01855 831358
E: edencoille@tiscali.co.uk
W: kinlochlevenbedandbreakfast.co.uk

Total number of rooms: 6

Prices from:

Single:	**£50.00**	Double:	**£32.00**
Twin:	**£32.00**	Family room:	**£32.00**

Mallaig, Inverness-shire

Anchorage

Map Ref: 3F11

58031

★★★
B&B

Open: March-October

Gillies Park, Mallaig, Inverness-shire PH41 4QU
T: 01687 462454
E: anchoragemallaig@btopenworld.com
W: anchoragemallaig.co.uk

Total number of rooms: 3

Prices from:

Double: **£25.00-30.00**

Important: Prices stated are estimates and may be subject to amendments.

Mallaig, Inverness-shire

Seaview- Mallaig

Map Ref: 3F11 54062

Open: March-November

Main Street, Mallaig, Inverness-shire PH41 4QS

T: 01687 462059

E: info@seaviewguesthousemallaig.com

W: seaviewguesthousemallaig.com

Total number of rooms: 3

Prices from:

Single:	**£30.00**	Double:	**£25.00**
Twin:	**£25.00**	Family room:	**£25.00**

Onich, by Fort William

Tom-Na-Creige

Map Ref: 3G12 81362

Open: All year

Onich, Fort William PH33 6RY

T: 01855 821547

E: info@tom-na-creige.co.uk

W: tom-na-creige.co.uk

The house in the heart of the Highlands overlooks Loch Linnhe with stunning views of Glencoe and the Isle of Mull. Three of the four bedrooms are ensuite all with good views and hot drinks making facilities. Our hearty Highland breakfast is the perfect start to your day.

Total number of rooms: 4

Prices from:

Single:	**£33.00-40.00**	Double:	**£27.50**
Twin:	**£25.00**	Family room:	**£27.50**
Children (5-12):	**£15.00**		

Plockton, Ross-shire

Hill View

Map Ref: 3F9 30506

Open: All year excl Xmas

2 Frithard Road, Plockton, Ross-shire IV52 8TQ

T: 01599 544226

E: cameron_sybil@yahoo.co.uk

Total number of rooms: 3

Prices from:

Double:	**£27.50**	Twin:	**£27.50**

by Plockton, Wester Ross

Soluis Mu Thuath

Map Ref: 3F9 43723

Open: All year

Braeintra, by Achmore, by Plockton, Lochalsh
Wester Ross IV53 8UP

T: 01599 577219

E: soluismuthuath@btopenworld.com

W: highlandsaccommodation.co.uk

Set amidst open countryside with views over surrounding mountains. Excellent centre for North West of Scotland including Skye, Applecross and Torridon. No smoking. Evening meal available. Suitable for disabled accommodation.

Total number of rooms: 5

Prices from:

Single:	**£35.00**	Double:	**£25.00**
Twin:	**£25.00**	Family room:	**£25.00**

Breakish, Isle of Skye

Fernlea

Map Ref: 3F10

25826

Open: All year excl Xmas and New Year

11 Upper Breakish, Breakish, Isle of Skye IV42 8PY

T: 01471 822107

E: fernlea11@btinternet.com

W: isleofskye.net/fernlea

Total number of rooms: 3

Prices from:

Single: **£45.00** Twin: **£30.00**

Breakish, Isle of Skye

Tir Alainn

Map Ref: 3F10

61323

Open: All year

8 Upper Breakish, Breakish, Isle of Skye IV42 8PY

T: 01471 822366

E: tiralainn@btinternet.com

W: visitskye.com

Total number of rooms: 3

Prices from:

Single: **£35.00** Double: **£30.00**

Family room: **£28.00**

Broadford, Isle of Skye

Tigh an Dochais

Map Ref: 1E10

70523

Open: March-November

13 Harrapool, Broadford, Isle of Skye IV49 9AQ

T: 01471 820022

E: hopeskye@btinternet.com

W: skyebedbreakfast.co.uk

Architect designed contemporary coastal home with stunning sea and mountain views, floor to ceiling windows in bedrooms and guest lounge plus cathedral ceiling allow light to flood in. Guests are surrounded by the outdoors. Excellent breakfasts using the best of local produce. Large ensuite bedrooms open out to the beach.

Total number of rooms: 3

Prices from:

Single: **£60.00** Double: **£40.00**

Twin: **£40.00**

by Carbost, Isle of Skye

Crossal House

Map Ref: 3E8

21453

Open: All year excl Xmas and New Year

Glen Drynoch, Carbost, Isle of Skye IV47 8SP

T: 01478 640745

E: andrea@richardson9031.freeserve.co.uk

W: crossal.co.uk

Set in lovely scenic location with panoramic views of the Cuillin Mountains. Crossall House offers comfortable homely accommodation and is centrally located for touring the island with Portree, the island's capital, only 15 minutes drive and the Talisker Distillery just 5 minutes away. A paradise for walkers, climbers, birdwatchers and photographers.

Total number of rooms: 2

Prices from:

Double: **£26.00** Twin: **£26.00**

Important: Prices stated are estimates and may be subject to amendments.

Dunvegan, Isle of Skye
Roskhill Barn

Map Ref: 3D9

AWAITING GRADING

Open: All year excl Xmas and New Year 11262

Roskhill Barn, Roskhill, Dunvegan, Isle of Skye IV55 8ZD
T: 01470 521755
E: skyeholidays@aol.com
W: bedbreakfastskye.co.uk

Beautifully located near Dunvegan, Roskhill is ideal for touring the north of Skye. Experience the luxury of our cosy two bedroom apartment and enjoy a hearty cooked breakfast served in your own private dining area. Extremely comfortable accommodation is complemented by friendly service in this unique self-contained environment

Total number of rooms: 2

Prices from:
Single: **£40.00** Double: **£32.00**
Twin: **£32.00**

Dunvegan, Isle of Skye
Uiginish Farmhouse

Map Ref: 3D9

★★★ ARMHOUSE

Open: May-September 62404

Uiginish, Dunvegan, Isle of Skye IV55 8ZR
T: 01470 521431
E: heather@uiginish.co.uk

Total number of rooms: 3

Prices from:
Single: **£30.00** Double: **£26.00**
Twin: **£26.00**

Kyleakin, Isle of Skye
Blairdhu House

Map Ref: 3F9

Open: April-October 15389

Old Kyle Farm Road, Kyleakin, Isle of Skye IV14 8PR
T: 01599 534760
E: enquiries@blairdhuhouse.co.uk
W: blairdhuhouse.co.uk

Beautifully situated house amidst spectacular scenery. Minutes from Skye Bridge and five minutes from the lovely fishing village of Kyleakin. All rooms ensuite. Ideal base to stay when visiting Skye.

Total number of rooms: 6

Prices per room from:
Double: **£60.00** Twin: **£60.00**

Kyleakin, Isle of Skye
Corran Guest House

Map Ref: 3F9

Open: March-October 20496

Kyleakin, Isle of Skye IV41 8PL
T: 01599 534859
E: b&b@corranskye.co.uk
W: corranskye.co.uk

Total number of rooms: 4

Prices from:
Single: **£40.00** Double: **£30.00**
Twin: **£30.00**

Portree, Isle of Skye

Dalriada

Map Ref: 3E9

★★★ GUEST HOUSE

Open: All year excl Xmas and New Year

22096

Achachork, Portree, Isle of Skye IV51 9HT

T: 01478 612397

E: duncan.brown1@tiscali.co.uk

W: dalriadaguesthouse.co.uk

Enjoy a warm welcome and tasty breakfast in our comfortable home with relaxing guest lounge. All rooms ensuite. We are situated in a peaceful rural location with panoramic views, just 1½ miles from Portree. Dalriada makes an ideal base to explore the island and experience it's many delights.

Total number of rooms: 6

Prices from:

Single: **£25.00** Double: **£25.00**

Twin: **£25.00** Family room: **£25.00**

Portree, Isle of Skye

Stonefield

Map Ref: 3E9

★★★★ B&B

Open: All year excl Xmas and New Year

67942

Oronsay Court, Portree, Isle of Skye IV51 9TL

T: 01478 611636

E: douglas@stonefieldskye.co.uk

W: stonefieldskye.co.uk

Stonefield - Isle of Skye bed and breakfast style accommodation. Stonefield is a modern, spacious house a few minutes walk from the centre of Portree. Rosemary and Douglas Bruce promise a warm welcome to their house, great hospitality and a hearty breakfast - a perfect base for your visit to the magical Isle of Skye.

Total number of rooms: 2

Prices from:

Double: **£35.00** Twin: **£35.00**

Portree, Isle of Skye

Tir Alainn-Kildonan

Map Ref: 3E9

★★★★ B&B

Open: All year excl Xmas and New Year

79539

2a Kildonan, Edinbane, Portree, Isle of Skye IV51 9PU

T: 01470 582335

E: stay@skyebnb.co.uk

W: skyebnb.co.uk

In Gaelic 'Tir Alainn' means beautiful land. Situated at the head of Loch Greshornish with views across the Atlantic towards the Outer Hebrides it is easy to see how it is so named. Tir Alainn is a purpose built Bed and Breakfast offering ample parking, double, twin and family accommodation with ensuite bathrooms.

Total number of rooms: 3

Prices per room from:

Double: **£59.00** Twin: **£59.00**

Family room: **£100.00**

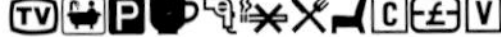

Important: Prices stated are estimates and may be subject to amendments.

Struan, Isle of Skye

Glenside

Map Ref: 3D9

Open: March-October
4 Lower Totarder, Struan, Isle of Skye IV56 8FW
T: 01470 572253

28344

Total number of rooms: 3

Prices from:

Double: **£25.00** Twin: **£25.00**

Uig, Isle of Skye

Cnoc Preasach

Map Ref: 3D8

Open: March-October
2 Peinlich, Glenhinnisdale, Isle of Skye IV51 9UY
T: 01470 542406

19855

Total number of rooms: 3

Prices from:

Single: **£25.00** Double: **£25.00**
Twin: **£25.00** Family room: **£25.00**

Uig, Isle of Skye

Mrs Mary MacLeod

Map Ref: 3D8

Open: March-October
11 Earlish, Uig, Portree, Isle of Skye IV51 9XL
T: 01470 542319

44654

Total number of rooms: 3

Prices from:

Single: **£20.00** Double: **£20.00**
Twin: **£20.00** Family room: **£55.00pr**

by Spean Bridge, Inverness-shire

Riverside House

Map Ref: 3H12

Open: All year excl Xmas and New Year
Invergloy, by Spean Bridge, Inverness-shire PH34 4DY
T: 01397 712684
E: enquiries@riversidelodge.org.uk
W: riversidelodge.org.uk

51706

Be a guest in our house. Very comfortable, ensuite room with double and single bed. 12 acres woodland gardens, private beach on Loch Lochy, river gorge. Perfect location for walking, cycling, touring or just relaxing! A bird watchers paradise, free fishing. The ultimate Highland location.

Total number of rooms: 1

Prices from:

Family room: **£35.00**

For everything you need to know about skiing and snowsports in Scotland call 0845 22 55 121

ski-scotland.com

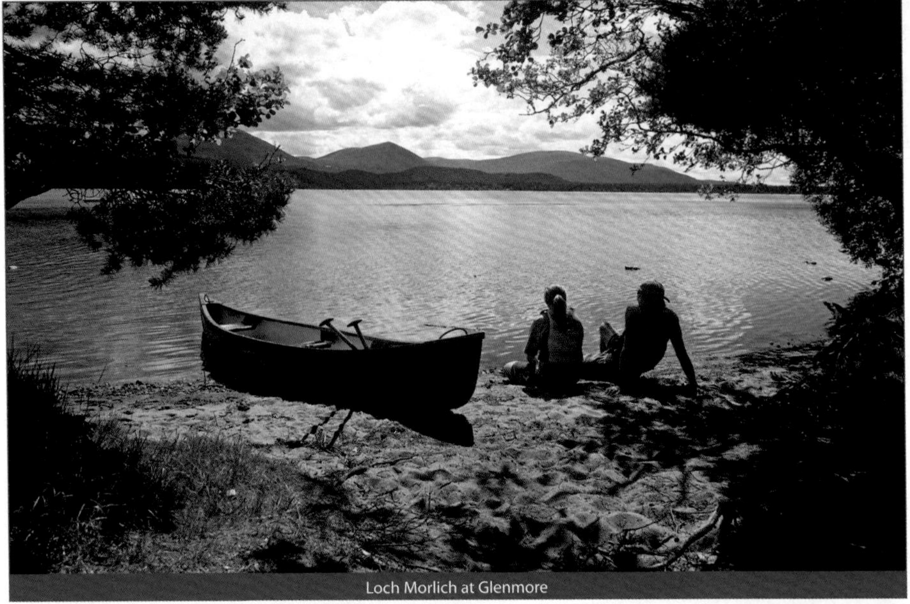

Loch Morlich at Glenmore

Moray, Aviemore and the Cairngorms

From the active lifestyle of Aviemore and the majestic beauty of the Caringorms; to the lure of Malt Whisky Country and the golden beaches of the Moray coast this is an area as contrasting as it is captivating.

There's inspiring landscape and diverse wildlife to spot so join ranger guided walks in the Cairngorms National Park or on the Moray Coast or spend an evening looking for pine marten and deer in a nature hide.

For watersports, including canoeing, sailing and windsurfing, head for Loch Insh or Loch Morlich. Hillwalkers will find the Cairngorm range is always a challenge while the more leisurely can wander to their heart's content in Rothiemurchus Estate, Culbin Forest, Craigellachie National Nature Reserve, Glenlivet Estate and many other hidden gems.

For exciting mountain bike action try cycling at Moray Monster Trails or Laggan Wolftrax and ski in the winter at CairnGorm Mountain and The Lecht. There are also lots of opportunities for golfing and fishing. You can even take a steam train trip from Aviemore to Boat of Garten and Broomhill or you can ascend Cairn Gorm on the funicular railway.

Laggan Wolftrax mountain bike trails, near Laggan,Strathspey

DON'T MISS

1 The **Cairngorms National Park** offers many events and activities throughout the year which are suitable for all ages and abilities. Visitor centres and ranger bases have leaflets, guides and trail maps to help you make the most of your time in the Park, and Visitor Information Centres throughout the area will be able to provide you with local information on events, attractions and activities.

2 At the heart of the beautiful Cairngorms National Park is the **CairnGorm Mountain Railway**. It takes 8 minutes from bottom to top, where an interactive exhibition tells the history and ecology of the surrounding area and you can see some stunning panoramic views of the National Park. Have a bite to eat and take in the view stretching from the Cairngorm plateau to the Monadliath Mountains and beyond.

3 **The Malt Whisky Trail** invites you to enjoy the wide-ranging flavour of eight malts as you wind your way through Speyside. Also on the trail is the family owned Speyside Cooperage where you can watch oak whisky barrels being constructed using traditional methods (see number 20).

4 Step back in time to the **Highland Folk Museum** with sites in Kingussie and Newtonmore, where you can experience over 400 years of Highland life. Re-constructions of an 18th century Highland township and 20th century working croft can be seen at Newtonmore. Both locations have programmes of live demonstrations and activities where you can see traditional skills and crafts in action.

5 **Johnstons** is the only Scottish mill to transform cashmere from fibre to garment and its story is told in their visitor centre and interactive exhibition in Elgin. They also have an engaging tour, tempting food hall and courtyard shop.

6 When **ospreys** returned to breed in Scotland the ancient Caledonian pinewood of Loch Garten was their first choice. Watch these magnificent birds bring fish to their chicks from the RSPB hide or on non-invasive CCTV. The reserve also has some excellent walks where you can spot red squirrels, crested tits and dragonflies. The ospreys are in residence from April till August but birds like capercaillie, redstart and goldeneye fill the calendar.

FOOD AND DRINK

eatscotland.com

7 At **The Old Bridge Inn**, on the outskirts of Aviemore, the staff are friendly and the service is excellent. A selection of meat, game and fish awaits and all dishes are cooked simply and with flair. The dining room adjacent to the bar area allows more formal and romantic dining with its open fire, and the puddings are all home-made and vary from day to day.

8 At the Speyside Heather Centre, near Dulnain Bridge, **The Clootie Dumpling** is the perfect opportunity to sample its namesake, a Scottish delicacy. This traditional and versatile pudding can be enjoyed in a variety of different ways from sweet to savoury. The recipe has a mixture of spices, carrots, apple, raisins and more, all mixed together in a 'cloot' (muslin cloth), steamed for hours and served with accompaniments.

9 Dine at **Craggan Mill** in the picturesque water mill near Grantown-on-Spey. Fine dining in a relaxed environment offers you the choice of bistro lunch or à la carte evening meal – all prepared from local, seasonal produce. Local artists exhibit paintings for view and sale within the restaurant and gallery.

10 **Minmore House Hotel** is an EatScotland Silver awarded restaurant set amid the spectacular scenery of the Glenlivit estate in Speyside. Their restaurant specialises in fine Scottish produce using only fresh, local ingredients, including some from their own kitchen garden.

7

13

14

ACTIVITIES

11 Up to 30km of fun-packed mountain biking awaits at the **Moray Monster Trails**. They work as three independent sites all linked to each other. So for those with a truly monster appetite and stamina to match, try all three sites end to end, from Fochabers to Craigellachie. For the more leisurely, the green-graded trail is at Quarrelwood, by Elgin.

12 **Inch Marshes Bird Reserve** is a birdwatching paradise! Around half of all British goldeneyes nest at Inch Marshes in spring. You're also likely to see lapwings, redshanks and curlews, as well as oystercatchers, snipe and wigeon. In winter, the marshes host flocks of whooper swans and greylag geese. Roe deer, wildcats, otters and foxes may all be seen along the edges of the marshes.

13 Enjoy year-round outdoor fun and action at the **Lecht Multi-Activity Centre**. With summer action on quad bikes, fun karts, dévalkarts and chairlift rides, winter is covered by skiing, snowboarding and tubing.

14 Take a step back in time and travel by steam engine. The **Strathspey Railway** runs from Aviemore to Broomhill (also known as Glenbogle from the TV series Monarch of the Glen) and affords beautiful views of the Cairngorms from the carriage window. To make the trip really special, you can even have afternoon tea on board.

WALKS

visitscotland.com/walking

15 **Glenmore Forest Park** has a range of walks from all-ability trails suitable for pushchairs, to longer walks through beautiful woodland which open out to give fantastic views of the Cairngorm Mountains. The Visitor Centre provides an audio-visual presentation plus café, toilets and shop.

16 Walking from **Hopeman to Lossiemouth** as part of the **Moray Coastal Trail** follows a route along the top of cliffs, giving privileged views into sandy coves and rocky headlands. There are lots of opportunities to venture onto beaches where you can relax and take in extensive views across the Moray Firth to the Black Isle and Helmsdale about 50 miles away.

17 There are a variety of waymarked trails throughout the **Rothiemurchus Estate**, with maps available from the visitor centre. The estate is teeming with Highland wildlife, including the red squirrel and the rare capercaillie, with guided tours available courtesy of Scottish Natural Heritage. Free tours on Tuesdays.

18 **Culbin Forest** meets the Moray coast between Nairn and Forres and offers cycling and walking on gentle paths with junction markers so you can make it up as you go along. Bird-watching and even the opportunity to spot otters is on offer as is a magnificent view from the 20m viewing tower at Hill 99 – a 99ft sand dune.

ATTRACTIONS

19 The **Cairngorm Reindeer Centre** is home to the only reindeer herd in the country and you can encounter the animals grazing in their natural environment. During the guided visits you can wander freely among the reindeer, stroking and feeding them. These friendly deer are a delight to all ages and, if you feel especially fond of one, you might be able to adopt it!

20 In the heart of Malt Whisky Country lies the **Speyside Cooperage**; the only working cooperage in the UK where you can experience the ancient art of producing whisky barrels.Based in Craigellachie the family owned company produces the finest casks and you can see the workers using traditional methods and tools.

Aviemore, Inverness-shire

Ardlogie Guest House

Map Ref: 4C10

76065

Open: All year

Dalfaber Road, Aviemore, Inverness-shire PH22 1PU

T: 01479 810747

E: ardlogie@btinternet.com

W: ardlogie.co.uk

Total number of rooms: 5

Prices from:

Single:	**£38.00**	Double:	**£28.00**
Twin:	**£28.00**	Family room:	**£28.00**

Aviemore, Inverness-shire

Cairn Eilrig Bed and Breakfast

Map Ref: 4C10

17397

Open: All year

Glenmore, Aviemore, Inverness-shire PH22 1QU

T: 01479 861223

E: mary@cairneilrig.com

W: bedandbreakfast-aviemore-glenmore.com

For a relaxing or active break, base yourself in this secluded home 7 miles from Aviemore in Glenmore Forest Park. All rooms with panoramic views to Cairngorm Mountains and Loch Morlich. Local knowledge on surrounding area and activities. Tea/coffee available in stunning conservatory, full Scottish breakfasts, wireless connection available.

Total number of rooms: 2

Prices from:

Double:	**£24.00**	Twin:	**£24.00**
Family room:	**£24.00**		

Aviemore, Inverness-shire

Cairngorm Guest House

Map Ref: 4C10

17434

Open: All year excl Xmas

Grampian Road, Aviemore, Inverness-shire PH22 1RP

T: 01479 810630

E: enquiries@cairngormguesthouse.com

W: cairngormguesthouse.com

Peter, Gail and staff invite you to our lovely Victorian home in the Cairngorm National Park. Some rooms on ground floor, some with mountain views, some with kingsize beds. 24 hour access, drying/storage, private parking. Real fire in guest lounge. All amenities – 10 minute walk. Ideal location.

Total number of rooms: 12

Prices from:

Single:	**£45.00**	Double:	**£30.00**
Twin:	**£30.00**	Family room:	**£90.00pr**

Aviemore, Inverness-shire

Carn Mhor

Map Ref: 4C10

69293

★★★ B&B

Open: All year

The Shieling, Aviemore, Inverness-shire PH22 1QD

T: 01479 811004

E: info@carnmhor.co.uk

W: carnmhor.co.uk

Total number of rooms: 5

Prices from:

Single:	**£40.00**	Double:	**£27.50**
Twin:	**£27.50**	Family room:	**£27.50**

Important: Prices stated are estimates and may be subject to amendments.

Aviemore, Inverness-shire
Eriskay
Map Ref: 4C10

25057

Open: All year excl Xmas

Craig na Gower Avenue, Aviemore
Inverness-shire PH22 1RW
T: 01479 810717
E: enquiry@eriskay-aviemore.co.uk
W: eriskay-aviemore.co.uk

Eriskay is a family run business situated in the centre of Aviemore offering comfortable accommodation in a quiet location. An ideal spot for walking, bird-watching, cycling, pony-trekking and touring or just relaxing in a friendly relaxed atmosphere. Perfect base for summer and winter pursuits.

Total number of rooms: 3

Prices from:
Single: **£30.00** Double: **£27.50**
Twin: **£27.50**

Aviemore, Inverness-shire
Vermont Guest House
Map Ref: 4C10

62832

Open: All year

Grampian Road, Aviemore, Inverness-shire PH22 1RP
T: 01479 810470
E: info@vermontguesthouse.co.uk
W: vermontguesthouse.co.uk

A warm welcome awaits you at our small six bedroom house. Ideally situated at quiet end of main road, only five minute walk to bars, restaurants and shops. All rooms have TV's, tea/coffee facilities and full Scottish breakfast. Opposite bus stop to take you to Cairngorms. Parking at rear of house.

Total number of rooms: 6

Prices from:
Single: **£40.00** Double: **£27.50**
Twin: **£27.50** Family room: **£70.00pr**

Carrbridge, Inverness-shire
The Cairn Hotel
Map Ref: 4C9

17400

Open: All year excl Xmas day

Main Road, Carrbridge, Inverness-shire PH23 3AS
T: 01479 841212
E: info@cairnhotel.co.uk
W: cairnhotel.co.uk

Enjoy the country pub atmosphere, log fire, malt whiskies, real ales and affordable food in this family owned village centre Inn. Close to the historic bridge, a perfect base for touring the Cairngorms, Whisky Trail and Loch Ness. Free Wi-Fi available.

Total number of rooms: 7

Prices from:
Single: **£26.00** Double: **£26.00**
Twin: **£26.00** Family room: **£70.00**

Dalwhinnie, Inverness-shire

Balsporran Cottages

Map Ref: 4B11

Open: All year excl Xmas

14107

Drumochter Pass, Dalwhinnie,
Inverness-shire PH19 1AF
T: 01528 522389
E: ann@balsporran.com
W: balsporran.com

A relaxed, informal, family run bed and breakfast set amidst the Grampian mountains. Ideally placed for touring the Cairngorms, cycling, walking, fishing or just chilling out.

Total number of rooms: 3			
Prices from:			
Single:	**£30.00**	Double:	**£30.00**
Twin:	**£30.00**		

Elgin, Moray

Richmond Bed and Breakfast

Map Ref: 4D8

Open: All year excl Xmas and New Year

51608

48 Moss Street, Elgin, Moray IV30 1LT
T: 01343 542561
E: info@elginbedandbreakfast.co.uk
W: elginbedandbreakfast.co.uk

Alison and Jock extend a warm welcome to their tastefully refurbished Victorian town house, located near railway station and town centre. Enjoy a hearty breakfast of local produce in our whisky themed dining room. Relax in the lovely sunken garden. Private parking. Short breaks available.

Total number of rooms: 3			
Prices from:			
Single:	**£35.00**	Double:	**£27.00**
Twin:	**£27.00**	Family room:	**£68.00pr**

Forres, Moray

Bain Springfield B&B

Map Ref: 4C8

Open: All year, Xmas and New Year by arrangement

55616

Croft Road, Forres, Moray IV36 3JS
T: 01309 676965
E: catherinebain@tinyworld.co.uk
W: springfieldb-b.co.uk

Total number of rooms: 2			
Prices from:			
Single:	**£35.00**	Double:	**£30.00**
Twin:	**£30.00**		

Get the most out of your stay...

Visitor Information Centres are staffed by people 'in the know', offering friendly advice, helping to make your stay in Scotland the most enjoyable ever... whatever your needs!

Live it. Visit Scotland.
visitscotland.com/wheretofindus

Important: Prices stated are estimates and may be subject to amendments.

Forres, Moray

Mayfield Bed and Breakfast

Map Ref: 2C8

★★★★ B&B

74672

Open: All year excl Xmas and New Year

Victoria Road, Forres, Moray IV36 3BN
T: 01309 671541
E: sarah@mayfieldforres.co.uk
W: mayfieldforres.co.uk

Quiet location, perfect base from which to explore Moray. Close to beaches, woods, golf courses and the Whisky Trail. Family run B&B. Vegetarians catered for. Pets by prior arrangement. Accommodation is very spacious and comfortable.

Total number of rooms: 2

Prices per room from:
Single: **£40.00** Double: **£60.00**

Grantown-on-Spey, Moray

An Cala Guest House

Map Ref: 4C9

★★★★★ GUEST HOUSE

11944

Open: All year excl Xmas

Woodlands Terrace, Grantown-on-Spey
Morayshire PH26 3JU
T: 01479 873293
E: ancala@globalnet.co.uk
W: ancala.info

Lovely large Victorian house overlooking woods yet within 12 minute walk of town centre. King and superking doubles and beautiful kingsize Castle Grant 4 poster bed. All rooms ensuite, onsite parking, freeview TVs and free WiFi access. In Cairngorm National Park.

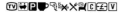

Total number of rooms: 4

Prices from:
Double: **£35.00-40.00** Twin: **£35.00-40.00**
Family room: **£32.00**

Grantown-on-Spey, Moray

Balliefurth Farm

Map Ref: 4C9

★★★ FARMHOUSE

74021

Open: May-October

Grantown-on-Spey, Moray PH26 3NH
T: 01479 821636
E: a.maclennan@totalise.co.uk
W: scottishholidayhomes.co.uk

A warm welcome awaits you to our beautiful home, a working, family run, beef and sheep farm in the Highlands of Scotland. Taste the dinners and breakfasts incorporating our own beef and lamb and other produce sourced from the same farmer's market where we sell our produce.

Total number of rooms: 2

Prices from:
Single: **£42.50** Double: **£32.50**
Twin: **£32.50**

Grantown-on-Spey, Moray

Dunallan House

Map Ref: 4C9

★★★★ GUEST HOUSE

77401

Open: All year

Woodside Avenue, Grantown on Spey
Morayshire PH26 3JN
T: 01479 872140
E: enquiries@dunallan.com
W: dunallan.com

Stay in comfortable and spacious accommodation, all our bedrooms are ensuite with great attention to detail and comfort. Beautiful breakfast and sitting rooms with log-fires. We offer an extensive breakfast menu including fresh fruit, organic yoghurt and cereal, local smoked salmon and the full Scottish cooked breakfast. Your perfect Highland stay!

Total number of rooms: 7

Prices from:

Single: **£40.00** Double: **£30.00**
Twin: **£30.00** Family room: **£80.00pr**

Grantown-on-Spey, Moray

Garden Park Guest House

Map Ref: 4C9

★★★ GUEST HOUSE

27235

Open: All year

Woodside Avenue, Grantown-on-Spey
Moray PH26 3JN
T: 01479 873235
E: gardenpark@waitrose.com
W: garden-park.co.uk

Total number of rooms: 5

Prices from:

Single: **£30.00** Double: **£29.00**
Twin: **£29.00**

Kincraig, Inverness-shire

Braeriach Guest House

Map Ref: 4C10

★★★★ GUEST HOUSE

16028

Open: All year

Braeriach Road, Kincraig, Kingussie
Inverness-shire PH21 1NA
T: 01540 651369
E: fiona@braeriachgh.com
W: braeriachgh.com

Set in a beautiful riverside location with stunning views of the Cairngorm Mountains beyond. Accommodation is very comfortable with all rooms decorated to a high standard. Enjoy a very tasty breakfast overlooking the River Spey and mountains or on outdoor patio when weather permits.

Total number of rooms: 3

Prices from:

Single: **£50.00** Double: **£38.00**
Twin: **£38.00**

Kincraig, Inverness-shire

Insh House Guest House

Map Ref: 4C10

★★★ GUEST HOUSE

26768

Open: Boxing Day-end October

Kincraig, Kingussie, Inverness-shire PH21 1NU
T: 01540 651377
E: inshhouse@btinternet.com
W: kincraig.com/inshhouse

Total number of rooms: 5

Prices from:

Single: **£26.00-30.00** Double: **£26.00-30.00**
Twin: **£26.00-30.00** Family room: **£26.00-30.00**

Important: Prices stated are estimates and may be subject to amendments.

Kingussie, Inverness-shire

The Hermitage Guest House

Map Ref: 4B11

59243

Open: All year

Spey Street, Kingussie, Inverness-shire PH21 1HN
T: 01540 662137
E: thehermitage@clara.net
W: thehermitage-scotland.com

Total number of rooms: 5			
Prices per room from:			
Single:	**£40.00**	Double:	**£60.00**
Twin:	**£60.00**	Family room:	**£70.00**

Newtonmore, Inverness-shire

Alvey House

Map Ref: 4B11

11819

Open: All year

Golf Course Road,
Newtonmore, Inverness-shire PH20 1AT
T: 01540 673260
E: enquiries@alveyhouse.co.uk
W: alveyhouse.co.uk

Total number of rooms: 7			
Prices from:			
Single:	**£24.50**	Double:	**£24.50**
Twin:	**£24.50**	Family room:	**£24.50**

Newtonmore, Inverness-shire

The Rumblie

Map Ref: 4B11

60279

Open: All year

Laggan, Newtonmore PH20 1AH
T: 01528 544766
E: mail@rumblie.com
W: rumblie.com

The Rumblie is a friendly and relaxed Highland home within the Cairngorms National Park, ideally situated for exploring the area with mountain biking and lots of walking opportunities (cycle store and well equipped drying room). All bedrooms are beautifully decorated, spacious and well equipped with mountain views. Two rooms have king size beds and one ground floor twin room. Freeview satellite LCD TV with DVD player, hospitality tray and adjustable central heating, all with ensuite facilties. Comfortable lounge and dining sunroom with our focus on organic and Fairtrade products. No single supplements applied and dinner available by arrangement.

Total number of rooms: 3			
Prices from:			
Double:	**£30.00**	Twin:	**£30.00**

visitscotland.com/walking

For everything you need to know about walking in Scotland and for a brochure Call 0845 22 55 121
Scotland. Created for Walking

Warebeth Beach, Stromness, Orkney

THE OUTER ISLANDS

Outer Hebrides, Orkney, Shetland

There's something very special about island holidays and Scotland has so many wonderful islands to explore.

On an island holiday, you can leave all the stresses of mainland life far behind. You don't have to settle for just one destination either – try a bit of island hopping, there's a lot of choice.

A different pace

At Scotland's western edge, the Outer Hebrides look out to the Atlantic swell and life moves at a relaxed pace. In this last Gaelic stronghold, a warm welcome awaits.

You can get there by ferry from Oban or from Uig on Skye – ferry prices to the Outer Hebrides have been reduced for 2009. Or travel by plane - fly to Barra and you'll land on the beach at low tide!

Lewis is the largest of the Outer Hebrides with a busy town at Stornoway and historical sites like the standing stones at Calanais stretching back over 3,000 years. It's distinctly different from the more mountainous Harris. Don't forget to visit the traditional weavers making wonderful Harris Tweed.

North and South Uist, Benbecula, Eriskay and Barra are all well worth a visit too and each has its own attractions.

Life at the crossroads

Island life can also be experienced in Scotland's two great northern archipelagos. Some 70 islands make up Orkney with 21 inhabited. Shetland, at the crossroads where the Atlantic meets the North Sea, has over 100 islands and is home to around 22,000 people and well over a million seabirds.

In Orkney, you can see the oldest houses in northern Europe at Papa Westray, dating back to 3800 BC.

The influence of the Vikings in these parts is everywhere. Orcadians spoke Old Norse until the mid 1700s and the ancient Viking Parliament used to meet at Scalloway in Shetland.

These islands enjoy long summer days and at midsummer it never really gets dark. You can even play midnight golf in the 'Simmer Dim'.

In winter, the nights are long but the islanders have perfected the art of indoor life. Musicians fill the bars and community halls and there always seems to be something to celebrate.

Two great unmissable events are the winter fire festival of Up Helly Aa in Lerwick, Shetland and the Ba' in Kirkwall, Orkney, where up to 400 players take to the streets for a game of rough and tumble that is somewhere between football, rugby and all-out war.

Have a wild time

Orkney and Shetland are a joy for wildlife watchers. There are millions of birds to observe as well as otters, seals, dolphins and whales. Being surrounded by sea, angling, yachting, sea kayaking, cruising and diving are readily available.

B&B establishments are an important part of island life and there are many superb places to stay including traditional crofts, farms, villas, seaside cottages and other family homes. Once you've made your choice, however, you should book quickly as island holidays are always a popular choice.

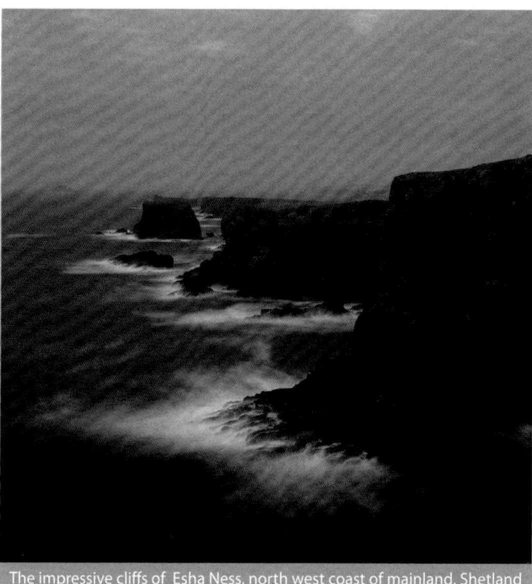

The impressive cliffs of Esha Ness, north west coast of mainland, Shetland

What's On?

Orkney Jazz Weekend
24 – 26 April 2009
A weekend of jazz with local and visiting performers.
stromnesshotel.com

Shetland Folk Festival
30 April – 3 May 2009
The UK's most northerly folk festival is regarded a prestigious event for performers, locals and visitors alike.
shetlandfolkfestival.com

Orkney Folk Festival
21 – 24 May 2009
The best in modern and traditional folk music.
orkneyfolkfestival

Johnsmas Foy
18 – 28 June 2009
Recently revived festival that used to mark the arrival of the Dutch herring fleet in Shetland.
johnsmasfoy.com

St Magnus Festival
19 – 24 June 2009, Kirkwall
Midsummer celebration of the Arts.
stmagnusfestival.co.uk

Lewis Golf Week
July 2009, Stornoway
A week of golf at Stornoway Golf Club.

Taransay Fiddle Week
July 2009
Learn new skills from leading fiddlers.

Creative Connections
3 - 9 August 2009
Learn arts and crafts, traditional fiddle playing and the art of storytelling.

Harris Arts Festival
August 2009 – various dates
Celebrate arts and crafts on the island.

DON'T MISS

1 The combination of peace and tranquillity that can be found throughout the Outer Hebrides, blended with the vibrant nature of the people and their language, has been a true inspiration to many. This is demonstrated in the islands' crafts, music and culture. Arts venues such as **An Lanntair** in Stornoway and **Taigh Chearsabhagh** in Uist often attract internationally renowned performers.

2 The 5,000 year old **Calanais Standing Stones** on the west side of Lewis are one of the most famous landmarks in the Outer Hebrides. Second only to Stonehenge, these mystical stones are unique in their cross-shaped layout which has caused endless fascinating debate. Check out the visitor centre to form your own opinion!

3 **Seallam!** Visitor Centre in Northton at the southern end of the beautiful Isle of Harris provides a variety of exhibitions for both first-time and returning visitors. Browse among exhibits about the history and natural environment of the Hebrides, and find out what has influenced the development of the various island communities. Whether you wish to spend an hour or a whole day, there is plenty to occupy your attention. There is even a tea and coffee bar and a small craft-shop.

4 The area around **Loch Druidibeg** on South Uist is a National Nature Reserve with many different habitats including freshwater, brackish lagoon, dune, machair, peatland and scrub woodland. The loch itself is shallow but very large, with many islands: one of which is home to a resident colony of herons. The greylag geese which breed around the loch contribute to the resident population that remain in the Uists all year. Birds of prey include golden eagle, hen harriers, kestrel, peregrine and merlin.

5 **Kisimul Castle** is a sight to behold, situated in the bay of Castlebay Village on Barra. The stronghold of the MacNeils of Barra, this is the only surviving medieval castle in the Hebrides. Day tickets to visit the castle can be obtained at the local Visitor Information Centre.

2

8

9

ACTIVITIES

7 There are five official **golf** courses in the Hebrides: in Barra, Uist, Benbecula, Harris and Lewis. The 9-hole course at Scarista on Harris, in particular, is legendary for its stunning setting and challenging situation. You may think it's an easy option but the small greens, massive sand dunes and ever-present Atlantic winds combine for an enjoyable round!

8 The **surf** around the Hebrides is so good that the area is now on the map for international lovers of the sport. With over 70 beaches from white shell sands to pebble shores and almost always empty, it really is a surfer's paradise. The Isle of Lewis is positioned so it receives swells from almost every direction and is classed as having the most consistent surf in Europe.

9 With some of the most beautiful coastline in Britain and warmer water temperatures, the Hebrides is the perfect wilderness to explore by **kayak**. See otters, dolphins and puffins as you glide through the crystal clear waters around the islands. The coastline is a labyrinth of complex bays, inlets, dramatic cliffs, secret coves, sandy beaches and offshore islands.... a sea paddler's paradise.

10 The Outer Hebrides is a game angler's dream location and will fill you with all the emotions and pleasures associated with this wonderful and rewarding sport. Whether you are a solitary angler, form part of a larger group or simply looking for a tranquil family vacation, the Outer Hebrides has it all - namely, some of the best summer salmon and trout **fishing** in Europe set amidst spectacular scenery.

DON'T MISS

1 **Skara Brae** (B9056, 19 miles from Kirkwall) is an unrivalled example of life in Stone Age Orkney. Without doubt the best preserved village in western Europe, the houses contain stone beds, dressers, hearths and drains, giving a fantastic insight into how life was 5,000 years ago. Together with several other historical sites, it is part of a designated World Heritage Site.

2 Discovered in 1958, the **Tomb of the Eagles** is a 5,000 year old tomb containing ceremonial tools, beds, talons and other bones of the white-tailed eagle, pottery and working tools.

3 In the heart of Orkney's main town, Kirkwall, lies **St Magnus Cathedral**. It was built in 1137 by Earl Rognvald, in memory of his cousin Magnus who was earlier murdered by another cousin, Haakon, co-ruler at that time. Today the beautiful sandstone building continues to be a place of worship for the local people.

4 **The Pier Arts Centre** was reopened in 2007 and houses a remarkable collection of 20th century British art. The Collection charts the development of modern art in Britain and includes key work by Barbara Hepworth, Ben Nicholson and Naum Gabo amongst others.

5 Orkney is blessed with an abundance of birds and marine **wildlife**. Late spring sees the arrival of thousands of breeding seabirds including everybody's favourite – the colourful puffin. Grey seals breed in huge numbers around the coast in late autumn, while whales, dolphins and porpoises are regularly sighted off-shore throughout the summer. Wildlife is everywhere, and with a diverse range of professional guiding services there is something to suit everyone.

HISTORY AND HERITAGE

6 **The Ring of Brodgar** and the **Standing Stones of Stenness** (both just off the B9055) are also included within the World Heritage Site. Undeniably mystical, these spiritual places reward visitors with a real sense of ancient times.

7 **Maeshowe** is a central feature of the Neolithic Orkney World Heritage Site. A chambered cairn (off the A965), it is considered to be one of the finest architectural achievements of its time, around 5,000 years ago. Timed ticketing is in operation, allowing the informative guides to point out all the interesting aspects of the site, including Viking graffiti.

8 The **Broch of Gurness** at Aikerness (A966) is a well-organised Iron Age village, giving fascinating insight into community life 2,000 years ago.

9 Travel across the first of the Churchill Barriers to see an artistic phenomenon at the **Italian Chapel**. Built by Italian POWs in WWII, using only the most modest of materials, the intricate interior is all the more impressive.

DON'T MISS

1 Whatever your interests, there is something to suit every taste in Shetland. Our beautiful landscape is perfect for **walkers** – offering everything from coastal treks to energetic hikes. There are over 300 lochs holding brown trout and sea fishing is superb.

2 **Midsummer** is an especially magical time in Shetland when there are almost 19 hours of daylight to enjoy. It never really gets dark at this time of year – the other five hours between sunrise and sunset are filled with an eerie lingering twilight that's known locally as the "Simmer Dim".

3 Ever since **bird watching** became a popular British leisure pursuit in the late 19th century, Shetland's been famous, among those in the know, as the place to enjoy sensational seabird colonies and amazing rarities. If you want a close-up view of tens of thousands of breeding gannets, alongside guillemots, puffins, razorbills, kittiwakes and fulmars, then head for Sumburgh Head, Noss or Hermaness Nature Reserves.

4 Built on the historic site of Hay's Dock, is the impressive new **Shetland Museum and Archives** offers a rich insight into the development of Shetland from its geological beginnings to present day. See the museum's outstanding collection of historic boats hanging in the dramatic three-storey boat hall.

5 The accessibility of Shetland's coastline is ideal for **sea kayakers**. There are hundreds of miles of cliffs and deserted beaches as well as some of Europe's finest sea caves. Enjoy stunning cliff scenery, stack, arches and sheltered inlets. There are large colonies of seals and seabirds, most of them easily reachable by sea.

3

8

ATTRACTIONS

6 One of the best places to enjoy the cliff scenery by road is **Eshaness Lighthouse**, perched above a precipice of volcanic lava. A short walk away is an impressive collapsed cave, Da Hols o' Scraada ('the Devil's Caves'). Nearby is Da Grind o' da Navir ('Gate of the Borer'), a huge gateway in the cliffs where the sea has ripped out a huge chunk of rock and hurled it inland.

7 **Shetland Crofthouse**, Boddam, is a typical thatched crofthouse of the 19th century restored with traditional materials. The layout of the house is similar to Norse houses from 1,000 years earlier. The sweet smell of peat smoke, thick walls and cramped living space will instantly take you back to life in 1870s.

8 The broch, or fortified Iron Age tower, on the little island of Mousa is the only one in the world to have survived almost complete for more than 2,000 years. Built as a refuge against raiding local tribes, **Mousa Broch** is a wonder of archaeology, not to mention ornithology. Tiny storm petrels nest in its stone, visiting the broch only after dark – a night excursion to hear their eerie calls is an experience not to be missed.

9 A recent archaeological dig at **Old Scatness Broch**, next to Sumburgh Airport, has revealed one of Britain's most exciting Iron Age villages, with many buildings standing at or near roof height and some still even 'decorated' with yellow clay! Buried for nearly 2,000 years, the site is rich in artefacts and remarkably well preserved.

MAP

Live it. Visit Scotland.
visitscotland.com/wheretofindus

©Collins Bartholomew Ltd 2008

VISITOR INFORMATION CENTRES

Visitor Information Centres are staffed by people 'in the know' offering friendly advice, helping to make your stay in Scotland the most enjoyable ever . . . whatever your needs!

Outer Hebrides		
Stornoway	26 Cromwell Street, Stornoway, Isle of Lewis, HS1 2DD	Tel: 01851 703088
Orkney		
Kirkwall	The Travel Centre, West Castle Street, Kirkwall, Orkney KW15 1GU	Tel: 01856 872856
Shetland		
Lerwick	Market Cross, Lerwick, Shetland, ZE1 0LU	
Sumburgh (Airport)	Wilsness Terminal, Sumburgh Airport, Shetland ZE3 9JP	Tel: 01595 693434

LOCAL KNOWLEDGE • WHERE TO STAY • ACCOMMODATION BOOKING • PLACES TO VISIT • THINGS TO DO • MAPS AND GUIDES • TRAVEL ADVICE • ROUTE PLANNING • WHERE TO SHOP AND EAT • LOCAL CRAFTS AND PRODUCE • EVENT INFORMATION • TICKETS

For information and ideas about exploring Scotland in advance of your trip, call our booking and information service **0845 22 55 121** or go to **visitscotland.com**

If calling from outside the UK and Ireland **+44 1506 832 121** From Ireland **1800 932 510**

A £4 booking fee applies for accommodation bookings made via a Visitor Information Centre and through our booking and information service.

Kirkwall, Orkney

Sanderlay Guest House

Map Ref: 5B12

52953

Open: All year excl Xmas

2 Viewfield Drive, Kirkwall, Orkney KW15 1RB
T: 01856 875587
E: enquiries@sanderlay.co.uk
W: sanderlay.co.uk

Total number of rooms: 8

Prices from:

Single:	**£35.00**	Double:	**£30.00**
Twin:	**£30.00**	Family room:	**£25.00**

Shapinsay, Orkney

Hilton Farmhouse B&B

Map Ref: 5C12

30618

Open: All year

Shapinsay, Orkney KW17 2EA
T: 01856 711239
E: info@hiltonorkneyfarmhouse.co.uk
W: hiltonorkneyfarmhouse.co.uk

Relax, enjoy and savour in a beautiful island location with a warm welcome. Relaxed, you will enjoy great food freshly prepared from homegrown or local produce. Dine in our new lounge and conservatory restaurant with panoramic sea views over Orkney's main shipping channel, Balfour Village and harbour. Island package tours available.

Total number of rooms: 2

Prices from:

Single:	**£35.00**	Double:	**£30.00**
Twin:	**£30.00**		

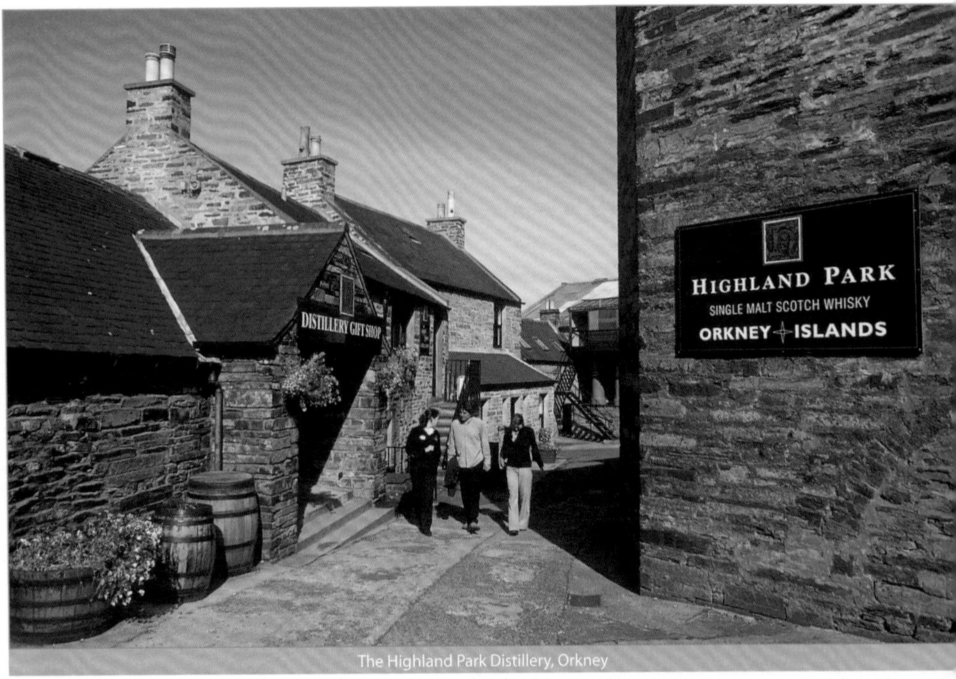

The Highland Park Distillery, Orkney

Important: Prices stated are estimates and may be subject to amendments.

Directory of all VisitScotland Assured Serviced Establishments, ordered by location.

Establishments highlighted have an advertisement in this guide.

Aberdeen

Name	Address	Telephone	Grade	Type	Access
20 Louisville Avenue	Aberdeen, Aberdeenshire, AB10 6TX	01224 319812	★★★	Bed & Breakfast	
Abbotswell Guest House	28 Abbotswell Crescent, Aberdeen, Aberdeenshire, AB12 5AR	01224 871788	★★★	Guest House	
Aberdeen Guest House	218 Great Western Road, Aberdeen, Aberdeenshire, AB10 6PD	01224 211733	★★★	Guest House	
Adelphi Guest House	8 Whinhill Road, Aberdeen, Aberdeenshire, AB11 7XH	01224 583078	★★★	Guest House	
Aldersyde Guest House	138 Bon Accord Street, Aberdeen, Aberdeenshire, AB11 6TX	01224 580012	★★★	Guest House	
Aldridge	60 Hilton Drive, Aberdeen, Aberdeenshire, AB24 4NP	01224 485651	★★★	Bed & Breakfast	
Antrim Guest House	157 Crown Street, Aberdeen, Aberdeenshire, AB11 6HT	01224 590987	★★	Guest House	
Arden Guest House	61 Dee Street, Aberdeen, Aberdeenshire, AB10 2EE	01224 580700	★★★	Guest House	
Arkaig Guest House	43 Powis Terrace, Aberdeen, Aberdeenshire, AB25 3PP	01224 638872	★★★	Guest House	
Armadale Guest House	605 Holburn Street, Aberdeen, Aberdeenshire, AB10 7JN	01224 580636	★★★	Guest House	
Ashgrove Guest House	34 Ashgrove Road, Aberdeen, Aberdeenshire, AB25 3AD	01224 484861	★★★	Guest House	
Beeches	193 Great Western Road, Aberdeen, Aberdeenshire, AB10 6PS	01224 586413	★★★	Guest House	
Bimini Guest House	69 Constitution Street, Aberdeen, Aberdeenshire, AB24 5ET	01224 646912	★★★	Guest House	
Brentwood Villa	560 King Street, Aberdeen, Aberdeenshire, AB24 5SR	01224 480633	★★★	Guest House	
Burnett Guest House	75 Constitution Street, Aberdeen, Aberdeenshire, AB24 5ET	01224 647995	★★★	Guest House	
Butler's Islander Guest House	122 Crown Street, Aberdeen, Aberdeenshire, AB11 6HJ	01224 212411	★★★	Guest House	
Cedars Guest House	339 Great Western Road, Aberdeen, Aberdeenshire, AB10 6NW	01224 583225	★★★	Guest House	
Crombie House	University of Aberdeen, Aberdeen, Aberdeenshire, AB24 3TS	01224 273444	★★	Campus	(Assisted wheelchair access)
Dun Laoire	430 King Street, Aberdeen, Aberdeenshire, AB24 3BS	01224 634406	★★★	Bed & Breakfast	
Dunrovin Guest House	168 Bon-Accord Street, Aberdeen, Aberdeenshire, AB11 6TX	01224 586081	★★★	Guest House	
Ellenville Guest House	50 Springbank Terrace, Aberdeen, Aberdeenshire, AB11 6LR	01224 213334	★★★	Guest House	
Fairview	112 Fairview Circle, Aberdeen, Aberdeenshire, AB22 8YR	01224 824622	★★	Bed & Breakfast	
Furain Guest House	92 North Deeside Road, Peterculter, Aberdeen, Aberdeenshire, AB14 0QN	01224 732189	★★★	Guest House	
Granville Guest House	401 Great Western Road, Aberdeen, Aberdeenshire, AB10 6NY	01224 313043	★★★	Guest House	
Kildonan Guest House	410 Great Western Road, Aberdeen, Aberdeenshire, AB10 6NR	01224 316115	★★★	Guest House	
King's Hall	University of Aberdeen, Aberdeen, Aberdeenshire, AB24 3FX	01224 273444	★★	Campus	(Unassisted wheelchair access)
Macleans B&B	8 Boyd Orr Avenue, Aberdeen, Aberdeenshire, AB12 5RG	01224 248726	★★	Bed & Breakfast	
Merkland Guest House	12 Merkland Road East, Aberdeen, Aberdeenshire, AB24 5PR	01224 634451	★★	Guest House	
Noble Guest House	376 Great Western Road, Aberdeen, Aberdeenshire, AB10 6PH	01224 313678	★★★	Guest House	
Open Hearth Guest House	349 Holburn Street, Aberdeen, Aberdeenshire, AB10 7FQ	01224 591675	★★	Guest House	

Unassisted wheelchair access   Assisted wheelchair access   Access for visitors with mobility difficulties

Bronze Green Tourism Award   Silver Green Tourism Award   Gold Green Tourism Award

For further information on our Green Tourism Business Scheme please see page 9.

Penny Meadow	189 Great Western Road, Aberdeen, Aberdeenshire, AB10 6PS	01224 588037	★★★★	Guest House	
Roselea House	12 Springbank Terrace, Aberdeen, Aberdeenshire, AB10 2LS	01224 583060	★★★	Guest House	
Royal Crown Guest House	111 Crown Street, Aberdeen, Aberdeenshire, AB11 2HN	01224 586461	★★★	Guest House	
St Elmo	64 Hilton Drive, Aberdeen, Aberdeenshire, AB24 4NP	01224 483065	★★★★	Guest House	
Struan	Echt, Westhill, Aberdeen, Aberdeenshire, AB32 6UL	01330 860799	★★★★	Bed & Breakfast	
The Globe Inn	13-15 North Silver Street, Aberdeen, Aberdeenshire, AB10 1RJ	01224 624258	★★★	Inn	
The Jays Guest House	422 King Street, Aberdeen, Aberdeenshire, AB24 3BR	01224 638295	★★★★	Guest House	
Travelodge Aberdeen	9 Bridge Street, Aberdeen, Aberdeenshire, AB11 6JL	08719 846117	AWAITING GRADING		
Travelodge Aberdeen Aiport	Burnside Drive Off Riverview Drive, Dyce, Aberdeen, Aberdeenshire, AB21 0HW	0871 984 6309	AWAITING GRADING		

By Aberdeen

Travelodge Aberdeen Bucksburn	A96 Inverurie Road, Bucksburn, By Aberdeen, Aberdeenshire, AB21 0HW	08719 846118	AWAITING GRADING		
Craibstone Estate	Scottish Agricultural College,Craibstone Estate, Bucksburn, By Aberdeen,	01224 711012	★★	Campus	
Old Mill Inn	South Deeside Road, Maryculter, By Aberdeen, Aberdeenshire, AB12 5FX	01224 733212	★★★	Inn	
Avalon B&B	17 Denhead Crescent, Potterton, By Aberdeen, Aberdeenshire, AB23 8UA	01358 742619	★★★	Bed & Breakfast	
Parkview	Potterton, By Aberdeen, Aberdeenshire, AB23 8UY	01358 743299	★★★	Bed & Breakfast	
Viewfield	Panmure Gardens, Potterton, By Aberdeen, Aberdeenshire, AB23 8UG	01358 742605	★★★	Bed & Breakfast	
Kilnhall	Strawberry Field Road, Westhill, By Aberdeen, Aberdeenshire, AB32 6TB	01224 279640	★★★★	Guest House	

Aberdour

The Cedar Inn	20 Shore Road, Aberdour, Fife, KY3 0TR	01383 860310	★★	Inn	

Aberfeldy

6 The Beeches	Kenmore Road, Aberfeldy, Perthshire, PH15 2BZ	01887 829490	★★★★	Bed & Breakfast	
Ardtalnaig Lodge	Ardtalnaig, Aberfeldy, Perthshire, PH15 2HX	01567 820771	★★★	Bed & Breakfast	
Ardtornish	Kenmore Street, Aberfeldy, Perthshire, PH15 2BL	01887 820629	★★★	Bed & Breakfast	
Balnearn House	Crieff Road, Aberfeldy, Perthshire, PH15 2BJ	01887 820431	★★★	Guest House	
Cedar House	30a Chapel Street, Aberfeldy, Perthshire, PH15 2AS	01887 820779	★★★	Bed & Breakfast	
Coshieville House	By Keltneyburn, Aberfeldy, Perthshire, PH15 2NE	01887 830319	★★★	Guest House	
Fernbank House	Kenmore Street, Aberfeldy, Perthshire, PH15 2BL	01887 820486	★★★★	Bed & Breakfast	
Lurgan Farm	Edradynate, Aberfeldy, Perthshire, PH15 2JX	01887 840451	★★	Farmhouse	
Old Police Station	30 Chapel Street, Aberfeldy, Perthshire, PH15 2AS	01887 822980	★★★	Bed & Breakfast	
Tigh'n Eilean	Taybridge Drive, Aberfeldy, Perthshire, PH15 2BP	01887 820109	★★★★	Bed & Breakfast	
Tomvale	Tom of Cluny, Aberfeldy, Perthshire, PH15 2JT	01887 820171	★★★	Farmhouse	Assisted wheelchair access

Unassisted wheelchair access   Assisted wheelchair access   Access for visitors with mobility difficulties
Bronze Green Tourism Award   Silver Green Tourism Award   Gold Green Tourism Award

For further information on our Green Tourism Business Scheme please see page 9.

Directory of all VisitScotland Assured Serviced Establishments, ordered by location.
Establishments highlighted have an advertisement in this guide.

By Aberfeldy

Ailean Chraggan Hotel, Weem	By Aberfeldy, Perthshire, PH15 2LD	01887 820346	★★★	Inn	

Aberfoyle

Craigmore Guest House	Lochard Road, Aberfoyle, Stirlingshire, FK8 3SZ	01877 382536	★★★	Guest House	
Crannaig House	Trossachs Road, Aberfoyle, Stirlingshire, FK8 3SR	01877 382276	★★★	Guest House	Assisted wheelchair access; Gold Green Tourism Award
Inverard Lodge B&B	Lochard Road, Aberfoyle, Stirlingshire, FK8 3TD	01877 389113	★★★	Bed & Breakfast	
StoneyPark	Lochard Road, Aberfoyle, Stirlingshire, FK8 3SZ	01877 382208	★★★	Bed & Breakfast	
The Bield	Trossachs Road, Aberfoyle, Perthshire, FK8 3SX	01877 382351	★★★★	Bed & Breakfast	
The Forth Inn	Main Street, Aberfoyle, Perthshire, FK8 3UQ	01877 382372	★★★	Inn	Bronze Green Tourism Award

Aberlady

Kilspindie House Hotel	High Street, Aberlady, Longniddry, EH32 0RE	01875 870682	★★★	Restaurant with Rooms	

Aberlour

Lynwood Bed and Breakfast	Elchies, Craigellachie, Aberlour, Moray, AB38 9SQ	01340 871801	★★★★	Bed & Breakfast	
Norlaggan	22 High Street, Aberlour, Moray, AB38 9QD	01340 871270	★★★	Bed & Breakfast	

Aberuthven

Kilrymont	8 Loanfoot Park, Aberuthven, Perthshire, PH3 1JF	01764 662660	★★★★	Bed & Breakfast	
Smiddy Haugh Hotel	Main Road, Aberuthven, Perthshire, PH3 1HE	01764 662013	★★	Inn	

Aboyne

Chesterton House	Formaston Park, Aboyne, Aberdeenshire, AB34 5HF	013398 86740	★★	Bed & Breakfast	Access for visitors with mobility difficulties
Dinnet House	Aboyne, Aberdeenshire, AB34 5LN	01339 885332	★★★★	Bed & Breakfast	
Glendavan House	Dinnet, Aboyne, Aberdeenshire, AB34 5LU	013398 81610	★★★★★	Bed & Breakfast	
Newton of Drumgesk	Dess, Aboyne, Aberdeenshire, AB34 5BL	01339 886203	★★	Bed & Breakfast	
The Commercial Hotel	The Square,Tarland, Aboyne, Aberdeenshire, AB34 4TX	01339 881922	★★★	Inn	

By Acharacle

Tigh A'Ghobhainn	Kilchoan, By Acharacle PH36 4LH	01972 570771	★★★	Bed & Breakfast	

Achmore, Isle of Lewis

Cleascro House	Achmore, Isle of Lewis HS2 9DU	01851 860302	★★★★	Guest House	

by Achmore, Isle of Lewis

Soluis Mu Thuath	Braeintra, by Achmore, Isle of Lewis IV53 8UP	01599 577219	★★★	Guest House	Access for visitors with mobility difficulties

Achnasheen

Merlinwood	Kinlochewe, Achnasheen, Ross-shire, IV22 2PA	01445 760346	★★★	Bed & Breakfast	

Unassisted wheelchair access · Assisted wheelchair access · Access for visitors with mobility difficulties
Bronze Green Tourism Award · Silver Green Tourism Award · Gold Green Tourism Award

For further information on our Green Tourism Business Scheme please see page 9.

Torridon Inn	Torridon, Achnasheen, Ross-shire, IV22 2EY	01445 791242	★★★	Inn	

By Achnasheen

Hillhaven Bed & Breakfast	Kinlochewe, By Achnasheen, Ross-Shire, IV22 2PA	01445 760204	★★★	Bed & Breakfast	
The Sheiling	3 Achgarve, Laide, By Achnasheen, Ross-shire, IV22 2NS	01445 731487	★★★★	Bed & Breakfast	
Old Smiddy Guest House	Laide, By Achnasheen, Ross-shire, IV22 2NB	01445 731696	★★★★	Bed & Breakfast	

Aignish, Isle of Lewis

Ceol-Na-Mara	1a, Aignish, Isle of Lewis HS2 0PB	01851 870339	★★★	Bed & Breakfast	

Airdrie

Easter Glentore Farm	Slamannan Road, Greengairs, Airdrie, Lanarkshire, ML6 7TJ	01236 830243	★★★★	Farmhouse	Silver Green Tourism Award
Knight's Rest	150 Clark Street, Airdrie, Lanarkshire, ML6 6DZ	01236 606193	★★★	Guest House	
Shawlee Cottage	108 Luachope Street, Chapellhall, Airdrie, Lanarkshire, ML6 8SW	01236 753774	★★★	Bed & Breakfast	

By Airdrie

Craigpark House B&B	57 Airdrie Road, Caldercruix, By Airdrie, Lanarks, ML6 8PA	01236 843211	★★★	Bed & Breakfast	

Alexandria, Loch Lomond

Albannach	274 Main Street, Alexandria, Loch Lomond, West Dumbartonshire, G83 0NU	01389 603345	★★★★	Bed & Breakfast	
Cloudside	Overton Road, Alexandria, Loch Lomond, Dunbartonshire, G83 0LJ	01389 601588	★★★★	Bed & Breakfast	
The Inverbeg Inn	Luss, Alexandria, Loch Lomond, Argyll, G83 8PD	01436 860678	AWAITING GRADING		

Alford

Bydand Bed & Breakfast	18 Balfour Road, Alford, Aberdeenshire, AB33 8NF	019755 63613	★★★	Bed & Breakfast	

Allanton

Allanton Inn	Main Street, Allanton, Scottish Borders, TD11 3JZ	01890 818260	★★★	Inn	

Alloa

Breacan House	West End Gardens, Alloa, Clackmannanshire, FK10 1LN	01259 724786	★★★★	Bed & Breakfast	
The Royal Oak Hotel	7 Bedford Place, Alloa, Clackmannanshire, FK10 1LJ	01259 722423	★★	Inn	

Alloway, Ayr

Garth Madryn	71 Maybole Road, Alloway, Ayr, Ayrshire, KA7 4TB	01292 443346	★★★	Bed & Breakfast	
The Wytchery	10 Doonvale Place, Alloway, Ayr, Ayrshire, KA6 6FD	01292 442070	★★★★	Bed & Breakfast	

Alness

Tullochard Guest House	37 Obsdale Road, Alness, Ross-shire, IV17 0TU	01349 882075	★★★	Guest House	

Alyth

Alyth Hotel	6 Commercial Street, Alyth, Perthshire, PH11 8AT	01828 632447	★★	Inn	

Unassisted wheelchair access · Assisted wheelchair access · Access for visitors with mobility difficulties
Bronze Green Tourism Award · Silver Green Tourism Award · Gold Green Tourism Award
For further information on our Green Tourism Business Scheme please see page 9.

Old Stables	2 Losset Road, Alyth, Perthshire, PH11 8BT	01828 632547	★★★★	Bed & Breakfast	
Tigh Na Leigh	22-24 Airlie Street, Alyth, Perthshire, PH11 8AD	01828 632372	★★★★★	Guest House	

Annan

East Upper Priestside	Cummentrees, Annan, Dumfriesshire, DG12 5PX	01387 259219	★★★	Farmhouse	
Rowanbank	20 St Johns Road, Annan, Dumfriesshire, DG12 5AW	01461 204200	★★	Guest House	
The Old Rectory Guest House	12 St Johns Road, Annan, Dumfriesshire, DG12 6AW	01461 202029	★★★	Guest House	

Anstruther

8 Melville Terrace	Anstruther, Fife, KY10 3EW	01333 310453	★★★	Bed & Breakfast	
Barnsmuir Farmhouse	Crail, Anstruther, Fife, KY10 3XB	01333 450342	★★★	Bed & Breakfast	
Beaumont Lodge	43 Pittenweem Road, Anstruther, Fife, KY10 3DT	01333 310315	★★★★	Bed & Breakfast	
Crichton House	High Street West, Anstruther, Fife, KY10 3DJ	01333 310219	★★★	Bed & Breakfast	
Far Reaches B&B	32 Pickford Crescent, Cellardyke, Anstruther, Fife, KY10 3AL	01333 310448	★★★★	Bed & Breakfast	
Laggan House	The Cooperage, Anstruther, Fife, KY10 3AW	01333 311170	★★★★	Bed & Breakfast	
No 6 Urquhart Wynd	Cellardyke, Anstruther, Fife, KY10 3BN	01333 310939	★★★★	Bed & Breakfast	
Spalefield Lodge	Spalefield, Anstruther, Fife, KY10 3LB	01333 310036	★★★	Bed & Breakfast	
The Bakehouse & The Granary	18/20 Shore Street, Anstruther, Fife, KY10 3EA	01333 312200	★★★	Restaurant with Rooms	
The Sheiling	32 Glenogil Gard, Anstruther, Fife, KY10 3ET	01333 310697	★★★	Bed & Breakfast	
The Spindrift	Pittenween Road, Anstruther, Fife, KY10 3DT	01333 310573	★★★★	Guest House	

Appin

Bealach House	Duror, Appin, Argyll, PA38 4BW	01631 740298	★★★★	Bed & Breakfast	

Applecross

Applecross Inn	Shore Street, Applecross, Strathcarron, IV54 8LR	01520 744262	★★★	Inn	Silver Green Tourism Award
Meall mo Chridhe	Camusterrach, Applecross, Ross-shire, IV54 8LU	01520 744432	★★★★	Bed & Breakfast	

Arbroath

Ashwell B&B	24 Hayswell Road, Arbroath, Tayside, DD11 1TU	01241 874258	★★★	Bed & Breakfast	
Blairdene Guest House	216 High Street, Arbroath, Angus, DD11 1HY	01241 872380	★★★	Guest House	
Croftsmuir Steading	Carmyllie, Arbroath, Angus, DD11 2RQ	01241 860245	AWAITING GRADING		
Harbour Nights Guest House	4 Shore, Arbroath, Angus, DD11 1PB	01241 434343	★★★★	Guest House	
The Old Vicarage B & B	2 Seaton Road, Arbroath, Angus, DD11 5DX	01241 430475	★★★★★	Bed & Breakfast	Bronze Green Tourism Award
Towerbank Guest House	9 James Street, Arbroath, Angus, DD11 1JP	01241 431343	★★	Guest House	

Unassisted wheelchair access Assisted wheelchair access Access for visitors with mobility difficulties
Bronze Green Tourism Award Silver Green Tourism Award Gold Green Tourism Award
For further information on our Green Tourism Business Scheme please see page 9.

By Arbroath

Copper Dell B&B	12 Cotton's Corner, Lethan Grange, By Arbroath, Angus, DD11 4QD	01241 890546	AWAITING GRADING		
Five Gables House	Elliot, By Arbroath, Angus, DD11 2PE	01241 871632	★★★	Bed & Breakfast	
Gordon's Restaurant With Rooms	Gordon's Restaurant, Main Street, Inverkeilor, By Arbroath, Angus, DD11 5RN	01241 830364	★★★★	Restaurant with Rooms	
Inishowen Guest House	Dundee Road, Elliot, By Arbroath, Angus, DD11 2PE	01241 871922	★★★★	Bed & Breakfast	

Archiestown

Spey Burn House B&B	61 High Street, , Archiestown, Moray, AB38 7QZ	01340 810543	★★★	Bed & Breakfast	

Ardgay

Corvost	Ardgay, Sutherland, IV24 3BP	01863 755317	★★	Bed & Breakfast	

Ardhasaig, Isle of Harris

Ardhasaig House	9 Ardhasaig, Ardhasaig, Isle of Harris, Western Isles, HS3 3AJ	01859 502500	★★★★	Restaurant with Rooms	Access for visitors with mobility difficulties

Ardmore

Anglers Retreat	1, Ardmore, South Uist, HS8 5QY	01870 610325	★★★	Guest House	

Ardnamurchan

Torr Solais	Kilchoan, Ardnamurchan, Argyll, PH36 4LH	01972 510 389	★★★★	Bed & Breakfast	

Ardrishaig

Dalriada	Glenburn Road, Ardrishaig, Argyll, PA30 8EU	01546 603345	★★★	Bed & Breakfast	
Allt-Na-Craig House	Tarbert Road, Ardrishaig, Argyll, PA30 8EP	01546 603245	★★★★	Guest House	

Ardrossan

Edenmore	47 Parkhouse Road, Ardrossan, Ayrshire, KA22 8AN	01294 462306	★★	Bed & Breakfast	

Arinagour, Isle of Coll

Isle of Coll Hotel	Arinagour, Isle of Coll , Isle of Coll, PA78 6SZ	01879 230334	★★★	Inn	Bronze Green Tourism Award

Arisaig

Cnoc-Na-Faire	Back of Keppoch, Arisaig, Inverness-shire, PH39 4NS	01687 450249	★★★★	Inn	
Leven House	Borrodale, Arisaig, Inverness-shire, PH39 4NR	01687 450238	★★★★	Bed & Breakfast	
The Old Library Lodge	Main Street , Arisaig, Inverness-shire, PH39 4NH	01687 450651	★★★	Restaurant with Rooms	
Kilmartin Farm Guesthouse	Kinloid Farm, Kilmartin, Arisaig, Inverness-shire, PH39 4NS	01687 450366	★★★	Bed & Breakfast	

Aros, Isle of Mull

Arle Lodge	Aros, Isle of Mull PA72 6JS	01680 300299	★★	Guest House	
Caorann	Aros Mains, Aros, Isle of Mull PA72 6JS	01680 300355	★★★	Bed & Breakfast	
Fascadail	Salen, Aros, Isle of Mull PA72 6JB	01680 300444	★★★	Bed & Breakfast	

Unassisted wheelchair access   Assisted wheelchair access   Access for visitors with mobility difficulties
Bronze Green Tourism Award   Silver Green Tourism Award   Gold Green Tourism Award
For further information on our Green Tourism Business Scheme please see page 9.

Arrochar

Argyll View	Main Street, Arrochar G83 7AA	01301 702932	★★★★	Bed & Breakfast	
Ashfield House	Arrochar G83 7AA	01301 702287	★★★	Bed & Breakfast	
Ben Bheula	Succoth, Arrochar G83 7AL	01301 702184	AWAITING GRADING		
Braemor B&B	Braeside, Arrochar G83 7AA	01301 702 535	★★★★	Bed & Breakfast	
Burnbrae	Shore Road, Arrochar G83 7AG	01301 702988	★★★★	Bed & Breakfast	
Clisham Cottage Bed and Breakfast	Inverarnan, By Ardlui, Arrochar G83 7DX	01301 704339	★★	Bed & Breakfast	
Cruachan B&B	Shore Road, Arrochar G83 7BB	01301 702521	★★★★	Bed & Breakfast	
Fascadail Country Guest House	Shore Road, Arrochar G83 7AB	01301 702344	★★★	Guest House	
Lomond View	Tarbet, Arrochar G83 7DG	01301 702477	★★★★	Bed & Breakfast	
Long Shadows	Succoth, Arrochar G83 7AL	01301 702546	★★★★	Bed & Breakfast	
Rowantree Cottage	Main Street, Arrochar G83 7AA	01301 702882	★★★	Bed & Breakfast	
Stuckgowan Cottage	Tarbert, Arrochar G83 7DH	01301 702451	★★★	Bed & Breakfast	
Village Inn	Main Street, Arrochar G83 7AX	01301 702279	★★★	Inn	🚶

by Arrochar

33 Ballyhennan Crescent	Tarbet, by Arrochar G83 8DA	01301 702213	★★	Bed & Breakfast	

Ascog, Isle of Bute

Balmory Hall	Ascog, Isle of Bute PA20 9LL	01700 500669	★★★★★	Bed & Breakfast	

Athelstaneford

Fidra House	Athelstaneford, East Lothian, EH39 5BE	01620 880777	★★★★★	Bed & Breakfast	

Auchterarder

Alma House	Hunter Street, Auchterarder, Perthshire, PH3 1PA	01764 662894	★★★★	Bed & Breakfast	
Basset Cottage	20 Townhead, Auchterarder, Perthshire, PH3 1AH	01764 662237	★★★	Bed & Breakfast	
Easterton Farm	Blackford, Auchterarder, Perthshire, PH4 1RQ	01764 682268	★★★	Bed & Breakfast	
Greystanes	Western Road, Auchterarder, Perthshire, PH3 1JJ	01764 664239	★★★★	Bed & Breakfast	🚶
The Parsonage Guest House	111 High Street, Auchterarder, Perthshire, PH3 1AA	01764 662392	★★★	Bed & Breakfast	

Auldgirth

Low Kirkbride Farmhouse B&B	Low Kirkbride, Auldgirth, Dumfriesshire, DG2 0SP	01387 820258	★★★	Farmhouse	Silver Green Tourism Award

Aultbea

Burnside	48 Mellon Charles, Aultbea, Ross-shire, IV22 2JL	01445 731270	★★★	Bed & Breakfast	
Mellondale Guest House	47 Mellon Charles, Aultbea, Ross-shire, IV22 2JL	01445 731326	★★★★	Guest House	

Unassisted wheelchair access · Assisted wheelchair access · 🚶 Access for visitors with mobility difficulties
Bronze Green Tourism Award · Silver Green Tourism Award · Gold Green Tourism Award
For further information on our Green Tourism Business Scheme please see page 9.

Tranquility	21 Mellon Charles, Aultbea, Ross-shire, IV22 2JN	01445 731241	★★★	Bed & Breakfast		

Aviemore

Ardlogie Guest House	Dalfaber Road, Aviemore, Inverness-shire, PH22 1PU	01479 810747	★★★	Guest House		
Cairn Eilrig	Glenmore, Aviemore, Inverness-shire, PH22 1QU	01479 861223	★★★	Bed & Breakfast		
Cairngorm Guest House	Grampian Road, Aviemore, Inverness-shire, PH22 1RP	01479 810630	★★★	Guest House		Silver Green Tourism Award
Carn Mhor B&B	The Sheiling, Aviemore, Inverness-shire, PH22 1QD	01479 811004	★★★	Bed & Breakfast		
Corrour House	Inverdruie, Aviemore, Inverness-shire, PH22 1QH	01479 810220	★★★★	Guest House		
Dunroamin	Craig Na Gower, Aviemore, Inverness-shire, PH22 1RW	01479 810698	★★★	Bed & Breakfast		
Eriskay	Craig-Na-Gower, Aviemore, Inverness-shire, PH22 1RW	01479 810717	★★★	Bed & Breakfast		
Junipers	5 Dellmhor, Aviemore, Inverness-shire, PH22 1QW	01479 810405	★★★	Guest House		
Kinapol Guest House	Dalfaber Road, Aviemore, Inverness-shire, PH22 1PY	01479 810513	★★★	Guest House		
Macdonald Academy	Aviemore Highland Resort, Aviemore, Inverness-shire, PH22 1PF	01479 810781	★★★	Lodge	Assisted wheelchair access	Silver Green Tourism Award
MacKenzies Highland Inn	125 Grampian Road, Aviemore, Inverness-shire, PH22 1RL	01479 810672	★	Inn		
Ravenscraig Guest House	141 Grampian Road, Aviemore, Inverness-shire, PH22 1RP	01479 810278	★★★★	Guest House	Access for visitors with mobility difficulties	Silver Green Tourism Award
Strathspey House	Grampian Road, Aviemore, Inverness-shire, PH22 1RP	01479 812453	★★★★	Bed & Breakfast		
The Garden Suite	115 Dalnabay, Silverglades, Aviemore, Inverness-shire, PH22 1TA	01479 812293	★★★★	Bed & Breakfast		
The Old Ministers House	Rothiemurchus, Aviemore, Inverness-shire, PH22 1QH	01479 812181	★★★★	Guest House		
The Rowan Tree Country Hotel	Loch Alvie, Aviemore, Inverness-shire, PH22 1QB	01479 810207	★★★	Inn		
Vermont Guest House	Grampian Road, Aviemore, Inverness-shire, PH22 1RP	01479 810470	★★★	Guest House		
Waverley	35 Strathspey Avenue, Aviemore, Inverness-shire, PH22 1SN	01479 811226	★★★	Bed & Breakfast	Access for visitors with mobility difficulties	

By Aviemore

Dell Druie Guest House	Dell Druie, Inverdruie, By Aviemore, Inverness-shire, PH22 1QH	07918 636257	★★★★	Bed & Breakfast

Avoch

Ardvreckan	Knockmuir Brae, Avoch, Ross-shire, IV9 8RD	01381 621523	★★★★	Bed & Breakfast

Ayr

Ayrs & Graces	1 Netherauchendrane, High Maybole Road, Ayr, Ayrshire, KA7 4EE	01292 440028	AWAITING GRADING	
Belmont	15 Park Circus, Ayr, Ayrshire, KA7 2DJ	01292 265588	★★★	Guest House
Berkeley House	1 Barns Street, Ayr, Ayrshire, KA7 1XB	01292 287888	AWAITING GRADING	
Burnside Guest House	14 Queens Terrace, Ayr, Ayrshire, KA7 1DU	01292 263912	★★★★	Guest House
Bythesea Guest House	16 Queens Terrace, Ayr, Ayrshire, KA7 1DU	01292 282365	★★★★	Guest House
Canterholm Guest House	9 Racecourse Road, Ayr, Ayrshire, KA7 2DG	01292 880919	★★★	Bed & Breakfast

Unassisted wheelchair access · Assisted wheelchair access · Access for visitors with mobility difficulties
Bronze Green Tourism Award · Silver Green Tourism Award · Gold Green Tourism Award

For further information on our Green Tourism Business Scheme please see page 9.

Coila Guest House	10 Holmston Road, Ayr, Ayrshire, KA7 3BB	01292 262642	★★★★	Guest House	
Craggallan Guest House	8 Queens Terrace, Ayr, Ayrshire, KA7 1DU	01292 264998	★★★★	Guest House	
Craigholm	7 Queens Terrace, Ayr, Ayrshire, KA7 1DU	01292 261470	★★★	Guest House	
Craigie Guest House	46 Craigie Road, Ayr, Ayrshire, KA8 0HA	01292 282175	★★★	Bed & Breakfast	
Daviot House	12 Queen's Terrace, Ayr, Ayrshire, KA7 1DU	01292 269678	★★★★	Guest House	
Dunduff Farm	Dunure, Ayr, Ayrshire, KA7 4LH	01292 500225	★★★★	Bed & Breakfast	
Dunlay House	1 Ailsa Place, Ayr, Ayrshire, KA7 1JG	01292 610230	★★★★	Guest House	
Dunn Thing Guest House	13 Park Circus, Ayr, Ayrshire, KA7 2DJ	01292 284531	★★★	Bed & Breakfast	
Eglinton Guest House	23 Eglinton Terrace, Ayr, Ayrshire, KA7 1JJ	01292 264623	★★	Guest House	
Failte	9 Prestwick Road, Ayr, Ayrshire, KA8 8LD	01292 265282	★★★	Bed & Breakfast	
Grange View Bed & Breakfast	3 Carrick Road, Ayr, Ayrshire, KA7 2RA	01292 266680	★★★	Bed & Breakfast	
Jac-Mar	23 Dalblair Road, Ayr, Ayrshire, KA7 1UF	01292 264798	★★★	Bed & Breakfast	
Kensington House	37 Miller Road, Ayr, Ayrshire, KA7 2AX	01292 266301	★★★	Bed & Breakfast	
Kilkerran Guest House	15 Prestwick Road, Ayr , Ayrshire , KA8 8LD	01292 266477	★★	Guest House	
Langley Bank Guest House	39 Carrick Road, Ayr, Ayrshire, KA7 2RD	01292 264246	★★★★	Guest House	
Leslie Anne Guest House	13 Castlehill Road, Ayr, Ayrshire, KA7 2HX	01292 265648	★★★	Bed & Breakfast	
Lochinver	32 Park Circus, Ayr, Ayrshire, KA7 2DL	01292 265086	★★★	Bed & Breakfast	
Miller House	36 Miller Road, Ayr, Ayrshire, KA7 2AY	01292 282016	★★★	Guest House	
No. 26 The Crescent	26 Bellevue Crescent, Ayr, Ayrshire, KA7 2DR	01292 287329	★★★★★	Guest House	
Nordek House	4 Bellevue Crescent, Ayr, Ayrshire, KA7 2DR	01292 262289	★★★★	Bed & Breakfast	
Perryston Farm	Dunure Road, Ayr, Ayrshire, KA7 4LD	01292 441315	★★★	Bed & Breakfast	
Queen's Guest House	10 Queen's Terrace, Ayr, Ayrshire, KA7 1DU	01292 265618	★★★	Guest House	
Richmond Guest House	38 Park Circus, Ayr, Ayrshire, KA7 2LD	01292 265153	★★★	Guest House	
St Andrews Hotel	7 Prestwick Road, Ayr, Ayrshire, KA8 8LD	01292 263211	★★	Inn	
Sunnyside	26 Dunure Road, Ayr, Ayrshire, KA7 4HR	01292 441234	★★★★	Bed & Breakfast	
The Beechwood Guest House	37/39 Prestwick Road, Ayr, Ayrshire, KA8 8LE	01292 262093	★★★	Guest House	
The Windsor	6 Alloway Place, Ayr, Ayrshire, KA7 2AA	01292 264689	★★	Guest House	

By Ayr

Muirburn House B&B	Annbank Road Annbank, By Ayr, Ayrshire, KA6 5AG	01292 521430	★★★★	Bed & Breakfast	
Alt-Na-Craig	Hollybush, By Ayr, Ayrshire, KA6 7EB	01292 560555	★★★★	Bed & Breakfast	Access for visitors with mobility difficulties

Unassisted wheelchair access   Assisted wheelchair access   Access for visitors with mobility difficulties
Bronze Green Tourism Award   Silver Green Tourism Award   Gold Green Tourism Award
For further information on our Green Tourism Business Scheme please see page 9.

Back, Isle of Lewis

Broad Bay House	Back, Isle of Lewis, Western Isles, HS2 0LQ	01851 820990	★★★★★	Guest House	♿	
Crowberry	43 Vatisker, Back, Isle of Lewis, Western Isles, HS2 0LF	01851 605004	★★★★	Guest House		
Ravenstar	24 Vatisker, Back, Isle of Lewis, Western Isles, HS2 0JS	01851 820517	★★★	Bed & Breakfast		
Seaside Villa	Back, Isle of Lewis, Western Isles, HS2 0LQ	01851 820208	★★★★	Bed & Breakfast		

Balallan, Isle of Lewis

Gledfield	5 Balallan, Balallan, Isle of Lewis, Western Isles, HS2 9PN	01851 830233	★★★	Bed & Breakfast		

Balerno

Haughhead Farm	Balerno, Midlothian, EH14 7JH	0131 4493875	★★	Farmhouse		
Newmills Cottage	472 Lanark Road West, Balerno, Midlothian, EH14 5AE	0131 449 4300	★★★★	Bed & Breakfast		

Balfron Station

Ballochruin Farm	Balfron Station, Balfron Station, Stirlingshire, G63 0LE	01360 440496	★★★★	Bed & Breakfast		

Balfour

Hilton Farmhouse	Shapinsay, Balfour, Orkney, KW17 2EA	01856 711239	★★★★	Farmhouse		

Ballachulish

Ardno House	Lettermore, Ballachulish, Argyll, PH49 4JD		★★★★	Bed & Breakfast		
Ballachulish House	Ballachulish, Argyll, PH49 4JX	01855 811266	★★★★★	Guest Accommodation		
Craiglinnhe House	Lettermore, Ballachulish, Argyll, PH49 4JD	01855 811270	★★★★	Guest House		
Fern Villa Guest House	Loan Fern, Ballachulish, Argyll, PH49 4JE	01855 811393	★★★	Guest House		
Lyn-Leven Guest House	West Laroch, Ballachulish, Argyll, PH49 4JP	01855 811392	★★★★	Guest House		
Strathassynt Guest House	Loan Fern, Ballachulish, Argyll, PH49 4JB	01855 811261	★★★	Guest House		

Ballater

Celicall	3 Braemar Road, Ballater, Aberdeenshire, AB35 5RL	013397 55699	★★★	Bed & Breakfast		
Creag Meggan	Bridge of Gairn, Ballater, Aberdeenshire, AB35 5UD	013397 55767	★★★	Bed & Breakfast		
Eastbank	50 Albert Road, Ballater, Aberdeenshire, AB35 5QU	013397 55742	★★★★	Bed & Breakfast		
Glenernan	37 Braemar Road, Ballater, Aberdeenshire, AB35 5RQ	01339 753111	★★★	Guest House	♿	
Langdale Bed and Breakfast	Hawthorn Place, Ballater, Aberdeen-shire, AB35 5QH	013397 55500	★★★★	Bed & Breakfast		
Moorside Guest House	26 Braemar Road, Ballater, Aberdeenshire, AB35 5RL	01339 755492	★★★★	Guest House	🚶	
Morvada House	28 Braemar Road, Ballater, Aberdeenshire, AB35 5RL	013397 56334	★★★★	Guest House		
Netherley Guest House	2 Netherley Place, Ballater, Aberdeenshire, AB35 5QE	013397 55792	★★★★	Guest House		
School House	Anderson Road, Ballater, Aberdeenshire, AB35 5QW	01339 756333	★★★★	Bed & Breakfast	🚶	Bronze Green Tourism Award

♿ Unassisted wheelchair access · Assisted wheelchair access · 🚶 Access for visitors with mobility difficulties
Bronze Green Tourism Award · Silver Green Tourism Award · Gold Green Tourism Award
For further information on our Green Tourism Business Scheme please see page 9.

Tangley House	41 Braemar Road, Ballater, Aberdeenshire, AB35 5RQ	01339 755624	★★★★	Bed & Breakfast	
The Auld Kirk	Braemar Road, Ballater, Aberdeenshire, AB35 5RQ	01339 755762	★★★	Restaurant with Rooms	
The Gordon Guest House	Station Square, Ballater, Aberdeenshire, AB35 5QB	013397 55996	★★★★	Guest House	
The Green Inn	9 Victoria Road, Ballater, Aberdeenshire, AB35 5QQ	01339 755701	★★★★	Restaurant with Rooms	
Woodside	Old Line Road, Ballater, Aberdeenshire, AB35 5UT	01339 756351	★★★	Bed & Breakfast	

by Ballater

The Inver Hotel	Crathie, by Ballater, Aberdeenshire, AB35 5XN	01339 742345	★★★	Inn	

Ballindalloch

Woodville	Ballindalloch, Banffshire, AB37 9AD	01807 500396	★★★★	Bed & Breakfast	

Balloch

8 Balloch Road	Balloch, Dunbartonshire, G83 8SR	01389 750436	★★★	Bed & Breakfast	
Aird House	1 Ben Lomond Walk, Balloch, Dunbartonshire, G83 8RJ	01389 754464	★★★	Bed & Breakfast	
Argyll Lodge	16 Luss Road, Balloch, Dunbartonshire, G83 0RH	01389 759020	★★★	Bed & Breakfast	
Barton Bed and Breakfast	12 Balloch Road, Balloch, Dunbartonshire, G83 8SR	01389 759653	★★★	Bed & Breakfast	Access for visitors with mobility difficulties
Dumbain Farm	Balloch, Dunbartonshire, G83 8DS	01389 752263	★★★	Bed & Breakfast	
Glyndale	6 Mackenzie Drive, Balloch, Dunbartonshire, G83 8HL	01389 758238	★★★	Bed & Breakfast	
Gowanlea	Drymen Road, Balloch, Dunbartonshire, G83 8HS	01389 752456	★★★★	Bed & Breakfast	
Millhall	Old Luss Road, Balloch, Dunbartonshire, G83 8QP	01389 750451	★★★	Bed & Breakfast	
Monday Cottage	29 Torrinch Drive, Balloch, Dunbartonshire, G83 8JL	01389 759932	★★★	Bed & Breakfast	
Norwood Guest House	60 Balloch Road, Balloch, Dunbartonshire, G83 8LE	01389 750309	★★★	Guest House	
Oakvale	Drymen Road, Balloch, Dunbartonshire, G83 8JY	01389 751615	★★★	Bed & Breakfast	
Palombo's of Balloch	40 Balloch Road, Balloch, Dunbartonshire, G83 8LE	01389 753501	★★★	Restaurant with Rooms	
Restil	Riverside, Balloch, Dunbartonshire, G83 8LF	01389 753105	★★	Bed & Breakfast	
St Blanes	Drymen Road, Balloch, Dunbartonshire, G83 8JY	01389 729 661	★★★	Bed & Breakfast	
The Reivers	Drymen Road, Balloch, Dunbartonshire, G83 8HS	01204 362606	★★★	Bed & Breakfast	
Tigh Mo Ghraidh	16 Endrick Drive, Balloch, Dunbartonshire, G83 8HY	01389 752312	★★★★	Bed & Breakfast	Bronze Green Tourism Award
Time Out	24 Balloch Road, Balloch, Dunbartonshire, G83 8LE	07957 436731	★★★	Guest House	
Tullie Inn	Balloch Road, Balloch, Dunbartonshire, G83 8SW	01389 752052	★★★	Inn	
Tullichewan Farm	Upper Stoneymollan Road, Balloch, Loch Lomond, G83 8QY	01389 711190	★★★★	Bed & Breakfast	
Whitecraigs Cottage	Stirling Road, Balloch, Dunbartonshire, G83 8NA	01389 757811	★★★	Bed & Breakfast	
Woodvale	Drymen Road, Balloch, Dunbartonshire, G83	01389 755771	★★★	Bed & Breakfast	

Unassisted wheelchair access   Assisted wheelchair access   Access for visitors with mobility difficulties
Bronze Green Tourism Award   Silver Green Tourism Award   Gold Green Tourism Award
For further information on our Green Tourism Business Scheme please see page 9.

By Balloch

Braeburn Cottage	West Auchencarroch Road, By Balloch, Dunbartonshire, G83 9LU	01389 710998	★★★	Bed & Breakfast

Ballygrant, Isle of Islay

Kilmeny	Ballygrant, Isle of Islay PA45 7QW	01496 840668	★★★★★	Guest House

Balmaha

Mar Achlais	Milton of Buchanan, Balmaha, Stirlingshire, G63 0JE	01360 870300	★★★	Bed & Breakfast

Banchory

Birchlea Cottage	Strachan, Banchory , Aberdeenshire , AB31 6NL	01330 824132	★★★★	Bed & Breakfast
Crossroads Hotel	Lumphanan, Banchory, Aberdeenshire, AB31 4RH	01339 883275	★★	Inn
Davont	Crathes , Banchory, Aberdeenshire, AB31 5JE	01330 844600	★★★	Bed & Breakfast
Gable End	73 High Street, Banchory, Aberdeenshire, AB31 5TJ	01330 824666	★★★	Bed & Breakfast
Lochton	Durris, Banchory, Kincardineshire , AB31 6DB	01330 844543	★★★	Bed & Breakfast
The Old West Manse	71 Station Road, Banchory, Kincardineshire, AB31 5YD	01330 822202	★★★★	Bed & Breakfast
Wester Durris Cottage	Kirkton of Durris, Banchory, Kincardineshire, AB31 3BQ	01330 844638	★★	Bed & Breakfast

By Banchory

Mapleview	Lumphanan, By Banchory, Kincardineshire, AB31 4RH	013398 83481	★★★	Bed & Breakfast
Dorena	Strachan, By Banchory, Kincardineshire, AB31 6NL	01330 822540	★★★★	Bed & Breakfast

Banff

Bryden	Boyndie, Banff, Aberdeenshire, AB45 2LD	01261 861742	★★★★	Bed & Breakfast
Gardenia House	19 Castle Street, Banff, Banff & Buchan, AB45 1DH	01261 812675	★★★	Guest House
The Trinity and Alvah Manse	21 Castle Street, Banff, Aberdeen-shire, AB45 1DH	01261 812244	★★★	Guest House

Bankfoot

Forest Lodge	Forestry Place, Bankfoot, Perthshire, PH1 4BN	01738 787150	★★★	Bed & Breakfast

Bannockburn

Laurinda	66 Ochilmount, Ochilview, Bannockburn, Stirlingshire, FK7 8PJ	01786 815612	★★★	Bed & Breakfast

Barvas, Isle of Lewis

Rockvilla	Barvas, Isle of Lewis, Isle of Lewis, HS2 0QY	01851 840286	★★★	Bed & Breakfast

Bathgate

Hillview	35 The Green, Bathgate, West Lothian, EH48 4DA	01506 654830	★★	Bed & Breakfast

By Bathgate

East Badallan Farm	Fauldhouse, By Bathgate, West Lothian, EH47 9AG	01501 770251	★★★	Farmhouse

Unassisted wheelchair access   Assisted wheelchair access   Access for visitors with mobility difficulties
Bronze Green Tourism Award   Silver Green Tourism Award   Gold Green Tourism Award
For further information on our Green Tourism Business Scheme please see page 9.

Tarrareoch Farm	Station Road, Armadale, By Bathgate, West Lothian, EH48 3BJ	01501 730404	★★★	Bed & Breakfast

Bayherivagh, Isle of Barra

Heathbank Hotel	Bayherivagh, Isle of Barra, Isle of Barra, HS9 5YQ	01871 890266	★★★	Inn

Beauly

Archdale Guest House	High Street, Beauly, Inverness-shire, IV4 7BT	01463 783043	★★	Guest House
Broomhill	Kiltarlity, Beauly, Inverness-shire, IV4 7JH	01463 741447	★★★	Bed & Breakfast
Cnoc End	Croyard Road, Beauly, Inverness-shire, IV4 7DJ	01463 782230	★★★★	Bed & Breakfast
Cruachan	Wester Balblair, Beauly, Inverness-shire, IV4 7BQ	01463 782479	★★★	Bed & Breakfast

By Beauly

Rheindown Farm	By Beauly, Inverness-shire, IV4 7AB	01463 782461	★★★	Bed & Breakfast
Kerrow House	Cannich, By Beauly, Inverness-shire, IV4 7NA	01456 415243	★★★	Bed & Breakfast
Westward	Cannich, By Beauly, Inverness-shire, IV4 7LT	01456 415708	★★★	Bed & Breakfast
Ardgowan Lodge Guest House	Wester Phoineas, By Beauly, Inverness-shire, IV4 7BA	01463 741745	★★★★	Bed & Breakfast

Beith

Shotts Farm	Barrmill, Beith, Ayrshire, KA15 1LB	01505 502273	★★★	Farmhouse

Benbecula

Bainbhidh	9 Lionacleit, Benbecula, Western Isles, HS7 5PY	01870 602532	★★	Bed & Breakfast
Borve Guest House	5 Torlum, Benbecula, Western Isles, HS7 5PP	01870 602685	★★★★	Guest House
Creag Liath	15 Griminish, Benbecula, Western Isles, HS7 5QA	01870 602992	★★★★	Bed & Breakfast
Lionacleit Guest House	27 Liniclate, Benbecula, Western Isles, HS7 5PY	01870 602176	★★★	Guest House

Benderloch, by Oban

Ardchoille	Benderloch, by Oban, Argyll, PA37 1ST	01631 720432	★★★	Bed & Breakfast
Hawthorn	Keil Croft, Benderloch, by Oban, Argyll, PA37 1QS	01631 720452	★★★★	Bed & Breakfast
Rowantree Cottage B & B	Keil Farm, Benderloch, by Oban, Argyll, PA37 1QP	01631 720433	★★★	Bed & Breakfast

Bernera

Garymilis	Kirkibost, Bernera, Isle of Lewis, Outer Hebrides, HS2 9LX	01851 612341	★★★	Bed & Breakfast

Bernsdale, Isle of Skye

Lochview	45 Park, Bernsdale, Isle of Skye, Inverness-shire, IV51 9NT	01470 532736	★★★★	Bed & Breakfast

Berwick-upon-Tweed

Banrach	Tweedhill, Berwick-upon-Tweed, Berwickshire, TD15 1XQ	01289 386851	★★★★	Bed & Breakfast

♿ Unassisted wheelchair access ♿ Assisted wheelchair access 🚶 Access for visitors with mobility difficulties
Bronze Green Tourism Award Silver Green Tourism Award Gold Green Tourism Award
For further information on our Green Tourism Business Scheme please see page 9.

Biggar

Allershaw House	Daerside, By Elvonfoot, Biggar, Lanarkshire, ML12 6TJ	01864 505050	★★★★	Farmhouse	
Cormiston Farm	Cormiston Road, Biggar, South Lanarkshire, ML12 6NS	01899 221507	★★★★	Bed & Breakfast	
Cuil Darach	7 Langvout Gate, Biggar, South Lanarkshire, ML12 6UF	01899 221259	★★★★	Bed & Breakfast	
Elphinstone Hotel	145 High Street, Biggar, Lanarkshire, ML12 6DL	01899 220044	★★	Inn	
Victoria Lodge	Tweedsmuir, Biggar, Peeblesshire, ML12 6QP	01899 880293	★★★★★	Bed & Breakfast	

By Biggar

The Glenholm Centre	Broughton, By Biggar, Lanarkshire, ML12 6JF	01899 830408	★★★	Guest House	♿ Gold Green Tourism Award
Skirling House	Skirling, By Biggar, Lanarkshire, ML12 6HD		★★★★★	Guest House	
High Meadows B&B	Meadowflats Road,Tthankerton, By Biggar, Lanarkshire, ML12 6NF	01899 308872	★★★	Bed & Breakfast	

Birnam, by Dunkeld

The Birnam Guest House	4 Murthly Terrace, Birnam, by Dunkeld, Perthshire, PH8 0BG	01350 727201	★★★	Guest House	
Byways	Perth Road, Birnam, by Dunkeld, Perthshire, PH8 0DH	01350 727542	★★★	Bed & Breakfast	
Tayburn House	Perth Road, Birnam, by Dunkeld, Perthshire, PH8 0BQ	01350 728822	★★★	Bed & Breakfast	

Birsay

Choin	Birsay, Orkney, KW17 2ND	01856 721488	★★★★	Bed & Breakfast	
Linkshouse	Birsay, Orkney, KW17 2LX	01856 721221	★★★★	Bed & Breakfast	
Primrose Cottage	Birsay, Orkney, KW17 2NB	01856 721384	★★★	Bed & Breakfast	

Bishopton

The Millers House	Formakin, Bishopton, Renfrewshire, PA7 5NX	01505 862417	★★★★	Bed & Breakfast	

Blackburn

Cruachan Guest House	78 East Main Street, Blackburn, West Lothian, EH47 7QS	01506 655221	★★★	Bed & Breakfast	

Blackwaterfoot, Isle of Arran

Morvern	Blackwaterfoot, Isle of Arran, Isle of Arran, KA27 8EU	01770 860254	★★	Bed & Breakfast	

Blair Atholl

Dalgreine Guest House	Bridge of Tilt, Blair Atholl, Perthshire, PH18 5SX	01796 481276	★★★★	Guest House	
Ptarmigan House	Bridge of Tilt, Blair Atholl, Perthshire, PH18 5SZ	01796 481269	★★★	Guest House	
The Firs	St Andrews Crescent, Blair Atholl, Perthshire, PH18 5TA	01796 481256	★★★	Guest House	Silver Green Tourism Award

Blairgowrie

Bankhead	Clunie, Blairgowrie, Perthshire, PH10 6SG		★★★	Farmhouse	
Broadmyre Motel	Carsie, Blairgowrie, Perthshire, PH10 6QW	01250 873262	★★	Guest House	

♿ Unassisted wheelchair access ♿ Assisted wheelchair access 🚶 Access for visitors with mobility difficulties
Bronze Green Tourism Award Silver Green Tourism Award Gold Green Tourism Award
For further information on our Green Tourism Business Scheme please see page 9.

Establishment	Address	Telephone	Grading	Type	Facilities
Dalhenzean Lodge	Glenshee, Blairgowrie, Perthshire, PH10 7QD	01250 885217	★★★★	Bed & Breakfast	
Drumellie Meadow	Wester Essendy, Blairgowrie, Perthshire, PH10 6RD	01250 884282	★★★★	Bed & Breakfast	
Eildon Bank	Perth Road, Blairgowrie, Perthshire, PH10 6ED	01250 873648	★★★	Bed & Breakfast	
Garfield House	Perth Road, Blairgowrie, Perthshire, PH10 6ED	01250 872999	★★★	Bed & Breakfast	
Gilmore House	Perth Road, Blairgowrie, Perthshire, PH10 6EJ	01250 872791	★★★★	Bed & Breakfast	
Glenisla Hotel	Kirkton of Glenisla, Blairgowrie, Perthshire, PH11 8PH	01575 582223	★★	Inn	
Glenkilrie Bed and Breakfast	Blacklunans, Blairgowrie, Perthshire, PH10 7LR	01250 882241	★★★	Bed & Breakfast	
Glensheiling House	Hatton Road, Blairgowrie, Perthshire, PH10 7HZ	01250 874605	★★★★	Guest House	
Heathpark House	Coupar Angus Road, Blairgowrie, Perthshire, PH10 6JT	01250 870700	★★★★	Bed & Breakfast	
Heathpark Lodge	Coupar Angus Road, Blairgowrie, Perthshire, PH10 6JT	01250 874929	★★★★	Bed & Breakfast	
Holmrigg	Wester Essendy, Blairgowrie, Perthshire, PH10 6RD	01250 884309	★★★	Bed & Breakfast	Access for visitors with mobility difficulties
Ivybank Guest House	Boat Brae, Blairgowrie, Perthshire, PH10 7BH	01250 873056	★★★★	Guest House	
Lunanbrae	Essendy, Blairgowrie, Perthshire, PH10 6RA	01250 884224	★★★★	Bed & Breakfast	
Miramichi	Golf Course Road, Blairgowrie, Perthshire, PH10 6LQ	01250 873310	★★★	Bed & Breakfast	
Ridgeway	Wester Essendy, Blairgowrie, Perthshire, PH10 6RA	01250 884734	★★★	Bed & Breakfast	
Rosebank House	Balmoral Road, Blairgowrie, Perthshire, PH10 7AF	01250 872912	★★★	Guest House	
Shocarjen House	Balmoral Road, Blairgowrie, Perthshire, PH10 7AF	01250 870525	★★★★	Bed & Breakfast	
West Freuchies	Kirkton of Glenisla, Blairgowrie, Perthshire, PH11 8PG	01575 582716	★★★★	Bed & Breakfast	

By Blairgowrie

Establishment	Address	Telephone	Grading	Type	Facilities
Burrelton Park Inn	High Street, Burrelton, By Blairgowrie, Perthshire, PH13 9NX	01828 670206	★	Inn	
Meikleour Hotel	Meikleour, By Blairgowrie, Perthshire, PH2 6EB	01250 883206	★★★★	Inn	
The Laurels Guest House	Golf Course Road, Rosemount, By Blairgowrie, Perthshire, PH10 6LH	01250 874920	★★★	Guest House	

Boat of Garten

Establishment	Address	Telephone	Grading	Type	Facilities
Granlea House	Deshar Road, Boat of Garten, Inverness-shire, PH24 3BN	01479 831601	★★★	Guest House	
Heathbank House	Drumuillie Road, Boat of Garten, Inverness shire, PH24 3BD	01479 831234	★★★	Guest House	Silver Green Tourism Award
Moorfield House	Deshar Road, Boat of Garten, Inverness-shire, PH24 3BN	01479 831646	★★★★	Guest House	Silver Green Tourism Award
The Boat House	Deishar Road, Boat of Garten, Inverness-shire, PH24 3BN	01479 831484	★★★	Guest House	Access for visitors with mobility difficulties

Bogside, Wishaw

Establishment	Address	Telephone	Grading	Type	Facilities
Herdshill Guest House	224 Main Street, Bogside, Wishaw, Lanarkshire, ML2 8HA	01698 381579	★★★	Guest House	

Bo'ness

Establishment	Address	Telephone	Grading	Type	Facilities
Carriden House	Carriden Brae, Bo'ness, West Lothian, EH51 9SN	01506 829811	★★★	Guest House	

Unassisted wheelchair access · Assisted wheelchair access · Access for visitors with mobility difficulties
Bronze Green Tourism Award · Silver Green Tourism Award · Gold Green Tourism Award

For further information on our Green Tourism Business Scheme please see page 9.

Bonhill

Sunnyside B & B	35 Main street, Bonhill, Dunbartonshire, G83 9JX	01389 750282	★★★	Bed & Breakfast	

Bowmore, Isle of Islay

Lambeth Guest House	Jamieson Street, Bowmore, Isle of Islay, Argyll, PA43 7HL	01496 810597	★★	Guest House	
The Harbour Inn and Restaurant	The Square, Bowmore, Isle of Islay, Argyll, PA43 7JR	01496 810330	★★★★	Restaurant with Rooms	

Brae, Shetland

Westayre B&B	Muckle Roe, Brae, Shetland, Shetland, ZE2 9QW	01806 522368	★★★★	Bed & Breakfast	

Braemar

Braemar Lodge	Glenshee Road, Braemar, Aberdeenshire, AB35 5YQ	013397 41627	★★★	Guest House	
Callater Lodge Guest House	9 Glenshee Road, Braemar, Aberdeenshire, AB35 5YQ	01339 741275	AWAITING GRADING		
Clunie Lodge Guest House	Cluniebank Road, Braemar, Aberdeenshire, AB35 5ZP	013397 41330	★★★	Guest House	
Craiglea	Hillside Road, Braemar, Aberdeenshire, AB35 5YU	013397 41641	★★★	Guest House	
Cranford Guest House	15 Glenshee Road, Braemar, Aberdeenshire, AB35 5YQ	01339 741675	★★★	Guest House	
Dalmore House	Fife Brae, Braemar, Aberdeenshire, AB35 5NS	013397 41225	★★★	Bed & Breakfast	
Gordons Restaurant & Bed & Breakfast	20 Mar Road, Braemar, Aberdeenshire, AB35 5YL	01339 741247	★★★	Bed & Breakfast	Silver Green Tourism Award
Moorfield House	Chapel Brae, Braemar, Aberdeenshire, AB35 5YT	01339 741244	★★★	Restaurant with Rooms	
Schiehallion Guest House	10 Glenshee Road, Braemar, Aberdeenshire, AB35 5YQ	013397 41679	★★★	Guest House	

Branahuie, Stornoway

Holm View Guest House	18 Bhraighe Road, Branahuie, Stornoway, Isle of Lewis, HS2 0BQ	01851 706826	★★★★	Guest House	

Breakish, Isle of Skye

Maltby B&B	12 Upper Breakish, Breakish, Isle of Skye, Inverness-shire, IV42 8PY	01471 822642	★★★	Bed & Breakfast	
Ruisgarry	10 Upper Breakish, Breakish, Isle of Skye, Inverness-shire, IV42 8PY	01471 822 850	★★★★	Bed & Breakfast	

Breasclete, Isle of Lewis

Loch Roag Guest House	22A Breasclete, Breasclete, Isle of Lewis, Western Isles, HS2 9EF	01851 621357	★★★★	Guest House	

Brechin

Blibberhill Farm	Brechin, Angus, DD9 6TH	01307 830323	★★★	Bed & Breakfast	
Gramarcy House	6 Airlie Street, Brechin, Angus, DD9 6JP	01356 622240	★★★★	Bed & Breakfast	
Liscara	3A Castle Street, Brechin, Angus, DD9 6JW	01356 625584	★★★★	Bed & Breakfast	
No23 B&B	23 Church Street, Brechin, Angus, DD9 6HB	01356 622672	★★★	Bed & Breakfast	

By Brechin

Brathinch Farm	By Brechin, Angus, DD9 7QZ	01356 648292	★★★	Bed & Breakfast	

Unassisted wheelchair access   Assisted wheelchair access   Access for visitors with mobility difficulties
Bronze Green Tourism Award   Silver Green Tourism Award   Gold Green Tourism Award
For further information on our Green Tourism Business Scheme please see page 9.

Newtonmill House	By Brechin, Angus, DD9 7PZ	01356 622533	★★★★	Bed & Breakfast	
Ballabeg Guest House	14 Keir Street, Bridgend, By Brechin, Angus, PH2 7HJ	01738 620434	★★★	Bed & Breakfast	
Alexandra Lodge	Inveriscandye Road, Edzell, By Brechin, Angus, DD9 7TN	01356 648266	★★★★	Bed & Breakfast	
Doune Guest House	24 High Street, Edzell, By Brechin, Angus, DD9 7TA	01356 648201	★★★	Bed & Breakfast	
Kinnaber	Ramsay Street, Edzell, By Brechin, Angus, DD9 7TT	01356 648051	★★★★	Bed & Breakfast	
Negara Bed & Breakfast	35 High Street, Edzell, By Brechin, Angus, DD9 7TA	01356 647463	★★★	Bed & Breakfast	
North Esk Lodge	18A High Street, Edzell, By Brechin, Angus, DD9 7TA	01356 647409	★★★	Bed & Breakfast	
The Glebe Bed & Breakfast	5 The Glebe, Edzell, By Brechin, Angus, DD9 7SZ	01356 647278	★★★★	Bed & Breakfast	

Bressay

Maryfield House Hotel	Bressay, Shetland, ZE2 9EL	01595 820207	★	Restaurant with Rooms	
Northern Lights Holistic Spa	Sound View Uphouse, Bressay, Shetland, ZE2 9ES	01595 820733	★★★★	Guest House	♿

Bridge of Allan

Knockhill Guest House	Bridge of Allan, Stirlingshire, FK9 4ND	01786 833123	★★★★	Guest House	🚶
Lynedoch	7 Mayne Avenue, Bridge of Allan, Stirlingshire, FK9 4QU	01786 832178	★★★	Bed & Breakfast	🚶

Bridge of Earn

Bronton Cottage B&B	Edinburgh Road, Bridge of Earn, Perthshire, PH2 9PP	01738 815997	★★★	Bed & Breakfast	
The Last Cast	Main Street, Bridge of Earn, Perthshire, PH2 9PL	01738 812578	★★	Guest House	

Bridge of Orchy

Bridge of Orchy Hotel	Bridge of Orchy, Argyll, PA36 4AD	01838 400208	★★★★	Inn	

Bridge of Walls

Pomona	Gruting, Bridge of Walls, Shetland, ZE2 9NR	01595 810438	★★	Bed & Breakfast	

Bridge of Weir

The Sycamores	20 Kilmacolm Road, Bridge of Weir, Renfrewshire, PA11 3PU	01505 613137	★★★★	Bed & Breakfast	

Bridgend, Isle of Islay

The Meadows	Claggan Farm,, Bridgend, Isle of Islay, Argyll, PA44 7PZ	01496 810567	★★★★	Guest House	🚶
2 Mulindry Cottages	Bridgend, Isle of Islay, Argyll, PA44 7PZ	01496 810397	AWAITING GRADING		🚶

Brig O' Turk

Burnt Inn House	Brig O' Turk, Perthshire, FK17 8HT	01877 376212	★★★	Bed & Breakfast	

Broadford, Isle of Skye

Benview	6 Black Park, Broadford, Isle of Skye, Inverness-shire, IV49 9AE	01471 822445	★★★	Bed & Breakfast	
Berabhaigh Bed & Breakfast	3 Lime Park, Broadford, Isle of Skye, Inverness-shire, IV49 9AE	01471 822372	★★★★	Bed & Breakfast	

♿ Unassisted wheelchair access ♿ Assisted wheelchair access 🚶 Access for visitors with mobility difficulties
Bronze Green Tourism Award Silver Green Tourism Award Gold Green Tourism Award
For further information on our Green Tourism Business Scheme please see page 9.

Braigh A' Roid	Heaste Road, Harrapool, Broadford, Isle of Skye, Inverness-shire, IV49 9AQ	01471 820221	★★★★	Bed & Breakfast	
Dunmara B&B	1, Dunan, Broadford, Isle of Skye, Inverness-shire, IV49 9AJ	01471 820319	★★★	Bed & Breakfast	
Fearnoch	1/2 of 16, Torrin, Broadford, Isle of Skye, Inverness-shire, IV49 9BA	01471 822717	★★★	Bed & Breakfast	
Hillview	Black Park, Broadford, Isle of Skye, Inverness-shire, IV49 9AE	01471 822083	★★★★	Bed & Breakfast	
Lime Stone Cottage	4 Lime Park, Broadford, Isle of Skye, Inverness-shire, IV49 9AE	01471 822142	★★★	Bed & Breakfast	
Scalpay View	2 Arddorch, Broadford, Isle of Skye, Inverness-shire, IV49 9AJ	01471 820229	★★★	Bed & Breakfast	
Seaview	Shore Road, Broadford, Isle of Skye, Inverness-shire, IV49 9AB	01471 820308	★★★	Guest House	🚶
Slapin View	Torrin, Broadford, Isle of Skye, Inverness-shire, IV49 9BA	01471 822672	★★	Farmhouse	
Strathgorm	15 Upper Breakish, Broadford, Isle of Skye, Inverness-shire, IV42 8PY	01471 822508	★★★★	Bed & Breakfast	
The Skye Picture House	Ard Dorch, Broadford, Isle of Skye, Inverness-shire, IV49 9AJ	01471 822531	★★★	Bed & Breakfast	
Tigh an Dochais	13 Harrapool, Broadford, Isle of Skye, Inverness-shire, IV49 9AQ	01471 820022	★★★★★	Bed & Breakfast	
Tir Alainn	8 Upper Breakish, Broadford, Isle of Skye, Inverness-shire, IV42 8PY	01471 822366	★★★★	Bed & Breakfast	

By Broadford, Isle of Skye

Luib House	Luib, By Broadford, Isle of Skye, Inverness-shire, IV49 9AN	01471 820334	★★★	Bed & Breakfast	
Fernlea	11 Upper Breakish, By Broadford, Isle of Skye, Inverness-shire, IV42 8PY	01471 822107	★★★	Bed & Breakfast	

Brodick

Alltan	Knowe Road, Brodick, Isle of Arran, KA27 8BY	01770 302937	★★★★	Bed & Breakfast	Silver Green Tourism Award
Bay View	Brodick, Brodick, Isle of Arran, KA27 8JU	01770 302178	★★	Bed & Breakfast	
Belvedere Guest House	Alma Road, Brodick, Isle of Arran, KA27 8AZ	01770 302397	★★★	Guest House	🚶
Carrick Lodge	Pier Lodge, Brodick, Isle of Arran, KA27 8BH	01770 302550	★★★	Guest House	
Crovie	Corriegills, Brodick, Isle of Arran, KA27 8BL	01770 302193	★★★	Bed & Breakfast	
Dunvegan House	Shore Road, Brodick, Isle of Arran, KA27 8AJ	01770 302811	★★★★	Guest House	
Glenartney	Mayish Road, Brodick, Isle of Arran, KA27 8BX	01770 302220	★★★	Guest House	Gold Green Tourism Award
Glencloy Farm Guest House	Glen Cloy,, Brodick, Isle of Arran, KA27 8DA	01770 302351	★★★	Guest House	
Glenn House	Brodick, Isle of Arran, KA27 8DW	01770 302 092	★★★	Bed & Breakfast	
Invercloy	Shore Road, Brodick, Isle of Arran, KA27 8AJ	01770 302225	★★★	Guest House	
Rosaburn Lodge	Brodick, Isle of Arran, KA27 8DP	01770 302383	★★★	Bed & Breakfast	
Strathwhillan House	Strathwhillan Road, Brodick, Isle of Arran, KA27 8BQ	01770 302331	★★★	Guest House	🚶
The Barn	Glencloy, Brodick, Isle of Arran, KA27 3DA	01770 303615	★★★	Bed & Breakfast	

Brora

Baldovie	Harbour Road, Brora, Sutherland, KW9 6QF	01408 621920	★★★	Bed & Breakfast	

♿ Unassisted wheelchair access ♿ Assisted wheelchair access 🚶 Access for visitors with mobility difficulties
Bronze Green Tourism Award Silver Green Tourism Award Gold Green Tourism Award
For further information on our Green Tourism Business Scheme please see page 9.

Glenaveron	Golf Road , Brora, Sutherland, KW9 6QS	01408 621601	★★★★	Bed & Breakfast	Assisted wheelchair access; Bronze Green Tourism Award
Inverbrora Farmhouse	Brora, Sutherland, KW9 6NJ	01408 621208	★★★★	Bed & Breakfast	
Seaforth	Achrimsdale, Brora, Sutherland, KW9 6LT	01408 621793	★★★	Bed & Breakfast	

Broughty Ferry, Dundee

Redwood Guest House	89 Monifieth Road, Broughty Ferry, Dundee, Tayside, DD5 2SB	01382 736550	★★★★	Guest House
No 1 Kerrington Crescent	Broughty Ferry, Dundee, Tayside, DD5 2TS	01382 480489	★★★	Bed & Breakfast
Invergarth	79 Camphill Road, Broughty Ferry, Dundee, Tayside, DD5 2NA	01382 736278	★★★	Bed & Breakfast

Broxburn

Bankhead Farm	Dechmont, Broxburn, West Lothian, EH52 6NB	01506 811209	★★★★	Guest House

Bruichladdich, Isle of Islay

Anchorage	Bruichladdich, Isle of Islay, Argyll, PA49 7UN	01496 850540	★★	Bed & Breakfast
An Taigh Odsa	Main Street, Bruichladdich, Isle of Islay, Argyll, PA49 7UN	01496 850587	AWAITING GRADING	
Loch Gorm House	Bruichladdich, Isle of Islay, Argyll, PA49 7UN	01496 850139	★★★★★	Bed & Breakfast

Buchlyvie

Buchlyvie Bed and Breakfast	1 Station Road, Buchlyvie, Stirlingshire, FK8 3NA	01360 850580	AWAITING GRADING	

Buckie

Kintrae	39 East Church Street, Buckie, Morayshire, AB56 1ES	01542 839755	★★★★	Bed & Breakfast
Rosemount	62 East Church Street, Buckie, Banffshire, AB56 1ER	01542 833434	★★★★	Bed & Breakfast

Bunavoneadar, Isle of Harris

Benview	Bunavoneadar, Isle of Harris, Eilean Siar, HS3 3AL	01859 502279	★★★★	Bed & Breakfast

Bunessan Isle of Mull

Ardness House	Tiraghoil, Bunessan Isle of Mull, Argyll, PA67 6DU	01681 700260	★★★	Bed & Breakfast
Ardtun House	Bunessan Isle of Mull, Argyll, PA67 6DG	01681 700264	★★★	Bed & Breakfast
Dunan	Bunessan Isle of Mull, Argyll, PA67 6DH	01681 700665	★★	Bed & Breakfast
Newcrofts	Bunessan Isle of Mull, Argyll, PA67 6DS	01681 700471	★★★	Farmhouse
Oran-Na-Mara	Bunessan,Isle of Mull, Isle of Mull, Argyll, PA67 6DG	01681 700087	★★★★	Bed & Breakfast

Burnmouth

White Craggs	Hillfield, Burnmouth, Berwickshire, TD14 5SU	01890 781397	★★★	Bed & Breakfast

Burntisland

Bay View B&B	65 Kinghorn Road, Burntisland, Fife, KY3 9EB	01592 872699	AWAITING GRADING	
Gruinard	148 Kinghorn Road, Burntisland, Fife, KY3 9JU	01592 873877	★★★★	Bed & Breakfast

Unassisted wheelchair access Assisted wheelchair access Access for visitors with mobility difficulties
Bronze Green Tourism Award Silver Green Tourism Award Gold Green Tourism Award
For further information on our Green Tourism Business Scheme please see page 9.

Martins Lodge	60 Aberdour Road, Burntisland, Fife, KY3 0EN	01592 870481	★★★	Bed & Breakfast	
No 69 Cromwell Road	Burntisland, Fife, KY3 9EL	01592 874969	★★★	Bed & Breakfast	

Burray

Ankersted	Burray, Orkney, KW17 2SS	01856 731217	★★★	Bed & Breakfast	

Cairndow

Cairndow Stagecoach Inn	Cairndow, Argyll, PA26 8BN	01499 600286	★★	Inn	

Cairnryan, Stranraer

Cairnryan House	Main Street, Cairnryan, Stranraer, Wigtownshire, DG9 8QX	01581 200624	★★★	Guest House	
The Homestead	Cairnryan, Stranraer, Wigtownshire, DG9 8QX	01581 200203	★★★	Bed & Breakfast	
Rhins of Galloway	A77 Coast Road, Cairnryan, Stranraer, Wigtownshire, DG9 8QU	01581 200294	★★★	Guest House	

Callander

Abbotsford Lodge Guest House	Stirling Road, Callander, Perthshire, FK17 8DA	0877 330066	★★★	Guest House	
Annfield House	18 North Church Street, Callander, Perthshire, FK17 8EG	01877 330204	★★★★	Guest House	
Arden House	Bracklinn Road, Callander, Perthshire, FK17 8EQ	01877 330235	★★★★	Guest House	
Brook Linn Country House	Leny Feus, Callander, Perthshire , FK17 8AU	01877 330103	★★★★	Guest House	
Corriemar	Lagrannoch, Callander, Perthshire, FK17 8LE	01877 330827	★★★	Bed & Breakfast	
Dunmor House	Leny Road, Callander, Perthshire, FK17 8AL	01877 330756	★★★★	Guest House	
Leighton House	162 Main Street, Callander, Perthshire, FK17 8BG	0877 330291	★★★	Bed & Breakfast	
Lubnaig House	Leny Feus, Callander, Perthshire, FK17 8AS	01877 330376	★★★★	Guest House	
Riverside House	Leny Road, Callander, Perthshire, FK17 8AJ	01877 330049	AWAITING GRADING		
Riverview House	Leny Road, Callander, Perthshire, FK17 8AL	01877 330635	★★★	Guest House	
Roslin Cottage	Stirling Road, Callander, Perthshire, FK17 8LE	01877 339787	★★★	Bed & Breakfast	
Southfork Villa	25 Cross Street, Callander, Perthshire, FK17 8EA	01877 330831	★★★★	Guest House	
The Crags Hotel	101 Main Street, Callander, Perthshire, FK17 8BQ	01877 330257	★★★	Guest House	Access for visitors with mobility difficulties
The Knowe	Ancaster Road, Callander, Perthshire, FK17 8EL	01877 330076	★★★★	Guest House	
The Old Rectory Guest House	Leny Road, Callander, Perthshire, FK17 8AL	01877 339215	★★★	Guest House	Access for visitors with mobility difficulties
Westerton	Leny Road, Callander, Perthshire, FK17 8AJ	01877 330147	★★★★	Bed & Breakfast	
Auchenlaich Farmhouse Guest House	Keltie Bridge, Callander, Perthshire, FK17 8LQ	01877 331683	★★★★	Guest House	

By Callander

Frennich House	Brig O'Turk, Kilmahog, By Callander, Perthshire, FK17 8HT	01877 376274	★★★★	Bed & Breakfast	Silver Green Tourism Award

Unassisted wheelchair access · Assisted wheelchair access · Access for visitors with mobility difficulties
Bronze Green Tourism Award · Silver Green Tourism Award · Gold Green Tourism Award
For further information on our Green Tourism Business Scheme please see page 9.

Callanish

Eshcol Guest House	21 Breasclete, Callanish, Lewis, Outer Hebrides, HS2 9DY	01851 621357	★★★★	Guest House

Calvine

The Struan Inn	Calvine, Perthshire, PH18 5UB	01796 483208	★★	Inn

Campbeltown

Oatfield House	Campbeltown, Argyll, PA28 6PH	01586 551551	★★★★	Bed & Breakfast
Redknowe	Witchburn Road, Campbeltown, Argyll, PA28 6PD	01586 550374	★★★	Bed & Breakfast
Rosemount	Low Askomil, Campbeltown, Argyll, PA28 6EN	01586 553552	★★★	Bed & Breakfast
Westbank Guest House	Dell Road, Campbeltown, Argyll, PA28 6JG	01586 553660	★★★	Guest House

By Campbeltown

Pennyseorach Farm	Southend, By Campbeltown, Argyll, PA28 6RF	01586 830217	★★★	Bed & Breakfast
Ormsary Farm	Southend, By Campbeltown, Argyll, PA28 6RN	01586 830665	★★★	Bed & Breakfast

Canisbay

Bencorragh House	Upper Gills, Canisbay, Caithness, KW1 4YD	01955 611449	★★★	Farmhouse

Canonbie

Byreburnfoot Country House B&B	Byreburnfoot, Canonbie, Dumfriesshire, DG14 0RA	01387 371209	★★★★	Bed & Breakfast
Cross Keys Hotel	Main Road, Canonbie, Dumfriesshire, DG14 0SY	013873 71205	★★★	Inn
Four Oaks	Canonbie, Dumfriesshire, DG14 0TF	01387 371329	★★★	Bed & Breakfast

Carbost, Isle of Skye

Ardtreck Cottage	28 Fiskavaig, Carbost, Isle of Skye, Inverness-shire, IV47 8SN	01478 640744	★★★★	Bed & Breakfast
Fineviews	11B Portnalong, Carbost, Isle of Skye, Inverness-shire, IV47 8SL	01470 640309	★★★	Bed & Breakfast
Phoenix House Bed & Breakfast	Phoenix House, Carbost, Isle of Skye, Inverness-shire, IV47 8SR	01478 640775	★★★★	Bed & Breakfast
The Rowans	Portnalong, Carbost, Isle of Skye, Inverness-shire, IV47 8SL	01478 640478	★★★★	Bed & Breakfast

Cardross

Ben Rhydding	3 Richie Avenue, Cardross G82 5LL	01389 841659	★★★	Bed & Breakfast

Carluke

Wallace Hotel	1 Yieldshields Road, Carluke, Lanarkshire, ML8 4QG	01555 773000	★★	Restaurant with Rooms
Burnhead Farm	Carluke, Lanarkshire, ML8 4QN	01555 771320	★★★	Bed & Breakfast

Carnoustie

Carnoustie Coach House B&B	Carlogie Road, Carnoustie, Angus, DD7 6LD	01241 857319	★★	Bed & Breakfast 🚶
Morven House	28 West Path, Carnoustie, Angus, DD7 7SN	01241 852385	★★★★	Bed & Breakfast

Unassisted wheelchair access · Assisted wheelchair access · Access for visitors with mobility difficulties
Bronze Green Tourism Award · Silver Green Tourism Award · Gold Green Tourism Award
For further information on our Green Tourism Business Scheme please see page 9.

Park House	12 Park Avenue, Carnoustie, Angus, DD7 7JA	01241 852101	★★★★★	Bed & Breakfast	
Poppy House	2B Dalhousie Street, Carnoustie, Angus, DD7 6EJ	01241 410214	★★★	Bed & Breakfast	
Seavview Guest House	29 Ireland Street, Carnoustie, Angus, DD7 6AS	01241 851092	★★★★	Guest House	
The Old Manor	Panbride, Carnoustie, Angus, DD7 6JP	01241 854804	★★★★	Bed & Breakfast	

Carnwath

Carnwath Vineyard B&B	120 Main Street, Carnwath, Lanarkshire, ML11 8HR	01555 840156	★★★	Bed & Breakfast	
Walston Mansion Farmhouse	Walston, Carnwath, Lanarkshire, ML11 8NF	01899 810334	★★★	Bed & Breakfast	

Carradale

Dunvalanree	Portrigh Bay, Carradale, Argyll, PA28 6SE	01583 431226	★★★★	Restaurant with Rooms	♿ Silver Green Tourism Award
Kiloran Guest House	Carradale, Argyll, PA28 6QG	01583 431795	★★★	Guest House	

Carrbridge

Birchwood	12 Rowan Park, Carrbridge, Inverness-shire, PH23 3BE	01479 841393	★★★	Bed & Breakfast	
Caberfeidh Guest House	Station Road, Carrbridge, Inverness-shire, PH23 3AN	01479 841638	★★★	Bed & Breakfast	
Carrmoor Guest House	Carr Road, Carrbridge, Inverness-shire, PH23 3AD	01479 841244	★★★	Guest House	
Craigellachie House	Main Street, Carrbridge, Inverness-shire, PH23 3AS	01479 841641	★★★★	Guest House	
The Cairn Hotel	Main Road, Carrbridge, Inverness-shire, PH23 3AS	01479 841212	★★★	Inn	Bronze Green Tourism Award

Carronbridge

Lochend Farm	Carronbridge, Stirlingshire, FK6 5JJ	01324 822778	★★★	Bed & Breakfast	

Castle Douglas

Airds Farmhouse	Crossmichael, Castle Douglas, Kirkcudbrightshire, DG7 3BG	01556 670418	★★★	Farmhouse	
Albion House	49 Ernespie Road, Castle Douglas, Kirkcudbrightshire, DG7 1LD	01556 502360	★★★★	Bed & Breakfast	
Balcary Mews	Balcary Bay, Auchencairn, Castle Douglas, Kirkcudbrightshire, DG7 1QZ	01556 640276	★★★★	Bed & Breakfast	
Craigadam	Castle Douglas, Kirkcudbrightshire, DG7 3HU	01556 650233	★★★★	Farmhouse	
Crown Hotel	King Street, Castle Douglas, Kirkcudbrightshire, DG7 1AA	01556 502031	★★	Inn	
Croys	Bridge of Urr, Castle Douglas, Kirkcudbrightshire, DG7 3EX	01556 650237	★★★★	Bed & Breakfast	
Douglas House B&B	63 Queen Street, Castle Douglas, Kirkcudbrightshire, DG7 1HS	01556 503262	★★★★	Bed & Breakfast	Assisted wheelchair access
Hillowton House	Castle Douglas, Kirkcudbrightshire, DG7 3EL	07707 507543	AWAITING GRADING		
Kings Arms Hotel	St Andrew Street, Castle Douglas, Kirkcudbrightshire, DG7 1EL	01556 502626	★★★	Inn	
Market Inn Hotel	6/7 Queen Street, Castle Douglas, Kirkcudbrightshire, DG7 1HX	01556 505070	★★★	Inn	
Rangemhor	Springholm, Castle Douglas, Kirkcudbrightshire, DG7 3LP	01556 650296	★★★	Bed & Breakfast	
Smithy House	The Buchan, Castle Douglas, Kirkcudbrightshire, DG7 1TH	01556 503841	★★★★	Bed & Breakfast	

♿ Unassisted wheelchair access   Assisted wheelchair access   Access for visitors with mobility difficulties
Bronze Green Tourism Award   Silver Green Tourism Award   Gold Green Tourism Award
For further information on our Green Tourism Business Scheme please see page 9.

The Craig	44 Abercromby Road, Castle Douglas, Kirkcudbrightshire, DG7 1BA	01556 504840	★★★	Bed & Breakfast	
TheBreakPad, Benmore	King Street, Castle Douglas, Kirkcudbrightshire, DG7 1LB	01556 502693	★★★	Bed & Breakfast	

By Castle Douglas

Bluehill Farm	Auchencairn, By Castle Douglas, Kirkcudbrightshire, DG7 1QW	01556 640228	★★★★	Farmhouse	
Deeside	42 Main Street, Crossmichael, By Castle Douglas, Kirkcudbrightshire, DG7 3AU	01556 670239	★★★	Bed & Breakfast	
Chipperkyle Bed and Breakfast	Chipperkyle, Kirkpatrick, Durham, By Castle Douglas, Kirkcudbrightshire, DG7	01556 650223	★★★★	Bed & Breakfast	

Castle Kennedy

Plantings Inn	Castle Kennedy, Wigtownshire, DG9 8SQ	01581 400633	★★★	Inn	

Castlebay, Isle of Barra

Gearadhmor	123 Craigston, Castlebay, Isle of Barra, HS9 5XS	01871 810688	★★	Bed & Breakfast	
Ocean View	78 Borve, Castlebay, Isle of Barra, HS9 5XR	01871 810590	★★★	Bed & Breakfast	
Orosay	170/2 Earsary, Castlebay, Isle of Barra, HS9 5UR	01871 810564	★★★	Bed & Breakfast	

Castletown

Greenland House	Main Street, Castletown, Caithness, KW14 8TU	01847 821694	★★★	Guest House	

Ceann Dibig, Isle Of Harris

Rodean	Ceann Dibig, Isle Of Harris, Western Isles, HS3 3HQ	01859 502079	★★★	Bed & Breakfast	

Cellardyke

Kilrenny Mill Farmhouse	Cellardyke, Fife, KY10 3JW	01333 311272	★★★	Bed & Breakfast	

Ceres

Braemount	Bridgend, Ceres, Fife, KY15 5LS	01334 828169	★★★★	Bed & Breakfast	
Meldrums Hotel	56 Main Street, Ceres, Fife, KY15 5NA	01334 828286	★★	Inn	

Clackmannan

Tower House	10 Main Street, Clackmannan, Clackmannanshire, FK10 4JA	01259 213889	★★★	Bed & Breakfast	

Clarencefield

Farmers Inn	Main Street, Clarencefield, Dumfriesshire, DG1 4NF	01387 870675	★★	Inn	

Coaltown of Balgonie

Hollytree B&B	122 Main Street, Coaltown of Balgonie, Fife, KY7 6HZ	01592 774498	★★★	Bed & Breakfast	

Coldingham

Dunlaverock	Coldingham Bay, Coldingham, Berwickshire, TD14 5PA	01890 771450	★★★★	Guest House	🚶
Priory View	Eyemouth Road, Coldingham, Eyemouth, Berwickshire, TD14 5NH	01890 771525	★★★	Guest House	

♿ Unassisted wheelchair access ♿ Assisted wheelchair access 🚶 Access for visitors with mobility difficulties
Bronze Green Tourism Award Silver Green Tourism Award Gold Green Tourism Award
For further information on our Green Tourism Business Scheme please see page 9.

Directory of all VisitScotland Assured Serviced Establishments, ordered by location.

Establishments highlighted have an advertisement in this guide.

Coldstream

Fernyrig Farm	Birgham, Coldstream, Berwickshire, TD12 4NB	01890 830251	★★★	Bed & Breakfast	
Haymount Guest House	Duns Road, Coldstream, Berwickshire, TD12 4DP	01890 883619	★★★★	Bed & Breakfast	
Old School House	Birgham, Coldstream, Berwickshire, TD12 4NF	01890 830612	★★★	Bed & Breakfast	
Saint Foin	Birgham, Coldstream, Berwickshire, TD12 4NH	01890 830209	★★★★	Bed & Breakfast	

By Coldstream

Nisbet House	Main Street, Leitholm, By Coldstream, Berwickshire, TD12 4JL	01890 840279	★★★★	Bed & Breakfast	

Colinsburgh

Craigdene	20 Main Street, Colinsburgh, Leven, KY9 1LR	01333 340408	AWAITING GRADING		

Collin

Travelodge Dumfires	A75 Annan Road, Collin, Dumfries and Galloway, DG1 3SE	08719 846134	AWAITING GRADING		

Comrie

Drumearn Cottage	The Ross, Comrie, Perthshire, PH6 2JU	01764 670030	★★★★	Bed & Breakfast	🚶
St Margaret's	Braco Road, Comrie, Perthshire, PH6 2HP	01764 670413	★★★	Bed & Breakfast	

Connel, by Oban

Achnamara	Old Shore Road, Connel, Oban, Argyll, PA37 1DT	01631 710705	★★★★	Bed & Breakfast	
Grove House	Main Street, Connel, Argyll, PA37 1PA	01631 710599	AWAITING GRADING		
Ronebhal Guest House	Connel, Argyll, PA37 1PJ	01631 710310	★★★★	Guest House	
Rosebank	Connel, by Oban, Argyll, PA37 1PA	01631 710316	★	Bed & Breakfast	
Wide Mouthed Frog	Dunstaffnage Marina, Connel, by Oban, Argyll, PA37 1PX	01631 567005	★★★	Restaurant with Rooms	♿

Coupar Angus

Red House Hotel	Station Road, Coupar Angus, Perthshire, PH13 9AL	01828 628500	★★★	Inn	🚶

Cowie

Stillrovin In Scotland	Stillrovin,Bannockburn Road, Cowie, Stirlingshire, FK7 7BG	01786 818899	AWAITING GRADING		

Coylton

The Kyle Hotel	40-42 Main Street, Coylton, Ayrshire, KA6 6JW	01292 570312	★★★	Inn	
Woodside Farmhouse	Dalrymple Road, Coylton, Ayrshire, KA6 6HQ	01292 570254	★★★	Bed & Breakfast	

Craigellachie

Highlander Inn	Victoria Street, Craigellachie, Speyside, AB38 9SR	01340 881446	★★★	Inn	
Speybank	S [DLeslie Terrace, Craigellachie, Morayshire, AB38 9SY	01340 871888	★★★	Bed & Breakfast	

♿ Unassisted wheelchair access   Assisted wheelchair access   🚶 Access for visitors with mobility difficulties
Bronze Green Tourism Award   Silver Green Tourism Award   Gold Green Tourism Award
For further information on our Green Tourism Business Scheme please see page 9.

Craigendoran, Helensburgh

The County Lodge Hotel	Old Luss Road, Craigendoran, Helensburgh, Dunbartonshire, G84 7BH	01436 672034	AWAITING GRADING		

Craignure, Isle of Mull

Clachan House	Lochdon, Craignure Isle of Mull, Argyll, PA64 6AP	01680 812439	★★★	Bed & Breakfast	
Dee-Emm Bed & Breakfast	Druim Mhor,, Craignure Isle of Mull, Argyll, PA65 6AY	01680 812440	★★★	Bed & Breakfast	
Pennygate Lodge	Craignure Isle of Mull, Argyll, PA65 6AY	01680 812333	★★★	Guest House	

Crail

Caiplie Guest House	53 High Street, Crail, Fife, KY10 3RA	01333 450564	★★★	Guest House	
Golf Hotel	4 High Street, Crail, Fife, KY10 3TD	01333 450206	★★★	Inn	
Marine Hotel	54 Nethergate, Crail, Fife, KY10 3TZ	01333 450207	★★★	Guest House	
The Hazelton	29 Marketgate, Crail, Fife, KY10 3TH	01333 450250	★★★	Guest House	
The Honeypot Guest House	6 High Street South, Crail, Fife, KY10 3TD	01333 450935	AWAITING GRADING		

Crianlarich

Ewich House	Strathfillan, Crianlarich, Perthshire, FK20 8RU	01838 300300	★★★★	Guest House	
Glenardran	Crianlarich, Perthshire, FK20 8QS	01838 300236	★★★	Guest House	
Inverardran House	A85, Crianlarich, Perthshire, FK20 8QS	01838 300240	★★★	Guest House	
Northumbria Guest House	Glenfalloch Road, Crianlarich, Perthshire, FK20 8RJ	01838 300253	★★★	Bed & Breakfast	
Riverside Guest House	Tigh Na Struith, Crianlarich, Perthshire, FK20 8RU	01838 300235	★★	Guest House	
Strathfillan House	Tyndrum, Crianlarich, Perthshire, FK20 8RU	01838 400228	★★	Bed & Breakfast	
The Lodge House	Crianlarich, Perthshire , FK20 8RU	01838 300276	★★★★	Guest House	
The Luib Hotel	Glendochart, Crianlarich, Perthshire, FK20 8QT	01567 820664	AWAITING GRADING		
West Highland Lodge	Crianlarich, Perthshire, FK20 8RU	01838 300283	★★★	Guest House	

by Crianlarich

Tyndrum Lodge	Tyndrum, by Crianlarich, Perthshire, FK20 8RY	01838 400219	★★	Inn	

Crieff

Arduthie House	Perth Road, Crieff, Perthshire, PH7 3EQ	01764 653113	★★★★	Guest House	
Comely Bank Guest House	32 Burrell Street, Crieff, Perthshire, PH7 4DT	01764 653409	★★★	Guest House	Assisted wheelchair access
Fendoch Guest House	Sma' Glen, Crieff, Perthshire, PH7 3LW	01764 655619	★★★	Guest House	Access for visitors with mobility difficulties
Galvelbeg House	Perth Road, Crieff, Perthshire, PH7 3EQ	01764 655061	★★★	Guest House	
Galvelmore House	Galvelmore Street, Crieff, Perthshire, PH7 4BY	01764 655721	★★★	Bed & Breakfast	Silver Green Tourism Award
Glencairn B&B	Broich Terrace, Crieff, Perthshire, PH7 3BD	01764 655700	★★★	Bed & Breakfast	

Unassisted wheelchair access · Assisted wheelchair access · Access for visitors with mobility difficulties
Bronze Green Tourism Award · Silver Green Tourism Award · Gold Green Tourism Award
For further information on our Green Tourism Business Scheme please see page 9.

Kingarth	Perth Road, Crieff, Perthshire, PH7 3EQ	01764 652060	★★★	Guest House	
Merlindale	Perth Road, Crieff, Perthshire, PH7 3EQ	01764 655205	★★★★	Bed & Breakfast	
The Crieff Hotel	45-47 East High Street, Crieff, Perthshire, PH7 3HY	01764 652632	★★	Inn	
The Rowans	New Fowlis, Crieff, Perthshire, PH7 3NH	01764 683720	★★★★	Bed & Breakfast	
Yann's At Glenearn House	Perth Road, Crieff, Perthshire, PH7 3EQ	01764 650111	★★★★	Restaurant with Rooms	

by Crieff

Cultoquhey House	Gilmerton, by Crieff, Perthshire, PH7 3NE	01764 653253	★	Guest House	
Foulford Inn	Sma'Glen, by Crieff, Perthshire, PH7 3LN	01764 652407	★★	Inn	

Crocketford

Lochview Motel & Restaurant	Crocketford, Dumfries & Galloway, DG2 8RF	01556 690281	★	Lodge	

Culbokie

Ben Wyvis Views	Bydand, Culbokie, Black Isle, Ross-shire, IV7 8JH	01349 877430	★★★★	Bed & Breakfast	
Solus Or	Harmonology Centre,Findon Hill, Culbokie, Black Isle, Ross-shire, IV7 8JH	01349 877828	★★★★	Bed & Breakfast	Silver Green Tourism Award

by Culbokie

Cam-mont House	No 2 Balloan, by Culbokie, Black Isle, Ross-shire, IV7 8HU	01349 877061	★★★★	Bed & Breakfast	

Cullen

Crannoch Hotel	12 Blantyre Street, Cullen, Morayshire, AB56 4RQ	01542 840210	★★★	Inn	
Norwood House	11 Seafield Place, Cullen, Banffshire, AB56 4TE	01542 840314	★★★	Guest House	

Culloden Moor

Bayview	Culloden Moor, Inverness-shire, IV1 2BP	01463 790386	★★★	Bed & Breakfast	

Cumbernauld

Greenacres House	Palacerigg, Cumbernauld, Lanarkshire, G67 3HU	01236 724281	★★	Bed & Breakfast	

Cumnock

Laigh Tarbeg Farm	Ochiltree, Cumnock, Ayrshire, KA18 2RL	01290 700242	★★★★	Farmhouse	

Cunningsburgh

Windrush	Cunningsburgh, Shetland, ZE2 9HE	01950 477408	★★★	Bed & Breakfast	

Cupar

Fairway	Blebo Craigs, Cupar, Fife, KY15 5UF	01334 850371	★★★★	Bed & Breakfast	
Gorno Grove House	By Strathmiglo, Cupar, Fife, KY14 7SE	01337 860483	★★★★	Bed & Breakfast	
Ladeddie Barns B&B	Pitscottie, Cupar, Fife, KY15 5TX	01334 828357	★★	Bed & Breakfast	
Mansfield	52 South Road, Cupar, Fife, KY15 5JF	01334 655120	★★★★	Bed & Breakfast	

Unassisted wheelchair access · Assisted wheelchair access · Access for visitors with mobility difficulties
Bronze Green Tourism Award · Silver Green Tourism Award · Gold Green Tourism Award
For further information on our Green Tourism Business Scheme please see page 9.

Westfield House	Westfield Road, Cupar, Fife, KY15 5TD	07951 710668	AWAITING GRADING		

By Cupar

The Peat Inn	By Cupar, Fife, KY15 5LH	01334 840206	★★★★★	Restaurant with Rooms	
Osnaburgh	84 Main Street, Dairsie, By Cupar, Fife, KY15 4SS	01334 870603	★★★	Bed & Breakfast	
Robins Nest	29 Main Street, Dairsie, By Cupar, Fife, KY15 4SR	01334 871466	★★★★	Bed & Breakfast	

Dailly

Strathtalus	4 Brunston Wynd, Dailly, Ayrshire, KA26 9GA	01465 811425	★★★	Bed & Breakfast	

Dalbeattie

East Daylesford B&B	Colvend, Dalbeattie, Kirkcudbrightshire, DG5 4QA	01556 630483	★★★	Bed & Breakfast	
Heritage Guest House	273 High Street, Dalbeattie, Dumfries and Galloway, DG5 4DW	01556 610817	★★★★	Bed & Breakfast	
Rosemount	Kippford, Dalbeattie, Kirkcudbrightshire, DG5 4LN	01556 620214	★★★★	Guest House	
Springfield B&B	Colvend, Dalbeattie, Kirkcudbright-Shire, DG5 4QA	01556 630403	★★★	Bed & Breakfast	
Trewan	97 William Street, Dalbeattie, Kirkcudbrightshire, DG5 4EE	01556 612337	★★★	Bed & Breakfast	

by Dalbeattie

Millbrae House	Rockcliffe, by Dalbeattie, Dumfries and Galloway, DG5 4QG	01556 630217	★★★★	Bed & Breakfast	

Dalcataig

Lann Dearg Studios	Lann Dearg, Dalcataig, Invermoriston, IV63 7YG	01456 459083	★★★★	Bed & Breakfast	

Dalcross

Easter Dalziel Farm	Dalcross, Inverness-shire, IV2 7JL	01667 462213	★★★	Farmhouse	

Dalgety Bay

11 The Beeches	Dalgety Bay, Fife, KY11 9SN	01383 822167	★★★★	Bed & Breakfast	
The Coach House	1 Hopeward Mews, Dalgety Bay, Fife, KY11 9TB	01383 823584	★★★★	Bed & Breakfast	

Dalkeith

Newbattle Abbey College	Newbattle Road, Dalkeith , Midlothian, EH22 3LL	0131 663 1921	★★	Campus	
Strathcairn	3 Eskview Grove, Dalkeith, Midlothian, EH22 1JW	0131 663 1208	★★★	Bed & Breakfast	
Wester Cowden Farmhouse	Dalkeith, Midlothian, EH22 2QA	0131 663 3052	★★★★	Bed & Breakfast	

Dalmally

Craigroyston	Dalmally, Argyll, PA33 1AA	01838 200234	★★★	Bed & Breakfast	Gold Green Tourism Award
Strathorchy	Dalmally, Argyll, PA33 1AE	01838 200373	★★★	Bed & Breakfast	

Dalry

Langside Farm	By Dalry, Dalry, North Ayrshire, KA24 5JZ	01294 834 402	★★★★	Bed & Breakfast	Gold Green Tourism Award

Unassisted wheelchair access · Assisted wheelchair access · Access for visitors with mobility difficulties
Bronze Green Tourism Award · Silver Green Tourism Award · Gold Green Tourism Award
For further information on our Green Tourism Business Scheme please see page 9.

Dalrymple

Kirkton Inn	1-3 Main Street, Dalrymple, Ayrshire, KA6 6DF	01292 560241	★★	Inn

by Dalwhinnie

Balsporran Cottages	Drumochter Pass, by Dalwhinnie, Inverness-shire, PH19 1AF	01528 522389	★★★	Bed & Breakfast

Darvel

Gowanbank House	Darvel, East Ayrshire, KA17 0LL	01560 322538	★★★	Bed & Breakfast

Denny

Drum Farm	Carronbridge, Denny, Stirlingshire, FK6 5JL	01324 825518	★★	Bed & Breakfast

by Denny

Woodcockfaulds Farm	Thorney Dyke Road, by Denny, Stirlingshire, FK6 6RH	01786 811985	★★★	Bed & Breakfast

Dervaig Isle of Mull

Bellachroy Hotel	Dervaig, Dervaig Isle of Mull, Argyll, PA75 6QW	01688 400314	★★★	Inn
Calgary Hotel	Dervaig Isle of Mull, Argyll, PA75 6QW	01688 400256	★★★	Restaurant with Rooms
Cuin Lodge	Dervaig Isle of Mull, Argyll, PA75 6QL	01688 400346	★★★	Bed & Breakfast
Druimnacroish	Dervaig Isle of Mull, Argyll, PA75 6QW	01688 400274	★★★	Guest House
Glen Bellart House	Dervaig Isle of Mull, Argyll, PA75 6QJ	01688 400282	★★	Bed & Breakfast
Glenview	Dervaig Isle of Mull, Argyll, PA75 6QJ	01688 400239	★★★★	Bed & Breakfast

Dingwall

Fairfield House	Craig Road, Dingwall, Ross-shire, IV15 9LE	01349 864965	★★★	Bed & Breakfast
Moydene	Craig Road, Dingwall, Ross-shire, IV15 9LF	01349 864754	★★★★	Bed & Breakfast

By Dingwall

Autumn Gold Bed & Breakfast	Balblair, By Dingwall, Ross-shire, IV7 8LR	01381 610725	★★★★	Bed & Breakfast
Newton Croft Bed & Breakfast	103 Newton Of Ferintosh, Conon Bridge, By Dingwall, Ross-shire, IV7 8AS	01349 861442	★★★★	Bed & Breakfast

Dollar

Leys Farm	Muckhart, Dollar , Clackmannanshire, FK14 7JL	01259 781313	★★★	Bed & Breakfast

By Dollar

Kennels Cottage	Dollar Beg, By Dollar, Clacks, FK14 7PA	01259 742476	★★★★	Bed & Breakfast

Doonfoot, Ayr

Greenan Lodge	39 Dunure Road, Doonfoot, Ayr, Ayrshire, KA7 4HR	01292 443939	★★★★	Bed & Breakfast

Dornoch

Auchlea	Balnapolaig Muir, Dornoch, Sutherland, IV25 3HY	01862 811524	★★★	Bed & Breakfast

♿ Unassisted wheelchair access ♿ Assisted wheelchair access Access for visitors with mobility difficulties
Bronze Green Tourism Award Silver Green Tourism Award Gold Green Tourism Award
For further information on our Green Tourism Business Scheme please see page 9.

Hillview	Evelix Road, Dornoch, Sutherland, IV25 3RD	01862 810151	★★★★	Bed & Breakfast	
Kyleview House B&B	Evelix Road, Dornoch, Sutherland, IV25 3HR	01862 810999	★★★★	Bed & Breakfast	
Tordarroch	Castle Street, Dornoch, Sutherland, IV25 3SN	01862 810855	★★★	Bed & Breakfast	

By Dornoch

Corven	Station Road Embo, By Dornoch, Sutherland, IV25 3PT	01862 810128	★★	Bed & Breakfast	

Dounby

Ashleigh	Howaback Road, Dounby, Orkney, KW17 2JA	01856 771378	★★★★	Bed & Breakfast	Access for visitors with mobility difficulties
Smithfield Hotel	Dounby, Orkney, KW17 2HT	01856 771215	★★	Inn	

Doune

Glenardoch House	Castle Road, Doune, Perthshire, FK16 6EA	01786 841489	★★★★	Bed & Breakfast	

Drumnadrochit

Aslaich	East Lewiston, Drumnadrochit, Inverness-shire, IV63 6UJ	01456 459466	★★★	Bed & Breakfast	Silver Green Tourism Award
Benleva Hotel	Drumnadrochit, Inverness-shire, IV63 6UH	01456 450080	★★	Inn	
Bradys	30 Kilmore Road, Drumnadrochit, Inverness, IV63 6TS	01456 450071	★★★	Bed & Breakfast	
Bridgend House	The Green, Drumnadrochit, Inverness-shire, IV63 6TX	01456 450865	★★★★	Bed & Breakfast	
Cruachan	Milton, Drumnadrochit, Inverness-shire, IV63 6UA	01456 450574	★★★	Bed & Breakfast	
Drumbuie Farm	Loch Ness, Drumnadrochit, Inverness-shire, IV63 6XP	01456 450634	★★★★	Bed & Breakfast	
Drumnadrochit Hotel	Drumnadrochit, Inverness-shire, IV63 6TU	01456 450218	★★★	Inn	
Elmbank	Lewiston, Drumnadrochit, Inverness-shire, IV63 6UW	01456 450372	★★★	Bed & Breakfast	
Glen Rowan House	West Lewiston, Drumnadrochit, Inverness-shire, IV63 6UW	01456 450235	★★★	Bed & Breakfast	
Glenkirk	Drumnadrochit, Inverness-shire, IV63 6TZ	01456 450802	★★★★	Bed & Breakfast	
Kilmore Farmhouse	Drumnadrochit, Inverness-shire, IV63 6UF	01456 450524	★★★★	Bed & Breakfast	
Knowle B&B	136 Balmacaan Road, Drumnadrochit, Inverness-shire, IV63 6UP	01456 450646	★★★	Bed & Breakfast	
Loch Ness Inn	Lewiston, Drumnadrochit, Inverness-shire, IV63 6UW	07889 496092	★★★	Inn	
Rowan Cottage B&B	10 West Lewiston, Drumnadrochit, Inverness-shire, IV63 6UW	01456 450944	★★★★	Bed & Breakfast	
Woodlands	East Lewiston, Drumnadrochit, Inverness-shire, IV63 6UJ	01456 450356	★★★★	Guest House	Assisted wheelchair access

By Drumnadrochit

Tigh na Bruaich B&B	Glen Urquhart, By Drumnadrochit, Inverness-shire, IV63 6TH	01456 459341	★★★★	Bed & Breakfast	

Drymen

Elmbank	10 Stirling Road, Drymen, Stirlingshire, G63 0BN	01360 661016	AWAITING GRADING		
Green Shadows	Buchanan Castle Estate, Drymen, Stirlingshire, G63 0HX	01360 660289	★★★★	Bed & Breakfast	

Unassisted wheelchair access · Assisted wheelchair access · Access for visitors with mobility difficulties
Bronze Green Tourism Award · Silver Green Tourism Award · Gold Green Tourism Award

For further information on our Green Tourism Business Scheme please see page 9.

Name	Address	Telephone	Grading	Type	
Hillview	The Square, Drymen, Stirlingshire, G63 0BL	01360 661000	★★★	Bed & Breakfast	
Overmains	Balmaha Road, Drymen, Stirlingshire, G63 0HY	01360 660374	★★★★	Bed & Breakfast	

By Drymen

Name	Address	Telephone	Grading	Type	
Croftburn Bed & Breakfast	Croftamie, By Drymen, Stirlingshire, G63 0HA	01360 660796	★★★	Bed & Breakfast	Silver Green Tourism Award
Anchorage Cottage	Rowardennan, Nr Drymen, Glasgow, G63 0AW	01360 870394	★★★★	Bed & Breakfast	

Drynoch, Isle of Skye

Name	Address	Telephone	Grading	Type	
Bla Bheinn	Crossal, Drynoch, Isle of Skye, Inverness-shire, IV47 8SP	01478 640269	★★★★	Bed & Breakfast	
Crossal House	Drynoch, Isle of Skye, Inverness-shire, IV47 8SP	01478 640745	★★★	Bed & Breakfast	

Dufftown

Name	Address	Telephone	Grading	Type	
Braehead Villa	Braehead Terrace, Dufftown, Banffshire, AB55 4AN	01340 820461	★★★	Bed & Breakfast	Access for visitors with mobility difficulties
Davaar	Church Street, Dufftown, Banffshire, AB55 4AR	01340 820464	★★★	Bed & Breakfast	
Gowan Brae	19 Church Street, Dufftown, Banffshire, AB55 4AR	01340 821344	★★★	Guest House	
Tannochbrae Guest House & Scotts Restaurant	22 Fife Street, Dufftown, Banffshire, AB55 4AL	01340 820541	★★★	Guest House	
Fernbank House	Parkmore, Dufftown, Banffshire, AB55 4DL	01340 820136	★★★	Bed & Breakfast	
Nashville	8A Balvenie Street, Dufftown, Banffshire, AB55 4AB	01340 820553	★★★	Bed & Breakfast	

Dumbarton

Name	Address	Telephone	Grading	Type	
Kilmalid House	17 Glenpath, Dumbarton, Dunbartonshire, G82 2QL	01389 732030	★★★	Bed & Breakfast	
Positano	71 Glasgow Road, Dumbarton, Dunbartonshire, G82 1RE	01389 731943	★★★	Bed & Breakfast	

Dumfries

Name	Address	Telephone	Grading	Type	
Alva House	Mainsriddle, Dumfries, Dumfries & Galloway, DG2 8AG	07871 391104	★★★	Bed & Breakfast	
Burnett House	4 Lovers Walk, Dumfries, Dumfries & Galloway, DG1 1LP	01387 263164	★★★	Bed & Breakfast	
Craignair	5 Newall Terrace, Dumfries, Dumfries & Galloway, DG1 1LN	01387 251796	★★★	Bed & Breakfast	
Dumfries Villa	33 Lovers Walk, Dumfries, Dumfries & Galloway, DG1 1LR	01387 248609	★★★	Bed & Breakfast	
East Brae Cottage	Crocketford, Dumfries, Dumfries & Galloway, DG2 8QE	01556 690296	★★	Bed & Breakfast	
Glenaldor House	5 Victoria Terrace, Dumfries, Dumfries & Galloway, DG1 1NL	01387 264248	★★★	Bed & Breakfast	
Glenure Bed and Breakfast	43 Moffat Road, Dumfries, Dumfries & Galloway, DG1 1NN	01387 252373	★★★	Bed & Breakfast	
Grovewood House	Kirkbean, Dumfries, Dumfries & Galloway, DG2 8DW	01387 880721	★★★	Bed & Breakfast	
Hamilton House	12 Moffat Road, Dumfries, Dumfries & Galloway, DG1 1NJ	01387 266606	★★★★	Guest House	
Huntingdon House	18 St Marys Street, Dumfries, Dumfries & Galloway, DG1 1LZ	01387 254893	★★★★	Guest House	
Inverallochy	15 Lockerbie Road, Dumfries, Dumfries & Galloway, DG1 3AP	01387 267298	★★★	Bed & Breakfast	
Lochenlee Guest House	32 Ardwall Road, Dumfries, Dumfries & Galloway, DG1 3AQ	01387 265153	★★★	Guest House	

Unassisted wheelchair access · Assisted wheelchair access · Access for visitors with mobility difficulties
Bronze Green Tourism Award · Silver Green Tourism Award · Gold Green Tourism Award
For further information on our Green Tourism Business Scheme please see page 9.

Merlin	2 Kenmure Terrace, Dumfries, Dumfries & Galloway, DG2 7QX	01387 261002	★★★	Bed & Breakfast	
Millhill Farm	The Glen, Dumfries, Dumfries & Galloway, DG2 8PX	01387 730472	★★★★	Farmhouse	
Nithcairn House	52 Annan Road, Dumfries, Dumfries & Galloway, DG1 3EQ	01387 240082	★★★★	Bed & Breakfast	
Rivendell	105 Edinburgh Road, Dumfries, Dumfries & Galloway, DG1 1JX	01387 252251	★★★★	Guest House	
Torbay Lodge	31 Lovers Walk, Dumfries, Dumfries & Galloway, DG1 1LR	01387 253922	★★★★	Guest House	🚶
Wallamhill House	Kirkton, Dumfries, Dumfriesshire, DG1 1SL	01387 248249	★★★★	Bed & Breakfast	🚶
White Hart Hotel	Brewery Street, Dumfries, Dumfries & Galloway , DG1 2RP	01387 253337	★★	Inn	

By Dumfries

Averon House	Rashgill Park, Quarry Road, Locharbriggs, By Dumfries, Dumfries & Galloway, DG1	01387 711875	★★★★	Bed & Breakfast
Southpark Country House	Quarry Road, Locharbriggs, By Dumfries DG1 1QG	01387 711188	★★★★	Bed & Breakfast
Abbey Arms Hotel	1 The Square, New Abbey, By Dumfries, Dumfriesshire, DG2 8BX	01387 850489	★★	Inn
Smithy House	Torthorwald, By Dumfries, Dumfriesshire, DG1 3PT	01387 750518	★	Bed & Breakfast

Dunbar

Springfield Guest House	Belhaven Road, Dunbar, East Lothian, EH42 1NH	01368 862502	★★★	Guest House
Thorntonloch House Bed & Breakfast	Thorntonloch House, Dunbar, East Lothian, EH42 1QS	01368 840683	★★★★	Bed & Breakfast
Woodside	13 North Street, Belhaven, Dunbar, East Lothian, EH42 1NU	01368 862384	★★★★	Bed & Breakfast

Dunbeath

Tormore Farm	Dunbeath, Caithness, KW6 6EH	01593 731240	★★	Farmhouse

Dunblane

Ciar Mhor	Auchinlay Road, Dunblane, Perthshire, FK15 9JS	01786 823371	★★★	Bed & Breakfast

Dundee

Aberlaw Guest House	230 Broughty Ferry Road, Dundee, Angus, DD4 7JP	01382 456929	★★★	Guest House
Alcorn Guest House	5 Hyndford Street, Dundee, Angus, DD2 1HQ	01382 668433	★★★	Guest House
Anderson's Guest House	285 Perth Road, Dundee, Angus, DD2 1JS	01382 668585	★★★	Guest House
Ardmoy	359 Arbroath Road, Dundee, Angus, DD4 7SQ	01382 453249	★★★	Bed & Breakfast
Ashvilla	216 Arbroath Road, Dundee, Angus, DD4 7RZ	01382 450831	★★★	Bed & Breakfast
Balmuirfield House	Harestane Road, Dundee, Angus, DD3 0NU	01382 818444	★★★★	Bed & Breakfast
Cullaig Guest House	1 Rosemount Terrace, Dundee, Angus, DD3 6JQ	01382 322154	★★★	Guest House
Errolbank Guest House	9 Dalgleish Road, Dundee, Angus, DD4 7JN	01382 462118	★★★	Guest House
Grosvenor Hotel	1 Grosvenor Road, Dundee, Angus, DD2 1LF	01382 642991	★★★	Guest House
St Leonard B&B	22 Albany Terrace, Dundee, Angus, DD3 6HR	01382 227146	★	Guest House

♿ Unassisted wheelchair access ♿ Assisted wheelchair access 🚶 Access for visitors with mobility difficulties
Bronze Green Tourism Award Silver Green Tourism Award Gold Green Tourism Award
For further information on our Green Tourism Business Scheme please see page 9.

Name	Address	Telephone	Grading	Type	Facilities
Strathdon Guest House	277 Perth Road, Dundee, Angus, DD2 1JS	01382 665648	★★★	Guest House	
The Grampian	295 Perth Road, Dundee, Angus, DD2 1JS	01382 667785	★★★	Guest House	
Travelodge Dundee	A90 Kingsway, Dundee, Angus, DD2 4TD	08719 846135	AWAITING GRADING		
Travelodge Dundee Central	152-158 West Marketgait, Dundee, Angus, DD1 1NJ	08719 846301	AWAITING GRADING		
West Park Centre	319 Perth Road, Dundee, Angus, DD2 1NN	01382 647177	★★★	Campus	Unassisted wheelchair access
Your Hotel	296a Strathmore Avenue, Dundee, Angus, DD3 6SP	01382 826000	★★	Lodge	Unassisted wheelchair access

Dunfermline

Name	Address	Telephone	Grading	Type	Facilities
Bell House	23 Maitland Street, Dunfermline, Fife, KY12 8HE	01383 723701	★★★	Bed & Breakfast	
Carneil Farm	Carnock, Dunfermline, Fife, KY12 9JJ	01383 850285	★★★★	Farmhouse	
Clarke Cottage Guest House	139 Halbeath Road, Dunfermline, Fife, KY11 4LA	01383 735935	★★★	Guest House	Access for visitors with mobility difficulties
Grange Farmhouse	Grange Road, Dunfermline, Fife, KY11 3DG	01383 733125	AWAITING GRADING		
Hillview House	9 Aberdour Road, Dunfermline, Fife, KY11 4PB	01383 726278	★★★★	Bed & Breakfast	
Pitreavie Guest House	3 Aberdour Road, Dunfermline, Fife, KY11 4PB	01383 724244	★★★	Guest House	
Roscobie Farmhouse	Dunfermline, Fife, KY12 0SG	01383 731571	★★★★	Farmhouse	

Dunkeld

Name	Address	Telephone	Grading	Type	Facilities
Hatton Grange	Lower Hatton, Dunkeld, Perthshire, PH8 0ET	01350 727137	★★★	Bed & Breakfast	
Letter Farm	Loch of the Lowes, Dunkeld, Perthshire, PH8 0HH	01350 724254	★★★★	Farmhouse	Silver Green Tourism Award
The Bridge Bed & Breakfast	10 Bridge Street, Dunkeld, Perthshire, PH8 0AH	01350 727068	★★★★	Bed & Breakfast	
Upper Hatton	Dunkeld, Perthshire, PH8 0ER	07762 276693	★★★	Bed & Breakfast	

By Dunkeld

Name	Address	Telephone	Grading	Type	Facilities
The Birnam Guest House	4 Murthly Terrace, Birnam, By Dunkeld, Perthshire, PH8 0BG	01350 727201	★★★	Guest House	
Byways	Perth Road, Birnam, By Dunkeld, Perthshire, PH8 0DH	01350 727542	★★★	Bed & Breakfast	
Tayburn House	Perth Road, Birnam, By Dunkeld, Perthshire, PH8 0BQ	01350 728822	★★★	Bed & Breakfast	

Dunoon

Name	Address	Telephone	Grading	Type	Facilities
Ardtully Guest House	297 Marine Parade, Hunters Quay, Dunoon, Argyll, PA23 3HN	01369 702478	★★★	Guest House	
Bay House	West Bay Promenade, Dunoon, Argyll, PA23 7HU	01369 704832	★★★	Guest House	Bronze Green Tourism Award
Blairmore House	Blairmore, Dunoon, Argyll, PA23 8TH	01369 840090	★★★	Bed & Breakfast	
Craigen	85 Argyll Street, Dunoon, Argyll, PA23 7DH	01369 702307	★★	Guest House	
Craigieburn	Alexandra Parade, East Bay, Dunoon, Argyll, PA23 8AN	01369 702048	★★	Guest House	
Dhailling Lodge	155 Alexandra Parade, Dunoon, Argyll, PA23 8AW	07051 130655	★★★★	Guest House	
Eileagan	47 Kilbride Road, Dunoon, Argyll, PA23 7LN	01369 707047	★★★★	Bed & Breakfast	

Unassisted wheelchair access · Assisted wheelchair access · Access for visitors with mobility difficulties
Bronze Green Tourism Award · Silver Green Tourism Award · Gold Green Tourism Award
For further information on our Green Tourism Business Scheme please see page 9.

Foxbank	Marine Parades, Hunters Quay, Dunoon, Argyll, PA23 8HJ	01369 703858	★★	Bed & Breakfast	
Mayfair Hotel	7 Clyde Street, Kirn, Dunoon, Argyll, PA23 8DX	01369 703803	★★★	Guest House	
Milton Tower Guest House	West Bay , Dunoon, Argyll, PA23 7LD	01369 705785	★★★	Guest House	
Sebright	41A Alexandra Parade, Dunoon, Argyll, PA23 8AF	01369 702099	★★	Guest House	
St Ives Hotel	West Bay, Dunoon, Argyll, PA23 7HU	01369 702400	★★	Guest House	
The Cedars	51 Alexandra Parade, East Bay, Dunoon, Argyll, PA23 8AF	01369 702425	★★★★	Guest House	
The Watermill	Glendaruel, Dunoon, Argyll, PA22 3AB	01369 820203	★★★★	Bed & Breakfast	
Undercliff Bed and Breakfast	275 Marine Parade, Hunters Quay, Dunoon, Argyll, PA23 8HN	01369 704688	★★★	Bed & Breakfast	
Vaila	277 Argyll Street, Dunoon, Argyll, PA23 7QY	01369 707540	★★	Bed & Breakfast	
Undercliff Bed and Breakfast	275 Marine Parade, Hunters Quay, Dunoon, Argyll, PA23 8HN	01369 704688	★★★	Bed & Breakfast	

By Dunoon

Duncreggan House	Blairmore, By Dunoon, Argyll, PA23 9TG	07973 129490	★★★	Bed & Breakfast	
The Cot House Hotel	by Sandbank, Kilmun, By Dunoon, Argyll, PA23 8QS	01369 840260	★★	Inn	
St Munns Old Manse	Shore Road, Kilmun, By Dunoon, Argyll, PA23 8SD	01369 840311	★★★	Bed & Breakfast	
Coylet Inn	Loch Eck, By Dunoon, Argyll, PA23 8SG	01369 840426	★★★	Inn	

Duns

Claymore House	8 Langtongate, Duns, Berwickshire, TD11 3AE	01361 883652	★★	Bed & Breakfast	
Crosshall Farm	Greenlaw, Duns, Berwickshire, TD10 6UL	0189084 0220	★★★★	Farmhouse	
Maines North Lodge	Chirnside, Duns, Berwickshire, TD11 3LD	01890 819171	★★★★	Bed & Breakfast	
Ravelaw Farmhouse	Ravelaw, Duns, Berwickshire, TD11 3NQ	01890 870207	★★★★	Farmhouse	

Dunscore

Boreland Farm	Dunscore, Dumfriesshire, DG2 0XA	01387 820287	★★★	Farmhouse	

Dunsyre

Dunsyre Mains Farm	Dunsyre, Lanarkshire, ML11 8NQ	01899 810251	★★★	Bed & Breakfast	

Duntrune

Main Wing	Duntrune House, Duntrune, Dundee, DD4 0PJ	01382 350 239	★★★★	Bed & Breakfast	🚶 Silver Green Tourism Award

Dunure

The Dunure Inn	9-11 Harbour View, Dunure, Ayrshire, KA7 4LN	01292 500549	★★★	Inn	

Dunvegan, Isle of Skye

Achalochan House	1/3 / 4 Ose, Dunvegan, Isle of Skye, Inverness-shire, IV56 8FJ	01470 572323	★★★★	Bed & Breakfast	
Ardmorn	Roskhill, Dunvegan, Isle of Skye, Inverness-shire, IV55 8ZD	01470 521354	★★★★	Bed & Breakfast	

Unassisted wheelchair access · Assisted wheelchair access · Access for visitors with mobility difficulties
Bronze Green Tourism Award · Silver Green Tourism Award · Gold Green Tourism Award
For further information on our Green Tourism Business Scheme please see page 9.

Balmeanach House	M [DBalmeanach, Struan, Dunvegan, Isle of Skye, Inverness-shire, IV56 8FH	01470 572320	★★★★	Bed & Breakfast
Roskhill House	Roskhill, Dunvegan, Isle of Skye, Inverness-shire, IV55 8ZD	01470 521317	★★★	Guest House
Silverdale	14 Skinidin, Dunvegan, Isle of Skye, Inverness-shire, IV55 8ZS	01470 521251	★★★★	Bed & Breakfast
The Tables	Main Street, Dunvegan, Isle of Skye, Inverness-shire, IV55 8WA	01470 521404	★★	Guest House
Uiginish Farmhouse	Dunvegan, Isle of Skye, Inverness-shire, IV55 8ZR	01470 521431	★★★	Farmhouse

By Dunvegan, Isle of Skye

Three Chimneys	Colbost, By Dunvegan, Isle of Skye, Inverness-shire, IV55 8ZT	01470 511258	★★★★★	Restaurant with Rooms

Durness

Morven	Lerin, Durness, Sutherland, IV27 4QB	01971 511252	★★★	Bed & Breakfast
Wild Orchid Guest House	Durine, Durness, Sutherland, IV27 4PN	01971 511280	★★★	Guest House

Dysart

Merchant House	44 East Quality Street, Dysart, Fife, KY1 2TN	01592 659177	★★★	Bed & Breakfast

Earlston

Broomfield House	10 Thorn Street, Earlston, Berwickshire, TD4 6DR	01896 848084	★★★	Guest House

East Calder

Ashcroft Farmhouse	7 Raw Holdings, East Calder, West Lothian, EH53 0ET	01506 881810	★★★★	Guest House
Overshiel Farm	East Calder, West Lothian, EH53 0HT	01506 880469	★★★	Bed & Breakfast
Whitecroft	7 Raw Holdings, East Calder, West Lothian, EH53 0ET	01506 882494	★★★	Bed & Breakfast

East Kilbride

Creighton Grove	29 Brouster Hill, East Kilbride, Lanarkshire, G74 1AJ	01355 234998	★★	Bed & Breakfast
East Rogerton Lodge	Markethill Road, East Mains, East Kilbride, Lanarkshire	01355 263176	★★	Bed & Breakfast

East Linton

Crauchie Farmhouse	East Linton, East Lothian, EH40 3EB	01620 860124	★★★★	Bed & Breakfast
Linton Hotel	3 Bridgend, East Linton, East Lothian, EH40 3AF	01620 860202	★★★	Restaurant with Rooms

Eastriggs

The Graham Arms Guest House	The Rand, Eastriggs, Dumfriesshire, DG12 6NL	01461 40031	★★★	Guest House	🚶

Ecclefechan

Carlyle House	Main Street, Ecclefechan, Dumfriesshire, DG11 3DG	01576 300322	★	Bed & Breakfast

Eday

Roadside	Eday, Orkney, KW17 2AA	01857 622303	★★★	Bed & Breakfast

♿ Unassisted wheelchair access ♿ Assisted wheelchair access 🚶 Access for visitors with mobility difficulties
Bronze Green Tourism Award Silver Green Tourism Award Gold Green Tourism Award
For further information on our Green Tourism Business Scheme please see page 9.

Eddleston

The Horseshoe Inn	Eddleston, Peebleshire, EH45 8QP	01721 730225	★★★★	Restaurant with Rooms	

Edinbane, Isle of Skye

Ashaig B&B	3 Kildonan, Edinbane, Isle of Skye, Inverness-shire, IV51 9PU	01470 582336	★★★★	Bed & Breakfast	

Edinburgh

Edinburgh First	Chancellor Court, Pollock Halls, 18 Holyrood Park Road, Edinburgh EH16 5AY	0131 651 2007	★★★	Campus	Assisted wheelchair access
10 Baberton Mains Rise	Edinburgh EH14 3HG	0131 442 3619	★★	Bed & Breakfast	
11 Belford Place	Edinburgh, Midlothian, EH4 3DH	0131 332 9704	★★★★	Bed & Breakfast	
2 Seton Place	Edinburgh EH9 2JT	0131 667 6430	★★★	Bed & Breakfast	
21 Mayfield Road	Newington, Edinburgh EH9 2NQ	0131 667 8435	★★★	Bed & Breakfast	
21 West Mayfield	Edinburgh EH9 1TQ	0131 668 2148	★★★★	Bed & Breakfast	
27 Braid Crescent	Edinburgh EH10 6AX	0131 447 5830	★★★	Bed & Breakfast	
37 Howe Street	Edinburgh, Midlothian, EH3 6TF	0131 557 3487	★★	Bed & Breakfast	
38 Dublin Street	Edinburgh, Lothian, EH3 6NN	0131 557 1789	★★★★	Bed & Breakfast	
3A Clarence Street	Edinburgh EH3 5AE	0131 557 9368	★★	Bed & Breakfast	
46A Drumbrae South	Edinburgh, Lothian, EH12 8SZ	0131 539 0909	★★	Bed & Breakfast	
7 Cambridge Gardens	Edinburgh, Lothian, EH6 5DH	0131 554 6196	★★	Bed & Breakfast	
A Room In Leith	146/8 Commercial Street, Edinburgh EH6 6LB	0131 553 2704	★★★★	Bed & Breakfast	
A'Abide'an'Abode	18 Moat Place, Edinburgh EH14 1PP	0131 443 5668	★★★	Bed & Breakfast	
Aaran Lodge Guest House	30 Milton Road East, Edinburgh, Midlothian, EH15 2NW	0131 657 5615	★★★★	Guest House	
Aaron Lodge	128 Old Dalkeith Road, Edinburgh EH16 4SD	0131 664 2755	★★★★	Guest House	
Abbey Lodge Hotel	137 Drum Street, Gilmerton, Edinburgh EH17 8RJ	0131 6649548	★★	Guest House	Access for visitors with mobility difficulties
Abbotsford Guest House	36 Pilrig Street, Edinburgh EH6 5AL	0131 554 2706	★★★	Guest House	
Abbotshead House	40 Minto Street, Edinburgh EH9 2BR	0131 668 1658	★★	Guest House	
Abcorn Guest House	4 Mayfield Gardens, Edinburgh EH9 2BU	0131 667 6548	★★★	Guest House	
Abercorn Guest House	1 Abercorn Terrace, Edinburgh, East Lothian, EH15 2DD	0131 6696139	★★★★	Guest House	
Acer Lodge Guest House	425 Queensferry Road , Edinburgh, Midlothian, EH4 7NB	0131 3362554	★★★★	Guest House	
Adam Drysdale House	42 Gilmore Place, Edinburgh, Midlothian, EH3 9NQ	0131 2288952	★★	Bed & Breakfast	
Adria House	11-12 Royal Terrace, Edinburgh EH7 5AB	0131 556 7875	★★★	Guest House	
Afton Guest House	1 Hartington Gardens, Edinburgh EH10 4LD	0131 229 1019	★★★	Guest House	
Airdenair Guest House	29 Kilmaurs Road, Edinburgh EH16 5DB	0131 668 2336	★★★	Guest House	

♿ Unassisted wheelchair access Assisted wheelchair access Access for visitors with mobility difficulties
Bronze Green Tourism Award Silver Green Tourism Award Gold Green Tourism Award
For further information on our Green Tourism Business Scheme please see page 9.

Airlie Guest House	29 Minto Street, Edinburgh EH9 1SB	0131 667 3562	★★★	Guest House	
Albyn Town House	16 Hartington Gardens, Edinburgh EH10 4LD	0131 229 6459	★★★	Guest House	
Allburys	8 Magdal Crescent, Edinburgh, Lothian, EH12 5BE	0131 337 1043	★★★★	Bed & Breakfast	
Allison House	17 Mayfield Gardens, Edinburgh EH9 2AX	0131 667 8049	★★★★	Guest House	
Alloway Guest House	96 Pilrig Street, Edinburgh EH6 5AY	0131 554 1786	★★★	Guest House	
Allt nan Craobh	28 Cammo Road, Edinburgh EH4 8AP	0131 339 3613	★★★★	Bed & Breakfast	
Almond House	52 Glasgow Road, Edinburgh, Midlothian, EH12 8HN	0131 467 4588	★★★	Bed & Breakfast	
Alness Guest House	27 Pilrig Street, Edinburgh EH6 5AN	0131 554 1187	★★	Guest House	
Amaragua Guest House	10 Kilmaurs Terrace, Edinburgh, Lothian, EH16 5DR	0131 667 6775	★★★★	Guest House	Silver Green Tourism Award
Appin House	4 Queens Crescent, Edinburgh, Midlothian, EH9 2AZ	0131 668 2947	★★	Guest House	
Ardblair Guest House	1 Duddingston Crescent, Milton Road, Edinburgh, Lothian, EH15 3AS	0131 6203081	★★★	Guest House	
Ardenlee Guest House	9 Eyre Place, Edinburgh EH3 5ES	0131 5562838	★★★	Guest House	
Ardgarth Guest House	1 St Mary's Place, Portobello, Edinburgh EH15 2QF	0131 669 3021	★★★	Guest House	Unassisted wheelchair access
Ardleigh Guest House	260 Ferry Road, Edinburgh EH5 3AN	0131 552 1833	★★★	Guest House	
Ardmor House	74 Pilrig Street, Edinburgh, Lothians, EH6 5AS	0131 554 4944	★★★★	Guest House	
Ard-Na-Said	5 Priestfield Road, Edinburgh, Lothian, EH16 5HH	0131 667 8754	★★★★	Guest House	
Aros House	1 Salisbury Place, Edinburgh EH9 1SL	0131 667 1585	★★★	Bed & Breakfast	
Arrandale Guest House	28 Mayfield Gardens, Edinburgh, Lothian, EH9 2BZ	0131 622 2232	★★★	Guest House	
Ascot Garden	154 Glasgow Road, Edinburgh, Lothian, EH12 8LS	0131 339 2092	★★★	Bed & Breakfast	
Ascot Guest House	98 Dalkeith Road, Edinburgh EH16 5AF	0131 667 1500	★	Guest House	
Ashdene House	23 Fountainhall Road, Edinburgh EH9 2LN	0131 6676026	★★★★	Guest House	Gold Green Tourism Award
Ashgrove House	12 Osborne Terrace, Edinburgh EH12 5HG	0131 337 5014	★★★	Guest House	
Ashlyn Guest House	42 Inverleith Row, Edinburgh EH3 5PY	0131 552 2954	★★★	Guest House	
Auld Reekie Guest House	16 Mayfield Gardens, Edinburgh EH9 2BZ	0131 667 6177	★★★	Guest House	
Aurora Bed & Breakfast	70 North Gyle Terrace, Edinburgh, Lothian, EH12 8JY	07742 661545	★★	Bed & Breakfast	
Averon Guest House	44 Gilmore Place, Edinburgh EH3 9NQ	0131 229 9932	★★	Guest House	
Ayden Guest House	70 Pilrig Street, Edinburgh EH6 5AS	0131 554 2187	★★★★	Guest House	
Aynetree Guest House	12 Duddingston Crescent, Milton Road, Edinburgh EH15 3AS	0131 258 2821	★★★	Guest House	
B&B Harrison	58 Buckstone Terrace, Edinburgh, Lothian, EH10 6RQ	0131 4451430	★★★	Bed & Breakfast	
Badjao B&B	21 Moat Place, Edinburgh, Midlothian, EH14 1PP	0131 443 3170	★★	Bed & Breakfast	
Baird, Lee, Ewing and Turner House	18 Holyrood Park Road, Edinburgh EH16 5AY	0131 651 2011	★★	Campus	

Unassisted wheelchair access · Assisted wheelchair access · Access for visitors with mobility difficulties
Bronze Green Tourism Award · Silver Green Tourism Award · Gold Green Tourism Award

For further information on our Green Tourism Business Scheme please see page 9.

Directory of all VisitScotland Assured Serviced Establishments, ordered by location.
Establishments highlighted have an advertisement in this guide.

Name	Address	Telephone	Grading	Type	Facilities
Ballantrae Hotel At The West End	6 Grosvenor Crescent, Edinburgh, Midlothian, EH12 5EP	0131 225 7033	AWAITING GRADING		
Balmore House	34 Gilmore Place, Edinburgh, Lothian, EH3 9NQ	0131 2211331	★★★★	Guest House	
Barrosa Guest House	21 Pilrig Street, Edinburgh EH6 5AN	0131 554 3700	★★	Guest House	
Ben Craig House	3 Craigmillar Park, Edinburgh EH16 5PG	0131 667 2593	★★★	Guest House	Access for visitors with mobility difficulties
Ben Cruachan	17 McDonald Road, Edinburgh, Midlothian, EH7 4LX	0131 556 3709	★★★★	Guest House	
Ben Doran	11 Mayfield Gardens, Edinburgh, Lothian, EH9 2AX	0131 667 8488	★★★★	Guest House	
Bield B&B	3 Orchard Brae West, Edinburgh, Midlothian, EH4 2EW	0131 3325119	★★★★	Bed & Breakfast	
Birch Tree House	419 Queensferry Road, Edinburgh EH4 7NB	0131 336 4790	★★	Bed & Breakfast	
Blinkbonny House	23 Blinkbonny Gardens, Edinburgh, Lothian, EH4 3HG	0131 467 1232	★★★	Bed & Breakfast	
Bonnington Guest House	202 Ferry Road, Edinburgh EH6 4NW	0131 554 7610	★★★★	Guest House	
Brae Guest House	119 Willowbrae Road, Edinburgh EH8 7HN	0131 661 0170	★★★	Guest House	
Brae Lodge Guest House	30 Liberton Brae, Edinburgh, Lothian, EH16 6AF	0131 6722876	★★★	Guest House	Access for visitors with mobility difficulties
Brig O'Doon Guest House	262 Ferry Road, Edinburgh EH5 3AN	0131 552 3953	★★★	Guest House	
Briggend Guest House	19 Old Dalkeith Road, Edinburgh, Midlothian, EH16 4TE	0131 258 0810	★★★	Guest House	
Brodie's Guest House	22 East Claremont Street, Edinburgh EH7 4JP	0131 556 4032	★★★	Guest House	
Brothaig House	18 Craigmillar Park, Edinburgh EH16 5PS	0131 667 2202	★★★	Guest House	
Burns Guest House	67 Gilmore Place, Edinburgh EH3 9NU	0131 229 1669	★★★	Guest House	
Capital Guest House	7 Mayfield Road, Newington, Edinburgh EH9 2NG	0131 466 0717	★★★	Guest House	
Carrington	38 Pilrig Street, Edinburgh EH6 5AN	0131 554 4769	★★★	Guest House	
Casa Buzzo Guest House	8 Kilmaurs Road, Edinburgh EH16 5DA	0131 667 8998	★★★	Guest House	
Castle Park Guest House	75 Gilmore Place, Edinburgh EH3 9NU	0131 229 1215	★★	Guest House	
Castle View	30 Castle Street, Edinburgh, Lothian, EH2 3HT	0131 226 5784	★★★	Guest House	
Ceol-na-Mara	50 Paisley Crescent, Edinburgh EH8 7JQ	0131 661 6337	★★★	Bed & Breakfast	
Charleston House Guest House	38 Minto Street, Edinburgh EH9 2BS	0131 667 6589	★★★	Guest House	Bronze Green Tourism Award
Clan Walker Guest House	96 Dalkeith Road, Edinburgh, Lothian , EH16 5AF	0131 667 1244	★★★	Guest House	
Classic Guest House	50 Mayfield Road, Edinburgh EH9 2NH	0131 6675847	★★★	Guest House	
Cloughley B&B	36 Upper Gray Street, Edinburgh, Lothian, EH9 1SW	0131 667 3565	★★★	Bed & Breakfast	
Cluaran House	47 Leamington Terrace, Edinburgh EH10 4JS	0131 221 0047	★★★★	Guest House	
Craigellachie	21 Murrayfield Avenue, Edinburgh EH12 6AU	0131 337 4076	★★★★	Guest House	
Craigmore Bed & Breakfast	20 Craigs Road, Edinburgh, Mid Lothian, EH12 8EL	0131 339 4225	★★★★	Bed & Breakfast	Silver Green Tourism Award
Craigmoss Guest House	62 Pilrig Street, Edinburgh EH6 4HS	0131 554 3885	★★★★	Guest House	

Unassisted wheelchair access   Assisted wheelchair access   Access for visitors with mobility difficulties
Bronze Green Tourism Award   Silver Green Tourism Award   Gold Green Tourism Award
For further information on our Green Tourism Business Scheme please see page 9.

Crioch Guest House	23 East Hermitage Place, Edinburgh EH6 8AD	0131 554 5494	★★★	Guest House	
Cruachan Guest House	53 Gilmore Place, Edinburgh, Midlothian, EH3 9NT	0131 229 6219	★★★	Guest House	
Davenport House	58 Great King Street, Edinburgh, Lothian, EH3 6QY	0131 558 8495	★★★★	Guest House	
Dene Guest House	7 Eyre Place, Edinburgh EH3 5ES	0131 556 2700	★★★	Guest House	
Doocote House	15 Moat Street, Edinburgh EH14 1PE	0131 443 5455	★★★	Bed & Breakfast	
Dorstan House	7 Priestfield Road, Edinburgh EH16 5HJ	0131 667 6721	★★★	Guest House	
Dovecot House	6 Dovecot Road, Edinburgh, Midlothian, EH12 7LE	0131 4677467	★★★★	Bed & Breakfast	
Drumfin	35 Orchard Road South, Edinburgh, Mid Lothian, EH4 3JA	0131 3328209	★★★	Bed & Breakfast	
Dunedin Guest House	8 Priestfield Road, Edinburgh, Lothian, EH16 5HH	0131 6681949	★★★★	Guest House	
Duthus Lodge	5 West Coates, Edinburgh, Lothian, EH12 5JG	0131 337 6876	★★★	Guest House	
Ecosse International	15 MacDonald Road, Edinburgh EH7 4LX	0131 556 4967	★★★	Guest House	
Edinburgh Brunswick	7 Brunswick Street, Edinburgh EH7 5JB	0131 556 1238	★★	Guest House	
Edinburgh House	11 Mcdonald Road, Edinburgh EH7 4LX	0131 556 3434	★★★	Guest House	
Elas Guest House	10 Claremont Crescent, Edinburgh EH7 4HX	0131 556 1929	★	Guest House	
Elder York Guest House	38 Elder Street, Edinburgh EH1 3DX	0131 556 1926	★★★	Guest House	
Emerald House	3 Drum Street, Edinburgh, Lothian, EH17 8GG	0131 664 5918	AWAITING GRADING		
Falcon Crest Guest House	70 South Trinity Road, Edinburgh EH5 3NX	0131 552 5294	★	Guest House	
Flat 6	4 Hillside Street, Edinburgh, Lothian, EH7 5HR	0131 557 8702	★★★	Bed & Breakfast	
Four Twenty Guest House	420 Ferry Road, Edinburgh EH5 2AD	0131 552 2167	★	Guest House	
Frasers B&B	7 Bellevue Place, Edinburgh EH7 4BS	0131 556 5123	★★★	Bed & Breakfast	
Frederick House	42 Frederick Street, Edinburgh EH2 1EX	0131 226 1999	★★★	Lodge	
Gifford House	103 Dalkeith Road, Edinburgh EH16 5AJ	0131 667 4688	★★★★	Guest House	
Gil-Dun Guest House	9 Spence Street, Edinburgh EH16 5AG	0131 667 1368	★★★★	Guest House	
Gillis	100 Strathearn Road, Edinburgh EH9 1BB	0131 623 8933	★★★	Guest House	Assisted wheelchair access
Gladstone Guest House	90 Dalkeith Road, Edinburgh EH16 5AF	0131 6674708	★★★	Guest House	
Glenalmond Guest House	25 Mayfield Gardens, Edinburgh EH9 2BX	0131 668 2392	★★★★	Guest House	
Glendevon	50 Glasgow Road, Edinburgh EH12 8HN	0131 539 0491	★★★	Bed & Breakfast	
Glenfarrer House	36 Farrer Terrace, Edinburgh EH7 6SG	0131 669 1265	★★	Bed & Breakfast	
Granville Guest House	13 Granville Terrace, Edinburgh EH10 4PQ	0131 229 1676	★★	Guest House	
Grosvenor Gardens	The Grosvenor Gardens, Edinburgh, Midlothian, EH12 5JU	0131 3133415	★★★	Guest House	
Halcyon Hotel	8 Royal Terrace, Edinburgh EH7 5AB	0131 556 1033	★★	Guest House	

Unassisted wheelchair access · Assisted wheelchair access · Access for visitors with mobility difficulties
Bronze Green Tourism Award · Silver Green Tourism Award · Gold Green Tourism Award
For further information on our Green Tourism Business Scheme please see page 9.

Directory of all VisitScotland Assured Serviced Establishments, ordered by location.

Establishments highlighted have an advertisement in this guide.

Halidon	19 Lismore Crescent, Edinburgh EH8 7DL	0131 6612959	★★★	Bed & Breakfast	
Harvest Guest House	33, Straiton Place, Edinburgh EH15 2BA	0131 657 3160	★	Guest House	
Heriott Park Guest House	254/256 Ferry Road, Edinburgh EH5 3AN	0131 552 3456	★★★	Guest House	
Highfield Guest House	83 Mayfield Road, Edinburgh EH9 3AE	0131 667 8717	★★★★	Guest House	
Holland House	18 Holyrood Park Road, Edinburgh EH16 5AY	0131 651 2007	★★	Campus	🚶
Ingleneuk	31 Drumbrae North, Edinburgh EH4 8AT	0131 317 1743	★★★	Bed & Breakfast	
Ivy House Guest House	7 Mayfield Gardens, Edinburgh EH9 2AX	0131 667 3411	★★	Guest House	
Joppa Turrets Guest House	1 Lower Joppa(at Beech end of Morton St), Edinburgh EH15 2ER	0131 669 5806	★★★	Guest House	
Judy Guest House	2 St Catherines Gardens, Edinburgh EH12 7AZ	0131 334 6159	★★	Guest House	
Kabayan	31 Craigs Garden, Edinburgh, Lothian, EH12 8HA	07907 326879	★★	Bed & Breakfast	
Kaimes Guest House	12 Granville Terrace, Edinburgh EH10 4PQ	0131 478 2779	★★	Guest House	
Kariba Guest House	10 Granville Terrace, Edinburgh EH10 4PQ	0131 229 3773	★★★	Guest House	
Kelly's Guest House	3 Hillhouse Road, Edinburgh, Lothian, EH4 3QP	0131 3323894	★★★	Guest House	🚶
Kenvie Guest House	16 Kilmaurs Road, Edinburgh EH16 5DA	0131 668 1964	★★★	Guest House	
Kew House	1 Kew Terrace, Murrayfield, Edinburgh EH12 5JE	0131 313 0700	★★★★★	Guest House	
Kilmaurs House	9 Kilmaurs Road, Edinburgh EH16 5DA	0131 667 8315	★★★	Guest House	
Kingsburgh House	2 Corstorphine Road, Murrayfield, Edinburgh, Midlothian, EH12 6HN	0131 313 1679	★★★★★	Guest House	
Kingsley Guest House	30 Craigmillar Park, Edinburgh EH16 5PS	0131 667 3177	★★★	Guest House	
Kingsway Guest House	5 East Mayfield, Edinburgh, Midlothian, EH9 1SD	0131 667 5029	★★★	Guest House	
Kirklea Guest House	11 Harrison Road, Edinburgh EH11 1EG	0131 337 1129	★★★	Guest House	
Lauderville House	52 Mayfield Road, Edinburgh EH9 2NH	0131 667 7788	★★★★	Guest House	
Lindsay Guest House	108 Polwarth Terrace, Edinburgh, Midlothian, EH11 1NN	0131 337 1580	★★★	Guest House	🚶
MacIntosh Guest House	21 Downie Terrace, Edinburgh, Lothian, EH12 7AU	0131 334 3108	★★	Guest House	
Mackenzie Guest House	2 East Hermitage Place, Edinburgh EH6 8AA	0131 554 3763	★★★★	Guest House	
Masson House	18 Holyrood Park Road, Edinburgh EH16 5AY	0131 651 2007	★★	Campus	🚶
Mayfield Lodge	75 Mayfield Road, Edinburgh EH9 3AA	0131 6628899	★★★	Guest House	
McCrae's	44 East Claremont Street, Edinburgh, Midlothian, EH7 4JR	0131 556 2610	★★★	Bed & Breakfast	
Md's B&B	20 Hillview, Queensferry Road, Edinburgh, Midlothian, EH4 2AF	0131 478 3228	★★★★	Bed & Breakfast	
Menzies Guest House	33 Leamington Terrace, Edinburgh EH10 4PX	0131 229 4629	★★	Guest House	
Mingalar	2 East Claremont Street, Edinburgh, Midlothian, EH7 4JP	0131 556 7000	★★★	Guest House	
Morita	3 Mayfield Gardens, Edinburgh, Lothian, EH9 2AX	0131 667 1337	★★	Bed & Breakfast	

♿ Unassisted wheelchair access ♿ Assisted wheelchair access 🚶 Access for visitors with mobility difficulties
Bronze Green Tourism Award Silver Green Tourism Award Gold Green Tourism Award

For further information on our Green Tourism Business Scheme please see page 9.

MW Guesthouse	94 Dalkeith Road, Edinburgh, Mid Lothian, EH16 5AF	0131 662 9265	AWAITING GRADING		
MW Town House	11 Spence Street, Edinburgh, Mid Lothian, EH16 5AG	0131 655 1530	★★★★	Guest House	
Newington Lodge	222 Dalkeith Road, Edinburgh EH16 5DT	0131 667 0910	★★	Bed & Breakfast	
No 4 Hill Street	4 Hill Street, Edinburgh EH2 3JZ	0131 2258884	★★★★	Guest House	
No 45	45 Gilmour Road, Edinburgh, Midlothian, EH16 5NS	0131 667 3536	★★★★	Bed & Breakfast	
No. 23 Mayfield	23 Mayfield Gardens, Edinburgh EH9 2BX	0131 667 5806	★★★★	Guest House	
No. 322 Leith Walk	322 Leith Walk, Edinburgh, Lothian, EH6 5BU	07747 643215	AWAITING GRADING		
Number 54	54 Orchard Drive, Edinburgh EH4 2DZ	0131 332 8810	★★★★	Bed & Breakfast	
Panda Villa	Edinburgh, Lothian, EH16 5DA	0131 667 5057	★★★	Bed & Breakfast	
Priestville Guest House	10 Priestfield Road, Edinburgh EH16 5HJ	0131 667 2435	★★★	Guest House	
Quaich Guest House	87 St John's Road, Edinburgh EH12 6NN	0131 334 4440	★★★	Bed & Breakfast	
Ravensdown Guest House	248 Ferry Road, Edinburgh, Midlothian, EH5 3AN	0131 552 5438	★★★	Guest House	
Relax Guest House	11 Eyre Place, Edinburgh, Scotland, EH3 5ES	0131 5561433	★★	Guest House	
Rick's	55A Frederick Street, Edinburgh EH2 1LH	0131 6227800	★★★★	Restaurant with Rooms	
Robert Bryson Hall	Riccarton, Edinburgh, Midlothian, EH14 4AS	0131 451 3504	★★	Campus	
Robertson Guest House	5 Hartington Gardens, Edinburgh EH10 4LD	0131 229 2652	★★★	Guest House	
Rosevale House	15 Kilmaurs Road, Edinburgh EH16 5DA	0131 667 4781	★★	Guest House	
Rowan Guest House	13 Glenorchy Terrace, Edinburgh EH9 2DQ	0131 667 2463	★★★	Guest House	
Sakura House	18 West Preston Street, Edinburgh EH8 9PU	0131 668 1204	★	Guest House	
San Marco	24 Mayfield Gardens, Edinburgh EH9 2BZ	0131 667 8982	★★★★	Guest House	
Sandaig Guest House	5 East Hermitage Place, Leith, Edinburgh EH6 8AA	0131 554 7357	★★★★	Guest House	
Sandeman House	33 Colinton Road, Edinburgh EH10 5DR	0131 447 8080	★★★★	Bed & Breakfast	
Sandilands House	25 Queensferry Road, Edinburgh EH4 3HB	0131 332 2057	★★★	Guest House	
Shalimar Guest House	20 Newington Road, Edinburgh EH9 1QS	0131 667 2827	★★	Guest House	
Sheridan Guest House	1 Bonnington Terrace, Edinburgh EH6 4BP	0131 554 4107	★★★	Guest House	
Sherwood Guest House	42 Minto Street, Edinburgh EH9 2BR	0131 667 1200	★★★★	Guest House	
Six Marys Place Guest House	Raeburn Place, Stockbridge, Edinburgh EH4 1JH	0131 332 8965	★★★	Guest House	Silver Green Tourism Award
Sonas Guest House	3 East Mayfield, Edinburgh EH9 1SD	0131 667 2781	★★★	Guest House	
South Lodge	2A Dovecot Road, Edinburgh EH12 7LG	0131 334 4651	★★	Bed & Breakfast	
Southside	8 Newington Road, Edinburgh EH9 1QS	0131 668 4422	★★★★	Guest House	
Spylaw Bank House	2 Spylaw Avenue, Edinburgh, Midlothian, EH13 0LR	0131 441 5022	★★★★	Bed & Breakfast	

Unassisted wheelchair access · Assisted wheelchair access · Access for visitors with mobility difficulties
Bronze Green Tourism Award · Silver Green Tourism Award · Gold Green Tourism Award
For further information on our Green Tourism Business Scheme please see page 9.

St Bernards Guest House	22 St Bernards Crescent, Edinburgh, Lothian, EH4 1NS	0131 3322339	★★	Guest House	
St Conan's Guest House	30 Minto Street, Edinburgh EH9 1SB	0131 667 8393	★★★	Guest House	
St Margaret's	13 Corstorphine High Street, Edinburgh, Midlothian, EH12 7SU	0131 334 7317	★★★★	Bed & Breakfast	
St Valery Guest House	36 Coates Gardens, Edinburgh EH12 5LE	0131 337 1893	★★★	Guest House	
Star Villa	36 Gilmore Place, Edinburgh EH3 9NQ	0131 229 4991	★★★	Guest House	
Stewart's Bed & Breakfast	21 Hillview, Queensferry Road, Blackhall, Edinburgh EH4 2AF	0131 539 7033	★★★	Bed & Breakfast	
Strathallan Guest House	44 Minto Street, Edinburgh, Lothian, EH9 2BR	0131 667 6678	★★★	Guest House	
Straven Guest House	3 Brunstane Road North, Edinburgh EH15 2DL	0131 669 5580	★★★	Guest House	Gold Green Tourism Award
Tailors Hall	139 Cowgate, Edinburgh, Lothian, EH1 1JS	0131 622 6801	★★	Inn	
Tania Guest House	19 Minto Street, Edinburgh EH9 1RQ	0131 667 4144	★★	Guest House	
Tankard Guest House	40 East Claremont Street, Edinburgh EH7 4JR	0131 556 4218	★	Guest House	
Tantallon Bed & Breakfast	17 Tantallon Place, Edinburgh, Lothian, EH9 1NZ	0131 667 1708	★★★★	Bed & Breakfast	
Terrace Hotel	37 Royal Terrace, Edinburgh EH7 5AH	0131 556 3423	★★	Guest House	
Teviotdale House	53 Grange Loan, Edinburgh EH9 2ER	0131 667 4376	★★★★	Guest House	
The Alexander Guest House	35 Mayfield Gardens, Edinburgh EH9 2BX	0131 258 4028	★★★★	Guest House	
The Bank Hotel	1 South Bridge, Edinburgh, Lothian, EH1 1LL	0131 556 9043	★★	Inn	
The Beresford	32 Coates Garden, Edinburgh EH12 5LE	0131 337 0850	★★	Guest House	
The Beverley	40 Murrayfield Avenue, Edinburgh EH12 6AY	0131 337 1128	★★★★	Guest House	
The Boisdale	9 Coates Gardens, Edinburgh EH12 5LG	0131 337 1134	★★★	Guest House	
The Broughton	37 Broughton Place, New Town, Edinburgh, Lothian, EH1 3RR	0131 558 9792	★★★	Guest House	
The Cameron Bed & Breakfast	5 Cameron Terrace, Edinburgh, Midlothian, EH16 5LD	0131 620 3126	★★	Bed & Breakfast	
The Conifers	56 Pilrig Street, Edinburgh EH6 5AS	0131 554 5162	★★★★	Bed & Breakfast	
The Corner House	1 Greenbank Place , Edinburgh EH10 6EW	0131 447 1077	★★★	Bed & Breakfast	
The Corstorphine Lodge	188 St Johns Road, Edinburgh, Lothians, EH12 8SG	0131 5394237	★★★	Guest House	
The Glenora Guest House	14 Rosebery Crescent, Edinburgh EH12 5JY	0131 337 1186	★★★★	Guest House	Bronze Green Tourism Award
The Hedges	19 Hillside Crescent, Edinburgh, Lothians, EH7 5EB	0131 478 9555	★★★★	Bed & Breakfast	
The Lairg	11 Coates Gardens, Edinburgh EH12 5LG	0131 3371050	★★★	Guest House	
The Laurels	320 Gilmerton Road, Edinburgh, Midlothian, EH17 7PR	0131 666 2229	★★★	Guest House	Access for visitors with mobility difficulties
The Lodge	6 Hampton Terrace, Edinburgh EH12 5JD	0131 3373682	★★★★	Guest House	
The McDonald Guest House	5 McDonald Road, Edinburgh, Midlothian, EH7 4LX	0131 557 5935	★★★	Guest House	
The Rosebery Guest House	13 Rosebery Crescent, Edinburgh EH12 5JY	0131 337 1085	★	Guest House	

Unassisted wheelchair access   Assisted wheelchair access   Access for visitors with mobility difficulties
Bronze Green Tourism Award   Silver Green Tourism Award   Gold Green Tourism Award

For further information on our Green Tourism Business Scheme please see page 9.

The Town House	65 Gilmore place, Edinburgh EH3 9NU	0131 229 1985	★★★★	Guest House	
The Victorian Townhouse	14 Eglinton Crescent, Edinburgh, Midlothian, EH12 5DD	0131 337 7088	★★★★	Bed & Breakfast	
The Walton	79 Dundas Street, Edinburgh, Lothian, EH3 6SD	0131 556 1137	★★★★	Guest House	
The Witchery by The Castle	Castlehill, The Royal Mile, Edinburgh, Lothian, EH1 2NF	0131 225 5613	★★★★★	Restaurant with Rooms	
Thistle House	1 Kilmaurs Terrace, Edinburgh EH16 5BZ	0131 667 2002	★★	Guest House	
Thrums	14-15 Minto Street, Edinburgh EH9 1RQ	0131 667 5545	★★★	Guest House	
Toby Carvery & Innkeepers Lodge Edin/Wes	114-116 St Johns Road, Edinburgh EH12 8AX	0870 2430500	★★★	Lodge	Unassisted wheelchair access
Travelodge Edinburgh Central	33 St Mary Street, Edinburgh, Midlothian, EH1 1TA	08719 846137	AWAITING GRADING		Assisted wheelchair access
Violet Bank House	167 Lanark Road West, Edinburgh, Midlothian, EH14 5NZ	0131 451 5103	★★★★★	Bed & Breakfast	
Western Manor House	92 Corstorphine Road, Edinburgh EH12 6JG	0131 538 7490	★★★	Guest House	

By Edinburgh

Ardbrae House	85 Drum Brae South, Corstorphine, By Edinburgh, Edinburgh, EH12 8TD	07875 623792	★★★	Bed & Breakfast	
Thistle Dhu	110 Glasgow Road, Corstorphine, By Edinburgh, Edinburgh, EH12 8LP	0131 3392862	★★★	Bed & Breakfast	
Riccarton Arms	198 Lanark Road West, Currie, By Edinburgh, Edinburgh, EH14 5NX	0131 449 2230	★★	Inn	

Elgin

Ardvorlich	125 South Street, Elgin, Moray, IV30 1JB	01343 556064	★★★	Bed & Breakfast	
Auchmillan	12 Reidhaven Street, Elgin, Moray, IV30 1QG	01343 549077	★★★	Guest House	
Moray Bank Bed and Breakfast	21 Institution Road, Elgin, Moray, IV30 1QT	01343 547618	★★★★	Bed & Breakfast	
Moraydale	276 High Street, Elgin, Moray, IV30 1AG	01343 546381	★★★	Guest House	
Richmond B&B	48 Moss Street, Elgin, Moray, IV30 1LT	01343 542561	★★★	Bed & Breakfast	
Southbank Guest House	36 Academy Street, Elgin, Moray, IV30 1LP	01343 547132	★★★	Guest House	
The Croft	10 Institution Road, Elgin, Moray, IV30 1QX	01343 546004	★★★★	Bed & Breakfast	
The Lodge	Duff Avenue, Elgin, Moray, IV30 1QS	01343 549981	★★★★	Guest House	
The Pines Guest House	East Road, Elgin, Moray, IV30 1XG	01343 552495	★★★★	Guest House	
West End Guest House	282 High Street, Elgin, Moray, IV30 1AQ	01343 549629	★★★	Guest House	

Errol

The Courtyard	West Inchmichael, Errol, Perthshire, PH2 7RS	01821 670435	★★★★	Bed & Breakfast	

Eskbank

Glenarch House	Melville Road, Eskbank, Dalkeith, EH22 3NJ	0131 6631478	★★★	Guest House	Access for visitors with mobility difficulties
The Guest House @ Eskbank	Rathaonn House, 45 Eskbank Road, Eskbank, Dalkeith EH22 3BH	0131 663 3291	★★★★	Guest House	

Unassisted wheelchair access · Assisted wheelchair access · Access for visitors with mobility difficulties
Bronze Green Tourism Award · Silver Green Tourism Award · Gold Green Tourism Award

For further information on our Green Tourism Business Scheme please see page 9.

Ettrick Valley

Tushielaw Inn	Ettrick Valley, Selkirkshire, TD7 5HT	01750 62205	★★	Inn

Ettrickbridge, by Selkirk

Cross Keys Inn	Main Street, Ettrickbridge, by Selkirk, Scottish Borders, TD7 5JN	01750 52224	★★★	Inn

by Evanton

Kiltearn House	Kiltearn House, Kiltearn, by Evanton, Ross-shire, IV16 9UY	01349 830 617	★★★★	Guest House

Evie

Stoo Bed & Breakfast	Stoo Costa, Evie, Orkney, KW17 2NN	01856 751761	★★★	Bed & Breakfast
Woodwick House	Evie, Orkney, KW17 2PQ	01856 751330	★★★	Guest House

Eyemouth

The Anchorage	Upper Houndlaw, Eyemouth, Berwickshire, TD14 5BU	01890 750307	★★★	Bed & Breakfast
Redhall Cottage	Eyemouth, Berwickshire, TD14 5SG	01890 781488	★★★★	Bed & Breakfast

Fair Isle

Fair Isle Bird Observatory Lodge	Fair Isle, Shetland, ZE2 9JU	01595 760258	★★	Guest House

48 Cromwell Road	Falkirk, Stirlingshire, FK1 1SF	01324 638227	★★★	Bed & Breakfast
Arbuthnot House	Dorrator Road, Falkirk, Stirlingshire, FK1 4BN	01324 634785	★★★★	Bed & Breakfast
Ashbank	105 Main Street, Redding, Falkirk, Stirlingshire, FK2 9UQ	01324 716649	★★★★	Guest House
Lismore House	Wester Bowhouse Farm, Maddiston, Falkirk , Stirlingshire , FK2 0BX	01324 720929	★★★★	Farmhouse
Rosie's B&B	115 Oswald Street, Falkirk, Stirlingshire, FK1 1QL	01324 634108	★★	Bed & Breakfast
Travelodge Falkirk	West Beancross Farm, Junction 5 M9, Falkirk, Stirlingshire, FK2 0XS	08719 846359	AWAITING GRADING	
Oaklands	32 Polmont Road, Laurieston, Falkirk, Stirlingshire, FK2 9QT	01324 610671	★★★★	Bed & Breakfast
Beancross	West Beancross Farm, Polmont, Falkirk, Stirlingshire, FK2 0XS	01324 718333	★★★	Restaurant with Rooms

Nr Falkirk

Bridgend Farm Country B&B	Moss Road, Near Airth, Nr Falkirk, Stirlingshire, FK2 8RT	01324 832060	AWAITING GRADING	

Falkland

Covenanter Hotel	Falkland, Fife, KY7 7BU	01337 857542	★★	Inn
Ladywell House	Falkland, Fife, KY15 7DE	01337 858414	★★★★	Bed & Breakfast

Falls of Truim

Crubenbeg House	Falls of Truim, By Newtonmore, PH20 1BE	01540 673300	★★★★	Guest House	♿

♿ Unassisted wheelchair access   Assisted wheelchair access   Access for visitors with mobility difficulties
Bronze Green Tourism Award   Silver Green Tourism Award   Gold Green Tourism Award
For further information on our Green Tourism Business Scheme please see page 9.

Fetlar

Gord Bed and Breakfast	Houbie, Fetlar, Shetland, ZE2 9DJ	01957 733227	★★★★	Bed & Breakfast	

Findhorn

Heath House	Findhorn, Moray, IV36 3WN	01309 691082	★★★★	Bed & Breakfast	

Finstown

Linnadale	Heddle Road, Finstown, Orkney, KW17 2EG	01856 761300	★★★★	Bed & Breakfast	

Fionnphort, Isle of Mull

Maolbhuidhe B&B	Maolbhuidhhe, Creich, Fionnphort, Isle of Mull, Argyll, PA66 6BP	01681 700718	★★★	Bed & Breakfast	
Achaban House	Fionnphort, Isle of Mull, Argyll, PA66 6BL	01681 700205	★★★	Guest House	
Abbey View	Fionnphort, Isle of Mull, Argyll, PA66 6BL	01681 700723	★★★	Bed & Breakfast	
Caol-Ithe	Fionnphort, Fionnphort, Isle of Mull, Argyll, PA66 6BL	01681 700375	★★★★	Bed & Breakfast	
Seaview	Fionnphort, Isle of Mull, Argyll, PA66 6BL	01681 700235	★★★★	Bed & Breakfast	Gold Green Tourism Award
Staffa House	Fionnphort, Isle of Mull, Argyll, PA66 6BL	01681 700677	★★★	Bed & Breakfast	

Flodda

Kyles Flodda Bed and Breakfast	3D Kyles, Flodda, Isle of Benbecula, HS7 5QR	01870 603145	★★★★	Bed & Breakfast	

by Fochabers

Castlehill Cottage	Blackdam, by Fochabers, Moray, IV32 7LJ	01343 820761	★★★	Bed & Breakfast	
Garmouth Hotel	South Road, Garmouth, by Fochabers, Moray, IV32 7LU	01343 870226	★★	Inn	

Fordoun

Cocketty Croft	Pitskelly, Fordoun, Kincardineshire, AB30 1LB	01561 320980	★★★	Bed & Breakfast	

Fordyce

Academy House	School Road, Fordyce, Banffshire, AB45 2SJ	01261 842743	★★★★★	Bed & Breakfast	

Forfar

34 Canmore Street	Forfar, Angus, DD8 3HT	01307 468285	★★★	Bed & Breakfast	
Atholl Cottage	2 Robertson Terrace , Forfar, Angus, DD8 3JN	01307 465755	★★★	Bed & Breakfast	
Newton Farmhouse Bed and Breakfast	Newton of Fothringham, Inverarity, Forfar, Angus, DD8 2JU	01307 820229	★★★	Bed & Breakfast	
West Mains of Turin	Rescobie, Forfar, Angus, DD8 2TE	01307 830229	★★★	Bed & Breakfast	

By Forfar

Hatton of Ogilvy	Glamis, By Forfar, Angus, DD8 1UH	01307 840229	★★★★	Bed & Breakfast	
Glencoul House	Justinhaugh, By Forfar, Angus, DD8 3SF	01307 860248	★★	Bed & Breakfast	
Kalulu House	East Murthill, Tannadice, By Forfar, Angus, DD8 3SF	01307 860205	★★★	Bed & Breakfast	

Unassisted wheelchair access · Assisted wheelchair access · Access for visitors with mobility difficulties
Bronze Green Tourism Award · Silver Green Tourism Award · Gold Green Tourism Award
For further information on our Green Tourism Business Scheme please see page 9.

Woodville	Heathercroft, Guthrie Street, Letham,, By Forfar, Angus, DD8 2PS	01307 818090	★★★	Bed & Breakfast	

Forgandenny

Battledown Bed & Breakfast	Off Station Road, Forgandenny, Perthshire, PH2 9EL	01738 812471	★★★★	Bed & Breakfast	♿

Forres

April Rise	16 Forbes Road, Forres, Moray, IV36 0HP	01309 674066	★★★	Bed & Breakfast
Caranrahd	Sanquhar Road, Forres, Moray, IV36 0DG	01309 672581	★★★	Bed & Breakfast
Invercairn House	Brodie, Forres, Moray, IV36 2TD	01309 641261	★★★	Bed & Breakfast
Mayfield	Victoria Road, Forres, Moray, IV36 3BN	01309 671541	★★★★	Bed & Breakfast
Milton of Grange Farm	Forres, Moray, IV36 2TR	01309 676360	★★★★	Farmhouse
Morven	Caroline Street, Forres, Moray, IV36 0AN	01309 673788	★★★	Bed & Breakfast
Sherston	Hillhead, Forres, Moray, IV36 2QT	01309 671087	★★★★	Bed & Breakfast
Springfield	Croft Road, Forres, Moray, IV36 3JS	01309 676965	★★★★	Bed & Breakfast
Uralla	Sanquhar Road, Forres, Moray, IV36 0DG	01309 672082	★★★★	Bed & Breakfast

By Forres

Brough House	Milton Brodie, by Forres, Moray, IV36 0UA	01343 850617	★★★★	Bed & Breakfast

Fort Augustus

Auchterawe Country House	Auchterawe, Fort Augustus, Inverness-shire, PH32 4BT	01320 366228	★★★	Bed & Breakfast
Cahirciveen	Canalside, Fort Augustus, Inverness-shire, PH32 4BA	01320 366202	★★★	Bed & Breakfast
Carn A' Chuilinn	Golf Course Road, Fort Augustus, Inverness-shire, PH32 4BY	01320 366387	★★★★	Bed & Breakfast
Cartref	Fort William Road, Fort Augustus, Inverness-shire, PH32 4BH	01320 366255	★★★	Bed & Breakfast
Hillside	1 The Steadings, Auchterawe, Fort Augustus, Inverness-shire, PH32 4BT	01320 366253	★★★	Bed & Breakfast
Lorien House	Station Road, Fort Augustus, Inverness-shire, PH32 4AY	01320 366736	★★★★	Bed & Breakfast
Mavisburn	2 The Steadings, Auchterawe, Fort Augustus, Inverness-Shire, PH32 4BT	01320 366417	★★★	Bed & Breakfast
Sonas	Fort Augustus, Inverness-shire, PH32 4BA	01320 366291	★★★★	Bed & Breakfast
St Josephs Bed & Breakfast	Fort William Road, Fort Augustus, Inverness-shire, PH32 4DW	01320 366771	★★★	Bed & Breakfast
Thistle Dubh	Auchterawe Road, Fort Augustus, Invernessshire, PH32 4BN	01320 366380	★★★	Bed & Breakfast
Tigh Na Mairi	Canalside, Fort Augustus, Inverness-shire, PH32 4BA	01320 366766	★★	Bed & Breakfast

Fort William

11 Castle Drive	Lochyside, Fort William, Inverness-shire, PH33 7NR	01397 702659	★★	Bed & Breakfast
16 Melantee	Claggan, Fort William, Inverness-shire, PH33 6PZ	01397 703870	★★	Bed & Breakfast
24 Henderson Row	Fort William, Inverness-shire, PH33 6HT	01397 702711	★★	Bed & Breakfast

4 Perth Place	Fort William, Inverness-shire, PH33 6UL	01397 706118	★★★	Bed & Breakfast	
6 Caberfeidh	Fassifern Road, Fort William, Inverness-shire, PH33 6BE	01397 703756	★★★	Bed & Breakfast	
81 Alma Road	Fort William, Inverness-shire, PH33 6HF	01397 703757	★★	Bed & Breakfast	
Achintee Farm Guest House	Achintee, Fort William, Inverness-shire, PH33 6TE	01397 702240	★★★	Bed & Breakfast	
Alma View	Alma Road, Fort William, Inverness-shire, PH33 6HD	01397 704115	★★★	Bed & Breakfast	
Alt-An Lodge	Achintore Road, Fort William, Inverness-shire, PH33 6RN	01397 704546	★★★	Bed & Breakfast	
Aonach Mor House	Torlundy, Fort William, Inverness-shire, PH33 6SW	01397 704525	★★★★	Bed & Breakfast	
Ardblair	Fassifern Road, Fort William, Inverness-shire, PH33 6LJ	01397 705832	★★★★	Bed & Breakfast	
Ardmory	Victoria Road, Fort William, Inverness-shire, PH33 6BH	01397 705943	★★★	Bed & Breakfast	
Argyll House	Hillside Estate, Fort William, Inverness-Shire, PH33 6RS	01397 700004	★★★★	Bed & Breakfast	
Aros Ard	Seafield Gardens, Fort William, Inverness-shire, PH33 6RJ	01397 704142	★★★★	Bed & Breakfast	
Balcarres	Seafield Gardens, Fort William, Inverness-shire, PH33 6RJ	01397 704444	★★★★	Bed & Breakfast	
Ben Nevis Guest House	Glen Nevis, Fort William, Inverness-shire, PH33 6PF	01397 708817	★★★	Guest House	
Ben View Guest House	Belford Road, Fort William, Inverness-shire, PH33 6ER	01397 702966	★★★	Guest House	
Berkeley House	Belford Road, Fort William, Inverness-shire, PH33 6BT	01397 701185	★★★	Guest House	
Blythedale	Seafield Gardens, Fort William, Inverness-shire, PH33 6RJ	01397 705523	★★★★	Bed & Breakfast	
Braeburn	Badabrie, Fort William, Inverness-shire, PH33 7LX	01397 772047	★★★★	Guest House	
Braeside House	Argyll Road, Fort William, Inverness-shire, PH33 6LF	01397 705466	★★★	Bed & Breakfast	
Carna B&B	Achintore Road, Fort William, Inverness-Shire, PH33 6RQ	01397 708995	AWAITING GRADING		
Carinbrook	Banavie, Fort William, Inverness-shire, PH33 7LX	01397 772318	★★★	Guest House	
Craig Nevis West	Belford Road, Fort William, Inverness-shire, PH33 6BU	01397 702023	★★	Guest House	Access for visitors with mobility difficulties
Crolinnhe	Grange Road, Fort William, Inverness-shire, PH33 6JF	01397 702709	★★★★★	Bed & Breakfast	
Cuilcheanna House	Onich, Fort William, Inverness-shire, PH33 6SD	01855 821226	★★★★	Guest House	
Distillery Guest House	North Road, Fort William, Inverness-shire, PH33 6LH	01397 700103	★★★★	Guest House	
Gara-Ni	Fassifern Road, Fort William, Invernes-shire, PH33 6BD	01397 701724	★★★	Bed & Breakfast	
Glen Loy Lodge	Banavie, Fort William , Inverness-shire, PH33 7PD	01397 712700	★★★	Guest House	
Glenaladale House	Achintore Road, Fort William, Inverness-shire, PH33 6RQ	01397 708609	★★★★	Bed & Breakfast	
Glengyle	Glen Nevis, Fort William, Inverness-shire, PH33 6PF	01397 708622	★★★★	Bed & Breakfast	
Glenlochy Guest House	Nevis Bridge, Fort William, Inverness-shire, PH33 6LP	01397 702909	★★★	Guest House	
Glentower Lower Observatory	Achintore Road, Fort William, Inverness Shire, PH33 6PQ	01397 704007	★★★★	Guest House	
Gowan Brae	Union Road, Fort William, Inverness-shire, PH33 6RB	01397 704399	★★★	Bed & Breakfast	

Guisachan Guest House	Alma Road, Fort William, Inverness-shire, PH33 6HA	01397 703797	★★★	Guest House	
Huntingtower Lodge	Druimarbin, Fort William, Inverness-shire, PH33 6RP	01397 700079	★★★★	Bed & Breakfast	
Innishfree	Lochyside, Fort William, Inverness-shire, PH33 7NX	01397 705471	★★★★	Bed & Breakfast	
Keirlee	36 Grange Road, Fort William, Inverness-shire, PH33 6JF	01397 702803	★★	Bed & Breakfast	
Kintail	Seafield Gardens, Fort William, Inverness-shire, PH33 6RJ	01397 701025	★★★★	Bed & Breakfast	
Lawriestone Guest House	Achintore Road, Fort William, Inverness-shire, PH33 6RQ	01397 700777	★★★★	Bed & Breakfast	
Leasona B & B	Torlundy, Fort William, Inverness-shire, PH33 6SW	01397 704661	★★★	Bed & Breakfast	
Lochan Cottage Guest House	Lochyside, Fort William, Inverness-shire, PH33 7NX	01397 702695	★★★★	Guest House	🚶
Lochview House	Heathercroft, off Argyll Terrace, Fort William, Inverness-shire, PH33 6RE	01397 703149	★★★	Guest House	
Melantee	Achintore Road, Fort William, Inverness-shire, PH33 6RW	01397 705329	★★	Bed & Breakfast	
Quaich Cottage	Upper Banavie, Fort William, Inverness-shire, PH33 7PB	01397 772799	★★★★	Bed & Breakfast	
Rhiw Goch	Top Locks, Banavie, Fort William, Inverness-shire, PH33 7LY	01397 772373	★★★	Bed & Breakfast	
Seangan Croft	Mursheirlich, Fort William, Inverness-shire, PH33 7PB	01397 773114	★★★★	Bed & Breakfast	
St Anthonys	Argyll Road, Fort William, Inverness-shire, PH33 6LF	01397 708496	★★★	Bed & Breakfast	
Stobahn	Fassifern Road, Fort William, Inverness-shire, PH33 6BD	01397 702790	★★★	Guest House	
Strathavon	Grange Road, Fort William, Inverness-shire, PH33 6JF	01397 705033	★★★	Bed & Breakfast	
Stronchreggan View Guest House	Achintore Road, Fort William, Inverness-shire, PH33 6RW	01397 704644	★★★	Guest House	
Taransay	Seafield Gardens, Fort William, Inverness-shire, PH33 6RJ	01397 703964	★★★★	Bed & Breakfast	
The Gantocks	Achintore Road, Fort William, Inverness-shire, PH33 6RN	01397 702050	★★★★★	Bed & Breakfast	
The Grange	Grange Road, Fort William, Inverness-shire, PH33 6JF	01397 705516	★★★★★	Bed & Breakfast	
Thistle Cottage	Torlundy, Fort William, Inverness-shire, PH33 6SN	01397 702428	★★★	Bed & Breakfast	
Tigh Na Faigh	Achintore Road, Fort William, Inverness-shire, PH33 6RN	01397 702079	★★★★	Bed & Breakfast	
Torlinnhe	Achintore Road, Fort William, Inverness-shire, PH33 6RN	01397 702583	AWAITING GRADING		
Valley House B&B	Torlundy, Fort William, Inverness-shire, PH33 6SN	01397 703804	★★★★	Bed & Breakfast	
Viewfield	Alma Road, Fort William, Inverness-shire, PH33 6HD	01397 704763	★★	Guest House	
Voringfoss	5 Stirling Place, Fort William, Inverness-shire, PH33 6UW	01397 704062	★★★★	Bed & Breakfast	
West Haven	Achintore Road, Fort William, Inverness-shire, PH33 6RW	01397 705500	★★★★	Bed & Breakfast	
Woodside	Tomacharich, Fort William, Inverness-shire, PH33 6SP	01397 705897	★★★	Bed & Breakfast	
Roneval	Tomonie, Banavie, Fort William, Inverness-shire, PH33 7LX	01397 772206	★★★	Bed & Breakfast	
Treetops	Badabrie, Banavie, Fort William, Inverness-shire, PH33 7LX	01397 772496	★★★★	Bed & Breakfast	
Taormina	Banavie, Fort William, Inverness-shire, PH33 7LY	01397 772217	★	Bed & Breakfast	

♿ Unassisted wheelchair access ♿ Assisted wheelchair access 🚶 Access for visitors with mobility difficulties
Bronze Green Tourism Award Silver Green Tourism Award Gold Green Tourism Award
For further information on our Green Tourism Business Scheme please see page 9.

Glenshian	Banavie, Fort William, Inverness-shire, PH33 7LX	01397 772174	★★★★	Bed & Breakfast		

By Fort William

The Inn at Ardgour	Ardgour, By Fort William, Inverness-shire, PH33 7AA	01855 841225	★★★	Inn	Access for visitors with mobility difficulties	
Ben Nevis View	Station Road, Corpach, By Fort William, Inverness-shire, PH33	01397 772131	★★★	Bed & Breakfast		
Kildonan	Station Road, Corpach, By Fort William, Inverness-shire, PH33 7JH	01397 772872	★★★	Bed & Breakfast		
Mansefield Guest House, Corpach	By Fort William, Inverness-shire, PH33 7LT	01397 772262	★★★★	Guest House		
The Neuk	Corpach, By Fort William, Inverness-shire, PH33 7LR	01397 772244	★★★	Bed & Breakfast		
Dailanna Guest House	Kinlocheil, By Fort William, Inverness-shire, PH33 7NP	01397 722253	★★★★	Bed & Breakfast		
Corrieview	Lochyside, By Fort William, Inverness-shire, PH33 7NX	01397 703608	★★★	Bed & Breakfast		
Rustic View	Lochyside, By Fort William, Inverness-shire, PH33 7NX	01397 704709	★★★★	Bed & Breakfast		
Mayfield	Happy Valley, Torlundy, By Fort William, Inverness-shire, PH33 6SN	01397 703 320	★★★★	Bed & Breakfast		
Ferndale	Tomacharich, Torlundy, By Fort William, Inverness-shire, PH33 6SP	01397 703593	★★★	Bed & Breakfast		

Fortrose

Hillhaven	Ordhill, Fortrose, Ross-shire, IV10 8RA	01381 620826	★★★	Bed & Breakfast		
Waters Edge	Canonbury Terrace, Fortrose, Ross-shire, IV10 8TT	01381 621202	★★★★★	Bed & Breakfast		

Foyers, Inverness

Craigdarroch House	South Loch Ness Side, Foyers, Inverness, Inverness-shire, IV2 6XU	01456 486400	★★★★	Restaurant with Rooms		

Fraserburgh

Findlays Hotel & Restaurant	Smiddyhill Road, Fraserburgh, Aberdeenshire, AB43 9WL	01346 519547	★★★	Restaurant with Rooms	Unassisted wheelchair access	

by Fraserburgh

Lonmay Old Manse	by Fraserburgh, Aberdeenshire, AB43 8UJ	01346 532227	★★★★★	Bed & Breakfast		

Gairloch

Gairloch View B&B	Gairloch View, Auchtercairn, Gairloch, Ross-shire, IV21 2BN	01445 712666	★★★★	Bed & Breakfast		
Heatherdale	Charleston, Gairloch, Ross-shire, IV21 2AH	01445 712388	★★★★	Bed & Breakfast		
Kerrysdale House	Gairloch, Rosshire, IV21 2AL	01445 712292	★★★★	Bed & Breakfast		Silver Green Tourism Award
Lochview	41 Lonemore , Gairloch, Ross-shire, IV21 2DB	01445 712676	★★★	Bed & Breakfast		
Strathlene	45 Strathmore, Lonmore, Gairloch, Ross-shire, IV21 2DB	01445 712170	★★★	Bed & Breakfast		

Galashiels

Craigielea	The Lawyer's Brae, Galashiels TD1 3JQ	01896 753838	★★★	Bed & Breakfast		
Ettrickvale	33 Abbotsford Road, Galashiels, Selkirkshire, TD1 3HW	01896 755224	★★★	Bed & Breakfast	Access for visitors with mobility difficulties	
Monorene	23 Stirling Street, Galashiels, Selkirkshire, TD1 1BY	01896 753073	★★★	Guest House		

Unassisted wheelchair access · Assisted wheelchair access · Access for visitors with mobility difficulties
Bronze Green Tourism Award · Silver Green Tourism Award · Gold Green Tourism Award
For further information on our Green Tourism Business Scheme please see page 9.

Sunnybrae B&B	160 Magdala Terrace, Galashiels, Selkirkshire, TD1 2HZ	01896 758042	★★★	Bed & Breakfast
Watson Lodge Guest House	15/16 Bridge Street, Galashiels, Selkirkshire, TD1 1SW	01896 750551	★★★	Guest House

Garelochhead

Mambeg Country Guest House	Mambeg, Garelochhead , Argyll & Bute, G84 0EN	01436 810136	★★★	Bed & Breakfast

Gartmore

Gartmore House	Gartmore, Stirling, FK8 3SZ	01877 382991	AWAITING GRADING	

Gartocharn

Ardoch Cottage	Main Street, Gartocharn, Dunbartonshire, G83 8NE	01389 830452	★★★★	Bed & Breakfast
The Hungry Monk	Main Street, Gartocharn, Dunbartonshire, G83 8RX	01389 830448	★★★	Inn
The Old School House	Gartocharn, Dunbartonshire, G83 8SB	01389 830373	★★★★	Bed & Breakfast

Garve

Birch Cottage	7 Station Road, Garve, Ross-shire, IV23 2PS	01997 414237	★★★	Bed & Breakfast
Hazelbrae House	Garve, Ross-shire, IV23 2PX	01997 414382	★★★	Bed & Breakfast
The Peatcutter's Croft	Croft 12, Badrallach, Dundonnell, Garve, Ross-Shire, IV23 2QP	01854 633797	★★★★	Bed & Breakfast

By Garve

Inchbae Lodge	By Garve, Ross-shire, IV23 2PH	01997 455269	★★	Guest House

Gatehouse of Fleet

The Bobbin Guest House	36 High Street, Gatehouse of Fleet, Kirkcudbrightshire, DG7 2HP	01557 814229	★★★	Guest House
The Ship Inn	1 Fleet Street, Gatehouse of Fleet, Dumfries & Galloway, DG7 2JT	01557 814217	★★★★	Inn

Gateside

Edenshead Stables	Main Street, Gateside, Fife, KY14 7ST	01337 868500	★★★★★	Bed & Breakfast

Girvan

Ardwell Farm	Girvan, Ayrshire, KA26 0HP	01465 713389	★★	Farmhouse
Garryloop	Penkill, Old Dailly, Girvan, South Ayrshire, KA26 9TG	01465 871393	★★★	Bed & Breakfast (Access for visitors with mobility difficulties)

By Girvan

Cosses Country House, Ballantrae	By Girvan, Ayrshire, KA26 0LR	01465 831363	★★★★★	Bed & Breakfast
Kings Arms Hotel	40 Main Street, Ballantrae, By Girvan, Ayrshire, KA26 0NB	01465 831202	★★	Inn
The Haven	75 Main Street, Ballantrae, By Girvan, Ayrshire, KA26 0NA	01465 831306	★★★	Bed & Breakfast
The King's Arms Hotel	1 Stinchar Road, Barr, By Girvan, Ayrshire, KA26 9TW	01465 861230	★★	Inn
Glengennet Farm	Barr, By Girvan, Ayrshire, KA26 9TY	01465 861220	★★★★	Farmhouse

Unassisted wheelchair access · Assisted wheelchair access · Access for visitors with mobility difficulties
Bronze Green Tourism Award · Silver Green Tourism Award · Gold Green Tourism Award
For further information on our Green Tourism Business Scheme please see page 9.

Glasgow

Adelaide's Guest House	209 Bath Street, Glasgow G2 4HZ	0141 248 4970	★★	Guest House		
Alison Guest House	26 Circus Drive, Glasgow G31 2JH	0141 556 1431	★★	Guest House		
Amadeus Guest House	411 North Woodside Road, Glasgow G20 6NN	0141 3398257	★★	Guest House		
Angus Hotel	966-970 Sauchiehall Street, Glasgow G3 7TH	0141 357 515	★★★	Lodge		
Belgrave Guest House	2 Belgrave Terrace, Glasgow G12 8JD	0141 337 1850	★★	Guest House		
Botanic Hotel	1 Alfred Terrace, Glasgow G12 8RF	01413 377007	★★★	Guest House		
Caledonian Court	Dobbies Loan, Glasgow G4 0JF	0141 3313980	★	Campus		
Claremont House	2 Broompark Circus, Glasgow, Lanarkshire, G31 2JE	0141 554 7312	★★★	Bed & Breakfast		
Clifton Hotel	27 Buckingham Terrace, Glasgow G12 8ED	0141 3348080	★★	Guest House		
Craigielea House	35 Westercraigs, Glasgow G31 2HY	0141 554 3446	★★	Bed & Breakfast		
Craigpark Guest House	33 Circus Drive, Glasgow G31 2JG	0141 554 4160	★★	Guest House		
Hampton Court Hotel	230 Renfrew Street, Glasgow G3 6TX	0141 332 6623	★★	Guest House		
Holly House	54 Ibrox Terrace, Glasgow G51 2TB	0141 427 5609	★★	Bed & Breakfast		
Kelvingrove Hotel	944 Sauchiehall Street, Glasgow G3 7TH	0141 339 5011	★★★	Guest House		
Laurel Bank, 96 Strathblane Road,	Milngavie, Glasgow G62 8HD	0141 584 9400	★★★	Bed & Breakfast		Silver Green Tourism Award
Lomond Hotel	6 Buckingham Terrace, Glasgow G12 8EB	0141 339 2339	★★	Guest House		
Manor Park Hotel	28 Balshagray Drive, Glasgow G11 7DD	0141 339 2143	★★★	Guest House		
McLays Guest House	268 Renfrew Street, Glasgow G3 6TT	0141 332 4796	★	Guest House		
Murray Hall	Collins Street, Glasgow G4 0NG	0141 553 4148	★	Campus		
Newton House Hotel	248-252 Bath Street, Glasgow G2 4JW	0141 3321666	★★★	Guest House		
Oak Tree Inn	Balmaha, Glasgow, Stirlingshire, G63 0JQ	01360 870357	★★★	Inn		
Queen Margaret Hall	55 Bellshaugh Road, Glasgow G12 0SQ	0141 334 2192	★★	Campus	Assisted wheelchair access	Bronze Green Tourism Award
Rab Ha's	83 Hutcheson Street, Glasgow G1 1SH	0141 5720400	★★	Inn		
The Alamo Guest House Ltd	46 Gray Street, Glasgow G3 7SE	0141 339 2395	★★★	Guest House		
The Belhaven Hotel	15 Belhaven Terrace, Glasgow G12 OTG	0141 339 3222	★★★	Guest House		
The Heritage	4-5 Alfred Terrace, Glasgow G12 8RF	07977 422428	AWAITING GRADING			
The Kelvin	15 Buckingham Terrace, Glasgow G12 8EB	0141 339 7143	★★	Guest House		
The Kirklee	11 Kensington Gate, Glasgow G12 9LG	0141 334 5555	★★★	Guest House		
The Merchant Lodge	52 Virginia Street, Glasgow G1 1TY	07779 299001	AWAITING GRADING			
The Piping Centre	30-34 McPhater Street, Glasgow G4 0HW	0141 353 0220	★★★	Restaurant with Rooms		

Unassisted wheelchair access · Assisted wheelchair access · Access for visitors with mobility difficulties
Bronze Green Tourism Award · Silver Green Tourism Award · Gold Green Tourism Award
For further information on our Green Tourism Business Scheme please see page 9.

The Sandyford	904 Sauchiehall Street, Glasgow G3 7TF	0141 334 0000	★★★	Lodge	
The Town House	4 Hughenden Terrace, Glasgow G12 9XR	0141 3570862	★★	Guest House	
The Townhouse Hotel	21 Royal Crescent, Glasgow G3 7SL	0141 332 9009	★★	Lodge	
The Victorian House Hotel	212 Renfrew Street, Glasgow G3 6TX	0141 332 0129	★★★	Lodge	
The Willow	228 Renfrew Street, Glasgow G3 6TX	0141 332 2332	★★	Guest House	
Travelodge Glasgow / Paisley Road	251 Paisley Road, Glasgow G5 8RA	08719 846142	AWAITING GRADING		
Travelodge Glasgow Central	5-11 Hill Street, Glasgow G3 6RP	08719 846335	AWAITING GRADING		
University of Strathclyde	Chancellors Hall, Rottenrow East, Glasgow G4 0NG	0141 553 4148	★	Campus	
Wolfson Hall	Kelvin Campus,West Scotland Science Park, Maryhill Road, Glasgow G20 0TH	0141 3303773	★	Campus	Assisted wheelchair access; Bronze Green Tourism Award
Victoria Hall Limited	171 Kyle Street, Glasgow, Strathclyde, G4 0JQ	0141 3544100	★	Campus	

By Glasgow

Auchenlea	153 Langmuir Road, Bargeddie, By Glasgow, Lanarkshire, G69 7RT	0141 771 6870	★★★	Guest House	
Bearsden Bed & Breakfast	6 New Kirk Road, Bearsden, By Glasgow G61 3SL	0141 9422424	★★	Bed & Breakfast	
Onslow Guest House	2 Onslow Drive, Dennistoun, By Glasgow G31 2LX	01415 546797	★★★	Guest House	
Seton Guest House	6 Seton Terrace, Dennistoun, By Glasgow G31 2HU	0141 556 7654	★★★	Guest House	

Glencoe, Ballachulish

Alltbeag	Tighphuirt, Glencoe, Ballachulish, Argyll, PH49 4HN	01855 811719	★★★★	Bed & Breakfast	
An Darag	Upper Carnoch, Glencoe, Ballachulish, Argyll, PH49 4HU	01855 811643	★★★	Bed & Breakfast	
Callart View B&B	Invercoe, Glencoe, Ballachulish, Argyll, PH49 4HP	01855 811259	★★★	Bed & Breakfast	
Clachaig Inn	Glencoe, Ballachulish, Argyll, PH49 4HX	01855 811252	★★	Inn	Bronze Green Tourism Award
Dorrington Lodge	6 Tigh Phuirst, Glencoe, Ballachulish, Argyll, PH49 4HN	01855 811653	★★★	Guest House	
Dunire	Glencoe, Ballachulish, Argyll, PH49 4HS	01855 811305	★★★	Guest House	
Kings House Hotel	Glencoe, Ballachulish, Argyll, PH49 4HY	01855 851 259	★	Inn	
Scorry Breac Guest House	Hospital Drive, Glencoe, Ballachulish, Argyll, PH49 4HT	01855 811354	★★★★	Guest House	
Signal Rock Cottage B&B	Torren, Glencoe, Ballachulish, Argyll, PH49 4HX	01855 811207	★★★	Bed & Breakfast	

Glendale

Carter's Rest	8/9 Upper Milovaig, Glendale, Isle of Skye, IV55 8WY	01470 511272	★★★★	Guest House	
Clach Ghlas	Lower Milovaig, Glendale, Isle of Skye, IV55 8NR	01470 511205	★★★★★	Bed & Breakfast	

Glenfarg

The Famous Bein Inn	Glenfarg, Perthshire, PH2 9PY	01577 830216	★★★	Inn	

Unassisted wheelchair access Assisted wheelchair access Access for visitors with mobility difficulties
Bronze Green Tourism Award Silver Green Tourism Award Gold Green Tourism Award
For further information on our Green Tourism Business Scheme please see page 9.

Glenforsa, Isle of Mull

Tigh An Solas	Rubha Nan Buth, Glenforsa, Isle of Mull, Argyll, PA72 6JN	01680 300506	★★★	Bed & Breakfast	

Glenhinnisdale Isle of Skye

Cnoc Preasach	2 Peinlich, Glenhinisdal, Snizort, Isle of Skye, Inverness-shire, IV51 9UY	01470 542406	★★★	Bed & Breakfast	

Glenkindie

The Smiddy House	Glenkindie, Aberdeenshire, AB33 8SS	01975 641216	★★★	Bed & Breakfast	

Glenmoriston

Cluanie Inn	Glenmoriston, Inverness-shire, IV63 7YW	01320 340238	★★★	Inn	

Glenrothes

Greenhead of Arnot	Leslie, Glenrothes, Fife, KY6 3JQ	01592 840459	★★★★	Bed & Breakfast	
Travelodge Glenrothes	Bank Head Park, Glenrothes, Fife, KY7 6GH	08719 846278	AWAITING GRADING		

By Glenrothes

The Priory	East End, Star of Markinch, By Glenrothes, Fife, KY7 6LQ	01592 754 566	★★★★	Bed & Breakfast	

Glenurquhart

Glenurquhart House	Marchfield, Glenurquhart, Inverness-shire, IV63 6TJ	01456 476234	★★★★	Restaurant with Rooms	

Gorebridge

Ivory House	14 Vogrie Road, Gorebridge, Midlothian, EH23 4HH	01875 820755	★★★★	Guest House	Assisted wheelchair access

Gourock

Berghaus	15 Turnberry Ave, Gourock, Renfrewshire, PA19 1JA	01475 634550	★★★	Bed & Breakfast	
Bed and Breakfast Castle Levan	Stirling Drive, Gourock, Renfrewshire, PA19 1AH	01475 659154	★★★	Bed & Breakfast	

Grangemouth

Grangeburn House	55 Bo'ness Road, Grangemouth, Stirlingshire, FK3 9BJ	01324 471301	★★★★	Guest House	

Grantown-on-Spey

An Cala Guest House	Woodlands Terrace, Grantown-on-Spey, Morayshire, PH26 3JU	01479 873 293	★★★★★	Guest House	Silver Green Tourism Award
Balliefurth Farm	Balliefurth Farm, Grantown-on-Spey+D1325, Morayshire, PH26 3NH	01479 821636	★★★	Farmhouse	Gold Green Tourism Award
Bellbec	Grantown-on-Spey, Morayshire, PH26 3NP	01479 873810	★★★★	Bed & Breakfast	
Brooklynn	Grant Road, Grantown-on-Spey, Morayshire, PH26 3LA	01479 873113	★★★★	Guest House	Silver Green Tourism Award
Dunallan House	Woodside Avenue, Grantown-on-Spey, Morayshire, PH26 3JN	01479 872140	★★★★	Guest House	
Garden Park Guest House	Woodside Avenue, Grantown-on-Spey, Morayshire, PH26 3JN	01479 873235	★★★	Guest House	
Haugh Hotel	Cromdale, Grantown-on-Spey, Morayshire, PH26 3LW	01479 872583	★★	Inn	
Holmhill House	Woodside Avenue, Grantown-on-Spey, Morayshire, PH26 3JR	01479 873977	★★★★	Guest House	Bronze Green Tourism Award

Unassisted wheelchair access · Assisted wheelchair access · Access for visitors with mobility difficulties
Bronze Green Tourism Award · Silver Green Tourism Award · Gold Green Tourism Award
For further information on our Green Tourism Business Scheme please see page 9.

Kinross Guest House	Woodside Avenue, Grantown-on-Spey, Morayshire, PH26 3JR	01479 872042	★★★★	Guest House	
Parkburn Guest House	High Street, Grantown-on-Spey, Morayshire, PH26 3EN	01479 873116	★★★	Guest House	
Rosehall Guest House	13 The Square, Grantown-on-Spey, Morayshire, PH26 3HG	01479 872721	★★★★	Guest House	
Rossmor Guest House	Woodlands Terrace, Grantown-on-Spey, Morayshire, PH26 3JU	01479 872201	★★★★	Guest House	
The Pines	Woodside Avenue, Grantown-on-Spey, Morayshire, PH26 3JR	01479 872092	★★★★★	Guest Accommodation	
Westhaven	South Street, Grantown-on-Spey, Morayshire, PH26 3HZ	01479 872471	★★★★	Bed & Breakfast	
Willowbank	High Street, Grantown-on-Spey, Morayshire, PH26 3EN	01479 872089	★★★	Guest House	[Access for visitors with mobility difficulties]

By Grantown-on-Spey

Rosegrove Guest House	Skye of Curr Road, Dulnain Bridge, By Grantown-on-Spey, Morayshire, PH26 3PA	01479 851335	★★★	Guest House	
Netherfield B&B	Skye of Curr Road, Dulnain Bridge, By Grantown-on-Spey, Morayshire, PH26 3PA	01479 851258	★★★★	Bed & Breakfast	

Greenock

Denholm B&B	22 Denholm Street, Greenock, Renfrewshire, PA16 8RJ	01475 781319	★★	Bed & Breakfast	
Heather Bed and Breakfast	24 Denholm Street, Greenock, Renfrewshire, PA16 8RJ	01475 724002	★★	Bed & Breakfast	
James Watt College	Waterfront Campus, Customhouse Way, Greenock, Renfrewshire, PA15 1EN	01475 731360	★★	Campus	[Unassisted wheelchair access]

Gretna Green

Alexander House	Glasgow road, Gretna Green, Dumfriesshire, DG16 5DU	01461 337056	★★★	Guest House	
Angus House	166 Central Avenue, Gretna Green, Dumfriesshire, DG16 5AF	01461 337533	★★★	Bed & Breakfast	
Barrasgate House	Millhill, Gretna Green, Dumfries and Galloway, DG16 5HU	01461 337577	★★★	Bed & Breakfast	
Days Inn	Welcome Break Service Area, M74, Gretna Green, Dumfriesshire, DG16 5HQ	01461 337566	AWAITING GRADING		[Unassisted wheelchair access]
Kirkcroft	Glasgow Road, Gretna Green, Dumfriesshire, DG16 5DU	01461 337403	★★★	Bed & Breakfast	
Rhone Villa	Gretna Green, Gretna Green, Dumfriesshire, DG16 5DY	01461 338889	★★★	Bed & Breakfast	[Access for visitors with mobility difficulties]
The Willows	Loanwath Road, Gretna Green, Dumfriesshire, DG16 5ES	01461 337996	★★★	Bed & Breakfast	[Assisted wheelchair access]

Grimsay

Shivinish	Scotvein, Grimsay, North Uist, HS6 5JA	01870 602481	★★★★	Bed & Breakfast	
Ardnastruban	Grimsay, North Uist, HS6 5HT	01870 602452	★★★★	Bed & Breakfast	

Grogarry, Isle of South Uist

Kinloch	Grogarry, Islof of South Uist, Isle Of South Uist, HS8 5RR	01870 620316	★★★	Bed & Breakfast	

Gruline, Isle of Mull

Barn Cottage and Stables	Gruline, Isle of Mull, Argyll, PA71 6HR	01680 300451	★★★	Bed & Breakfast	

Guardbridge

The Larches	7 River Terrace, Guardbridge, Fife, KY16 0XA	01334 838008	★★★	Bed & Breakfast	

Unassisted wheelchair access   Assisted wheelchair access   Access for visitors with mobility difficulties
Bronze Green Tourism Award   Silver Green Tourism Award   Gold Green Tourism Award

For further information on our Green Tourism Business Scheme please see page 9.

Guildtown

Oakwood House	Myreside, Guildtown, Perth, PH2 6DW	01821 650800	★★★★	Bed & Breakfast	

Gulberwick

Virdafjell	Shurton Brae, Gulberwick, Shetland, ZE2 9TX	01595 694336	★★★★	Bed & Breakfast	Access for visitors with mobility difficulties

Gullane

Kellagher B&B	6 The Pines, Gullane, East Lothian, EH31 2DT	01620 843348	★★★★	Bed & Breakfast	
Jadini Garden	Goose Green, Gullane, East Lothian, EH31 2BA	01620 843343	★★★	Bed & Breakfast	
Kilmory	Marine Street, Gullane, East Lothian, EH31 2AZ	01620 842332	★★★	Bed & Breakfast	
Saltcoats Farmhouse	Saltcoats Farm, Gullane, East Lothian, EH31 2AG	01620 842204	★★	Farmhouse	

Haddington

Carfrae	Garvald, Haddington, East Lothian, EH41 4LP	01620 830242	★★★★	Bed & Breakfast	
Eaglescairnie Mains	Haddington, East Lothian, EH41 4HN	01620 810491	★★★★	Farmhouse	Silver Green Tourism Award
Greeenfield Bed and Breakfast	26 Letham Mains Holdings, Haddington, East Lothian, EH41 4NW	01620 822458	★★★	Bed & Breakfast	
Orchard House	22 Letham Mains Holdings, Haddington, East Lothian, EH41 4HB	01620 824898	★★★	Bed & Breakfast	
Old Farmhouse B&B	Redskill Farm, Gifford, Haddington, East Lothian, EH41 4JN	01620 810406	★★★★	Farmhouse	

By Haddington

Fidra House	Athelstaneford, By Haddington, East Lothian, EH39 5BE	01620 880777	★★★★★	Bed & Breakfast	

Halbeath

Travelodge Dunfermline	Halbeath Junction, Halbeath, Fife, KY11 8PG	08719 846 287	AWAITING GRADING		

Hamilton

Avonclyde	15 Smithycroft, Hamilton, South Lanarkshire, ML3 7UL	01698 422917	★★★	Bed & Breakfast	
Reston House B&B	65A Clydesdale Street, Hamilton, South Lanarkshire, ML3 0DD	01698 330614	★★★	Bed & Breakfast	

Harray

Holland House	Harray, Orkney, KW17 2LQ	01856 771400	★★★★★	Bed & Breakfast	

Harris

Hirta House	Isle of Scalpay, Harris, Western Isles, HS4 3XZ	01859 540394	★★★★	Bed & Breakfast	
Dail na Mara	Isle of Scalpay, Harris, Western Isles, HS3 4XW	01859 540206	★★★	Bed & Breakfast	Access for visitors with mobility difficulties

Harthill

Blairmains	Harthill, Lanarkshire, ML7 5TJ	01501 751278	★★	Guest House	

Hawick

Billerwell Farm	Bonchester Bridge, Hawick, Roxburghshire, TD9 8JF	01450 860656	★★★★	Farmhouse	Silver Green Tourism Award

Unassisted wheelchair access · Assisted wheelchair access · Access for visitors with mobility difficulties
Bronze Green Tourism Award · Silver Green Tourism Award · Gold Green Tourism Award
For further information on our Green Tourism Business Scheme please see page 9.

Name	Address	Telephone	Grading	Type	Access	Green Tourism
Hizzy's Guest House	23 B&C North Bridge Street, Hawick, Roxburghshire, TD9 9DB	01450 372101	★★	Guest House		
Hopehill House	Wilton Crescent, Hawick, Roxburghshire, TD9 7EH	01450 375042	★★★	Bed & Breakfast		
Lynnwood Cottage B&B	12 Liddesdale Road, Hawick, Roxburgh, TD9 0ES	01450 372461	★★★★	Bed & Breakfast		
Mosspaul	Teviothead, Hawick, Roxburghshire, TD9 0LP	01450 850245	★★★	Restaurant with Rooms	Unassisted wheelchair access	
Oakwood House	Buccleuch Road, Hawick, Roxburghshire, TD9 0EH	01450 372814	★★★	Bed & Breakfast		
Rosemount	84 Weensland Road, Hawick, Roxburghshire, TD9 9PQ	01450 375405	★★★	Bed & Breakfast		
The Laurels	8 Princes Street, Hawick, Roxburghshire, TD9 7AY	01450 370002	★★★	Bed & Breakfast		
Whitchester Guest House	Hawick, Roxburghshire, TD9 7LN	01450 377477	★★★	Guest House	Assisted wheelchair access	Silver
Wiltonburn Farm	Hawick, Roxburghshire, TD9 7LL	01450 372414	★★★	Farmhouse		
The Steadings	Roundabouts Farm, Chesters, Hawick, Roxburghshire, TD9 8TH	01450 860730	★★★	Bed & Breakfast		

Helensburgh

Name	Address	Telephone	Grading	Type	Access	Green Tourism
4 Redclyffe Gardens	Helensburgh, Dumbartonshire, G84 9JJ	01436 677688	★★★	Bed & Breakfast		
Balmillig	64B Colquhoun Street, Helensburgh, Dumbartonshire, G84 9JP	01436 674922	★★★★	Bed & Breakfast		Gold
Bellfield	199 East Clyde Street, Helensburgh, Dumbartonshire, G84 7AJ	01436 673361	★★★★	Bed & Breakfast		
Eastbank	10 Hanover Street, Helensburgh, Dumbartonshire, G84 7AW	01436 673665	★★★	Bed & Breakfast		Bronze
Killin Cottage B&B	10 Lomond Street, Helensburgh, Dumbartonshire, G84 7PN	01436 670923	★★★	Bed & Breakfast		Silver
Larch View	10 Cumberland Avenue, Helensburgh, Dumbartonshire, G84 8QG	01436 674078	★★★	Bed & Breakfast		
Lethamhill	20 West Dhuhill Drive, Helensburgh, Dumbartonshire, G84 9AW	01436 676016	★★★★★	Bed & Breakfast		
Maybank	185 East Clyde Street, Helensburgh, Dumbartonshire, G84 7AG	01436 672865	★★★	Bed & Breakfast		
Ravenswood	32 Suffolk Street, Helensburgh, Dumbartonshire, G84 9PA	01436 672112	★★★★	Bed & Breakfast		
RSR Braeholm	31 East Montrose Street, Helensburgh, Dumbartonshire, G84 7HR	01436 671880	★★	Lodge	Access for visitors with mobility difficulties	
Shiloh Bed & Breakfast	201 East Clyde Street, Helensburgh, Dumbartonshire, G84 7AJ	01436 671005	★★★★	Bed & Breakfast		
Sinclair House	91/93 Sinclair Street, Helensburgh, Dumbartonshire, G84 8TR	01436 676301	★★★★	Guest House		Silver
The County Lodge Hotel	Old Luss Road, craigendoran, Helensburgh, Dunbartonshire, G84 7BH	01436 672034	AWAITING GRADING			
Westbank	122 West Clyde Street, Helensburgh, Dumbartonshire, G84 8ET	01436 674816	★★★★	Bed & Breakfast		

By Helensburgh

Name	Address	Telephone	Grading	Type	Access	Green Tourism
Timber Cottage	Pier Road, Rhu, By Helensburgh, Argyll and Bute, G84 8LH	01436 820611	★★★★	Bed & Breakfast		
Floral Cottage Guest House	Church Road, Rhu, By Helensburgh, Argyll and Bute, G84 8RW	01436 820687	★★★	Bed & Breakfast		

Helmsdale

Name	Address	Telephone	Grading	Type	Access	Green Tourism
Kindale House	5 Lillieshall Street, Helmsdale, Sutherland, KW8 6JF	01431 821415	★★★★	Guest House		
Broomhill House	Navidale Road, Helmsdale, Sutherland, KW8 6JS	01431 821259	★★★	Bed & Breakfast		

Unassisted wheelchair access   Assisted wheelchair access   Access for visitors with mobility difficulties
Bronze Green Tourism Award   Silver Green Tourism Award   Gold Green Tourism Award
For further information on our Green Tourism Business Scheme please see page 9.

Hillswick

Almara	Upper Urafirth, Hillswick, Shetland, ZE2 9RH	01806 503261	★★★★	Bed & Breakfast	Gold Green Tourism Award

Holm

Commodore Chalets	St Mary's, Holm, Orkney, KW17 2RU	01856 781319	★★★	Guest House

Hopeman

Ardent House	43 Forsyth Street, Hopeman, Moray, IV30 5SY	01343 830694	★★★★	Bed & Breakfast

Huntly

Dunedin Guest House	17 Bogie Street, Huntly, Aberdeenshire, AB5 5DX	01466 794162	★★	Guest House
Greenmount Guest House	43 Gordon Street, Huntly, Aberdeenshire, AB54 8EQ	01466 792482	★★★	Guest House
Hillview	Provost Street, Huntly, Aberdeenshire, AB54 5BB	01466 794870	★★★	Bed & Breakfast
New Marnoch	48 King Street, Huntly, Aberdeenshire, AB54 8HP	01466 792018	★★★★	Bed & Breakfast
Strathlene	MacDonald Street, Huntly AB54 8EW	01466 792664	★★★★	Bed & Breakfast

By Huntly

Drumdelgie House	Drumdelgie, By Huntly, Aberdeenshire, AB5 4TH	01466 760368	★★★★	Bed & Breakfast
Bandora	Yonder Bognie, Forgue, By Huntly, Aberdeenshire, AB54 6BR	01466 730375	★★★	Bed & Breakfast
Essie Croft	Rhynie, By Huntly, Aberdeenshire, AB54 4HN	01464 861120	★★★	Bed & Breakfast

Innerleithen

Caddon View	14 Pirn Road, Innerleithen, Peeblesshire, EH44 6HH	01896 830208	★★★★	Guest House
Glede Knowe	16 St Ronan's Terrace, Innerleithen, Scottish Borders, EH44 6RB	0775 2294346	★★★★	Guest House
The Old School House	Traquair, Innerleithen, Peeblesshire, EH44 6PP	01896 830425	★★	Bed & Breakfast
Traquair House	Innerleithen, Peeblesshire, EH44 6PW	01896 830323	★★★★	Bed & Breakfast

Inveraray

10 Argyll Court	Inveraray, Argyll, PA32 8UT	01499 302273	★★★	Bed & Breakfast
Arkland B&B	15 Arkland, Inveraray, Argyll, PA32 8UD	01499 302361	★★	Bed & Breakfast
Barn Park B&B	12 Barn Park, Inveraray, Argyll, PA32 8UP	01499 302483	★★★	Bed & Breakfast
Breagha Lodge	The Avenue, Inveraray, Argyll, PA32 8YX	01499 302061	★★★	Bed & Breakfast
Creag Dhubh	Inveraray, Argyll, PA32 8XT	01499 302430	★★★★	Guest House
Killean Farm House	Inveraray, Argyll, PA32 8XT	01499 302474	★★★	Guest House
Maggie's B&B	5 Queen Elizabeth Cottages, Furnace, Inveraray, Argyll, PA32 8XX	01499 500229	★★★	Bed & Breakfast
Rudha-Na-Craige	Rudha-Na-Craige, Inveraray, Argyll, PA32 8YX	01499 302668	★★★★	Guest House

Unassisted wheelchair access   Assisted wheelchair access   Access for visitors with mobility difficulties
Bronze Green Tourism Award   Silver Green Tourism Award   Gold Green Tourism Award
For further information on our Green Tourism Business Scheme please see page 9.

By Inverary

Claonairigh House	Bridge of Douglas, By Inverary, Argyll, PA32 8XT	01499 302160	★★★	Bed & Breakfast

Inverarnan

Beinglas Farm Campsite	Inverarnan, Ardlui, G83 7DX	01301 704281	★★★	Inn

Inverfarigaig

Evergreen	Inverfarigaig, Inverness-shire, IV2 6XR	01456 486717	★★★★	Bed & Breakfast

Invergarry

Ardgarry Farm	Faichem, Invergarry, Inverness-shire, PH35 4HG	01809 501226	★★★	Bed & Breakfast
Craigard Guest House	Invergarry, Inverness-Shire, PH35 4HG	01809 501258	★★	Guest House
Forest Lodge	South Laggan , Invergarry, Inverness-shire, PH34 4EA	01809 501219	★★★	Guest House

Inverinate

Mo-dhachaidh	Inverinate, Ross-shire, IV40 8HB	01599 511351	★★★	Bed & Breakfast

Inverkeithing

Elendil	10 Muckle Hill Park, Inverkeithing, Fife, KY11 1BX	01383 411367	★★★★	Bed & Breakfast
Inglewood Bed and Breakfast	42 Boreland Road, Inverkeithing, Fife, KY11 1DA	01383 410899	★★	Bed & Breakfast
The Roods	16 Bannerman Avenue, Inverkeithing, Fife, KY11 1NG	01383 415049	★★★	Bed & Breakfast

Inverkip

Inverkip Hotel	Main Street, Inverkip , Renfrewshire , PA16 OAS	01475 521478	★★★	Inn

Inverlussa Isle of Jura

Ardlussa House	Ardlussa Estate, Inverlussa Isle of Jura, Argyll, PA60 7XW	01496 820323	★	Bed & Breakfast

Invermoriston

Georgeston	Invermoriston, Inverness-shire, IV63 7YA	01320 351264	★★★	Bed & Breakfast
Riverbank Lodge	Invermoriston, Inverness-shire, IV63 7YA	01320 351287	★★★★	Bed & Breakfast
Tigh Na Bruach	Invermoriston, Inverness-shire, IV63 7YE	01320 351349	★★★★★	Bed & Breakfast

Inverness

14 Glenburn Drive	Inverness, Inverness-shire, IV2 4ND	01463 238832	★★	Bed & Breakfast
21 Crown Drive	Inverness, Inverness-shire, IV2 3QF	01463 232614	★★★	Bed & Breakfast
Aberfeldy Lodge Guest House	11 Southside Road, Inverness, Inverness-shire, IV2 3BG	01463 231120	★★★	Guest House
Abermar Guest House	25 Fairfield Road, Inverness, Inverness-shire, IV3 5QD	01463 239019	★★★	Guest House
Ach Aluinn Guest House	27 Fairfield Road, Inverness, Inverness-shire, IV3 5QD	01463 230127	★★★★	Guest House
Acorn House	Bruce Gardens, Inverness, Inverness-shire, IV3 5ED	01463 717021	★★★	Guest House

Unassisted wheelchair access   Assisted wheelchair access   Access for visitors with mobility difficulties
Bronze Green Tourism Award   Silver Green Tourism Award   Gold Green Tourism Award
For further information on our Green Tourism Business Scheme please see page 9.

Advie Lodge	31 Crown Drive, Inverness, Inverness-shire, IV2 3QQ	01463 237247	★★★★	Bed & Breakfast	
Amulree	40 Fairfield Road, Inverness, Inverness-shire, IV3 5QD	01463 224822	★★★	Bed & Breakfast	
An Grianan	11 Crown Drive, Inverness, Inverness-shire, IV2 3NW	01463 250530	★★★★	Bed & Breakfast	
Ardconnel House	21 Arconnel Street, Inverness, Inverness-shire, IV2 3EU	01463 240455	★★★★	Guest House	
Armadale Guest House	35 Greig Street, Inverness, Inverness-shire, IV3 5PX	01463 238970	★★	Bed & Breakfast	
Aros	5 Abertarff Road, Inverness, Inverness-shire, IV2 3NW	01463 235674	★★★	Bed & Breakfast	
Atherstone	42 Farifield Road, Inverness, Inverness-shire, IV3 5QD	01463 240240	★★★	Bed & Breakfast	
Avalon	46 Brookfield, Culloden Moor, Inverness, Inverness-shire, IV2 5GL	01463 798072	★★★★	Bed & Breakfast	
Avalon Guest House	79 Glenurquhart Road, Inverness, Inverness-shire, IV3 5PB	01463 239075	★★★★	Guest House	🚶
Balcroydon	6 Broadstone Park, Inverness, Inverness-shire, IV2 3LA	01463 221506	★★★	Bed & Breakfast	
Ballifeary Guest House	10 Ballifeary Road, Inverness, Inverness-shire, IV3 5PJ	01463 235572	★★★★	Guest House	
Bannerman Bed And Breakfast	47 Glenurquhart Road, Inverness, Inverness-shire, IV3 5NZ	01463 259199	★★★	Bed & Breakfast	
Bluebell House	31 Kenneth Street, Inverness, Inverness-shire, IV3 5DH	01463 238201	★★★★	Bed & Breakfast	
Brae Head	5 Crown Circus, Inverness, Inverness-shire, IV2 3NH	01463 224222	★★★	Bed & Breakfast	
Cambeth Lodge	49 Fairfield Road, Inverness, Inverness-shire, IV3 5QP	01463 231764	★★★	Bed & Breakfast	
Castleview Guest House	2A Ness Walk, Inverness, Inverness-shire, IV3 5NE	01463 241443	★★★	Guest House	
Cavell House	3 Moray Park,Island Bank Road, Inverness, Inverness-shire, IV2 4SX	01463 232850	★★★★	Bed & Breakfast	
Craig Villa	42 Kenneth Street, Inverness, Inverness-shire, IV3 5DH	01463 237568	★★★	Bed & Breakfast	
Craignay House	16 Ardross Street, Inverness, Inverness-shire, IV3 5NS	01463 226563	★★★	Guest House	
Craigside Lodge	4 Gordon Terrace, Inverness, Inverness-shire, IV2 3HD	01463 231576	★★★	Guest House	
Crathie	45 Old Edinburgh Road, Inverness, Inverness-shire, IV2 3PG	01463 238259	★★★	Bed & Breakfast	
Crown Guest House	19 Ardconnel Street, Inverness, Inverness-shire, IV2 3EU	01463 231135	★★★	Guest House	
Daisy Cottage	111 Ballifeary Road, Inverness, Inverness-shire, IV3 5PE	01463 234273	★★★	Bed & Breakfast	
Dalmore Guest House	101 Kenneth Street, Inverness, Inverness-shire, IV3 5QQ	01463 237224	★★★	Guest House	
Dionard	39 Old Edinburgh Road, Inverness, Inverness-shire, IV2 3HJ	01463 233557	★★★★	Bed & Breakfast	
Doric House	13 Denny Street, Inverness, Inverness-shire, IV2 3AP	01463 239498	★★★	Bed & Breakfast	
Dunhallin House	164 Culduthel Road, Inverness, Inverness-shire, IV2 4BH	01463 220824	★★★	Guest House	
Eden House	8 Ballifeary Road, Inverness, Inverness-shire, IV3 5PJ	01463 230278	★★★★	Guest House	
Eiland View Bed & Breakfast	Woodside of Culloden, Westhill, Inverness, Inverness-shire, IV2 5BP	01463 798900	★★★★	Bed & Breakfast	
Eildon Guest House	29 Old Edinburgh Road, Inverness, Inverness-shire, IV2 3HJ	01463 231969	★★★	Guest House	
Eilidh	39 Glenurquhart Road, Inverness, Inverness-shire, IV3 5NZ	01463 716106	★★★	Bed & Breakfast	

♿ Unassisted wheelchair access Assisted wheelchair access 🚶 Access for visitors with mobility difficulties
Bronze Green Tourism Award Silver Green Tourism Award Gold Green Tourism Award
For further information on our Green Tourism Business Scheme please see page 9.

Fairfield Villa	34 Fairfield Road, Inverness, Inverness-shire, IV3 5QD	01463 242243	★★★	Bed & Breakfast	
Fenton House	6 Crown Circus, Inverness, Inverness-shire, IV2 3NQ	01463 223604	★★★	Bed & Breakfast	
Fraser House	49 Huntly Street, Inverness, Inverness-shire, IV3 5HS	01463 716488	★★★	Guest House	
Furan Cottage	100 Old Edinburgh Road, Inverness, Inverness-shire, IV2 3HT	01463 712094	★★★	Guest House	
Glencairn and Ardross House	18-19 Ardross Street, Inverness, Inverness-shire, IV3 5NS	01463 232965	★★★	Guest House	Assisted wheelchair access
Glencoe	51 Fairfield Road, Inverness, Inverness-shire, IV3 5QP	01463 220345	★★★	Bed & Breakfast	
Glendoune B&B	24 Perceval Road, Inverness, Inverness-shire, IV3 5QE	01463 231493	★★★	Bed & Breakfast	
Heathcote B&B	59 Glenurquhart Road, Inverness, Inverness-shire, IV3 5PB	01463 243650	★★★	Bed & Breakfast	
Heronwood	16A Island Bank Road, Inverness, Inverness-shire, IV2 4QS	01463 243275	★★★	Bed & Breakfast	
Highfield House	62 Old Edinburgh Road, Inverness, Inverness-shire, IV2 3PG	01463 238892	★★★★	Bed & Breakfast	
Hornbeam	12A Lovat Road, Inverness, Inverness-shire, IV2 3NT	01463 225655	★★	Bed & Breakfast	
Inverglen	7 Abertarff Road, Inverness, Inverness-shire, IV2 3NW	01463 236281	★★★	Guest House	
Ivanhoe Guest House	68 Lochalsh Road, Inverness, Inverness-shire, IV3 8HW	01463 223020	★★	Guest House	
Kindeace	9 Lovat Road, Inverness, Inverness-shire, IV2 3NT	01463 241041	★★★	Bed & Breakfast	
Lakefield	21 Leys Drive, Inverness, Inverness-shire, IV2 3JB	01463 238352	★★★★	Bed & Breakfast	
Leanach Farm	Culloden Moor, Inverness, Inverness-shire, IV1 2EJ	01463 791027	★★★★	Farmhouse	
Logan Cottage	43 Ballifeary Road, Inverness, Inverness-shire, IV3 5PG	01463 235514	★★★★	Bed & Breakfast	
Lorne House	40 Crown Drive, Inverness, Inverness-shire, IV2 3QG	01463 236271	★★★★	Bed & Breakfast	
Lyndon	50 Telford Street, Inverness, Inverness-shire, IV3 5LE	01463 232551	★★★★	Bed & Breakfast	
Lynver	30 Southside Road, Inverness, Inverness-shire, IV2 3BG	01463 242906	★★★★	Bed & Breakfast	
Lynwilg	5 Green Drive, Inverness, Inverness-shire, IV2 4EX	01463 232733	★	Bed & Breakfast	
MacDonald House	1 Ardross Terrace, Inverness, Inverness-shire, IV3 5NQ	01463 232878	★★★	Guest House	
Malvern	54 Kenneth Street, Inverness, Inverness-shire, IV3 5PZ	01463 242251	★★★	Guest House	
Melness	8 Old Edinburgh Road, Inverness, Inverness-shire, IV2 3HF	01463 220963	★★★★	Bed & Breakfast	
Moray Park Guest House	1 Island Bank Road, Inverness, Inverness-shire, IV2 4SX	01463 233528	★★★	Guest House	
Ness Bank Guest House	7 Ness Bank, Inverness, Inverness-shire , IV2 4SF	01463 232939	★★★	Guest House	Silver Green Tourism Award
Park Hill Guest House	17 Ardconnel Street, Inverness, Inverness-shire, IV2 3EU	01463 223300	★★★	Guest House	
Pottery House	Dores, Inverness, Inverness-shire, IV2 6TR	01463 751267	★★★★	Bed & Breakfast	Gold Green Tourism Award
Riverview Guest House	2 Moray Park, Island Bank Road, Inverness, Inverness-shire, IV2 4SX	01463 235557	★★★★	Guest House	
Roseneath Guest House	39 Greig Street, Inverness, Inverness-shire, IV3 5PX	01463 220201	★★★	Guest House	
Rossmount B&B	32 Argyle Street, Inverness, Inverness-shire, IV2 3BB	01463 229749	★★★	Bed & Breakfast	

Unassisted wheelchair access · Assisted wheelchair access · Access for visitors with mobility difficulties
Bronze Green Tourism Award · Silver Green Tourism Award · Gold Green Tourism Award

For further information on our Green Tourism Business Scheme please see page 9.

Establishment	Address	Telephone	Grading	Type	Access	Green Tourism
Rowanvale Guest House	Culloden Moor, Inverness, Inverness-shire, IV2 5EG	01463 793073	★★★	Bed & Breakfast		
Royston Guest House	16 Millburn Road, Inverness, Inverness-shire, IV2 3PS	01463 231243	★★★	Guest House		
Silverwells Guest House	28 Ness Bank, Inverness, Inverness-shire, IV2 4SF	01463 222611	★★★★	Bed & Breakfast		
St Ann's House	37 Harrowden Road, Inverness, Inverness-shire, IV3 5QN	01463 236157	★★★	Guest House		
Strathmhor Guest House	99 Kenneth Street, Inverness, Inverness-shire, IV3 5QQ	01463 235397	★★★	Guest House		
Strathness House	4 Ardross Terrace, Inverness, Inverness-shire, IV3 5NQ	01463 232765	★★★	Guest House		
Sunnyholm	12 Mayfield Road, Inverness, Inverness-shire, IV2 4AE	01463 231336	★★★	Bed & Breakfast		
Talisker House	25 Ness Bank, Inverness, Inverness-shire, IV2 4SF	01463 236221	★★★	Guest House		
Tamarue	70a Ballifeary Road, Inverness, Inverness-shire, IV3 5PF	01463 239724	★★★	Bed & Breakfast		
The Alexander	16 Ness Bank, Inverness, Inverness-shire, IV2 4SF	01463 231151	★★★★	Guest House		
The Gatehouse	80 Old Edinburgh Road, Inverness, Inverness-shire, IV2 3PG	01463 234590	★★★★	Bed & Breakfast		
The Ghillies Lodge	16 Island Bank Road, Inverness, Inverness-shire, IV2 4QS	01463 232137	★★★★	Bed & Breakfast		
The Herons	Allanfearn, Inverness, Inverness-shire, IV2 7HY	01463 230644	★★★	Bed & Breakfast		
The Kemps	64 Telford Street, Inverness, Inverness-shire, IV3 5LE	01463 285780	★★★	Bed & Breakfast		
Travelodge Inverness	Stonyfield, A96 Inverness Road, Inverness, Inverness-shire, IV2 7PA	08719 864 285	AWAITING GRADING			
Travelodge Inverness Fairways	Castle Heather, Inverness, Inverness-shire, IV2 7PA	08719 846285	AWAITING GRADING			
Westhill House	Westhill, Inverness, Inverness-shire, IV2 5BP	01463 791009	★★	Bed & Breakfast		
Whinpark Guest House	17 Ardross Street, Inverness, Inverness-shire, IV3 5NS	01463 232549	★★★	Guest House		
White Lodge	15 Bishops Road, Inverness, Inverness-shire, IV3 5SB	01463 230693	★★★★	Guest House		
Wimberley House	1 Wimberley Way, Inverness, Inverness-shire, IV2 3XJ	01463 224430	★★★★	Bed & Breakfast		
Winston Guest House	10 Ardross Terrace, Inverness, Inverness-shire, IV3 5NQ	01463 234477	★★★	Guest House		
Wychway	3 Haugh Road, Inverness, Inverness-shire, IV2 4SD	01463 239399	★★★	Bed & Breakfast		

By Inverness

Establishment	Address	Telephone	Grading	Type	Access	Green Tourism
Stonea	3a Resaurie, Smithton, By Inverness, Inverness-shire, IV1 2NH	01463 791714	★★★	Bed & Breakfast		
Old North Inn	Kirkhill, By Inverness, Inverness-shire, IV5 7PX	01463 831296	★★	Inn		
The Lodge at Daviot Main, Daviot	By Inverness, Inverness-shire, IV2 5ER	01463 772215	★★★★★	Bed & Breakfast	Unassisted wheelchair access	Silver Green Tourism Award
Westerlea	Tower Brae South, Westhill, By Inverness, Inverness-shire, IV2 5BW	01463 792890	★★★	Bed & Breakfast		

Inverurie

Establishment	Address	Telephone	Grading	Type	Access	Green Tourism
5 Kirkton Park	Chapel of Gairloch, Inverurie, Aberdeenshire , AB51 5HF	01467 681281	★★★	Bed & Breakfast		
Breaslann Guest House	Old Chapel Road, Inverurie, Aberdeenshire, AB51 4QN	01467 621608	★★★	Guest House		
Broadsea	Burnhervie, Inverurie, Aberdeenshire, AB51 5LB	01467 681386	★★★	Farmhouse		

Unassisted wheelchair access · Assisted wheelchair access · Access for visitors with mobility difficulties
Bronze Green Tourism Award · Silver Green Tourism Award · Gold Green Tourism Award
For further information on our Green Tourism Business Scheme please see page 9.

Grant Arms Hotel	Monymusk, Inverurie, Aberdeenshire, AB51 7HJ	01467 651226	★★★	Inn	Assisted wheelchair access
Kingsgait	St Andrews Gardens, Inverurie, Aberdeenshire, AB51 3XT	01467 620431	★★★	Bed & Breakfast	
The Steading B&B	Fisherford, Inverurie, Aberdeenshire, AB51 8YS	01464 841476	★★	Bed & Breakfast	

By Inverurie

Fridayhill	Kinmuck, By Inverurie, Aberdeenshire, AB51 0LY	01651 882252	★★★★★	Bed & Breakfast	

Isle of Iona

Argyll Hotel	Iona, Isle of Iona, Argyll, PA76 6SJ	01681 700334	★★★	Restaurant with Rooms	Gold Green Tourism Award

Irvine

Laurelbank Guest House	3 Kilwinning Road, Irvine, Ayrshire, KA12 8RR	01294 277153	★★★	Guest House	
Mayfield Guest House	62 East Road, Irvine, Ayrshire, KA12 0BS	01294 279045	★★	Bed & Breakfast	

Isle of Colonsay

The Hannah's B&B	4 Uragaig, Isle of Colonsay, Argyll, PA61 7YT	01951 200150	★★★	Bed & Breakfast	

Isle of Eigg

Lageorna Guest House	Lageorna, Isle of Eigg, Inverness-shire, PH42 4RL	01687 482405	★★★★	Restaurant with Rooms	Silver Green Tourism Award

Isle Ornsay, Sleat, Isle of Skye

5 Drumfearn	Isle Ornsay, Sleat, Isle of Skye, Inverness-shire, IV43 8QZ	01471 820171	★★★	Bed & Breakfast	
Coille Challtainn	6 Duisdale Beag, Isle Ornsay, Sleat, Isle of Skye, Inverness-shire, IV43 8QU	01471 833230	★★★	Bed & Breakfast	

Jedburgh

Airenlea	The Boundaries, Jedburgh, Roxburghshire, TD8 6EX	07817 141705	★★★	Bed & Breakfast	
Allerton House	Oxnam Road, Jedburgh, Roxburghshire, TD8 6QQ	01835 869633	★★★★	Guest House	Access for visitors with mobility difficulties
Ancrum Craig	Jedburgh, Roxburghshire, TD8 6UN	01835 830280	★★★★	Bed & Breakfast	
Edgerston Mill	Jedburgh, Roxburghshire, TD8 6NF	01835 840343	★★★	Bed & Breakfast	
Fernlea	Allerton Place, Jedburgh, Roxburghshire, TD8 6LG	01835 862318	★★★★	Bed & Breakfast	
Harden Vale	Ancrum, Jedburgh TD8 6XH	01835 830280	★★★	Bed & Breakfast	
Meadhon House	48 Castlegate, Jedburgh, Roxburghshire, TD8 6BB	01835 862504	★★★	Guest House	
The School House	Edgerston, Jedburgh, Roxburghshire, TD8 6PW	01835 840627	★★★★★	Bed & Breakfast	
The Spinney Guest House	Langlee, Jedburgh, Roxburghshire, TD8 6PB	01835 863525	★★★★	Bed & Breakfast	
Willow Court	The Friars, Jedburgh, Roxburghshire, TD8 6BN	01835 863702	★★★★	Bed & Breakfast	

John O'Groats

Mill House	John O'Groats, Caithness, KW1 4YR	01955 611239	★★★	Bed & Breakfast	

♿ Unassisted wheelchair access   Assisted wheelchair access   Access for visitors with mobility difficulties
Bronze Green Tourism Award   Silver Green Tourism Award   Gold Green Tourism Award

For further information on our Green Tourism Business Scheme please see page 9.

Johnshaven

Ellington	Station Road, Johnshaven, Kincardineshire, DD10 0JD	01561 362756	★★★★	Bed & Breakfast

Keiss

Sinclair Bay Hotel	Main Street, Keiss, Caithness, KW1 4UY	01955 631233	★★	Inn

Keith

Chapelhill Croft	Grange, Keith, Banffshire, AB55 6LQ	01542 870302	★★★	Farmhouse
Craighurst Guest House	Seafield Avenue, Keith, Morayshire, AB55 5BS	01542 880345	★★★★	Bed & Breakfast
Earlsmount Fine Accommodation	Regent Street, Keith, Moray, AB55 5DY	01542 882609	★★★★	Bed & Breakfast
The Haughs	Keith, Banffshire, AB55 3QN	01542 882238	★★★	Farmhouse

Kelso

Bellevue House	Bowmont Street, Kelso, Roxburghshire, TD5 7DZ	01573 224588	★★★	Guest House
Edenbank House	Kelso, Scottish Borders, TD5 7SX	01573 226734	★★★★	Bed & Breakfast
Edenmouth Farm	Kelso, Roxburghshire, TD5 7QB	01890 830391	★★★	Bed & Breakfast
Inglestone House	Abbey Row, Kelso, Roxburghshire, TD5 7HQ	01573 225800	★★★	Guest House
Ivy Neuk	62 Horsemarket, Kelso, Roxburghshire, TD5 7AE	01573 226270	★★	Bed & Breakfast
Mill House B&B	Main Street, Kirk Yetholm, Kelso, Roxburghshire, TD5 8PE	01573 420604	★★★★	Bed & Breakfast
The Bield	Hume, Kelso, Roxburghshire, TD5 7TS	01573 470349	★★★	Bed & Breakfast
The Hermitage B&B	Hermitage Lane, Sheddon Park Road, Kelso, Roxburghshire, TD5 7AN	01573 229090	★★★★	Bed & Breakfast
Goldilands	Roxburgh Road, Heiton, Kelso, Roxburghshire, TD5 8TP	01573 450671	★★★	Bed & Breakfast

Nr Kelso

Eckford Hall Steading, Ekford	Nr Kelso, Roxburghshire, TD5 8LQ	07855 868342	★★★★★	Bed & Breakfast

Kilbride

Polochar Inn	Polachar, Kilbride , South Uist , HS8 5TT	01878 700215	★★★	Inn

Kilchoan

Tigh A'Ghobhainn	Kilchoan, By Acharacle, PH36 4LH	01972 570771	★★★	Bed & Breakfast
Torr Solais	Kilchoan, Ardnamurchan, PH36 4LH	01972 510 389	★★★★	Bed & Breakfast

Kilchrenan

Collaig House	Collaig House, Kilchrenan, Argyll, PA35 1HG	01866 833202	★★★★	Bed & Breakfast

Kildonan, Isle of Arran

Mare	6 The Keys, Kildonan, Isle Of Arran, KA27 8AS	07900 680930	★★★★	Bed & Breakfast

Unassisted wheelchair access Assisted wheelchair access Access for visitors with mobility difficulties
Bronze Green Tourism Award Silver Green Tourism Award Gold Green Tourism Award
For further information on our Green Tourism Business Scheme please see page 9.

Kilkenzie

Dalnaspidal Guest House	Tangy, Kilkenzie, Argyll, PA28 6QD	01586 820466	★★★★★	Guest House	♿

Killearnan

Wester Muckernich	Roadside, Killearnan, Muir-of-Ord, IV6 7SA	01349 861222	★★★★	Bed & Breakfast	

Killin

Ardlochay Lodge	Burnbank, Maragowan, Killin, Perthshire, FK21 8TN	01567 820962	★★★	Bed & Breakfast	
Breadalbane House	Main Street, Killin, Perthshire, FK21 8UT	01567 820134	★★★	Guest House	Bronze Green Tourism Award
Bridge of Lochay Hotel	Aberfeldy Road, Killin, Perthshire, FK21 8TS	01567 820272	★★★	Inn	
Craigbuie Guest House	Main Street, Killin, Perthshire, FK21 8UH	01567 820439	★★★	Guest House	
Dall Lodge Country House	Main Street, Killin, Perthshire, FK21 8TN	01567 820217	★★★★	Guest House	
Fairview House	Main Street, Killin, Perthshire, FK21 8UT	01567 820667	★★★	Guest House	
Succoth Farm	R [DArdeonaig, Killin, Perthshire, FK21 8SY	01567 820005	★★★★	Bed & Breakfast	
Am Bathach - 'The Barn'	Pine Cottage, Main Street, Killin, Perthshire, FK21 8UT	01567 820286	★★★	Bed & Breakfast	Silver Green Tourism Award
The Coach House Hotel	Lochay Road, Killin, Perthshire, FK21 8TN	01567 820349	★★	Inn	
Am Bathach - 'The Barn'	Pine Cottage, Main Street, Killin FK21 8UT	01567 820286	★★★	Bed & Breakfast	Silver Green Tourism Award

Kilmarnock

Dean Park Guest House	27 Wellington Street, Kilmarnock, Ayrshire, KA3 1DZ	01563 572794	★★★	Guest House	
East Langton Farm	Dunlop, Kilmarnock, Ayrshire, KA3 4DS	01560 482978	★★★	Bed & Breakfast	
Heughmill	Craigie, Kilmarnock, Ayrshire, KA1 5NQ	01563 860389	★★★★	Bed & Breakfast	
Tamarind	24 Arran Avenue, Kilmarnock, Ayrshire, KA3 1TP	01563 571788	★★★	Bed & Breakfast	
Travelodge Kilmarnock	Junction A71/A76/A77 Kilmarnock bypass, Kilmarnock, Ayrshire, KA1 5LQ	08719 846149	AWAITING GRADING		
West Tannacrieff	Fenwick, Kilmarnock, Ayrshire, KA3 6AZ	01560 600258	★★★★	Farmhouse	

By Kilmarnock

Underwood House	Craigie, By Kilmarnock, Ayrshire, KA1 5NG	01563 830887	★★★	Bed & Breakfast	

Kilmaurs

Aulton Farm	Kilmaurs, Ayrshire, KA3 2PQ	01563 538208	★★★	Farmhouse	

Kilpheder

Ard Na Mara	Kilpheder, South Uist, Western Isles, HS8 5TB	01878 700452	★★★	Bed & Breakfast	

Kilrenny

Invermay Cottage	Common Road, Kilrenny, Fife, KY10 3JQ	01333 312314	★★★	Bed & Breakfast	

Kilsyth

Establishment	Address	Telephone	Grading	Type	Access	Green Tourism
Allanfauld Farm	Kilsyth, North Lanarkshire, G65 9DF	01236 822155	★★★	Farmhouse		
Twechar Farm B&B	Twechar Farm, Kilsyth, East Dunbartonshire, G65 9LH	01236 823216	★★★	Farmhouse		

Kiltarlity

Establishment	Address	Telephone	Grading	Type	Access	Green Tourism
Cherry Trees	Kiltarlity, Kiltarlity, Inverness-shire, IV4 7JQ	01463 741368	★★★★	Farmhouse		

Kilwinning

Establishment	Address	Telephone	Grading	Type	Access	Green Tourism
Blairholme	45 Byres Road, Kilwinning, Ayrshire, KA13 6JU	01294 552023	★★	Bed & Breakfast		
High Smithstone Farmhouse	High Smithstone, Kilwinning, Ayrshire, KA13 6PG	01294 552361	★★★★	Farmhouse		

Kingsbarns

Establishment	Address	Telephone	Grading	Type	Access	Green Tourism
Kingsbarns Bed & Breakfast	3 Main Street, Kingsbarns, Fife, KY16 8SL	01334 880234	★★★	Bed & Breakfast		

Kingston-on-Spey

Establishment	Address	Telephone	Grading	Type	Access	Green Tourism
Bayview	Beach Road, Kingston-on-Spey, Moray, IV32 7NP		★★★	Bed & Breakfast		

Kingussie

Establishment	Address	Telephone	Grading	Type	Access	Green Tourism
Allt Gynack Guest House	Gynack Villa, 1 High Street, Kingussie, Inverness-shire, PH21 1HS	01540 661081	★★★	Guest House		
Arden House	Newtonmore Road, Kingussie, Inverness-shire, PH21 1HE	01540 661369	★★★★	Guest House		
Ardselma	The Crescent, Kingussie, Inverness-shire, PH21 1JZ		★★★	Bed & Breakfast		
Auld Alliance	East Terrace, Kingussie, Inverness-shire, PH21 1JS	01540 661506	★★★	Restaurant with Rooms		
Glengarry	East Terrace, Kingussie, Inverness-shire, PH21 1JS	01540 661386	★★★★	Bed & Breakfast		
Gowdenstane	Newtonmore Road, Kingussie PH21 1EH	01540 661944	★★★	Bed & Breakfast		
Homewood Lodge	Newtonmore Road, Kingussie, Inverness-shire, PH21 1HD	01540 661507	★★★★	Bed & Breakfast		Silver
Rowan House	Homewood, Newtonmore Road, Kingussie, Inverness-shire, PH21 1HD	01540 662153	★★★★	Bed & Breakfast		
Ruthven House	Ruthven, Kingussie, Inverness-shire, PH21 1NR	01540 661226	★★★★	Bed & Breakfast		
Ruthven Steadings	Ruthven, Kingussie, Inverness-shire, PH21 1NR	01540 662 328	★★★★	Bed & Breakfast		
Slemish B&B	Dunbarry Road, Kingussie, Inverness-shire, PH21 1JN	01540 662360	★★★★	Bed & Breakfast		Silver
St Helens	Ardbroilach Road, Kingussie, Inverness-shire, PH21 1JX	01540 661 430	★★★★	Bed & Breakfast		
The Cross at Kingussie	Tweed Mill Brae,Ardbroilach Road, Kingussie, Kingussie, PH21 1LB	01540 661166	★★★★	Restaurant with Rooms		Silver
The Hermitage Guest House	Spey Street, Kingussie, Inverness-shire, PH21 1HN	01540 662137	★★★★	Guest House	Mobility	Silver
West Wing of Clifton	Clifton, Middle Terrace, Kingussie, Inverness-shire, PH21 1EY	01540 661248	★★★★	Bed & Breakfast		

By Kingussie

Establishment	Address	Telephone	Grading	Type	Access	Green Tourism
Greenfield Croft	Insh, By Kingussie, Inverness-shire, PH21 1NT	01540 661010	★★★	Bed & Breakfast		
Braeriach Guest House	Kincraig, By Kingussie, Inverness-shire, PH21 1NA	01540 651369	★★★★	Guest House		

Unassisted wheelchair access · Assisted wheelchair access · Access for visitors with mobility difficulties
Bronze Green Tourism Award · Silver Green Tourism Award · Gold Green Tourism Award
For further information on our Green Tourism Business Scheme please see page 9.

Establishment	Address	Telephone	Grading	Category	
Insh House Guest House	Kincraig, By Kingussie, Inverness-shire, PH21 1NU	01540 651377	★★★	Guest House	🌿🌿
Suie Guest House	Kincraig, By Kingussie, Inverness-shire, PH21 1NA	01540 651 344	★★★	Guest House	

Kinlochbervie

Establishment	Address	Telephone	Grading	Category	
Old School Restaurant & Rooms	Inshegra, Kinlochbervie, Sutherland, IV27 4RH	01971 521383	★★★	Restaurant with Rooms	

Kinlochleven

Establishment	Address	Telephone	Grading	Category	
Edencoille	Garbhien Road, Kinlochleven, Argyll, PH50 4SE	01855 831358	★★★★	Guest House	
Hermon	5 Rob Roy Road, Kinlochleven, Argyll, PH50 4RA	01855 831383	★★★	Bed & Breakfast	
Highland Getaway	28 Leven Road, Kinlochleven, Argyll, PH50 4RP	01855 831506	★★★	Restaurant with Rooms	
Tailrace Inn	Riverside Road, Kinlochleven, Argyll, PH50 4QH	01855 831777	★★★	Inn	
Tigh-Na-Cheo	Garbien Road, Kinlochleven, Argyll, PH50 4SE	01855 831434	★★★★	Guest House	♿

Kinloch Rannoch

Establishment	Address	Telephone	Grading	Category	
The Gardens	Dunalastair, Kinloch Rannoch, Perthshire, PH16 5PB	01882 632434	★★★	Bed & Breakfast	

Kinnesswood

Establishment	Address	Telephone	Grading	Category	
Park House	Main Street, Kinnesswood, Perth & Kinross, KY13 9HN	01592 840237	★★★★	Bed & Breakfast	

Kinross

Establishment	Address	Telephone	Grading	Category	
Dalqueich Farmhouse	By Milnathort, Kinross, Perth & Kinross, KY13 0RG	01577 862599	★★★	Bed & Breakfast	
The Grouse and Claret	Heatheryford, Kinross KY13 0NQ	01577 864212	★★★	Restaurant with Rooms	
Travelodge Kinross M90	Turfhills Tourist Centre, Kinross, Perthshire, KY13 7NQ	08719 846151	AWAITING GRADING		♿

Kippford

Establishment	Address	Telephone	Grading	Category	
Roughfirth House	Roughfirth, Kippford, Dumfries & Galloway, DG5 4LJ	01556 620330	★★★	Bed & Breakfast	

Kirk Yetholm

Establishment	Address	Telephone	Grading	Category	
The Border Hotel	The Green, Kirk Yetholm, Scottish Borders, TD5 8PQ	01573 420237	★★★★	Inn	

Kirkbean

Establishment	Address	Telephone	Grading	Category	
Steamboat Inn	Carsethorn, Kirkbean, Dumfries, DG2 8DS	01387 880 631	★★★	Inn	

Kirkcaldy

Establishment	Address	Telephone	Grading	Category	
Ahaven	288 High Street, Kirkcaldy, Fife, KY1 1LB	01592 267779	★★★★	Bed & Breakfast	
Annies'Lan	36 Bennochy Road, Kirkcaldy, Fife, KY2 5RB	01592 262231	★★	Bed & Breakfast	
Ashgrove B&B	213 Nicol Street, Kirkcaldy, Fife, KY1 1PF	01592 268596	★★★	Bed & Breakfast	
Invertiel B&B	19 Bennochy Road, Kirkcaldy, Fife, KY2 5QJ	01592 264849	★★★★	Bed & Breakfast	
North Hall	143 Victoria Road, Kirkcaldy, Fife, KY1 1DQ	01592 268864	★★★★	Bed & Breakfast	
Scotties B&B	15 Bennochy Road, Kirkcaldy, Fife, KY2 5QU	01592 268596	★★★★	Bed & Breakfast	

♿ Unassisted wheelchair access ♿ Assisted wheelchair access Access for visitors with mobility difficulties
🌿 Bronze Green Tourism Award 🌿🌿 Silver Green Tourism Award 🌿🌿🌿 Gold Green Tourism Award
For further information on our Green Tourism Business Scheme please see page 9.

Kirkcudbright

1 Gordon Place	High Street, Kirkcudbright, Dumfries & Galloway, DG6 4LA	01557 330472	★★★	Bed & Breakfast		
Anchorlee	95 St Mary Street, Kirkcudbright, Dumfries & Galloway, DG6 4EL	01557 330197	★★★★	Bed & Breakfast		
Benutium	2 Rossway Road, Kirkcudbright, Dumfries & Galloway, DG6 4BS	01557 330788	★★★★	Bed & Breakfast		
Blaven	40 Fergus Road, Kirkcudbright, Dumfries & Galloway, DG6 4HN	01557 331415	★★★	Bed & Breakfast		
Dee Cottage	Tongland, Kirkcudbright, Dumfries & Galloway, DG6 4LT	01557 330338	★★★★	Bed & Breakfast		
Emahroo	109A High Street, Kirkcudbright, Dumfries & Galloway, DG6 4JG	01557 331279	★★★★	Bed & Breakfast		
Fludha Guest House	Tongland Road, Kirkcudbright, Dumfries & Galloway, DG6 4UU	01557 331443	★★★★★	Guest House	♿	
Gladstone House	48 High Street, Kirkcudbright, Dumfries & Galloway, DG6 4JX	01557 331734	★★★★	Guest House		
Kilkerran	Mansecroft, Twynholm, Kirkcudbright, Dumfries & Galloway, DG6 4NY	01557 860057	★★★	Bed & Breakfast		
Marks	Kirkcudbright, Dumfries & Galloway, DG6 4XR	01557 330254	★★★	Bed & Breakfast		
Number One Bed & Breakfast	1 Castle Gardens, Kirkcudbright, Dumfries & Galloway, DG6 4JE	01557 330540	★★★★	Bed & Breakfast		
Rivergarth	Tongland Road, Kirkcudbright, Dumfries & Galloway, DG6 4UT	01557 332054	★★★★	Bed & Breakfast	🚶	
Sassoon House	3 High St, Kirkcudbright, Dumfries & Galloway, DG6 4JZ	01557 330881	★★★★	Bed & Breakfast		
The Green Gate	46 High Street, Kirkcudbright, Dumfries & Galloway, DG6 4JX	01557 331895	★★★★	Bed & Breakfast		

Kirkintilloch

Bridgend Farm	Kirkintilloch, East Dunbartonshire, G66 1RT	0141 776 1607	★★★	Farmhouse

Kirkliston

Almondhill Guest House	7 Almondhill Cottages, Kirkliston, West Lothian, EH29 9EQ	0131 333 1570	★★★★	Bed & Breakfast

Kirkwall

1 Papdale Close	Kirkwall, Orkney, KW15 1QP	01856 874201	★★★	Bed & Breakfast		
Arundel	Inganis Road, Kirkwall, Orkney, KW15 1SP	01856 873148	★★★★	Bed & Breakfast		
Avalon House	Carness Road, Kirkwall, Orkney, KW15 1UE	01856 876665	★★★★	Guest House		
Bellavista	Carness Road, Kirkwall, Orkney, KW15 1UE	01856 872306	★★★	Guest House		
Berstane House	Kirkwall, Orkney, KW15 1SZ	01856 876277	AWAITING GRADING			
Bon Accord	New Scapa Road, Kirkwall, Orkney, KW15 1BT	01856 873034	★★★	Bed & Breakfast		
Brekkness Guest House	Muddisdale Road, Kirkwall, Orkney, KW15 1RS	01856 874317	★★★	Guest House		
Dunedin	Springfield Drive, Berstane Road, Kirkwall, Orkney , KW15 1XU	01856 872967	★★★	Bed & Breakfast		
Fairhaven	Ropewalk, Kirkwall, Orkney, KW15 1PX	01856 872944	★★★	Bed & Breakfast		
Kenila	Harray, Kirkwall, Orkney, KW17 2LE	01856 771431	★★★	Bed & Breakfast		
Lav'rockha Guest House	Inganess Road, Kirkwall, Orkney, KW15 1SP	01856 876103	★★★★	Guest House	♿	Gold Green Tourism Award

♿ Unassisted wheelchair access · Assisted wheelchair access · 🚶 Access for visitors with mobility difficulties
Bronze Green Tourism Award · Silver Green Tourism Award · Gold Green Tourism Award
For further information on our Green Tourism Business Scheme please see page 9.

Lerona	Cromwell Crescent, Kirkwall, Orkney, KW15 1LW	01856 874538	★★★	Bed & Breakfast	
Narvik	Weyland Terrace, Kirkwall, Orkney, KW15 1LS	01856 879049	★★★★	Bed & Breakfast	
Peter McKinlay B&B	13 Palace Road, Kirkwall, Orkney, KW15 1PA	01856 872249	★★★	Bed & Breakfast	
Polrudden Guest House	Peerie Sea Loan, Kirkwall, Orkney, KW15 1UH	01856 874761	★★★	Guest House	
Royal Oak Guest House	Holm Road, Kirkwall, Orkney, KW15 1PY	01856 873487	★★★	Guest House	
Sanderlay Guest House	2 Viewfield Drive, Kirkwall, Orkney, KW15 1RB	01856 875587	★★★	Guest House	
St Ola Hotel	Harbour Street, Kirkwall, Orkney, KW15 1LE	01856 875090	★★★	Guest House	
The Inn B&B	St Marys, Holm, Kirkwall, Orkney, KW17 2RU	01856 781786	★★★	Guest House	
The Shore, Rooms,Restaurant, Bar	Shore Street, Kirkwall, Orkney, KW15 1LG	01856 872200	★★★	Inn	

By Kirkwall

Ardconnel	Craigefield Road, St Ola, By Kirkwall, Orkney, KW15 1TB	01856 873885	★★★	Bed & Breakfast	
Crossford	Heathery Loan, St Ola, By Kirkwall, Orkney, KW15 1SY	01856 876142	★★★	Bed & Breakfast	

Kirriemuir

Crepto	Kinnordy Place, Kirriemuir, Angus, DD8 4JW	01575 572746	★★	Bed & Breakfast	
Lochside Lodge & Roundhouse Restaurant	Bridgend of Lintrathen, Kirriemuir, Angus, DD8 5JJ	01575 560340	★★★★	Restaurant with Rooms	Assisted wheelchair access
Muirhouses Farm	Kirriemuir, Angus, DD8 4QG	01575 573128	★★★★	Farmhouse	Silver Green Tourism Award

By Kirriemuir

Purgavie Farm	Lintrathen , By Kirriemuir, Angus, DD8 5HZ	01575 560213	★★★★	Farmhouse	
Falls of Holm	Lower Welton Farm, By Kirriemuir, Angus, DD8 5HY	01575 575867	★★★★	Bed & Breakfast	

Kyle of Lochalsh

Loch Aluinn B&B	7 Sconser, Kyle of Lochalsh, Inverness-shire, IV48 8TD	01478 650288	★★★★	Bed & Breakfast	
A'Chomraich	Plockton Road, Kyle of Lochalsh, Inverness-shire, IV40 8DA	01599 534210	★★	Bed & Breakfast	
Ardenlea	Church Road, Kyle of Lochalsh, Ross-shire, IV40 8DD	01599 534630	★★★★	Bed & Breakfast	

By Kyle of Lochalsh

Conchra House	Sallachy Road, Ardelve, By Kyle of Lochalsh, Ross-shire, IV40 8DZ	01599 555233	★★★	Guest House	
Sealladh Mara	Ardelve, Dornie, By Kyle of Lochalsh, Ross shire, IV40 8EY	01599 555296	★★★	Bed & Breakfast	
Eilean A Cheo	Ardelve, Dornie, By Kyle of Lochalsh, Ross shire, IV40 8DY	01599 555485	★★★	Guest House	
Balmacara Lodge B & B	Balmacara Square, Balmacara, By Kyle of Lochalsh, Ross-shire, IV40 8DP	01599 566282	★★★	Bed & Breakfast	
Ceol-Na-Mara	Reraig, Balmacara, By Kyle of Lochalsh, Ross-shire, IV40 8DH	01599 566208	★★★★	Bed & Breakfast	
Balmacara Mains Guest House	By Kyle of Lochalsh, Ross-Shire, IV40 8DN	01559 566242	★★★★	Guest House	
Galder	Glenelg, By Kyle of Lochalsh, Ross-shire, IV40 8JZ	01599 522 287	★★★	Bed & Breakfast	

Unassisted wheelchair access   Assisted wheelchair access   Access for visitors with mobility difficulties
Bronze Green Tourism Award   Silver Green Tourism Award   Gold Green Tourism Award

For further information on our Green Tourism Business Scheme please see page 9.

Glomach House	Ault-Na-Chruinne, Glenshiel, By Kyle of Lochalsh, Ross-shire, IV40 8HN	01599 511 222	★★★★	Bed & Breakfast	
Seadrift	Avernish, Nostie, By Kyle of Lochalsh, Ross-shire, IV40 8EQ	01599 555415	★★★	Bed & Breakfast	
Caberfeidh Guest House	Upper Ardelve, By Kyle of Lochalsh, Ross-shire, IV40 8DY	01599 555293	★★★	Guest House	

Kyleakin, Isle of Skye

17 Kyleside	Kyleakin, Isle of Skye, Inverness-shire, IV41 8PW	01599 534197	★★★	Bed & Breakfast	
Corran Guest House	Kyleakin, Isle of Skye, Inverness-shire	01599 534859	AWAITING GRADING		
Glenarroch	Main Street, Kyleakin, Isle of Skye, Inverness-shire, IV41 8PH	01599 534845	★★★	Guest House	
Mo-Dhachaidh	Old Kyle Farm Road, Kyleakin, Isle of Skye, Inverness-shire, IV41 8PR	01599 534724	★★★★	Bed & Breakfast	
Salento B&B	Old Kyle Farm Road, Kyleakin, Isle of Skye, Inverness-shire, IV41 8PR	01599 534771	★★★	Bed & Breakfast	
Witchwood House	Kyleakin, Isle of Skye, Inverness-shire, IV41 9PL	01599 530276	★★★	Bed & Breakfast	
Blairdhu House	Kyle Farm Road, Kyleakin, Isle of Skye, Inverness-shire, IV41 8PQ	01599 534760	★★★★	Guest House	

Kylesku

Newton Lodge	Kylesku, Sutherland, IV27 4HW	01971 502070	★★★★	Guest House	

Laggan

The Rumblie	Gergask Avenue, Laggan, Inverness-shire, PH20 1AH	01528 544766	★★★★	Guest House	Gold Green Tourism Award

Lagrannoch

Roslin Cottage	Stirling Road, Lagrannoch, Callander, FK17 8LE	01877 339787	★★★	Bed & Breakfast	

Lairg

77 Dalcharn	Tongue, Lairg, Sutherland, IV27 4XU	01847 611251	★★	Bed & Breakfast	
Lochview	Lochside, Lairg, Sutherland, IV27 4EH	01549 402578	★★★★	Bed & Breakfast	
Park House	Lairg, Sutherland, IV27 4AU	01549 402208	★★★★	Guest House	

By Lairg

Glengolly	Durine, Durness, By Lairg, Sutherland, IV27 4PN	01971 511255	★★★	Bed & Breakfast	
Ruddyglow Park Country House	Loch Assynt, By Lairg, Sutherland, IV27 4HB	01571 822216	★★★★★	Bed & Breakfast	Access for visitors with mobility difficulties
Glenaladale Bed And Breakfast	99A Laid, Loch Eriboll, By Lairg, Sutherland, IV27 4UN	01971 511329	★★★	Bed & Breakfast	
Fasgadh	Scouriemore, By Lairg, Sutherland, IV27 4TG	01971 502402	★★★	Bed & Breakfast	
Scourie Guest House	55 Scourie Village, By Lairg, Sutherland, IV27 4TE	01971 502001	★★★	Guest House	
Highland House	88 Station Road, By Lairg, Sutherland, IV27 4DH	01549 402414	★★★★	Bed & Breakfast	
Woodland Guest House	Woodland, Roseshall, By Lairg, Sutherland, IV27 4BD	01549 441715	★★	Bed & Breakfast	

Lamlash Bay, Isle of Arran

Lilybank	Shore Road, Lamlash Bay, Isle of Arran, KA27 8LS	01770 600230	★★★★	Guest House	Access for visitors with mobility difficulties

Unassisted wheelchair access Assisted wheelchair access Access for visitors with mobility difficulties
Bronze Green Tourism Award Silver Green Tourism Award Gold Green Tourism Award
For further information on our Green Tourism Business Scheme please see page 9.

Centre For The Earth Peace and Health	Holy Isle, Lamlash Bay, Isle of Arran, KA27 8GB	01770 601100	AWAITING GRADING		

Lanark

Clarkston Farm	Kirkfieldbank, Lanark, Lanarkshire, ML11 9UN	01555 663751	★★★	Farmhouse	
Corehouse Farm	Lanark, Strathclyde, ML11 9TQ	01555 661377	★★★	Farmhouse	Silver Green Tourism Award
Duneaton	159 Hyndford Road, Lanark, Lanarkshire, ML11 9BG	01555 665487	★★★	Bed & Breakfast	
Jerviswood Mains Farm	Lanark, Lanarkshire, ML11 7RL	01555 663987	★★★	Bed & Breakfast	
Kirkfield Mains	Kirkfieldbank, Lanark, South Lanarkshire, ML11 9UH	01555 660094	★★★★	Bed & Breakfast	
Scottish Equestrian Hotel	Lanark Race Course, Lanark, Lanarkshire, ML11 9TA	01555 661853	AWAITING GRADING		
St Catherines B&B	1 Kenilworth Road, Lanark, Lanarkshire, ML11 7BL	01555 662295	★★★	Bed & Breakfast	
Summerlea	32 Hyndford Road, Lanark, South Lanarkshire, ML11 9AE	01555 664 889	★★★	Bed & Breakfast	

Langholm

Border House	28 High Street, Langholm, Dumfriesshire, DG13 OJH	013873 80376	★★★	Bed & Breakfast
Bush of Ewes Farmhouse	Ewes, Langholm, Dumfriesshire, DG13 0HN	013873 81241	★★★	Farmhouse
Carnlea	16 Hillside Crescent, Langholm, Dumfries-shire, DG13 0EE	01387 380284	★★★	Bed & Breakfast
Wauchope Cottage	Wauchope Street, Langholm, Dumfriesshire, DG13 OAY	01387 380429	★★★	Bed & Breakfast

Largs

Broom Lodge	5 Broomfield Place, Largs, Ayrshire, KA30 8DR	01475 674290	★★★★	Bed & Breakfast
Glendarroch	24 Irvine Road, Largs, Ayrshire, KA30 8HW	01475 676305	★★★	Bed & Breakfast
Lilac Holm Guest House	14 Noddleburn Road, Largs, Ayrshire, KA30 8PY	01475 672020	★★★	Guest House
South Whittlieburn Farm	Brisbane Glen, Largs, Ayrshire, KA30 8SN	01475 675881	★★★★	Bed & Breakfast
St Leonard's Guest House	9 Irvine Road, Largs, Ayrshire, KA30 8JP	01475 673318	★★★	Bed & Breakfast
The Old Rectory	2 Aubrey Crescent, Largs, Ayrshire, KA30 8PR	01475 674405	★★★★	Bed & Breakfast
Tigh An Struan	29 Gogo Street, Largs, North Ayrshire, KA30 8BU	01475 670668	★★★	Guest House
Tigh-Na-Ligh	104 Brisbane Road, Largs, Ayrshire, KA30 8NN	01475 673975	★★★	Guest House
Whin-Park Guest House	16 Douglas Street, Largs, Ayrshire, KA30 8PS	01475 673437	★★★★	Guest House

By Largs

Ferry Row B&B	10 Ferry Row, Fairlie, By Largs, Ayrshire, KA29 0AJ	01475 568687	★★★	Bed & Breakfast

Lasswade

Droman House	Lasswade, Midlothian, EH18 1HA	0131 663 9239	★★	Bed & Breakfast

Lauder

Black Bull Hotel	9 Market Place, Lauder, Berwickshire, TD2 6SR	01578 722 208	★★	Inn

♿ Unassisted wheelchair access ♿ Assisted wheelchair access 🚶 Access for visitors with mobility difficulties
Bronze Green Tourism Award Silver Green Tourism Award Gold Green Tourism Award
For further information on our Green Tourism Business Scheme please see page 9.

Lornebank Homestay	10 East High Street, Lauder, Berwickshire, TD2 6SU	01578 722317	AWAITING GRADING			
No 16 Market Place	Market Place, Lauder, Berwickshire, TD2 6SR	01578 718776	★★★	Bed & Breakfast		

By Lauder

The Lodge at Carfraemill	Carfraemill, By Lauder, Berwickshire, TD2 6RA	01578 750750	★★★★	Restaurant with Rooms		

Laurencekirk

Netherton House Bed and Breakfast	Kintore Street, Auchenblae, Laurencekirk, Kincardineshire, AB30 1XP	01561 320587	★★★★	Bed & Breakfast		
The Redhall Arms Hotel	Station Road, Fordoun, Laurencekirk, Aberdeenshire, AB30 1NN	01561 320526	★★	Bed & Breakfast		

Lawers, Loch Tay

Ben Lawers Hotel	Lawers, Loch Tay, Perthshire, PH15 2PA	01567 820436	★★★	Inn		

Lerwick

Alderlodge Guest House	6 Clairmont Place, Lerwick, Shetland, ZE1 0BR	01595 695705	★★★	Guest House		
Breiview	43 Kanterstead Road, Lerwick, Shetland, ZE1 0RJ	01595 695956	★★★	Guest House		
Brentham House	7 Harbour Street, Lerwick, Shetland, ZE1 0LR	01950 460201	★★★★	Guest Accommodation		
Cee Aa	133 North Road, Lerwick, Shetland , ZE1 0PR	01595 693362	★★★	Bed & Breakfast		
Eddlewood Guest House	8 Clairmont Place, Lerwick, Shetland, ZE1 0BR	01595 692772	★★★	Guest House		
Fort Charlotte Guest House	1 Charlotte Street, Lerwick, Shetland, ZE1 OJL	01595 692140	★★★	Guest House		
Glen Orchy Guest House	20 Knab Road, Lerwick, Shetland, ZE1 0AX	01595 692031	★★★	Guest House	Access for visitors with mobility difficulties	Silver Green Tourism Award
Leeskol	4 Scalloway Road, Lerwick, Shetland, ZE1 0BT	01595 693135	★★	Bed & Breakfast		
No 4 Punds	Lerwick, Shetland, ZE1 0LP	01595 692155	★★★	Bed & Breakfast		
Roseville Bed & Breakfast	95 King Harald Street, Lerwick, Shetland, ZE1 0ER	01595 697128	★★★	Bed & Breakfast		
Seafield Farm	Lerwick, Shetland, ZE1 0RN	01595 69853	★★★	Bed & Breakfast		
Solheim Guest House	34 King Harald Street, Lerwick, Shetland, ZE1 0EQ	01595 695275	★★★	Guest House		
Westhall	Lower Sound, Lerwick, Shetland, ZE1 0RN	01595 694247	★★★★	Bed & Breakfast		

Lesmahagow

Dykecroft Farm	Lesmahagow, Lanarkshire, ML11 0JQ	01555 892226	★★	Farmhouse		

Letham

Whinney-Knowe	8 Dundee Street, Letham, Angus, DD8 2PQ	01307 818288	★★★	Bed & Breakfast		

Leuchars, by St Andrews

St Michaels Inn	St Michaels, Leuchars, by St Andrews, Fife, KY16 0DU	01334 839220	★★★	Inn		
The White House	Leuchars Lodge, Leuchars, by St Andrews, Fife, KY16 0EY	01334 838227	★★★★	Bed & Breakfast		

Unassisted wheelchair access · Assisted wheelchair access · Access for visitors with mobility difficulties
Bronze Green Tourism Award · Silver Green Tourism Award · Gold Green Tourism Award
For further information on our Green Tourism Business Scheme please see page 9.

Leven

Name	Address	Telephone	Grading	Type	Awards
Dunclutha	16 Victoria Road, Leven, Fife, KY8 4EX	01333 425515	★★★★	Guest House	
Fluthers Wood	Cupar Road, Leven , Fife, KY8 5NN	01333 351167	★★★	Bed & Breakfast	
Lomond Guest House	6 Church Road, Leven, Fife, KY8 4JE	01333 300930	★★★	Guest House	
Lorne House	Largo Road, Leven, Fife, KY8 4TB	01333 423255	★★★★	Bed & Breakfast	
Sandilands B&B	20 Leven Road, Lundin Links, Leven, Fife, KY8 6AH	01333 329881	★★★★	Bed & Breakfast	

Levenwick

Name	Address	Telephone	Grading	Type	Awards
Muckle Hus	Netherton, Levenwick, Shetland, ZE2 9HX	01950 422370	★★★★	Bed & Breakfast	
Shalders	Levenwick, Shetland, ZE2 9HX	01950 422229	★★★★	Bed & Breakfast	

Leverburgh, Isle of Harris

Name	Address	Telephone	Grading	Type	Awards
Grimisdale	Leverburgh, Isle of Harris, Western Isles, HS5 3TS	01859 520460	★★★★	Guest House	
Carminish House	1A Strond, Leverburgh, Isle of Harris, Western Isles, HS5 3UB	01859 520400	★★★★	Bed & Breakfast	Access for visitors with mobility difficulties
Sorrel Cottage	2 Glen, Leverburgh, Isle of Harris, Western Isles, HS5 3TY	01859 520319	★★★	Bed & Breakfast	

Linlithgow

Name	Address	Telephone	Grading	Type	Awards
26 Cameron Knowe	Philpstoun, Linlithgow, West Lothian, EH49 6RL	01506 834284	★★★	Bed & Breakfast	
Aran House	Woodcockdale Farm, Lanark Road, Linlithgow, West Lothian, EH49 6QE	01506 842088	★★	Bed & Breakfast	
Arden House	Belsyde, Linlithgow, West Lothian, EH49 6QE	01506 670172	★★★★★	Bed & Breakfast	Silver Green Tourism Award
Belsyde Farm	Lanark Road, Linlithgow, West Lothian, EH49 6QE	01506 842098	★★★★	Bed & Breakfast	Bronze Green Tourism Award
Bomains Farm	Linlithgow, West Lothian, EH49 7RQ	01506 822188	★★★★	Bed & Breakfast	
Cauldburn House	Belsyde, Linlithgow, West Lothian, EH49 6QE	01506 846132	★★★★	Bed & Breakfast	
Lumsdaine	Lanark Road, Linlithgow, West Lothian, EH49 6QE	01506 845001	★★★	Bed & Breakfast	
Strawberry Bank House	13 Avon Place, Linlithgow, West Lothian, EH49 6BL	01506 848372	★★★★	Bed & Breakfast	
The Star & Garter Hotel	1 High Street, Linlithgow, West Lothian, EH49 7AB	01506 846362	AWAITING GRADING		
Thornton	Edinburgh Road, Linlithgow, West Lothian, EH49 6AA	01506 844693	★★★★	Bed & Breakfast	
Rosebank	Blackness, Linlithgow, West Lothian, EH49 7WL	01506 834373	★★★	Bed & Breakfast	

Lintrathen, Kirriemuir

Name	Address	Telephone	Grading	Type	Awards
Purgavie Farm	Lintrathen, Kirriemuir, Angus, DD8 5HZ	01575 560213	★★★★	Farmhouse	

Livingston

Name	Address	Telephone	Grading	Type	Awards
Travelodge Livingston	The Hub, Almondvale Crescent, Livingston, West Lothian, EH54 6QX	08719 846288	AWAITING GRADING		

Loanhead

Name	Address	Telephone	Grading	Type	Awards
Aaron Glen Guest House	7 Nivensknowe Road, Loanhead, Midlothian, EH20 9AU	0131 440 1293	★★★	Guest House	Access for visitors with mobility difficulties

Unassisted wheelchair access · Assisted wheelchair access · Access for visitors with mobility difficulties
Bronze Green Tourism Award · Silver Green Tourism Award · Gold Green Tourism Award

For further information on our Green Tourism Business Scheme please see page 9.

Loch Broom

Braemore Square	Braemore, Loch Broom, Wester Ross, IV23 2RX	01854 655357	★★★★	Bed & Breakfast	Silver Green Tourism Award

Lochbuie, Isle of Mull

Laggan Farm	Lochbuie, Isle of Mull, Argyll, PA62 6AA	01680 814206	★★★★	Bed & Breakfast	

Lochdon, Isle of Mull

Birchgrove	Lochdon, Isle of Mull, Argyll, PA64 4AP	01680 812 364	★★★★	Bed & Breakfast	Access for visitors with mobility difficulties
Wild Cottage	Lochdon, Isle of Mull, Argyll & Bute, PA64 6AP	01680 812105	★★★	Bed & Breakfast	

Lochdonhead, Isle of Mull

Old Mill Cottage	Lochdonhead, Isle of Mull, Argyll, PA64 6AP	01680 812442	★★★★	Bed & Breakfast	Gold Green Tourism Award

Loch Fyne

West Loch Hotel	Tarbert , Loch Fyne, Argyll, PA29 6YF	01880 820283	★★	Inn	

Loch Goil

Rowan House B&B	The Drey, Carrick Castle, Loch Goil , Argyll, PA24 8AF	01301 703090	★★★★	Bed & Breakfast	

Loch Lomond

Culag Lochside Guest House	Luss, Loch Lomond, Argyll and Bute, G83 8PD	01436 860248	★★★★	Guest House	Access for visitors with mobility difficulties
Loaninghead Farm	Balfron Station, Loch Lomond, Argyll and Bute, G63 0SE	01360 440432	★★★★	Bed & Breakfast	Silver Green Tourism Award
Waters Edge Cottage	Duck Bay, Arden, Loch Lomond, Argyll and Bute, G83 8QZ	01389 850629	★★★★	Bed & Breakfast	

Loch Long

Dalkusha House	Arrochar, Loch Long, Argyll, G83 7AA	01301 702234	★★★★	Bed & Breakfast	

Loch Rannoch

Talladh-a-Bheithe Lodge	Loch Rannoch,by Pitlochry, Perthshire, PH17 2QW01882 633203	01882 633203	AWAITING GRADING		

Loch Torridon

Ferroch	Annat, Loch Torridon, Auchnasheen, IV22 2EU	01445 791451	★★★★	Bed & Breakfast	

Lochboisdale

Brae Lea House	Lasgair, Lochboisdale, Isle of South Uist, HS8 5TH	01878 700497	★★★	Guest House	
Croft House B&B	3 Milton, Lochboisdale, South Uist, HS8 5RY	01878 7102254	★★★	Bed & Breakfast	
Kiaora	405 North Smerclate, Lochboisdale, South Uist, Western Isles, HS8 5TU	01878 700382	★★★	Bed & Breakfast	

by Lochboisdale

Reineval	6 Milton, by Lochboisdale, South Uist, HS8 5RY	01878 710214	★★★	Bed & Breakfast	

Lochbroom, Ullapool

Torran	7A Loggie, Lochbroom, Ullapool, Ross-shire, IV23 2SG	01854 655227	★★★	Bed & Breakfast	

Unassisted wheelchair access · Assisted wheelchair access · Access for visitors with mobility difficulties
Bronze Green Tourism Award · Silver Green Tourism Award · Gold Green Tourism Award

For further information on our Green Tourism Business Scheme please see page 9.

Lochbuie, Isle of Mull

The Barn	Barrachandroman, Lochbuie, Isle of Mull, Argyll, PA62 6AA	01680 814220	★★★★	Bed & Breakfast	

Lochcarron

Lethame	7 Kirkton Avenue, Lochcarron, Ross-shire, IV54 8UE	01520 722451	★★★	Bed & Breakfast	
Lotta Dubh	Ardaneaskan, Lochcarron, Ross-shire, IV54 8YL	01520 722405	★★★	Bed & Breakfast	
Rockvilla Hotel	Main Street, Lochcarron, Ross-shire, IV54 8YB	01520 722379	★★★	Inn	

Lochearnhead

Lochearn House	Lochearnhead, Lochearnhead, Perthshire, FK19 8NR	01567 830380	★★★★	Guest House	
Mansewood Country House	Lochearnhead, Stirlingshire, FK19 8NS	01567 830213	★★★★	Guest House	

Lochend

Kimcraigan B&B	Kimcraigan, Lochend, Inverness-shire, IV3 8LA	01463 861474	★★★	Bed & Breakfast	

Locheport

Langass Lodge	Locheport, North Uist, HS6 5EX	01876 580285	★★★	Restaurant with Rooms	Gold Green Tourism Award

Lochgilphead

Auchenbeag	Tayvallich, Lochgilphead, Argyll, PA31 8PW	01546 870241	★★★	Bed & Breakfast	
Empire Travel Lodge	Union Street, Lochgilphead, Argyll, PA31 8JS	01546 602381	★★★	Lodge	Assisted wheelchair access
The Corran	Poltalloch Street, Lochgilphead, Argyll, PA31 8LR	01546 603866	★★★★	Bed & Breakfast	

By Lochgilphead

Bellanoch House	Bellanoch Yacht Basin, By Lochgilphead, Argyll, PA31 8SN	01546 830149	★★★★	Bed & Breakfast	
Ford House	Ford, By Lochgilphead, Argyll , PA31 8RH	01546 810273	★★★	Guest House	

Lochgoilhead

The Shore House Inn	Lochgoilhead, Argyll, PA24 8AA	01301 703340	★★★	Inn	

Lochinver

Ardmore House	Torbreck, Lochinver, Sutherland, IV27 4JB	01571 844310	★★★	Bed & Breakfast	
Ardsaile	Achmelvich, Lochinver, Sutherland, IV27 4SB	01571 844363	★★★★	Bed & Breakfast	
Davar	Lochinver, Sutherland, IV27 4LJ	01571 844501	★★★★	Bed & Breakfast	
Polcraig Guest House	Cruamer, Lochinver, Sutherland, IV27 4LD	01571 844429	★★★★	Guest House	
Stac Fada B&B	169 Stoer, Lochinver IV27 4JE	0845 3458849	★★★	Bed & Breakfast	
Veyatie	66 Baddidarroch, Lochinver, Sutherland, IV27 4LP	01571 844424	★★★★	Bed & Breakfast	Silver Green Tourism Award

by Lochinver

Cruachan Guest House	Stoer, by Lochinver, Sutherland, IV27 4JE	01571 855303	★★★★	Guest House	

Unassisted wheelchair access — Assisted wheelchair access — Access for visitors with mobility difficulties
Bronze Green Tourism Award — Silver Green Tourism Award — Gold Green Tourism Award
For further information on our Green Tourism Business Scheme please see page 9.

Lochmaben

The Crown Hotel	8 Bruce Street, Lochmaben, Dumfriesshire, DG11 1PD	01387 811750	★★	Inn	♿

Lochmaddy, Isle of North Uist

Carinish Inn	Carinish, Lochmaddy, Isle of North Uist, Western Isles, HS6 5EJ	01876 580673	★★★	Inn	
Redburn House	Lochmaddy, Isle of North Uist, Western Isles, HS6 5AA	01876 500301	★★★	Bed & Breakfast	Access for visitors with mobility difficulties
Sgeir Ruadh	Hougharry, Lochmaddy, Isle of North Uist, Western Isles, HS6 5DL	01876 510312	★★★	Bed & Breakfast	

Lochranza

Apple Lodge	Lochranza, Isle of Arran, KA27 8HJ	01770 830229	★★★★	Guest House	
Lochranza Hotel	Shore Road, Lochranza, Isle of Arran, KA27 8HL	01770 830223	★★★	Inn	

Lochs, Isle of Lewis

Clearview	44 Balallan, Lochs, Isle of Lewis HS2 9PT	01851 830472	★★★	Bed & Breakfast	
Glen House	77 Leurbost, Lochs, Isle of Lewis HS2 9NU	01851 860241	★★★	Bed & Breakfast	
Tighnabruaich	8 Balallan, Lochs, Isle of Lewis HS2 9PN	01851 830742	★★★	Bed & Breakfast	

Lochwinnoch

East Kerse Farm	Lochwinnoch, Renfrewshire, PA12 4DU	01505 502400	★★★	Farmhouse	
The Hungry Monk	Largs Road, Lochwinnoch, Renfrewshire, PA12 4JF	01505 843848	★★★★	Inn	

Lockerbie

Carik Cottage	Waterbeck, Lockerbie, Dumfriesshire, DG11 3EU	01461 600652	★★★★	Bed & Breakfast	
Nether Boreland	Boreland, Lockerbie, Dumfriesshire, DG11 2LL	01576 610248	★★★	Bed & Breakfast	
Torbeckhill Bungalow	Waterbeck, Lockerbie, Dumfriesshire, DG11 3EX	01461 600683	★★★★	Bed & Breakfast	

Logiealmond

Finlaggan House	Chapelhill, Logiealmond, Perthshire, PH1 3TH	01738 880234	★★★★	Bed & Breakfast	

Lossiemouth

Ardivot House B&B	Ardivot Farm, Lossiemouth, Moray, IV31 6RY	01343 811076	★★★	Farmhouse	
Carmania	45 St Gerardine's Road, Lossiemouth, Moray, IV31 6JX	01343 812276	★★★	Bed & Breakfast	
Ceilidh B&B	34 Clifton Road, Lossiemouth, Moray, IV31 6DP	01343 815848	★★★	Bed & Breakfast	♿
Links Lodge	Stotfield Road, Lossiemouth, Moray, IV31 6QS	01343 813815	★★★★	Guest House	Access for visitors with mobility difficulties
Lossiemouth House	33 Clifton Road, Lossiemouth, Moray, IV31 6DP	01343 813397	★★★	Bed & Breakfast	
Norland	Stotfield Road, Lossiemouth, Moray, IV31 6QP	01343 813570	AWAITING GRADING		

Lundin Links

No 18 Links Road	Links Road, Lundin Links KY8 6AU	01333 320497	★★★	Bed & Breakfast	Bronze Green Tourism Award

♿ Unassisted wheelchair access   Assisted wheelchair access   Access for visitors with mobility difficulties
Bronze Green Tourism Award   Silver Green Tourism Award   Gold Green Tourism Award
For further information on our Green Tourism Business Scheme please see page 9.

The Hamptons	Riverside, 14 Largo Road, Lundin Links, Fife, KY8 6DG	01333 329979	★★★★	Bed & Breakfast	

Luss

The Corries	Inverbeg, Luss, Loch Lomond, G83 8PD	01436 860275	★★★	Bed & Breakfast	
Doune of Glen Douglas Farm	Inverbeg, Luss, Loch Lomond, G83 8PD	01301 702312	★★★	Bed & Breakfast	
Shantron Farm House	Shantron Farm, Luss, Loch Lomond, G83 8RH	01389 850231	★★★	Bed & Breakfast	Bronze Green Tourism Award

By Luss

Polnaberoch	Arden, By Luss, Loch Lomond, G83 8RQ	01389 850615	★★★	Bed & Breakfast	

Lybster

Canisp House	Occumster, Lybster, Caithness, KW3 6BD	01593 721758	AWAITING GRADING		
The Croft House	Swiney, Lybster, Caithness, KW3 6BT	01593 721342	★★★	Bed & Breakfast	

Macduff

Monica & Martin's B&B	21 Gellymill Street, Macduff, Banffshire, AB44 1TN	01261 832336	★★★★	Bed & Breakfast	
The Park Hotel	Fife Street, Macduff, Banffshire, AB44 1YA	01261 832265	★★★	Guest House	

By Macduff

Palace Farm	Gamrie, By Macduff, Banffshire, AB45 3HS	01261 851261	★★★★	Farmhouse	

Macmerry

Adniston Manor	West Adniston Farm, Macmerry, East Lothian, EH33 1EA	01875 611190	★★★★	Guest House	Access for visitors with mobility difficulties

Mallaig

Anchorage	Gillies Park, Mallaig, Inverness-shire, PH41 4QS	01687 462454	★★★	Bed & Breakfast	
Garramore House	South Morar, Mallaig, Inverness-shire, PH40 4PD	01687 450268	★★	Guest House	
Seaview	Main Street, Mallaig, Inverness-shire, PH41 4QS	01687 462059	★★★	Guest House	
The Moorings	East Bay, Mallaig, Inverness-shire, PH41 4PQ	01687 462225	★★★	Guest House	
Western Isles Guest House	East Bay, Mallaig, Inverness-shire, PH41 4QG	01687 462320	★★★	Guest House	

By Mallaig

Doune Stone Lodges	Doune, Knoydart, By Mallaig, Inverness-shire, PH41 4PU	01687 462667	★★★	Restaurant with Rooms	

Markinch

Cruach Bed & Breakfast	Stobcross Road, Markinch, Fife, KY7 6ED	01592 751093	★★★	Bed & Breakfast	
Town House Hotel	1 High Street, Markinch, Fife, KY7 6DQ	01592 758459	★★★★	Restaurant with Rooms	
Shythrum Farm	Markinch, Fife, KY7 6HB	01592 758372	★★★	Bed & Breakfast	

Mauchline

Ardwell	103 Loundoun Street, Mauchline, Ayrshire, KA5 5BH	01290 552987	★★★	Bed & Breakfast	

Unassisted wheelchair access Assisted wheelchair access Access for visitors with mobility difficulties
Bronze Green Tourism Award Silver Green Tourism Award Gold Green Tourism Award
For further information on our Green Tourism Business Scheme please see page 9.

Treborane	Dykefield Farm, Mauchline, Ayrshire, KA5 6EY	01290 550328	★★	Bed & Breakfast	
Dykefield Farm	Mauchline, Ayrshire, KA5 6EY	01290 553170	★★	Farmhouse	

Meikleour

Meikleour Hotel	Meikleour, Perthshire, PH2 6EB	01250 883206	★★★★	Inn	

Melrose

Braidwood	Buccleuch Street, Melrose, Roxburghshire , TD6 9LD	01896 822488	★★★★	Guest House	
Dunfermline House	Buccleuch Street, Melrose, Roxburghshire, TD6 9LB	01896 822411	★★★	Guest House	
Easter Cottage	Lilliesleaf, Melrose, Roxburghshire, TD6 9JD	01835 870281	★★★★	Bed & Breakfast	Access for visitors with mobility difficulties
Fauhope House	Gattonside, Melrose, Roxburghshire, TD6 9LU	01896 823184	★★★★	Bed & Breakfast	
Fiorlin	Abbey Street, Melrose, Roxburghshire, TD6 9PX	01896 822984	★★★	Bed & Breakfast	
Old Abbey School	Waverley Road, Melrose, Roxburghshire, TD6 9SH	01896 823432	★★★	Bed & Breakfast	
Old Bank House	27 Buccleuch Street, Melrose, Roxburghshire, TD6 9LB	01896 823712	★★★★	Bed & Breakfast	

Mid Yell

Norwind	Mid Yell, Shetland, ZE2	01957 702312	★★★	Bed & Breakfast	

Midcalder

Redcraig Bed and Breakfast	Midcalder, Livingston, EH53 0JT	01506 884249	★★★★	Bed & Breakfast	

Millport

Denmark Cottage	8 Ferry Road, Millport, Isle of Cumbrae, KA28	01475 530958	★★★	Bed & Breakfast	
The Cathedral of the Isles	The College, Millport, Isle of Cumbrae, KA28 0HE	01475 530353	★★★	Guest House	Assisted wheelchair access
Westbourne	West Bay Road, Millport, Isle of Cumbrae, KA28 0HA	01475 530000	★★★	Bed & Breakfast	

Milton, South Uist

Caloraidh	Milton, Milton, South Uist, South Uist, HS8 5RY	01878 710365	★★★	Bed & Breakfast	Access for visitors with mobility difficulties

By Milton, Dumfries

Little Culmain (Bothy)	Crocketford Road, By Milton, Dumfries, Dumfries, DG2 8QP	01556 690 210	★★★	Farmhouse	

Milnathort

Mawcarse House	Mawcarse House, Milnathort, Kinross-shire, KY13 9SJ	01577 862220	★★★★	Farmhouse	

Milngavie, Glasgow

Auchenhowe Cottage B&B	9 Langbank Holdings, Milngavie, Glasgow, Dunbartonshire, G62 6EL	0141 956 4003	★★★	Bed & Breakfast	
Best Foot Forward @ West View	1 Dougalston Gardens South, Milngavie, Glasgow, Dunbartonshire, G62 6HS	0141 956 3046	★★★	Bed & Breakfast	
High Craigton Farm	Stockiemuir Road, Milngavie, Glasgow, Dunbartonshire, G62 7HA	0141 956 1384	★★	Farmhouse	
Tambowie Farm	Craigton Village, Milngavie, Glasgow, Dunbartonshire, G62 7HD	0141 956 1583	★★★	Bed & Breakfast	

Unassisted wheelchair access · Assisted wheelchair access · Access for visitors with mobility difficulties
Bronze Green Tourism Award · Silver Green Tourism Award · Gold Green Tourism Award
For further information on our Green Tourism Business Scheme please see page 9.

Milton

Milton Inn	Dumbarton Road , Milton, Dunbartonshire, G82 2DT	01389 761401	★★★	Inn	Access for visitors with mobility difficulties

Minard

Minard Castle	Minard, Argyll, PA32 8YB	01546 886272	★★★★	Bed & Breakfast	Assisted wheelchair access

Minnigaff

Flowerbank Guest House	Millcroft Road, Minnigaff, Wigtownshire, DG8 6PJ	01671 402629	★★★	Guest House

Moffat

Balmoral Hotel	High Street, Moffat, Dumfriesshire, DG10 9DL	01683 20288	★★★	Inn	
Blairdrummond House	School Lane, Moffat, Dumfriesshire, DG10 9AX	01683 221240	★★★★	Bed & Breakfast	
Bridge House	Well Road, Moffat, Dumfrieshire, DG10 9JT	01683 220558	★★★★	Guest House	
Buchan Guest House	Beechgrove, Moffat, Dumfriesshire, DG10 9RS	01683 220378	★★★	Guest House	
Dell-Mar	6 Beechgrove, Moffat, Dumfries & Galloway, DG10 9RS	01683 220260	★★★	Bed & Breakfast	
Fernhill	Grange Road, Moffat, Dumfriesshire, DG10 9HT	01683 220077	★★★★	Bed & Breakfast	
Hartfell House	Hartfell Crescent, Moffat, Dumfriesshire, DG10 9AL	01683 220153	★★★★	Guest House	
Limetree House	Eastgate, Moffat, Dumfriesshire, DG10 9AE	01683 220001	★★★★	Guest House	Access for visitors with mobility difficulties
Lochhouse Farm Retreat Centre	Beattock, Moffat, Dumfries & Galloway, DG10 9SG	01683 300451	★★★	Bed & Breakfast	Unassisted wheelchair access
Marchbankwood House	Beattock, Moffat, Dumfries & Galloway, DG10 9RG	01683 300118	★★★★	Guest House	
Morlich House	Ballplay Road, Moffat, Dumfriesshire, DG10 9JU	01683 220589	★★★★	Bed & Breakfast	
Queensberry House	Beechgrove, Moffat, Dumfriesshire, DG10 9RS	01683 220538	★★★★	Bed & Breakfast	
Rockhill Guest House	14 Beechgrove, Moffat, Dumfriesshire, DG10 9RS	01683 220283	★★★	Guest House	
Seamore House	Academy Road, Moffat, Dumfriesshire, DG10 9HW	01683 220404	★★★	Guest House	
Seven Oaks at 2 St. Mary's Church	a [D2 St. Mary's Church, Academy Road, Moffat, Dumfries & Galloway, DG10 9HP	01683 220584	★★★★	Bed & Breakfast	
Stag Hotel	22 High Street , Moffat, Dumfriesshire, DG10 9HL	01683 220343	★★	Inn	
Well View Hotel	Ballplay Road, Moffat, Dumfriesshire, DG10 9JU	01683 220184	★★★★	Restaurant with Rooms	
Wellstar	29 Well Street, Moffat, Dumfriess-shire, DG10 9DP	01683 220838	★★★	Bed & Breakfast	
Woodhead Farm	Moffat, Dumfriesshire, DG10 9LU	01683 220225	★★★★	Bed & Breakfast	

Moniaive

Causies Cross Guest House	10 High Street, Moniaive, Dumfries-shire, DG3 4HN	01848 200719	AWAITING GRADING

Monifieth

Ashlea Manor Guest House	2 Victoria Street, Monifieth, Dundee, DD5 4HP	01382 530015	★★★★	Bed & Breakfast

Unassisted wheelchair access   Assisted wheelchair access   Access for visitors with mobility difficulties
Bronze Green Tourism Award   Silver Green Tourism Award   Gold Green Tourism Award
For further information on our Green Tourism Business Scheme please see page 9.

Monikie

Craigton House B&B	Craigton Road, Monikie, Angus, DD5 3QN	01382 370570	★★★★	Bed & Breakfast	Access for visitors with mobility difficulties

Montrose

36 The Mall	Montrose, Angus, DD10 8SS	01674 673646	★★★★	Bed & Breakfast	
Fairfield	24 The Mall, Montrose, Angus, DD10 8NW	01674 676386	★★★	Bed & Breakfast	
Oaklands	10 Rossie Island Road, Montrose, Angus, DD10 9NN	01674 672018	★★★	Guest House	

By Montrose

Woodland Glade	5 Hillview Gardens, Inverbervie, By Montrose, Angus, DD10 0PX	01561 361567	★★★	Bed & Breakfast	
Eskview Farm	Nether Warburton, St Cyrus, By Montrose, Angus, DD10 0AQ	01674 830890	★★★	Bed & Breakfast	

Motherwell

Motherwell College Stewart Hall	Dalzell Drive, Motherwell, Lanarkshire, ML1 2DD	01698 261890	★	Campus	Unassisted wheelchair access

Muir of Ord

Dungrianach	Corrie Road, Muir of Ord, Ross-shire, IV6 7TN	01463 870316	★★★	Bed & Breakfast	
Fairburn Lodge & Activity Centre	Urray, Muir of Ord, Ross-shire, IV6 7UT	01997 433397	★★	Lodge	
Hillview Park	Muir-of-Ord, Ross-shire, IV6 7TU	01463 870787	★★★★	Bed & Breakfast	Access for visitors with mobility difficulties
Home Farm Bed and Breakfast	Highfield Mains, Muir of Ord, Ross-shire, IV6 7XN	01463 871779	★★★★	Bed & Breakfast	

Muirhead

West Adamston Farmhouse	West Adamston Farm, Muirhead, Dundee, DD2 5QX	01382 580215	★★★★	Bed & Breakfast	

Muirkirk

The Old Church Bed & Breakfast	Glasgow Road, Muirkirk, Ayrshire, KA18 3RN	01290 660045	★★★★	Bed & Breakfast	

Munlochy

Kinneskie House	Balnakyle, Munlochy, Ross-shire, IV8 8PF	01463 811779	★★★★	Bed & Breakfast	

Musselburgh

18 Woodside Gardens	Musselburgh, East Lothian, EH21 7LJ	0131 665 3170	★★	Bed & Breakfast	
19 Bridge Street	Musselburgh, East Lothian, EH21 6AA	0131 665 6560	★★	Bed & Breakfast	
8 Albert Terrace	Linkfield Road, Musselburgh, East Lothian, EH21 7LR	0131 665 3703	★★★	Bed & Breakfast	
Arden House	26 Linkfield Road, Musselburgh, East Lothian, EH21 7LL	0131 665 0663	★★★★	Guest House	
Carberry Tower	Musselburgh, East Lothian, EH21 8PY	0131 665 3135	AWAITING GRADING		Access for visitors with mobility difficulties
Eildon	109 Newbigging, Musselburgh, East Lothian, EH21 7AS	0131 665 3981	★★★	Bed & Breakfast	Gold Green Tourism Award
Travelodge Edinburgh Musselburgh	Service Area, A1 Old Craighall, Musselburgh, East Lothian, EH21 8RE	08719 846138	AWAITING GRADING		

Unassisted wheelchair access · Assisted wheelchair access · Access for visitors with mobility difficulties
Bronze Green Tourism Award · Silver Green Tourism Award · Gold Green Tourism Award
For further information on our Green Tourism Business Scheme please see page 9.

Nairn

Bracadale House	Albert Street, Nairn, Nairnshire, IV12 4HF	01667 452547	★★★★	Guest House	
Brackla Farmhouse	Cawdor, Nairn, Nairnshire, IV12 5QY	01667 404223	★★★★	Farmhouse	
Brighton House	Grant Street, Nairn, Nairnshire, IV12 4NN	01667 454670	★★★	Bed & Breakfast	
Cawdor House	7 Cawdor Street, Nairn, Nairnshire, IV12 4QD	01667 455855	★★★★	Guest House	
Glebe End	1 Glebe Road, Nairn, Nairnshire, IV12 4ED	01667 451659	★★★★	Bed & Breakfast	
Inveran	Seabank Road, Nairn, Nairnshire, IV12 4HG	01667 455666	★★★★	Bed & Breakfast	
Invernairne Guest House	Thurlow Road, Nairn, Nairnshire, IV12 4EZ	01667 452039	★★★	Guest House	
Redburn	Queen Street, Nairn, Nairnshire, IV12 4AA	01667 452238	★★★	Bed & Breakfast	

By Nairn

Covenanters' Inn	High Street, Auldearn, By Nairn, Nairnshire, IV12 5TG	01667 452456	★★★	Inn	♿

Ness, Isle of Lewis

The Cross Inn	Cross Ness, Ness, Isle of Lewis, Western Isles, HS2 0SN	01851 810152	★★★	Inn	♿

Nethybridge

Coire Choille B&B	Lettoch Road, Nethybridge, Inverness-shire, PH25 3DY	01479 821716	★★★	Bed & Breakfast	
Tigh Na Fraoch	Nethybridge, Inverness-shire, PH25 3DA	01479 821400	★★★★	Bed & Breakfast	

New Leeds

Rose Lodge	Longhill, New Leeds, Peterhead, AB42 4HX	01346 531148	★★★★	Bed & Breakfast	

Newburgh

Ninewells Farm	Woodriffe Road, Newburgh, Fife, KY14 6EY	01337 840307	★★★★	Bed & Breakfast

Newburgh, Ellon

Stevenson B&B	49 School Crescent, Newburgh, Ellon, Aberdeenshire, AB41 6BH	01358 789017	★★	Bed & Breakfast

Newcastleton

Liddesdale Hotel	17 Douglas Square, Newcastleton, Roxburghshire, TD9 0QD	01387 375255	★★★	Inn
Sorbietrees B&B	Newcastleton, Roxburghshire, TD9 0TL	01387 375 215	★★	Bed & Breakfast

Newmachar

The School House	5 School Road, Newmachar, Aberdeenshire, AB21 0WB	01651 862970	★★★★	Bed & Breakfast
Rosebank House	Mains of Torrykeith, Newmachar, Aberdeenshire, AB21 0QE	01651 862397	★★★★	Bed & Breakfast

Newport-on-Tay

Braemore	109b Tay Street, Newport-on-Tay, Fife, DD6 8AR	01382 542516	★★★★	Bed & Breakfast

Unassisted wheelchair access · Assisted wheelchair access · Access for visitors with mobility difficulties
Bronze Green Tourism Award · Silver Green Tourism Award · Gold Green Tourism Award
For further information on our Green Tourism Business Scheme please see page 9.

Newstead

No. 9, Townhead Way	Newstead, Melrose, TD6 9BU	01896 820435	★★★★	Bed & Breakfast	

Newton Stewart

Benera Bed and Breakfast	Corsbie Road, Newton Stewart, Wigtownshire, DG8 6JD	01671 403443	★★★	Bed & Breakfast	
Cherrytrees	Fairway Drive, Newton Stewart, Dumfries & Galloway, DG8 6PG	01671 402502	★★★	Bed & Breakfast	
Craiglemine Tigh	Whithorn, Newton Stewart, Wigtownshire, DG8 8NE	01988 500490	★★★	Bed & Breakfast	
Creebridge Lodge	Minnigaff , Newton Stewart, Wigtownshire, DG8 6NR	01671 402319	★★★	Bed & Breakfast	
East Culkae Farm House	Sorbie, Newton Stewart, Wigtownshire, DG8 8AS	01988 850214	★★★	Farmhouse	Access for visitors with mobility difficulties
Galloway Arms Hotel	Victoria Street, Newton Stewart, Wigtownshire, DG8 6DB	01671 402653	★★★	Inn	
Kilwarlin	4 Corvisel Road, Newton Stewart, Wigtownshire, DG8 6LN	01671 403047	★★★	Bed & Breakfast	
Ravenstone House	Whithorn, Newton Stewart, Wigtownshire, DG8 8DU	01988 700756	★★★★	Bed & Breakfast	
Rowallan	Corsbie Road, Newton Stewart, Wigtownshire, DG8 6JB	01671 402520	★★★	Guest House	
Stables Guest House	Corsbie Road, Newton Stewart, Wigtownshire, DG8 6JB	01671 402157	★★★	Guest House	
Tha Butchach	New Luce, Newton Stewart, Wigtonshire, DG8 0AW	01581 600217	★★	Bed & Breakfast	
The Steam Packet Inn	Harbour Row, Isle of Whithorn, Newton Stewart, Wigtownshire, DG8 8LL	01988 500334	★★	Inn	

By Newton Stewart

Cairnholy Farmhouse	Carsluith, By Newton Stewart, Wigtownshire, DG8 7EA	01557 840249	★★★	Bed & Breakfast	
Cherrytrees	59-6 St John Street, Creetown, By Newton Stewart, Wigtownshire, DG8 7JB	0167182 229	★★★	Bed & Breakfast	
The Haven	23 Harbour Street, Creetown, By Newton Stewart, Wigtownshire, DG8 7JJ	01671 820546	★★	Bed & Breakfast	

Newtonmearns

The Guest Rooms at Matherton	5 Matherton Avenue, Newtonmearns, Glasgow, G77 5EY	0141 639 8931	★★★	Bed & Breakfast	

Newtonmore

Alvey House	Golf Course Road, Newtonmore, Inverness-shire, PH20 1AT	01540 673260	★★★	Guest House	
Ard-Na-Coille	Kingussie Road, Newtonmore, Inverness-shire, PH20 1AY	01450 673214	★★★★★	Guest House	
Clune House	Main Street, Newtonmore, Inverness-shire, PH20 1DR	01540 673359	★★★	Bed & Breakfast	Silver Green Tourism Award
Coig Na Shee	Fort William Road, Newtonmore, Inverness-shire, PH20 1DG	01540 670109	★★★★	Guest House	
Glenavon House	Main Street, Newtonmore, Inverness-shire, PH20 1DR	01540 673701	★★★★	Bed & Breakfast	
Greenways	Golf Course road, Newtonmore, Inverness-shire, PH20 1AT	01540 670136	★★★★	Bed & Breakfast	
Larick House B&B	Golf Course Road, Newtonmore, Inverness-shire, PH20 1AT	01540 673762	★★★	Bed & Breakfast	

By Newtonmore

Crubenbeg House	Falls of Truim, By Newtonmore, Inverness-shire, PH20 1BE	01540 673300	★★★★	Guest House	Unassisted wheelchair access

Unassisted wheelchair access · Assisted wheelchair access · Access for visitors with mobility difficulties
Bronze Green Tourism Award · Silver Green Tourism Award · Gold Green Tourism Award
For further information on our Green Tourism Business Scheme please see page 9.

North Ballachulish

Creag Mhor Lodge	Onich , North Ballachulish, Inverness-shire, PH33 6RY	01855 821379	★★★★	Guest House
Highland View Bed & Breakfast	Highland View, Creag Dhu House, North Ballachulish, Inverness-shire, PH33 6RY	01855 821555	★★★★	Bed & Breakfast

North Berwick

12 Quality Street	North Berwick, East Lothian, EH39 4HP	01620 892529	★★★	Restaurant with Rooms
Drem Farmhouse	Drem, North Berwick, East Lothian, EH39 5AP	01620 850563	★★★★	Bed & Breakfast
Frances B&B	39a High Street, North Berwick, East Lothian, EH39 4HH	01620 890956	★★★	Bed & Breakfast
Glentruim	53 Dirleton Avenue, North Berwick, East Lothian, EH39 4BL	01620 890064	★★★	Bed & Breakfast
Melbourne Mews B&B	43 Melbourne Place, North Berwick, East Lothian, EH39 4JS	01620 890895	★★	Bed & Breakfast
The Glebe House	Law Road, North Berwick, East Lothian, EH39 4PL	01620 892608	★★★★	Bed & Breakfast
The Wing	13 Marine Parade, North Berwick, East Lothian, EH39 4LD	01620 893162	★★★	Bed & Breakfast
Troon	Dirleton Road, North Berwick, East Lothian, EH39 5DF	01620 893555	★★★	Bed & Breakfast

North Connel

Lochnell Arms Hotel	North Connel, Argyll, PA37 1RP	01631 710239	★★★	Inn

North Kessock

Anchor and Chain	Coulmore Bay, North Kessock, Inverness-shire, IV1 3XB	01463 731313	★★★	Restaurant with Rooms
Culbin	Drumsmittal, North Kessock, Inverness-shire, IV1 3XF	01463 731455	★★	Bed & Breakfast

North Lochs

Penuel	44 Crossbost, North Lochs, Isle Of Lewis, HS2 9NP	01851 860340	★★★	Bed & Breakfast

North Queensferry

Battery House	3 East Bay, North Queensferry, Fife, KY11 IJX	07905 584089	★★★	Bed & Breakfast
Northcraig Cottage	North Queensferry, North Queensferry, Fife, KY11 1JZ	01383 412299	★★★	Bed & Breakfast

North Ronaldsay

Observatory Guest House	North Ronaldsay, Orkney, KW17 2BE	01857 633200	★★★	Guest House	♿ (assisted)

North Tolsta

Hillside Cottage Bed and Breakfast	Hill Street, North Tolsta, Isle of Lewis, HS2 0NG	01851 890464	★★★	Bed & Breakfast

North Uist

Bonnie View	19 Carinish, North Uist, Western Isles, HS6 5EJ	01876 580211	★★★★	Bed & Breakfast
No. 19 Knockline	North Uist, Wesern Isles, HS6 5DT	01876 510390	AWAITING GRADING	
Old Shop House	Bayhead, North Uist, Western Isles, HS6 5DS	01876 510395	★★★	Bed & Breakfast
Rushlee House	Lochmaddy, North Uist, Western Isles, HS6 5AE	01876 500274	★★★★	Bed & Breakfast

♿ Unassisted wheelchair access ♿ Assisted wheelchair access Access for visitors with mobility difficulties
Bronze Green Tourism Award Silver Green Tourism Award Gold Green Tourism Award

For further information on our Green Tourism Business Scheme please see page 9.

Northbay

Airds Guest House	244 Bruernish, Northbay, Isle of Barra, HS9 5UY	01871 890720	★★★	Bed & Breakfast	⩚
Aros Cottage	190 Buaile-nam-Bodach, Northbay, Isle of Barra, HS9 5UT	01871 890355	★★★	Bed & Breakfast	

Oban

Alltavona	Corran Esplanade, Oban, Argyll, PA34 5AQ	01631 565067	★★★★	Guest House
Alt Na Craig	Glenmore Road, Oban, Argyll, PA34 4PG	01631 563637	★★★★	Guest House
Ard Struan	Croft Road, Oban, Argyll, PA34 5JN	01631 563689	★★★	Bed & Breakfast
Ards House	Connel, Oban, Argyll, PA37 1PT	01631 710255	★★★★	Guest House
Ardura	Duncraggan Road, Oban, Argyll, PA34 5DU	01631 562380	★★★	Bed & Breakfast
Aros Ard	Croft Drive, Oban, Argyll, PA34 5JN	01631 565500	★★★★	Bed & Breakfast
Ayres Guest House	3 Victoria Crescent, Oban, Argyll, PA34 5JL	01631 562260	★★	Guest House
Beech Grove Guest House	Croft Road, Oban, Argyll, PA34 5JL	01631 566111	★★★★	Guest House
Blair Villa South	Rockfield Road, Oban, Argyll, PA34 5DQ	01631 564813	★★★	Bed & Breakfast
Briarbank	Glencruitten Road, Oban, Argyll, PA34 4DN	01631 566549	★★★★	Bed & Breakfast
Clohass	Connel Road, Oban, Argyll, PA34 5TX	01631 563647	★★★	Bed & Breakfast
Corriemar	6 Esplanade, Oban, Argyll, PA34 5AQ	01631 562476	★★★★	Guest House
Don-Muir	Pulpit Hill, Oban, Argyll, PA34 4LX	01631 564536	★★★★	Bed & Breakfast
Dungallan Country House	Gallanach Road, Oban, Argyll, PA34 4PD	01631 563799	★★★★★	Guest House
Dunheanish Guest House	Ardconnel Road, Oban, Argyll, PA34 5DW	01631 566556	★★★	Guest House
Eredine	Ardconnel Road, Oban, Argyll, PA34 5DW	01631 563917	★★★	Bed & Breakfast
Glen Cottage	Longsdale Road, Oban, Argyll, PA34 5JU	01631 563420	★★★	Bed & Breakfast
Glenara Guest House	Rockfield Road, Oban, Argyll, PA34 5DQ	01631 563172	★★★★	Bed & Breakfast
Glenbervie Guest House	Dalriach Road, Oban, Argyll, PA34	01631 564770	★★★★	Guest House
Glenburnie	Esplanade, Oban, Argyll, PA34 5AQ	01631 562089	★★★★	Guest House
Glengorm	Dunollie Road, Oban, Argyll, PA34 5PH	01631 564386	★★★	Guest House
Glenrigh Guest House	The Esplanade, Oban, Argyll, PA34 5AQ	01631 562991	★★★★	Guest House
Glenroy Guest House	Rockfield Road, Oban, Argyll, PA34 5DQ	01631 562 585	★★★	Guest House
Gramarvin Guest House	Breadalbane Street, Oban, Argyll, PA34 5PE	01631 564622	★★★	Guest House
Greencourt Guest House	Benvoullin Road, Oban, Argyll, PA34 5EF	01631 563987	★★★★	Guest House
Hawthornbank Guest House	Dalriach Road, Oban, Argyll, PA34 5JE	01631 562041	★★★★	Guest House
Heatherfield House	Albert Road, Oban, Argyll, PA34 5EY	01631 562806	★★★★	Guest House

Unassisted wheelchair access   Assisted wheelchair access   Access for visitors with mobility difficulties
Bronze Green Tourism Award   Silver Green Tourism Award   Gold Green Tourism Award
For further information on our Green Tourism Business Scheme please see page 9.

High Cliff	35 Glencruitten Road, Oban, Argyll , PA34 4EW	01631 564134	★★★★	Guest House	
Inverasdale	Soroba Road, Oban, Argyll, PA34 4JY	01631 571031	★★★★	Bed & Breakfast	
Kathmore Guest House	Soroba Road, Oban, Argyll, PA34 4JF	01631 562104	★★★	Guest House	
Kelvin Hotel	Shore Street, Oban, Argyll, PA34 4LQ	01631 562150	★	Guest House	
Kilchrenan House	Corran Esplanade, Oban, Argyll, PA34 5AQ	01631 562663	★★★★	Guest House	
Lagganbeg Guest House	Dunollie Road, Oban PA34 5PH	01631 563151	★★★	Guest House	
Lagganbuie	Loch Feochan, Kilmore, Oban, Argyll, PA34 4QT	01631 770218	★★★★	Bed & Breakfast	
Latheron	Longsdale Road, Oban, Argyll, PA34 5JU	01631 564974	★★★	Bed & Breakfast	
Lochvoil House	Dunuaran Road, Oban, Argyll, PA34 4NE	01631 562645	★★★	Bed & Breakfast	
Lorne View	Ardconnel Road, Oban, Argyll, PA34 5DW	01631 567396	★★★	Bed & Breakfast	
Maridon House	Dunuaran Road, Oban, Argyll, PA34 4NE	01631 562670	★★★	Guest House	
Roseneath Guest House	Dalriach Road, Oban, Argyll, PA34 5EQ	01631 562929	★★★	Guest House	
Sabden Brook	Ardconnel Hill, Oban, Argyll, PA34 5DY	01631 562649	★★★	Bed & Breakfast	
Sgeir Mhaol Guest House	Soroba Road, Oban, Argyll, PA34 4JF	01631 562650	★★★	Guest House	
Shian Bed & Breakfast	Pulpit Drive, Oban, Argyll, PA34 4LE	01631 564763	★★★★	Bed & Breakfast	
St Anne's Guest House	Dunollie Road, Oban, Argyll, PA34 5PH	01631 562743	★★	Guest House	
Strathnaver Guest House	Dunollie Road, Oban, Argyll, PA34 5JQ	01631 63305	★★★	Guest House	
Strumhor	Connel, Oban, Argyll, PA37 1PJ	01631 710167	★★★	Bed & Breakfast	
Sutherland Guest House	Corran Esplanade, Oban, Argyll, PA34 5PN	01631 562539	★★	Guest House	
The Barriemore	Corran Esplanade, Oban, Argyll, PA34 5AQ	01631 566356	★★★★	Guest House	
The Manor House	Gallanoch Road, Oban, Argyll, PA34 4LS	01631 562087	★★★★	Restaurant with Rooms	
The Old Manse	Dalriach Road, Oban, Argyll, PA34 5JE	01631 564886	★★★★	Guest House	
Thornloe Guest House	Albert Road, Oban, Argyll, PA34 5EJ	01631 562879	★★★★	Guest House	Silver Green Tourism Award
Torlin Guest House	Glencruitten Road, Oban, Argyll, PA34 4EP	01631 570432	★★★	Bed & Breakfast	
Ulva Villa	Soroba Road, Oban, Argyll, PA34 4JF	01631 563042	★★★	Guest House	
Wellpark House	Esplanade, Oban, Argyll, PA34 5AQ	01631 562948	★★★	Guest House	
Willowdene	Glencruitten Road, Oban, Argyll, PA34 4EW	01631 563412	★★★	Bed & Breakfast	
Woodside Hotel	Tweeddale Street, Oban, Argyll, PA34 4DD	01631 562184	★	Inn	

By Oban

Blarcreen House	Ardchattan, By Oban, Argyll, PA37 1RG	01631 750272	★★★★	Bed & Breakfast
Ardchoille	Benderloch, By Oban, Argyll, PA37 1ST	01631 720432	★★★	Bed & Breakfast

Unassisted wheelchair access · Assisted wheelchair access · Access for visitors with mobility difficulties
Bronze Green Tourism Award · Silver Green Tourism Award · Gold Green Tourism Award

For further information on our Green Tourism Business Scheme please see page 9.

Hawthorn	Keil Croft, Benderloch, By Oban, Argyll, PA37 1QS	01631 720452	★★★★	Bed & Breakfast	
Rowantree Cottage B & B	Keil Farm, Benderloch, By Oban, Argyll, PA37 1QP	01631 720433	★★★	Bed & Breakfast	
An Struan	Benderloch, By Oban, Argyll, PA37 1ST	01631 720301	★★★★	Bed & Breakfast	
Innis Chonain	Benderloch, By Oban, Argyll, PA37 1RT	01631 720550	★★★	Bed & Breakfast	
Scotholm	Connel, By Oban, Argyll, PA37 1PG	01631 710549	★★★★	Bed & Breakfast	
Mactalla	Connel, By Oban, Argyll, PA37 1PJ	01631 710465	AWAITING GRADING		
Greenacre	Connel, By Oban, Argyll, PA31 1PJ	01631 710756	★★★	Guest House	
The Oyster Inn	Connel, By Oban, Argyll, PA37 1PJ	01631 710666	★★★★	Inn	
Garragh Mhor	Ellenabeich, Easdale, By Oban, Argyll, PA34 4RF	01852 300513	★★★	Bed & Breakfast	
Braeside Guest House	Kilmore, By Oban, Argyll, PA34 4QR	01631 770243	★★★★	Guest House	
Swallow Cottage	Musdale Road, Kilmore, By Oban, Argyll, PA34 4XX	01631 770286	★★	Bed & Breakfast	

Old Kilpatrick

4 Mount Pleasant Drive	Old Kilpatrick, Dunbartonshire, G60 5HJ	01389 876903	★	Bed & Breakfast	

Oldmeldrum

Cromlet Hill	South Road, Oldmeldrum, Aberdeenshire, AB51 0DW	01651 872315	★★★★	Bed & Breakfast	
The Redgarth	Kirkbrae, Oldmeldrum, Aberdeenshire, AB51 0DJ	01651 872353	★★★★	Inn	

Onich

Camus House	Lochside Lodge, Onich, Inverness-shire, PH33 6RY	01855 821200	★★★	Guest House	
The Woolly Rock Bed & Breakfast	North Ballachulish, Onich, Inverness-shire, PH33 6SA	01855 821338	★★★	Bed & Breakfast	
Tom-na-Creige	Onich, Inverness-shire, PH33 6RY	01855 821547	★★★	Bed & Breakfast	

Orphir, Stromness

Foin Haven	Germiston Road, Orphir, Stromness, Orkney, KW16 3HD	01856 811249	★★★	Bed & Breakfast	
Houton Bay Lodge	Houton Bay, Orphir, Scapa Flow, Orkney, KW17 2RD	01856 811320	★★★★	Inn	Access for visitors with mobility difficulties
Scorralee	Scorralee Road, Orphir, Orkney, KW17 2RF	01856 811268	★★★	Bed & Breakfast	Silver Green Tourism Award
The Noust	Orphir, Orkney, KW17 2RB	01856 811348	★★★	Bed & Breakfast	

Ose, Isle of Skye

Osedale House	10 Ose, Ose Isle of Skye IV56 8FJ	01470 872317	★★★	Bed & Breakfast	

Paisley

Ardgowan Town House Hotel	92 Renfrew Road, Paisley, Renfrewshire, PA3 4BJ	0141 889 4763	★★★	Guest House	Access for visitors with mobility difficulties
Ashtree House	9 Orr Square, Paisley, Renfrewshire, PA1 2DL	0141 8486411	★★★★	Guest House	
Dryesdale	37 Inchinnan Road, Paisley, Renfrewshire, PA3 2PR	0141 889 7178	★★	Guest House	

Unassisted wheelchair access Assisted wheelchair access Access for visitors with mobility difficulties
Bronze Green Tourism Award Silver Green Tourism Award Gold Green Tourism Award
For further information on our Green Tourism Business Scheme please see page 9.

Muirholm Bed & Breakfast	4 Calside Avenue, Paisley, Renfrewshire, PA2 6DO	01418 893854	★★★★★	Bed & Breakfast	
Scotscraig House	18 Park Road, Paisley, Renfrewshire, PA2 6JW	0141 8842082	★★★★★	Bed & Breakfast	
Travelodge Glasgow Airport	Marchburn Drive, Paisley, Glasgow, PA3 2SJ	08719 846335	★★★	Lodge	♿

Papa Westray

Beltane House	Papay Community Cooperative Ltd, Papa Westray, Orkney, KW17 2BU	01857 644321	★★	Guest House

Patthead

The Stair Arms Hotel	Ford, Patthead, Midlothian, EH37 5TX	01875 320277	★★	Inn

Peebles

Castlehill Knowe	Manor Valley, Peebles, Peeblesshire, EH45 9JN	01721 740218	★★★★	Bed & Breakfast
Craiguart Bed & Breakfast	Eshiels, Peebles, Borders, EH45 8LZ	01721 720219	★★★	Bed & Breakfast
Lindores	60 Old Town, Peebles, Peebles-shire, EH45 8JE	01721 722072	★★★	Guest House
Lyne Farmhouse	by Lyne Station, Peebles, Peebles-shire, EH45 8NR	01721 740255	★★★	Farmhouse
Rowanbrae	103 Northgate, Peebles, Peebles-shire, EH45 8BU	01721 721630	★★★★	Bed & Breakfast
Venlaw Farm	Peebles, Peebles-shire, EH45 8QG	01721 722040	★★★★	Bed & Breakfast
Viewfield	1 Rosetta Road, Peebles, Peebleshire, EH45 8JU	0721 721232	★★★	Bed & Breakfast
Whitestone House	Innerleithen Road, Peebles, Peeblesshire, EH45 8B	01721 720337	★★★	Bed & Breakfast
Whitie's	69 High Street, Peebles, Scottish Borders, EH45 8AN	01721 721605	★★★	Bed & Breakfast
Winkston Farmhouse	Edinburgh Road, Peebles, Peeblesshire, EH45 8PH	01721 721264	★★★	Farmhouse

Penicuik

Braidwood Farm	Penicuik, Midlothian, EH26 9LP	01968 679959	★★★	Bed & Breakfast
Peggyslea Farm	Nine Mile Burn, Penicuik, Midlothian, EH26 9LX	01968 660930	★★★★	Guest House

By Penicuik

Patieshill Farm	Carlops, By Penicuik, Midlothian, EH26 9ND	01968 660551	★★★	Farmhouse

Pennyghael, Isle of Mull

Craig Rowan	Pennyghael, Isle of Mull, Argyll, PA70 6HB	01681 704230	★★★★	Bed & Breakfast

Perth

Aaron	85 Glasgow Road, Perth, Perthshire, PH2 OPQ	01738 444728	★★★	Guest House
Achnacarry Guest House	3 Pitcullen Crescent, Perth, Perthshire, PH2 7HT	01738 621421	★★★★	Guest House
Ackinnoull Guest House	5 Pitcullen Crescent, Perth, Perthshire, PH2 7HT	01738 634165	★★★★	Guest House
Adam Guest House	6 Pitcullen Crescent, Perth, Perthshire, PH2 7HT	01738 627179	★★★	Guest House
Albert Villa Guest House	63 Dunkeld Road, Perth, Perthshire, PH1 5RP	01738 622730	★★★	Guest House

♿ Unassisted wheelchair access ♿ Assisted wheelchair access 🚶 Access for visitors with mobility difficulties
Bronze Green Tourism Award Silver Green Tourism Award Gold Green Tourism Award
For further information on our Green Tourism Business Scheme please see page 9.

Establishment	Address	Telephone	Grading	Type	Access	Green Tourism
Almond Villa Guest House	51 Dunkeld Road, Perth, Perthshire, PH1 5RP	01738 629356	★★★★	Guest House		
Ardfern House	15 Pitcullen Crescent, Perth, Perthshire, PH2 7HT	01738 637031	★★★★	Guest House		
Arisaig Guest House	4 Pitcullen Crescent, Perth, Perthshire, PH2 7HT	01738 628240	★★★★	Guest House	🚶	🍃🍃🍃
Beeches	2 Comely Bank, Perth, Perthshire, PH2 7HU	01738 624486	★★★	Bed & Breakfast		
Beechgrove Guest House	Dundee Road, Perth, Perthshire, PH2 7AQ	01738 636147	★★★★	Guest House		
Cherrybank B&B	217 Glasgow Road, Perth, Perthshire, PH2 0NB	01738 451982	★★★★	Guest House		
Cherrybank Inn	210 Glasgow Road, Perth, Perthshire, PH2 0NA	01738 624349	★★★	Inn	🚶	
Clifton House	36 Glasgow Road, Perth, Perthshire, PH2 0PB	01738 621997	★★★★	Guest House		
Clunie Guest House	12 Pitcullen Crescent, Perth, Perthshire, PH2 7HT	01738 623625	★★★★	Guest House		
Comely Bank Cottage	19 Pitcullen Crescent , Perth, Perthshire, PH2 7HT	01738 631118	★★★	Bed & Breakfast		
Dalvey	55 Dunkeld Road, Perth, Perthshire, PH1 5RP	01738 621714	★★★★	Bed & Breakfast		
Dunallan Guest House	10 Pitcullen Crescent, Perth, Perthshire, PH2 7TH	01738 622551	★★★★	Guest House		
Earnview Glenfoot	Glenfoot, By Abernethy, Perth, Perthshire, PH2 9LS	01738 850353	★★★	Bed & Breakfast		
Hazeldene Guest House	Strathmore Street, Perth, Perthshire, PH2 7HP	01738 623550	★★★★	Guest House		
Heidl Guest House	43 York Place, Perth, Perthshire, PH2 8EH	01738 635031	★★★	Guest House		
Marlehall B&B	99 Glasgow Road, Perth, Perthshire, PH2 0PQ	01738 633388	★★★★	Bed & Breakfast		
Marshall House	6 Marshall Place, Perth, Perthshire, PH2 8AH	01738 442886	★★★	Bed & Breakfast		
Northlees Farm	Kingfauns, Perth, Perthshire, PH2 7LJ	01738 860852	★★	Farmhouse		
Petra's B&B	4 Albany Terrace, Perth, Perthshire, PH1 2BD	01738 563050	★★★	Bed & Breakfast	🚶	
Pitcullen Guest House	17 Pitcullen Crescent, Perth, Perthshire, PH2 7HT	01738 626506	★★★	Guest House		
Rowanlea	87 Glasgow Road, Perth, Perthshire, PH2 0PQ	01738 621922	★★★★	Guest House		
Sunbank House	50 Dundee Road, Perth, Perthshire, PH2 7BA	01738 624882	★★★★	Guest House	🚶	
Taythorpe House	Isla Road, Perth, Perthshire, PH2 7HQ	01738 447994	★★★★	Bed & Breakfast		
The Gables Guest House	24 Dunkeld Road, Perth, Perthshire, PH1 5RW	01738 624717	★★★	Guest House		
The Townhouse	17 Marshall Place, Perth, Perthshire, PH2 8AG	01738 446179	★★★	Guest House		
Travelodge Perth Broxden Junction	Broxden Trunk Road Service Area, Perth, Perthshire, PH2 0PL	08719 846250	AWAITING GRADING			
Westview	49 Dunkeld Road, Perth, Perthshire, PH1 5RP	01738 627787	★★★★	Bed & Breakfast		

By Perth

Establishment	Address	Telephone	Grading	Type	Access	Green Tourism
Glencarse Hotel	Glencarse, By Perth, Perthshire, PH2 7LX	01738 860206	AWAITING GRADING		♿ (assisted)	
Greenacres	Logiealmond, By Perth, Perthshire, PH1 3TQ	01738 880302	★★★	Bed & Breakfast		🍃🍃🍃
Ballathie House Sportsman's Lodge	Kinclaven, Stanley, By Perth, Perthshire, PH1 4QN	01250 883268	★★★	Lodge		

♿ Unassisted wheelchair access ♿ (assisted) Assisted wheelchair access 🚶 Access for visitors with mobility difficulties
🍃 Bronze Green Tourism Award 🍃🍃 Silver Green Tourism Award 🍃🍃🍃 Gold Green Tourism Award
For further information on our Green Tourism Business Scheme please see page 9.

Newmill Farm	Stanley, By Perth, Perthshire, PH1 4PS	01738 828281	★★★	Farmhouse

Peterhead

Carrick Guest House	16 Merchant Street, Peterhead, Aberdeenshire, AB42 1DU	01779 470610	★★	Guest House
Durie House	Clola, Peterhead, Aberdeenshire, AB42 5BE	01771 622 823	★★★	Bed & Breakfast
Invernettie Guest House	South Road, Burnhaven, Peterhead, Aberdeenshire, AB42 0YX	01779 473530	★★★	Guest House
Pond View	Brucklay, Maud, Peterhead, Aberdeenshire, AB42 4QN	01771 613 675	★★★★	Bed & Breakfast

By Peterhead

Aden House	19 Abbey Street, Old Deer, By Peterhead, Aberdeenshire, AB42 5LN	01771 622573	★★★	Guest House
Bank House	6 Abbey Street, Old Deer, By Peterhead, Aberdeenshire, AB42 5LN	01771 623463	★★★	Bed & Breakfast
Greenbrae Farmhouse	Longside, By Peterhead, Aberdeenshire, AB42 4JX	01779 821051	★★★	Bed & Breakfast

Pirnhall

Travelodge Stirling	Service Area, Pirnhall, Stirling, FK7 8EU	08719 846178	AWAITING GRADING	

Pitlochry

Almond Lee	East Moulin Road, Pitlochry, Perthshire, PH16 5HU	01796 474048	★★★	Guest House
Annslea Guest House	164 Atholl Road, Pitlochry, Perthshire, PH16 5AR	01796 472430	★★★	Guest House
Ardvane	8 Lower Oakfield, Pitlochry, Perthshire, PH16 5DS	01796 472683	★★★★	Bed & Breakfast
Ashbank House	14 Tomcroy Terrace, Pitlochry, Perthshire, PH16 5JA	01796 472711	★★★	Bed & Breakfast
Atholl Villa Guest House	29/31 Atholl Road, Pitlochry, Perthshire, PH16 5BX	01796 473820	★★★	Guest House
Beinn Bhracaigh	Higher Oakfield, Pitlochry, Perthshire, PH16 5HT	01796 470355	★★★★	Guest House
Bridge House	53 Atholl Road, Pitlochry, Perthshire, PH16 5BL	01796 474062	★★★	Bed & Breakfast
Buttonboss Lodge	27 Atholl Road, Pitlochry, Perthshire, PH16 5BX	01796 472065	★★★	Guest House
Carra Beag Guest House	16 Toberargan Road, Pitlochry, Perthshire, PH16 5HG	01796 472835	★★★	Guest House
Craigatin House & Courtyard	165 Atholl Road, Pitlochry, Perthshire, PH16 5QL	01796 472478	★★★★	Guest House
Craigmhor Lodge	27 West Moulin Road, Pitlochry, Perthshire, PH16 5EF	01796 472123	★★★★	Guest House
Craigroyston Guest House	2 Lower Oakfield, Pitlochry, Perthshire, PH16 5HQ	01796 472053	★★★★	Guest House
Cuil -an- Daraich Guest House	2 Cuil -an- Daraich, Logierait, Pitlochry, Perthshire, PH9 0LH	01796 482750	★★★	Guest House
Dalshian House	Old Perth Road, Pitlochry, Perthshire, PH16 5TD	01796 472173	★★★	Guest House
Derrybeg Guest House	18 Lower Oakfield, Pitlochry, Perthshire, PH16 5DS	01796 472070	★★★★	Guest House
Dunmurray Lodge Guest House	72 Bonnethill Road, Pitlochry, Perthshire, PH16 5ED	01796 473624	★★★★	Guest House
Easter Croftinloan Farmhouse	Croftloan Farm, Pitlochry, Perthshire, PH16 5TA	01796 473454	★★★★	Guest House
Easter Dunfallandy Country House B&B	Dunfallandy, Pitlochry, Perthshire, PH16 5NA	01796 474128	★★★★★	Bed & Breakfast

Unassisted wheelchair access   Assisted wheelchair access   Access for visitors with mobility difficulties
Bronze Green Tourism Award   Silver Green Tourism Award   Gold Green Tourism Award
For further information on our Green Tourism Business Scheme please see page 9.

Farragon	Well Brae, Pitlochry, Perthshire, PH16 5HH	01796 470051	★★★★	Bed & Breakfast	
Fasganeoin Country House	Perth Road, Pitlochry, Perthshire, PH16 5DJ	01796 472387	★★★	Guest House	
Ferrymans Cottage	Port - Na - Craig, Pitlochry, Perthshire, PH16 5ND	01796 473681	★★★★	Bed & Breakfast	
Glen Garry	Armoury Road, Pitlochry, Perthshire, PH16 5AP	01796 474496	★★★	Bed & Breakfast	
Lavalette	Manse Road, Moulin, Pitlochry, Perthshire, PH16 5EP	01796 472364	★★★	Bed & Breakfast	
Macdonalds Restaurant & Guest House	140 Atholl Road, Pitlochry, Perthshire, PH16 5AG	01796 472170	★★★	Guest House	
Moville	Kinnaird, Pitlochry, Perthshire, PH16 5JL	01796 470100	★★★	Bed & Breakfast	
Roseburn B&B	15 West Moulin Road, Pitlochry, Perthshire, PH16 5EA	01796 470002	★★★★	Bed & Breakfast	
Rosehill	47 Atholl Road, Pitlochry, Perthshire, PH16 5BX	01796 472958	★★★	Guest House	
Strathgarry Hotel	113 Atholl Road, Pitlochry, Perthshire, PH16 5AG	01796 472469	★★★	Restaurant with Rooms	
The Dell B & B	11 Dixon Terrace, Pitlochry, Perthshire, PH16 5QX	01796 470306	★★★	Bed & Breakfast	
The Poplars	27 Lower Oakfield, Pitlochry, Perthshire, PH16 5DS	01796 472911	★★★	Guest House	🚶
The Rowans Bed and Breakfast	Ferry Road, Pitlochry, Perthshire, PH16 5DD	01796 474469	★★★★	Bed & Breakfast	
The Well House	11 Toberargan Road, Pitlochry, Perthshire, PH16 5HG	01796 472239	★★★★	Guest House	🚶
Tir Aluinn	10 Higher Oakfield, Pitlochry, Perthshire, PH16 5HT	01796 473811	★★★	Guest House	
Torrdarach House	Golf Course Road, Pitlochry, Perthshire, PH16 5AU	01796 472136	★★★★	Guest House	
Wellwood House	13 West Moulin Road, Pitlochry, Perthshire, PH16 5EA	01796 474288	★★★★	Guest House	
Wester Knockfarrie	Pitlochry, Perthshire, PH16 5DN	01796 472020	★★★★	Bed & Breakfast	
Windsor Gardens	5 Windsor Gardens, Pitlochry, Perthshire, PH16 5BE	01796 473562	★★★	Bed & Breakfast	
Woodburn House	Ferry Road, Pitlochry, Perthshire, PH16 5DD	01796 473818	★★★	Bed & Breakfast	
Woodshiel	23 West Moulin Road, Pitlochry, Perthshire, PH16 5EA	01796 470358	★★★	Bed & Breakfast	

By Pitlochry

Balbeagan	Balnaguard, By Pitlochry, Perthshire, PH9 0PY	01796 482627	★★★★	Bed & Breakfast

Pitscottie

South House	Pitscottie Vale, Dura Den, Pitscottie, Fife, KY15 5TJ	01334 828784	★★★	Bed & Breakfast

Pittenweem

Marie Philp	4 St Abbs Crescent, Pittenweem, Fife, KY10 2LT	01333 311964	★★★	Bed & Breakfast
Rooms@25	25 Charles Street, Pittenweem, Fife, KY10 2QH	01333 313306	★★★	Bed & Breakfast

Plockton

Creag Liath	Achnandarach, Plockton, Ross-shire, IV52 8TY	01599 544341	★★★★	Bed & Breakfast
Hillview B&B	2 Frithard Road, Plockton, Ross-shire, IV52 8TQ	01599 544226	★★★	Bed & Breakfast

♿ Unassisted wheelchair access   Assisted wheelchair access   🚶 Access for visitors with mobility difficulties
Bronze Green Tourism Award   Silver Green Tourism Award   Gold Green Tourism Award
For further information on our Green Tourism Business Scheme please see page 9.

Plockton Inn	Plockton, Ross-shire, IV52 8TW	01599 544222	★★★	Inn	
Tomac's	4 Firthard Road, Plockton, Ross-shire, IV52 8TQ	01599 544321	★★★	Bed & Breakfast	

by Plockton

Seann Bhruthach	Duirinish, by Plockton, Ross-shire, IV40 8BE	01599 544204	★★★	Bed & Breakfast	

Poolewe

Bruach Ard	7 Braes, Poolewe, Ross-shire, IV22 2LN	01445 781765	★★★	Bed & Breakfast	(Bronze Green Tourism Award)
Corriness House	Poolewe, Wester Ross, IV22 2JU	01445 781785	★★★★	Guest House	

Port Appin

Fasgadh Guest House	Port Appin, Argyll, PA38 4DE	01631 730374	★★★	Bed & Breakfast	

Port Charlotte, Islay of Islay

The Monachs	Nerabus, Port Charlotte, Islay of Islay, Argyll, PA48 7WE	01496 850049	★★★★★	Bed & Breakfast	

Port Ellen, Isle of Islay

40 Pier Road	Frederick Crescent, Port Ellen, Isle of Islay, Argyll, PA42 7DJ	01496 300502	★★★★	Bed & Breakfast	
Caladh Sona	53 Frederick Crescent, Port Ellen, Isle of Islay, Argyll, PA42 7BD	01496 302694	★★★	Bed & Breakfast	
Glenegedale House	Glenegedale, Port Ellen, Isle of Islay, Argyll, PA42 7AS	01496 300400	★★★★★	Guest House	
Kintra Farm	Kintra Beach, Port Ellen, Isle of Islay, Argyll, PA42 7AT	01496 302051	★★★	Bed & Breakfast	
The Trout Fly Bed & Breakfast	Charlotte Street, Port Ellen, Isle of Islay, Argyll, PA42 7DF	01496 302204	★★★	Bed & Breakfast	

Port of Menteith

Currach	Currach House, Port of Menteith, Stirling, FK8 3RA	01877 385699	★★★	Bed & Breakfast	
Inchie Farm	Port of Menteith, Stirling, FK8 3JZ	01877 385233	★★★	Bed & Breakfast	

Port William

Monreith Arms Hotel	The Square, Port William, Dumfries & Galloway, DG8 9SE	01988 700232	★★	Inn	

Portpatrick

Ard Choille Guest House	1 Blair Terrace, Portpatrick, Wigtownshire, DG9 8SY	01776 810313	★★★	Bed & Breakfast	
Braefield Guest House	Braefield Road, Portpatrick, Wigtownshire, DG9 8TA	01776 810255	★★★	Guest House	(Access for visitors with mobility difficulties)
Dunskey Guest House	Heugh Road, Portpatrick, Wigtownshire, DG9 8TD	01776 810241	★★	Guest House	
Rickwood House Hotel	Heugh Road, Portpatrick, Wigtownshire, DG9 8TD	01776 810270	★★★	Guest House	

Portree, Isle of Skye

11 Earlish	Portree, Isle of Skye, Inverness-shire, IV51 9XL	01470 542319	★★★	Bed & Breakfast	
25 Urquhart Place	Portree, Isle of Skye, Inverness-shire, IV51 9HJ	01478 612374	★★★	Bed & Breakfast	
9 Stormyhill Road	Portree, Isle of Skye, Inverness-shire, IV51 9DY	01478 613332	★★★	Bed & Breakfast	

Almondbank	Viewfield Road, Portree, Isle of Skye, Inverness-shire, IV51 9EU	01478 612696	★★★★	Guest House	
An Acarsaid	Viewfield Road, Portree, Isle of Skye, Inverness-shire, IV51 9ES	01478 612252	★★★	Bed & Breakfast	
An Airidh	6 Fisherfield, Portree, Isle of Skye, Inverness-shire, IV51 9EU	01478 612250	★★★	Guest House	
Auchendinny	Treaslane, Portree, Isle of Skye, Inverness-shire, IV51 9NX	01470 532470	★★★	Guest House	Assisted wheelchair access
Balloch	Viewfield Road, Portree, Isle of Skye, Inverness-shire, IV51 9ES	01478 612093	★★★★	Guest House	
Clynelish	Uigishadder, Portree, Isle of Skye, Inverness-shire, IV51 9LN	01470 532443	★★★	Bed & Breakfast	
Coolin View Guest House	Bosville Terrace, Portree, Isle of Skye, Inverness-shire, IV51 9DG	01478 611280	★★★	Guest House	
Cul Na Creagan	a, Portree, Isle of Skye, Inverness-shire, IV51 9LN	01478 611356	★★★	Bed & Breakfast	
Dalriada	Achachork, Portree, Isle of Skye, Inverness-shire, IV51 9HT	01478 612397	★★★	Guest House	
Drumorell	15 Fraser Crescent, Portree, Isle of Skye, Inverness-shire, IV51 9DS	01478 613058	★★★★	Bed & Breakfast	
Easdale	Bridge Road, Portree, Isle of Skye, Inverness-shire, IV51 9ER	01478 613244	★★★	Bed & Breakfast	
Eriskay	10 Achachork, Portree, Isle of Skye, Inverness-shire, IV51 9HT	01478 611199	★★★	Bed & Breakfast	
Feochan	11 Fisherfield, Portree, Isle of Skye, Inverness-shire, IV51 9EU	01478 613508	AWAITING GRADING		
Fishers Rock	5 Fisherfield, Viewfield Road, Portree, Isle of Skye, Inverness-shire, IV51 9EU	01478 612122	★★★	Bed & Breakfast	
Foreland	Stormyhill Road, Portree, Isle of Skye, Inverness-shire, IV51 9DT	01478 612752	★★★	Bed & Breakfast	
Givendale Guest House	Heron Place, Portree, Isle of Skye, Inverness-shire, IV51 9GU	01478 612183	★★★	Guest House	
Gleann an Ronnaich	Staffin Road, Portree, Isle of Skye, Inverness-shire, IV51 9HS	01478 611529	★★★	Bed & Breakfast	
Green Acres Guest House	Viewfield Road, Portree, Isle of Skye, Inverness-shire, IV51 9EU	01478 613175	★★★★	Guest House	
Heathfield	Achachork, Portree, Isle of Skye, Inverness-shire, IV51 9HT	01478 611125	★★★	Bed & Breakfast	
Heronfield	Heron Place, Portree, Isle of Skye, Inverness-shire, IV51 9GU	01478 613050	★★★	Bed & Breakfast	
Highfield	Viewfield Road, Portree, Isle of Skye, Inverness-shire, IV51 9ES	01478 612 781	★★★	Bed & Breakfast	
Meadowbank House	Seafield Place, Portree, Isle of Skye, Inverness-shire, IV51 9ES	01478 612059	★★★	Guest House	
Medina	Coolin Hills Gardens, Portree, Isle of Skye, Inverness-shire, IV51 9NB	01478 612821	★★★★	Bed & Breakfast	
Orasay	14 Idrigill, Uig, Portree, Isle of Skye, Inverness-shire, IV51 9XU	01470 542316	★★★	Bed & Breakfast	
Quiraing Guest House	Viewfield Road, Portree, Isle of Skye, Inverness-shire, IV51 9ES	01478 612870	★★★★	Guest House	
Rosebank House	Springfield Road, Portree, Isle of Skye, Inverness-shire, IV51 9QX	01478 612282	★★★	Guest House	
Sandgrounder Bed and Breakfast	13 Matheson Place, Portree, Isle of Skye, Inverness-shire, IV51 9JA	01478 612321	★★★	Bed & Breakfast	
Sgiathan Mara	Hill Place, Portree, Isle of Skye, Inverness-shire, IV51 9HS	01478 612927	★★★	Bed & Breakfast	
Stonefield	Oronsay Court, Portree, Isle of Skye, Inverness-shire, IV51 9TL	01478 611636	★★★★	Bed & Breakfast	
Tir Alainn - Kildonan	2A Kildonan, Edinbane, Portree, Isle of Skye, Inverness-shire, IV51 9PU	01470 582335	★★★★	Bed & Breakfast	
Viewfield House Hotel	Portree, Isle of Skye, Inverness-shire, IV51 9EU	01478 612217	★★★★	Guest House	Access for visitors with mobility difficulties

Unassisted wheelchair access · Assisted wheelchair access · Access for visitors with mobility difficulties
Bronze Green Tourism Award · Silver Green Tourism Award · Gold Green Tourism Award

For further information on our Green Tourism Business Scheme please see page 9.

Witch Hazel House	5 Achachork, Portree, Isle of Skye, Inverness-shire, IV51 9HT	01478 612548	★★★	Bed & Breakfast	
Woodlands	Viewfield Road, Portree, Isle of Skye, Inverness-shire, IV51 9EU	01478 612980	★★★★	Bed & Breakfast	

By Portree, Isle of Skye

52 Aird	Bernisdale, By Portree, Isle of Skye, Inverness-shire, IV51 9NU	01470 532471	★★	Bed & Breakfast	
Carnbeag	Earlish, By Portree, Isle of Skye, Inverness-shire, IV51 9XL	01470 542398	★★★	Bed & Breakfast	
Corran Guest House	Eyre, Kensaleyre, By Portree, Isle of Skye, Isle of Skye, Inverness-shire, IV51 9XE	01470 532311	★★★★	Guest House	
Dun Eighre Bed and Breakfast	Dun Eighre, Kensaleyre, By Portree, Isle of Skye, Portree, Isle of Skye, IV51 9XE	01470 532439	★★★	Bed & Breakfast	
Hillcroft	2 Treaslane, By Portree, Isle of Skye, Inverness-shire, IV51 9NX	01470 582304	★★★	Bed & Breakfast	
Peinmore House	By Portree, Isle of Skye, Inverness-shire, IV51 9LG	01478 612 574	★★★★	Guest House	
Torwood	1 Peiness, By Portree, Isle of Skye, Inverness-shire, IV51 9LW	01470 532479	★★★	Bed & Breakfast	
Cruinn Bheinn	4 Eyre, Snizort, By Portree, Isle of Skye, Inverness-shire, IV51 9XB	01470 532459	★★★★	Bed & Breakfast	

Portsoy

Harbour View House	School Hendry Street, Portsoy, Aberdeenshire, AB45 2RS	01261 843556	★★★★	Bed & Breakfast	

Prestwick

Afton-Lea	8 Ayr Road, Prestwick, Ayrshire, KA9 1RR	01292 474300	★★★	Bed & Breakfast	
Fernbank Guest House	213 Main Street, Prestwick, Ayrshire, KA9 1LH	01292 475027	★★★	Guest House	Bronze Green Tourism Award
Fionn Fraoch	64 Ayr Road, Prestwick, Ayrshire, KA9 1RR	01292 476838	★★★	Bed & Breakfast	
Firhill	3 Seabank Road, Prestwick, Ayrshire, KA9 1QS	01292 478225	★★★	Bed & Breakfast	
Golf View	17 Links Road, Prestwick, Ayrshire, KA9 1QG	01292 671234	★★★★	Guest House	
Kincraig Guest House	39 Ayr Road, Prestwick, Ayrshire, KA9 1SY	01292 479480	★★★	Guest House	
Knox	105 Ayr Road, Prestwick, Ayrshire, KA9 1TN	01292 78808	★★★	Bed & Breakfast	
No 6 The Crescent	Monkton Road, Prestwick, Ayrshire, KA9 1BQ	01292 471234	★★★	Bed & Breakfast	
The Dormie House	1A Mansfield Road, Prestwick, South Ayrshire, KA9 2DL	01292 477292	★★★★	Bed & Breakfast	

By Prestwick

The Barrels	52 Main Street, Monkton, By Prestwick, Ayrshire, KA9 2QL	01292 671391	★★★	Bed & Breakfast	

Quendale

Meadowbank Bed and Breakfast	Culster, Quendale, Shetland, ZE2 9JD	01950 460699	★★★	Bed & Breakfast	

Quoyloo

Hyval Farm B&B	North Dyke Road, Quoyloo, Orkney, KW16 3LS	01856 841522	★★★	Farmhouse	

Reston

The Craw Inn	Auchencrow, Reston, Berwickshire, TD14 5LS	01890 761293	★★★	Inn	

Unassisted wheelchair access Assisted wheelchair access Access for visitors with mobility difficulties
Bronze Green Tourism Award Silver Green Tourism Award Gold Green Tourism Award

For further information on our Green Tourism Business Scheme please see page 9.

Riccarton

Leonard Horner Hall	Edinburgh Conference Centre, Riccarton, Midlothian, EH14 4AS	0131 451 3118	★★	Campus	

Rosehearty

Hame Lea	1 Mid Street, Rosehearty, Aberdeenshire, AB43 7JS	01346 571145	★★★	Bed & Breakfast	

Rosewell

Hillwood	Rosewell, Midlothian, EH24 9AU	01314 482844	★★	Bed & Breakfast	
Orchard House B&B	The Walled Garden, Whitehill Road, Rosewell, Midlothian, EH24 9EQ	0131 440 4515	★★★★	Bed & Breakfast	Gold Green Tourism Award

Roslin

Original Rosslyn Inn	Main Street, Roslin, Midlothian, EH25 9LE	0131 440 2384	★★	Inn	
The Steading	Slatebarns, Chapel Loan, Roslin, Midlothian, EH25 9PU	0131 440 1608	★★★★	Bed & Breakfast	

Rosneath

Easter Garth	The Clachan, Rosneath, Argyll & Bute, G84 0RF	01436 831007	★★★	Guest House	

Rosyth

Backmarch House	54A Norval Place, Rosyth, Fife, KY11 2RJ	01383 412997	★★★★	Bed & Breakfast	
Cochranes Hotel	Hilton Road, Rosyth, Fife, KY11 2BA	01383 420101	AWAITING GRADING		

Rothesay

Argyle House	3 Argyle Place, Rothesay, Isle of Bute, PA20 0AZ	01700 502424	★★	Guest House	
Bayview Hotel	21-22 Mountstuart Road, Rothesay, Isle of Bute, PA20 9EB	01700 505411	★★★★	Guest House	
Bute House	4 West Princess Street, Rothesay, Isle of Bute, PA20 9AF	01700 502481	★★★	Guest House	
Craigewan	26 Auchnacloich Road, Rothesay, Bute, PA20 0EB	01700 504029	★★★	Bed & Breakfast	
Glendale Guest House	20 Battery Place, Rothesay, Isle of Bute, PA20 9DU	01700 502329	★★★★	Guest House	
Ivybank Villa	Westlands Road, Rothesay, Isle of Bute, PA2 0HX	01700 505064	★★★★	Bed & Breakfast	
The Commodore	12 Battery Place, Rothesay, Isle of Bute, PA20 9DP	01700 502178	★★★	Guest House	
The Moorings	7 Mountstuart, Rothesay, Bute, PA20 9DY	01700 502277	★★★	Bed & Breakfast	

Rothienorman

Rothie Inn	Main Street, Rothienorman, Aberdeenshire, AB51 8UD	01651 821206	★★★	Inn	

Rousay

The Taversoe	Frotoft, Rousay, Orkney, KW17 2PT	01856 821325	★★★	Inn	

Roy Bridge

Dunhafen B&B	4 Glenspean Park, Roy Bridge, Inverness-shire, PH31 4AS	01397 712830	★★★	Bed & Breakfast	
Homagen	Homagen, Roy Bridge, Inverness-shire, PH31 4AN	01397 712411	★★★	Bed & Breakfast	

Unassisted wheelchair access — Assisted wheelchair access — Access for visitors with mobility difficulties
Bronze Green Tourism Award — Silver Green Tourism Award — Gold Green Tourism Award
For further information on our Green Tourism Business Scheme please see page 9.

Roy Bridge Hotel	Roy Bridge, Inverness-shire, PH31 4AN	01397 712236	★★	Inn		

Salen, Isle of Mull

Ard Mhor House	Pier Road, Salen, Isle of Mull, Argyll, PA72 6JL	01680 300255	★★★	Guest House	Unassisted wheelchair access	
Aros View	Salen, Isle of Mull, Argyll, PA72 6JB	01680 300372	★★★	Bed & Breakfast		

Nr Salen, Isle of Mull

Gruline Home Farm	Gruline, Nr Salen, Isle of Mull, Argyll, PA71 6HR	01680 300581	★★★★★	Bed & Breakfast		Silver Green Tourism Award

Saline

Balnacraig B&B	Main Street, Saline, Fife, KY12 9TL	01383 852568	★★★★	Bed & Breakfast		
Kirklands House	Saline, Fife, KY12 9TS	01383 852737	★★★★	Bed & Breakfast		Silver Green Tourism Award

Saltcoats

Lochwood Farm	Saltcoats, Ayrshire, KA21 6NG	01294 552529	★★★★	Bed & Breakfast		

Sanday

Backaskaill B&B	Backaskaill, Sanday, Orkney, KW17 2BA	01857 600298	★★★	Bed & Breakfast		

Sandhead

Tigh-Na-Mara Hotel & Restaurant	Main Street, Sandhead, Dumfries & Galloway, DG9 9JF	01776 830210	★★★	Inn		

Sandwick

Carnan Beag	9 Lower Sandwick, Sandwick, Isle of Lewis, HS2 0AE	01851 704726	★★★★	Bed & Breakfast		
Orca Country Inn	Hoswick, Sandwick, Shetland, ZE2 9HL	01950 431226	★★★	Inn		
Solbrekke	Sandwick, Shetland, ZE2 9HP	01950 431410	★★	Bed & Breakfast		

Sanquhar

Newark	Sanquhar, Dumfriesshire, DG4 6HN	01659 50263	★★★	Farmhouse	Assisted wheelchair access	

Scalloway

Windward	Port Arthur, Scalloway, Shetland, ZE1 0UN	01595 880769	★★★	Bed & Breakfast		

Scalpay, Isle of Harris

Highcroft	6 Ardnakillie, Scalpay, Isle of Harris, Western Isles, HS4 3YB	01859 540305	★★★★	Bed & Breakfast		
New Haven	15 Scalpay, Scalpay, Isle of Harris, Western Isles, HS4 3XZ	01859 540325	★★★★	Bed & Breakfast		

Scarinish, Isle of Tiree

Tiree Scarinish Hotel	Scarinish, Isle of Tiree, Argyll, PA77 6UH	01879 220308	★★	Inn		

Scarista, Isle of Harris

Scarista House	Scarista, Isle of Harris, Isle of Harris, HS3 3HX	01859 550238	★★★★	Guest House		Bronze Green Tourism Award

Unassisted wheelchair access   Assisted wheelchair access   Access for visitors with mobility difficulties
Bronze Green Tourism Award   Silver Green Tourism Award   Gold Green Tourism Award

For further information on our Green Tourism Business Scheme please see page 9.

Scone

Perth Airport Skylodge	Norwell Drive, Perth Airport, Scone, Perthshire, PH2 6PL	01738 555700	★★★	Lodge	🚶

Scourie

Scourie Lodge	Scourie, Sutherland, IV27 4SX	01971 502248	★★★★	Bed & Breakfast

Nr Scousburgh

Setterbrae	Spiggie, Nr Scousburgh, Shetland, ZE2 9JE	01950 460468	★★★★	Bed & Breakfast

Seilebost Isle of Harris

Beul-na-Mara Bed and Breakfast	12 Seilebost, Seilebost Isle of Harris, Western Isles, HS3 3HP	01859 550205	★★★★	Bed & Breakfast

Selkirk

Buxton House B&B	Buxton, Selkirk, Scottish Borders, TD7 4PU	01750 24131	★★★★★	Bed & Breakfast
Ivy Bank	Hillside Terrace, Selkirk, Scottish Borders, TD7 4LT	01750 21270	★★	Bed & Breakfast
St Mary's House	Yarrow Feus, Selkirk, Scottish Borders, TD7 5NE	01750 82287	★★★	Bed & Breakfast
Sunnybrae House	75 Tower Street, Selkirk, Scottish Borders, TD7 4LS	0750 21156	★★★	Bed & Breakfast
The Firs	Manorhill Road, Philiphaugh, Selkirk, Scottish Borders, TD7 5LS	01750 20409	★★★★	Bed & Breakfast
Tower Street Guest House	29 Tower Street, Selkirk, Scottish Borders, TD7 4LR	01750 23222	★★★	Guest House

By Selkirk

Tushielaw Inn	Ettrick Valley, By Selkirk, Scottish Borders, TD7 5HT	0750 62205	★★	Inn
Cross Keys Inn	Main Street Ettrickbridge, By Selkirk, Scottish Borders, TD7 5JN	01750 52224	★★★	Inn
Cross Keys Inn	Main Street, Ettrickbridge, By Selkirk, Scottish Borders, TD7 5JN	01750 52224	★★★	Inn

Shieldaig

Aurora B&B	Aurora, Shieldaig, Ross-shire, IV54 8XN	01520 755246	★★★★	Bed & Breakfast

Shiskine, Isle of Arran

Croftlea	Shiskine, Isle of Arran, KA27 8EW	01770 860259	★★	Bed & Breakfast

Skene

4 Brodiach Court	Westhill, Skene, Aberdeenshire, AB32 6QY	01224 742749	★★★★	Bed & Breakfast

Sleat, Isle of Skye

Ord House	Ord, Sleat, Isle of Skye, Inverness-shire, IV44 8RN	01471 855212	★★★★★	Bed & Breakfast

Sorn

The Sorn Inn	Main Street, Sorn, East Ayrshire, KA5 6HU	01290 551305	★★★★	Restaurant with Rooms

South Boisdale, South Uist

363 Leth Meadhanach	South Boisdale, South Uist, Western Isles, HS8 5TE	01878 700586	★★★	Bed & Breakfast

♿ Unassisted wheelchair access ♿ Assisted wheelchair access 🚶 Access for visitors with mobility difficulties
Bronze Green Tourism Award Silver Green Tourism Award Gold Green Tourism Award
For further information on our Green Tourism Business Scheme please see page 9.

South Galson, Isle of Lewis

Galson Farm Guest House	South Galson, South Galson, Isle of Lewis, Western Isles, HS2 0SH	01851 850492	★★★★	Guest House	

South Lochs, Isle of Lewis

Planasker Old School	Marvig, South Lochs, Isle of Lewis, HS2 9QP	01851 880476	★★★★	Bed & Breakfast	

South Queensferry

Priory Lodge	8 The Loan, South Queensferry, West Lothian, EH30 9NS	0131 331 4345	★★★★	Guest House	Access for visitors with mobility difficulties

South Ronaldsay

The Creel Restaurant & Rooms	Front Road, St Margaret's Hope, South Ronaldsay, Orkney, KW17 2SL	01856 831311	★★★★	Restaurant with Rooms	

South Uist

Crossroads	Stoneybridge, South Uist, Western Isles, HS8 5SD	01870 620321	★★★	Bed & Breakfast	Unassisted wheelchair access
Kilchoan	445 Lochboisdale, South Uist, Western Isles, HS8 5TN	01878 700517	★★★	Bed & Breakfast	

Spean Bridge

Achnabobane Farmhouse	Spean Bridge, Inverness-shire, PH34 4EX	01397 712919	★★★	Farmhouse	
Coinachan	Gairlochy Road , Spean Bridge, Inverness-shire, PH34 4EG	01397 712 417	★★★★	Bed & Breakfast	
Coire Glas Guest House	Roybridge Road, Spean Bridge, Inverness-shire, PH34 4EU	01397 712272	★★★	Guest House	
Distant Hills Guest House	Roybridge Road, Spean Bridge, Inverness-shire, PH34 4EU	01397 712452	★★★★	Guest House	
Faegour House	Tirindrish, Spean Bridge, Inverness-shire, PH34 4EU	01397 712903	★★★★	Bed & Breakfast	
Inverour Guest House	Roy Bridge Road, Spean Bridge, Inverness-shire, PH34 4EU	01397 712218	★★★	Guest House	
Mahaar	Corriechoille Road, Spean Bridge, Inverness-shire, PH34 4EP	01397 712365	★★★	Bed & Breakfast	
Mehalah Riverside House	Lower Tirindrish, Spean Bridge, Inverness-shire, PH34 4EU	01397 712893	★★★★	Bed & Breakfast	
Old Smiddy Restaurant with Rooms	Roy Bridge Road, Spean Bridge, Inverness-shire, PH34 4EU	01397 712335	★★★★	Restaurant with Rooms	
Riverside	1 Lodge Gardens, Spean Bridge, Inverness-shire, PH34 4EN	01397 712702	★★★★	Bed & Breakfast	
Spean Lodge	Spean Bridge, Inverness-shire, PH34 4EP	01397 712004	★★★★	Bed & Breakfast	
Springburn	3 Stronaba, Spean Bridge, Inverness-shire, PH34 4DX	01397 712707	★★★★	Farmhouse	
The Braes Guest House	Spean Bridge, Inverness-shire, PH34 4EU	01397 71243	★★★	Guest House	Silver Green Tourism Award
The Heathers	Invergloy Halt, Spean Bridge, Inverness-shire, PH34 4DY	01397 712077	★★★★	Guest House	Access for visitors with mobility difficulties

By Spean Bridge

Dreamweavers	Mucomir, By Spean Bridge, Inverness-shire, PH34 4EQ	01397 712548	★★★★	Bed & Breakfast	Access for visitors with mobility difficulties
Riverside	Invergloy, By Spean Bridge, Inverness-shire, PH34 4DY	01397 712684	★★★★	Bed & Breakfast	

St Abbs

Springbank Cottage	The Harbour, St Abbs, Berwickshire, TD14 5PW	01890 771477	★★★	Bed & Breakfast	

Unassisted wheelchair access   Assisted wheelchair access   Access for visitors with mobility difficulties
Bronze Green Tourism Award   Silver Green Tourism Award   Gold Green Tourism Award

For further information on our Green Tourism Business Scheme please see page 9.

St Andrews

11 Queens Gardens	St Andrews, Fife, KY16 9TA	01334 478751	★★★★	Guest House
18 Queens Terrace	St Andrews, Fife, KY16 9QF	01334 478849	★★★★	Bed & Breakfast
30 Drumcarrow Road	St Andrews, Fife, KY16 8SE	01334 472036	★★★	Bed & Breakfast
Abbey Cottage	Abbey Walk, St Andrews, Fife, KY16 9LB	01334 473727	★★	Bed & Breakfast
Abbeyview	18 Priestden Place, St Andrews, Fife, KY16 8DW	01334 473389	★★★	Bed & Breakfast
Acorn B & B	16 Priestden Road, St Andrews, Fife, KY16 8DJ	01334 476009	★★★★	Bed & Breakfast
Amberside	4 Murray Park, St Andrews, Fife, KY16 9AW	01334 474644	★★★	Guest House
Anderson House	122 Lamond Drive, St Andrews, Fife, KY16 8DA	01334 477286	★★★	Bed & Breakfast
Anlaw House	21 Nelson Street, St Andrews, Fife, KY16 8AJ	01334 477994	★★★	Bed & Breakfast
Annandale Guest House	23 Murray Park, St Andrews, Fife, KY16 9AW	01334 475310	★★★★	Guest House
Arden House	2 Kilrymont Place, St Andrews, Fife, KY16 8DH	01334 475478	★★★	Bed & Breakfast
Arran House	5 Murray Park, St Andrews, Fife, KY16 9AW	01334 474 724	★★★	Guest House
Aslar House	120 North Street, St Andrews, Fife, KY16 9AF	01334 473460	★★★★	Guest House
Balrymonth B&B	6 Balrymonth Court, St Andrews, Fife, KY16 8XT	01334 470855	★★★	Bed & Breakfast
Bay Trees Bed and Breakfast	21 Cant Crescent, St Andrews, Fife, KY16 8NF	01334 470867	★★★★	Bed & Breakfast
Bell Craig	8 Murray Park, St Andrews, Fife, KY16 9AW	01334 472962	★★★	Guest House
Beveridge House	25 North Street, St Andrews, Fife, KY16 9PW	01334 477 453	★★★	Bed & Breakfast
Braeside House	25 Nelson Street, St Andrews, Fife, KY16 8AJ	01334 473375	★★★★	Bed & Breakfast
Brooksby House	Queens Terrace, St Andrews, Fife, KY16 9ER	01334 470723	★★★★★	Guest House
Brownlees	7 Murray Place, St Andrews, Fife, KY16 9AP	01334 473868	★★★★	Guest House
Burness House	1 Murray Park, St Andrews, Fife, KY16 9AW	01334 474314	★★★★	Guest House
Cambo House	Kingsbarns, St Andrews, Fife, KY16 8QD	01333 450313	★★★★	Bed & Breakfast
Cameron House	11 Murray Park, St Andrews, Fife, KY16 9AW	01334 72306	★★★★	Guest House
Castlemount	The Scores, St Andrews, Fife, KY16 9AR	01334 475579	★★★★	Bed & Breakfast
Charlesworth House	9 Murray Place, St Andrews, Fife, KY16 9AP	01334 476528	★★★★	Guest House
Cleveden Guest House	3 Murray Place, St Andrews, Fife, KY16 9AP	01334 474212	★★★★	Guest House
Craigmore Guest House	3 Murray Park, St Andrews, Fife, KY16 9AW	01334 472142	★★★★	Guest House
Deveron House	64 North Street, St Andrews, Fife, KY16 9AH	01334 473513	★★★	Guest House
Doune House	5 Murray Place, St Andrews, Fife, KY16 9AP	01334 475195	★★★★	Guest House
Drumtilly House	2 Drumcarrow Road, St Andrews, Fife, KY16 8SE	01334 470954	★★★	Bed & Breakfast

Unassisted wheelchair access — Assisted wheelchair access — Access for visitors with mobility difficulties
Bronze Green Tourism Award — Silver Green Tourism Award — Gold Green Tourism Award
For further information on our Green Tourism Business Scheme please see page 9.

Ducks Crossing	5 Dempster Terrace, St Andrews, Fife, KY16 9QQ	01334 477010	★★★	Bed & Breakfast	
Fairnie House	10 Abbey Street, St Andrews, Fife, KY16 9LA	01334 474094	★★★	Bed & Breakfast	
Five Pilmour Place	North Street, St Andrews, Fife, KY16 9HZ	01334 478665	★★★★	Guest House	
Glenderran Guest House	9 Murray Park, St Andrews, Fife, KY16 9AW	01334 477951	★★★★	Guest House	
Hayston Farm	Balmullo, St Andrews, Fife, KY16 0AJ	01334 870210	★★★	Bed & Breakfast	
Hillwood House	Cameron, St Andrews, Fife, KY16 8PD	01334 840396	★★★	Bed & Breakfast	
Hoppity House	38 Market Street, St Andrews, Fife, KY16 9NT	01334 461192	★★★	Bed & Breakfast	
Jules House B&B	22 Lindsay Gardens, St Andrews, Fife, KY16 8XD	01334 472735	★★★	Bed & Breakfast	
Kinburn Guest House	5 Kinburn Place, Double Dykes Road, St Andrews, Fife, KY16 9DT	01334 474711	★★★★	Bed & Breakfast	
Little Carron Cottage	St Andrews, Fife, KY16 8QN	01334 474039	★★★★	Bed & Breakfast	
Lorimer House	19 Murray Park, St Andrews, Fife, KY16 9AW	01334 476599	★★★★	Guest House	
McIntosh Hall	Abbotsford Crescent, St Andrews, Fife, KY16 9HT	01334 467000	★★	Campus	
Millhouse	2 Cauldside Farm Steading, St Andrews, Fife, KY16 9TY	01334 850557	★★★★	Bed & Breakfast	
Milton Lea B&B	by Balmullo, St Andrews, Fife, KY16 0AB	05602 988677	★★★★	Bed & Breakfast	
Montague House	21 Murray Park, St Andrews, Fife, KY16 9AW	01334 479 287	★★★	Guest House	
Nethan House	17 Murray Park, St Andrews, Fife, KY16 9AW	01334 472104	★★★★	Guest House	Silver Green Tourism Award
Ogstons on North Street	127 North Street, St Andrews, Fife, KY16 9AG	01334 473387	★★★	Inn	
Old Fishergate House	North Castle Street, St Andrews, Fife, KY16 9BG	01334 470874	★★★★	Bed & Breakfast	
Pitmilly West Lodge	Kingsbarns, St Andrews, Fife, KY16 8QA	01334 880581	★★★★	Bed & Breakfast	Access for visitors with mobility difficulties
Shandon House	10 Murray Place, St Andrews, Fife, KY16 9AP	01334 472412	★★★	Guest House	
Spinkieden	13 Cairnsden Gardens, St Andrews, Fife, KY16 8SQ	01334 475303	★★★	Bed & Breakfast	
Spinkstown Farmhouse	St Andrews, Fife, KY16 8PN	01334 473475	★★★★	Bed & Breakfast	
St Nicholas	East Sands, St Andrews, Fife, KY16 8LD	01334 473090	★★★	Bed & Breakfast	
Stravithie Castle	Stravithie, St Andrews, Fife, KY16 8LT	01334 880251	★★★	Bed & Breakfast	
The Grange Inn	Grange Road, St Andrews, Fife, KY16 8LJ	01334 472670	★★★	Restaurant with Rooms	
The Inn At Lathones	By Largoward, St Andrews, Fife, KY9 1JE	01334 840494	★★★★	Inn	
The New Inn	21 - 23 St Marys Street, St Andrews, Fife, KY16 8AZ	01334 461333	★★★	Inn	
The Old Station, Country Guest House	Stratvithie Bridge, St Andrews, Fife, KY16 8LR	01334 880505	★★★★	Guest House	Unassisted wheelchair access
The West Port	170 South Street, St Andrews, Fife, KY16 9EG	01334 473186	★★★	Inn	
The White Lodge	94 Hepburn Gardens, St Andrews, Fife, KY16 9LN	01334 475710	★★★★★	Bed & Breakfast	
Vardon House	22 Murray Park, St Andrews, Fife, KY16 9AW	01334 475787	★	Bed & Breakfast	

Unassisted wheelchair access · Assisted wheelchair access · Access for visitors with mobility difficulties
Bronze Green Tourism Award · Silver Green Tourism Award · Gold Green Tourism Award

For further information on our Green Tourism Business Scheme please see page 9.

Vicarsford Lodge	St Michaels, St Andrews, Fife, KY16 0DT	01334 834356	★★★	Bed & Breakfast	
West Acre Guest House	2 West Acre, St Andrews, Fife, KY16 9UD	01334 476720	★★★★	Bed & Breakfast	
Yorkston House	68-70 Argyle Street, St Andrews, Fife, KY16 9BU	01334 472019	★★★	Guest House	

By St Andrews

Anvil Cottage B&B	Radernie, By St Andrews, Fife, KY15 5LN	01334 840824	★★★★	Bed & Breakfast	
Barnhay	Kinaldy Meadows, By St Andrews, Fife, KY16 8NA	01334 477791	★★★★	Bed & Breakfast	
Edenside House	Edenside, By St Andrews, Fife, KY16 9QS	0133483 8108	★★★	Guest House	
Pinewood Country House	Tayport Road, St Michaels, By St Andrews, Fife, KY16 0DU	01334 839860	★★★★	Guest House	

St Boswells, Melrose

Clint Lodge Country House	Clinthill, St Boswells, Melrose, Roxburghshire, TD6 0DZ	01835 822027	★★★★	Guest House	
Mainhill	St Boswells, Melrose, Roxburghshire, TD6 0HG	01835 823788	★★★	Bed & Breakfast	
Whitehouse	St Boswells, Melrose, Roxburghshire, TD6 OED	01573 460343	★★★★★	Bed & Breakfast	

St Catherines

Thistle House	St Catherines, Argyll, PA25 8AZ	01499 302209	AWAITING GRADING		

St Fillans

Achray Cottage	St Fillans, Perthshire, PH6 2NF	01764 685383	★★★	Bed & Breakfast	

St. Margarets Hope

Westend B&B	Front Road, St. Margarets Hope, Orkney, KW17 2SL	01856 831877	★★★	Bed & Breakfast	
St. Margarets Cottage Bed & Breakfast	Church Road, St. Margarets Hope, Orkney, KW17 2SR	01856 831637	★★★	Bed & Breakfast	

St Michaels, by St Andrews

Pinewood Country House	Tayport Road, ST Michaels,by St Andrews, Fife, KY16 0DU	01334 839860	★★★★	Guest House	

Strathkinness, by St. Andrews

Bramley House	10 Bonfield Road, Strathkinness, by St. Andrews, Fife, KY16 9RP	01334 850362	AWAITING GRADING		
Hawthorne House	33 Main Street, Strathkinness, by St. Andrews, Fife, KY16 9RY	01334 850855	★★★★	Bed & Breakfast	
Mansedale House	35 Main Street, Strathkinness, by St. Andrews, Fife, KY16 9RY	01334 850850	★★★★	Bed & Breakfast	
Newton of Nydie Farmhouse	Strathkinness, by St. Andrews, Fife, KY16 9SL	01334 850204	★★★	Bed & Breakfast	
The Paddock	Sunnyside, Strathkinness, by St. Andrews, Fife, KY16 9XP	01334 850888	★★★★	Bed & Breakfast	Silver Green Tourism Award

Staffin, Isle of Skye

Gairloch View	3 Digg, Staffin, Isle of Skye, Inverness-shire, IV51 9LA	01470 562718	★★★	Bed & Breakfast	
Glenview	Culnacnoc, Staffin, Isle of Skye, Inverness-shire, IV51 9JH	01470 562248	★★	Restaurant with Rooms	

Unassisted wheelchair access — Assisted wheelchair access — Access for visitors with mobility difficulties
Bronze Green Tourism Award — Silver Green Tourism Award — Gold Green Tourism Award
For further information on our Green Tourism Business Scheme please see page 9.

Stein, Waternish, Isle of Skye

Stein Inn	MacLeods Terrace, Stein, Waternish, Isle of Skye, Inverness-shire, IV55 8GA	01470 592362	★★★	Inn	Gold Green Tourism Award

Stenness

Mill of Eyrland	Stenness, Orkney, KW16 3HA	01856 850136	★★★★	Bed & Breakfast

Stevenston

Ardeer Steading	Ardeer Mains Farm, Stevenston, Ayrshire, KA20 3DD	01294 465438	★★★★	Farmhouse

Stirling

10 Gladstone Place	Stirling, Stirlingshire, FK8 2NN	01786 472681	★★★★	Bed & Breakfast
14 Melville Terrace	Stirling, Stirlingshire, FK8 2NE	01786 475361	★★★	Bed & Breakfast
20 Manse Crescent	Stirling, Stirlingshire, FK7 9AJ	01786 463264	★★★	Bed & Breakfast
27 King Street	Stirling, Stirlingshire, FK8 1DN	01786 471082	★★	Bed & Breakfast
5 Randolph Terrace	Stirling, Stirlingshire, FK7 9AA	01786 472454	★★★	Bed & Breakfast
9 Glebe Crescent	Stirling, Stirlingshire, FK8 2JB	01786 473433	★★★	Bed & Breakfast
9 Maitland Crescent	St Ninians, Stirling, Stirlingshire, FK7 0DN	01786 474707	★★★	Bed & Breakfast
Alberts	10 Hillfoots Road, Causewayhead, Stirling, Stirlingshire, FK9 5LF	01786 478728	★	Bed & Breakfast
Allerton	75 Newhouse , Stirling, Stirlingshire, FK8 2AF	01786 465677	★★★	Bed & Breakfast
Barnsdale House	19 Barnsdale Road, St Ninians, Stirling, Stirlingshire, FK7 0PT	01786 461729	★★★	Bed & Breakfast
Brockville B&B	8 Deroran Place, Stirling, Stirlingshire, FK8 2PG	01786 475225	★★★	Bed & Breakfast
Burns View	1 Albert Place, Stirling, Stirlingshire, FK8 2QL	01786 451002	★★★	Guest House
Castlecroft Guest House	Ballengiech Road, Stirling, Stirlingshire, FK8 1TN	01786 474933	★★★	Guest House
Craigard	40 Causewayhead Road, Stirling, Stirlingshire, FK9 5EY	01786 460540	★★★	Bed & Breakfast
Craigquarter Farm	Stirling, Stirlingshire, FK7 9QP	01786 812668	★★★★	Farmhouse
Cressington	34 Causewayhead Road, Stirling, Stirlingshire, FK9 5EU	01786 462435	★★★	Bed & Breakfast
Firgrove	13 Clifford Road, Stirling, Stirlingshire, FK8 2AQ	01786 475805	★★★★	Bed & Breakfast
Forth Guest House	23 Forth Place, Riverside, Stirling, Stirlingshire, FK8 1UD	01786 471020	★★★★	Guest House
Garfield Guest House	12 Victoria Square, Stirling, Stirlingshire, FK8 2QZ	01786 473730	★★★	Guest House
Linden Guest House	22 Linden Avenue, Stirling, Stirlingshire, FK7 7PQ	01786 448850	★★★★	Guest House
Munro Guest House	14 Princes Street, Stirling, Stirlingshire, FK8 1HQ	01786 472685	★★★	Guest House
Neidpath B&B	24 Linden Avenue, Stirling, Stirlingshire, FK7 7PQ	01786 469017	★★★	Bed & Breakfast
No 31 Kenningknowes Road	Kenningknowes Road, Stirling, Stirlingshire, FK7 9JF	01786 475511	★★	Bed & Breakfast
OSTA	78 Upper Craigs, Stirling, Stirlingshire, FK8 2DT	01786 430890	★★★★	Restaurant with Rooms

Unassisted wheelchair access   Assisted wheelchair access   Access for visitors with mobility difficulties
Bronze Green Tourism Award   Silver Green Tourism Award   Gold Green Tourism Award
For further information on our Green Tourism Business Scheme please see page 9.

Queen's Guest House	26 Queen Street, Stirling, Stirlingshire, FK8 1HN	01786 471043	★★	Bed & Breakfast
Southfield	2 Melville Terrace, Stirling, Stirlingshire, FK8 2ND	01786 464872	★★★	Bed & Breakfast
St Alma	37 Causewayhead Road, Stirling, Stirlingshire, FK9 5EG	01786 465795	★★	Guest House
The Cottage	24 Park Place, Stirling, Stirlingshire, FK7 9JR	01786 478246	★★★	Bed & Breakfast
The Haven	24 Causewayhead Road, Stirling, Stirlingshire, FK9 5EU	01786 464060	★★★	Bed & Breakfast
The Old Tram House	42 Causeway Head Road, Stirling, Stirlingshire, FK9 5EY	01786 449774	★★★★	Bed & Breakfast
The Portcullis	Castle Wynd, Stirling, Stirlingshire, FK8 1AG	01786 472290	★★★	Inn
The Whitehouse	13 Glasgow Road, Stirling, Stirlingshire, FK7 0PA	01786 462636	★★★	Guest House
West Plean House	Denny Road, Stirling, Stirlingshire, FK7 8HA	01786 812208	★★★★	Bed & Breakfast

Stonehaven

Bayview B&B	1 Bayview Apartments, Beachgate, Stonehaven, Aberdeenshire, AB39 2BD	01569 766933	★★★★	Bed & Breakfast
Beachgate House	Beachgate Lane, Stonehaven, Kincardineshire, AB39 2BD	01569 763155	★★★★	Bed & Breakfast
Beachview B&B	7 Salmon Lane, Stonehaven, Kincardineshire, AB39 2NZ	01569 765267	★★★	Bed & Breakfast
Cardowan B&B	31 Slug Road, Stonehaven, Kincardineshire, AB39 2DU	01569 762759	★★★★	Bed & Breakfast
Dunnottar Mains Farm	Stonehaven, Kincardineshire, AB39 2TL	01569 762621	★★★★	Farmhouse
Gleniffer	15 Arduthie Road, Stonehaven, Aberdeenshire, AB39 2EH	01569 765272	★★★★	Bed & Breakfast
Johnston Lodge	26 Ann Street, Stonehaven, Aberdeenshire, AB39 2DA	01569 763586	★★★	Bed & Breakfast
Pitgaveny	Baird Street, Stonehaven, Aberdeenshire, AB39 2SP	01569 764719	★★★★	Bed & Breakfast
Station Hotel	Arduthie Road, Stonehaven, Kincardineshire, AB39 2NE	01569 762277	★★	Inn
Tewel Farmhouse	Stonehaven, Kincardineshire, AB39 3UU	01569 762306	★★	Farmhouse
The Ship Inn	5 Shore Head, Stonehaven, Aberdeen-Shire, AB39 2JY	01569 762 617	★★	Inn
Woodside of Glasslaw	Stonehaven, Aberdeenshire, AB39 3XQ	01569 763799	★★★	Guest House

By Stonehaven

Ambleside B&B	Ambleside, Netherley, By Stonehaven, Aberdeenshire, AB39 3RB	01569 731 105	★★★	Bed & Breakfast
Upper Crawton	Catterline, By Stonehaven, Kincardineshire, AB39 2TU	01569 750243	★★★	Bed & Breakfast

Stornoway, Lewis

26 Newton Street	Stornoway, Lewis, Isle of Lewis, HS1 2RE	01851 702824	★★★	Bed & Breakfast
Braighe House	20 Braighe Road, Stornoway, Lewis, Isle of Lewis, HS2 0BQ	01851 705287	★★★★★	Guest House
Fernlea	9 Matheson Road, Stornoway, Lewis, Isle of Lewis, HS1 2NQ	01851 702125	★★★★	Bed & Breakfast
Hal-O The Wynd	2 Newton Street, Stornoway, Lewis, Isle of Lewis, HS1 2RE	01851 706073	★★★	Guest House
Hebridean Guest House	61 Bayhead, Stornoway, Lewis, Isle of Lewis, HS1 2DZ	01851 702268	★★★	Guest House

Unassisted wheelchair access   Assisted wheelchair access   Access for visitors with mobility difficulties
Bronze Green Tourism Award   Silver Green Tourism Award   Gold Green Tourism Award
For further information on our Green Tourism Business Scheme please see page 9.

Jannel	5 Stewart Drive, Stornoway, Lewis, Isle of Lewis, HS1 2TU	01851 700100	★★★★	Bed & Breakfast
Lathamor	Bakers Road, Stornoway, Lewis, Isle of Lewis, HS2 0EA	01851 706093	★★★	Bed & Breakfast
Leumadair Guest House	7 Callanish, Stornoway, Lewis, Isle of Lewis, HS2 9DY	01857 621706	★★★★	Guest House
Number Six	Memorial Avenue, Stornoway, Lewis, Isle of Lewis, HS1 2QR	01851 703014	★★★★	Guest House
Primrose Villa	31 Lewis Street, Stornoway, Lewis, Isle of Lewis, HS1 2JL	01851 703387	★★	Bed & Breakfast
Sula Sgeir	6A Sand Street, Stornoway, Lewis, Isle of Lewis, HS1 2UE	01851 705893	★★★	Bed & Breakfast
The Croft House	6A Perceval Road, Stornoway, Lewis, Isle of Lewis, HS1 2UG	01851 701889	★★★	Bed & Breakfast
Westwinds	34 Newton Street, Stornoway, Lewis, Isle of Lewis, HS1 2RW	01851 703408	★★★	Bed & Breakfast

Strachur

Carraway	Old School Road, Strachur, Argyll & Bute, PA27 8DH	01369 860423	★★	Bed & Breakfast

Stranraer

Balyett House B&B	Cairnryan Road, Stranraer, Wigtownshire, DG9 8QL	0776 703395	★★★	Bed & Breakfast
Barnhills Farm	Kirkcolm, Stranraer, Wigtownshire, DG9 0QG	01776 853236	★★★★	Bed & Breakfast
Crosshaven Guest House	Lewis Street, Stranraer, Wigtownshire, DG9 7AL	01776 700598	★★★	Bed & Breakfast
Fernlea	Lewis Street, Stranraer, Wigtownshire, DG9 7AQ	01776 703037	★★★	Bed & Breakfast
Glenotter	Leswalt Road, Stranraer, Wigtownshire, DG9 0EP	01776 703199	★★★★	Bed & Breakfast
Harbour Guest House	11 Market Street, Stranraer, Wigtownshire, DG9 7RF	01776 704626	★★★	Guest House
Harbour Lights Guest House	7 Agnew Crescent, Stranraer, Wigtownshire, DG9 7JY	01776 706261	★★★	Guest House
Ivy House & Ferry Link	London Road, Stranraer, Wigtownshire, DG9 8ER	01776 704176	★★★	Guest House
Kildonan	Lochview Road, Stranraer, Wigtownshire, DG9 8HP	01776 704186	★★★★	Bed & Breakfast
Southpark Bed & Breakfast	London Road, Stranraer, Wigtownshire, DG9 8AD	01776 889706	★★	Bed & Breakfast
East Muntloch Croft B&B	Cairngaan Road, Drummore, Stranraer, Dumfries & Galloway, DG9 9HN	01776 840264	★★★★	Bed & Breakfast

By Stranraer

East Challoch Farmhouse	Dunragit, By Stranraer, Dumfries & Galloway, DG9 8PY	01581 400391	★★★	Farmhouse

Strath, Gairloch

Newton House	Mihol Road, Strath, Gairloch, Ross-shire, IV21 2BX	01445 712007	★★★★	Bed & Breakfast
Tregurnow	57 Lonemore, Strath, Gairloch, Ross-Shire, IV21 2DB	01445 712116	★★★★	Bed & Breakfast

Strathaven

Rissons at Springvale	18 Lethame Road, Strathaven, Lanarkshire, ML10 6AD	01357 521131	★★★	Restaurant with Rooms 🚶
The Steading	East Coldstream, Strathaven, Lanarkshire, ML10 6SU	01357 522326	★★★	Bed & Breakfast
The Sheiling	Lesmahagow Road, Strathaven, Lanarkshire, ML10 6DA	01357 520477	★★	Bed & Breakfast

♿ Unassisted wheelchair access   Assisted wheelchair access   🚶 Access for visitors with mobility difficulties
Bronze Green Tourism Award   Silver Green Tourism Award   Gold Green Tourism Award
For further information on our Green Tourism Business Scheme please see page 9.

Strathdon

The Colquhonnie House Hotel	Strathdon, Aberdeenshire, AB36 8UN	01975 651210	★★★	Inn	Bronze Green Tourism Award
Auld Cummerton	Glen Nochty, Bellabeg, Strathdon, Aberdeenshire, AB36 8UP	01975 651337	★★★★★	Bed & Breakfast	

Strathpeffer

Birch Lodge	Strathpeffer, Ross-shire, IV14 9BA	01997 420118	★★★	Bed & Breakfast
Craigvar	The Square, Strathpeffer, Ross-shire, IV14 9DL	01997 421622	★★★★	Bed & Breakfast
Garden House	Garden House Brae, Strathpeffer, Ross-shire, IV14 9BJ	01997 421242	★★★	Guest House
White Lodge	The Square, Strathpeffer, Ross-shire, IV14 9AL	01997 421730	★★★★	Bed & Breakfast

Strathtay

Bendarroch House	Strathtay, Perthshire, PH9 0PG	01887 840420	★★★	Guest House
Dundarave Guest House	Dundarave, Strathtay, Perthshire, PH9 0PG	01887 840277	★★★★	Guest House
Creagan House	Callander, Strathyre, Perthshire, FK18 8ND	01877 384638	★★★★★	Restaurant with Rooms

Stromness

45 John Street	Stromness, Orkney, KW16 3AD	01856 850949	★★★	Bed & Breakfast	
Asgard	Cairston Road, Stromness, Orkney, KW16 3JS	01856 851699	★★★★	Bed & Breakfast	
Burnmouth	Cairston Road, Stromness, Orkney, KW16 3JS	01856 850186	★★	Bed & Breakfast	
Ferry Inn	John Street, Stromness, Orkney, KW16 3AA	01856 850280	★★	Inn	
Ferrybank	2 North End Road, Stromness, Orkney, KW16 3AG	01856 851250	★★★★	Bed & Breakfast	
Lindisfarne	Stromness, Orkney, KW16 3LL	01856 850 828	★★★	Bed & Breakfast	
Millers House & Harbourside B&B	7 & 13 John Street, Stromness, Orkney, KW16 3AD	01856 851969	★★★	Guest House	Silver Green Tourism Award
Olnadale	Innertown, Stromness, Orkney, KW16 3JW	01856 850418	★★★	Bed & Breakfast	
Orca Guest House	76 Victoria Street, Stromness, Orkney, KW16 3BS	01856 850447	★★	Guest House	
Quoydale	Hoy, Stromness, Orkney, KW16 3NJ	01856 791315	★★★	Bed & Breakfast	
Thira	Innertown, Stromness, Orkney, KW16 3JP	01856 851181	★★★★	Bed & Breakfast	

Strontian, By Acharacle

Otterburn B&B	Strontian, Strontian, By Acharacle, Argyll, PH36 4HZ	01967 402138	★★★★	Bed & Breakfast
Heatherbank	Upper Scotstown, Strontian, By Acharacle, Argyll, PH36 4JB	01967 402201	★★★★	Guest House

Struan, Isle of Skye

Glenside	4 Lower Totarder, Struan, Isle of Skye, Inverness-shire, IV56 8FW	01470 572253	★★★	Bed & Breakfast
Grianan	One Balmeanach, Struan, Isle of Skye, Inverness-shire, IV56 8FH	01470 572374	★★★	Bed & Breakfast
The Old Byre	Ose, Struan, Isle of Skye, Inverness-shire, IV56 8FJ	01470 572730	★★★	Bed & Breakfast

Unassisted wheelchair access · Assisted wheelchair access · Access for visitors with mobility difficulties
Bronze Green Tourism Award · Silver Green Tourism Award · Gold Green Tourism Award
For further information on our Green Tourism Business Scheme please see page 9.

Ullinish Country Lodge	Struan, Isle of Skye, Inverness-shire, IV56 8FD	01470 572214	★★★★★	Restaurant with Rooms	
Swinton					
The Wheatsheaf at Swinton	Main Street, Swinton, Berwickshire, TD11 3JJ	01890 860257	★★★★	Restaurant with Rooms	[Unassisted wheelchair access]
Tain					
Carringtons	Morangie Road, Tain, Ross-shire, IV19 1PY	01862 892635	★★★	Bed & Breakfast	
Cartomie	Edderton, Tain, Ross-shire, IV19 1LB	01862 821599	★★★	Bed & Breakfast	
Dunbius Guest House	Morangie Road, Tain, Ross-shire, IV19 1HP	01862 894902	★★★	Guest House	
Golf View Guest House	13 Knockbreck Road, Tain, Ross-shire, IV19 1BN	01862 892856	★★★★	Guest House	
Morangie B&B	Morangie Road, Tain, Ross-shire, IV19 1PY	01862 893855	★★★	Bed & Breakfast	
Edderton Inn	Station Road, Edderton, Tain, Ross-shire, IV19 1LB	01862 821588	★★★	Inn	[Assisted wheelchair access]
Talmine					
Cloisters	Church Holme, Talmine, Sutherland, IV27 4YP	01847 601286	★★★★	Bed & Breakfast	[Assisted wheelchair access]
Tarbert, Argyll					
Ardglass	Garvel Road, Tarbert, Argyll, PA29 6TR	01880 820884	★★★	Bed & Breakfast	
Dunivaig B&B	Pier Road, Tarbert, Argyll, PA29 6UG	01880 820896	★★★	Bed & Breakfast	
Barr Na Criche	Tarbert, Argyll, PA29 6YA	01880 820833	★★★	Bed & Breakfast	
Rhu House	Tarbert, Argyll, PA29 6YF	01880 820231	★★★	Bed & Breakfast	
Struan House B&B	Harbour Street, Tarbert, Argyll, PA29 6UD	01880 820190	★★★★	Bed & Breakfast	
By Tarbert, Argyll					
Dunultach	Clachan, by Tarbert, Argyll, PA29 6XW	01880 740650	★★★★	Bed & Breakfast	
Kilberry Inn	Kilberry, by Tarbert, Argyll, PA29 6YD	01880 770223	★★★★	Restaurant with Rooms	
Tarbert, Isle of Harris					
Langracleit	Kendebig, Tarbert, Isle of Harris, Western Isles, HS3 3HQ	01859 502413	★★★	Bed & Breakfast	
Ceol Na Mara Guest House	7 Direclete, Tarbert, Isle of Harris, Western Isles, HS3 3DP	01859 502464	★★★★	Guest House	[Bronze Green Tourism Award]
Avalon	12 West Side, Tarbert, Isle of Harris, Western Isles, HS3 3BG	01859 502334	★★★★	Bed & Breakfast	
Hill Crest	Leachkin, Tarbert, Isle of Harris, Western Isles, HS3 3AH	01859 502119	★★★★	Bed & Breakfast	
MacLeod Motel	Manse Road, Tarbert, Isle of Harris, Western Isles, HS3 3DJ	01859 502364	AWAITING GRADING		
Tarbert, Loch Lomond					
Aye Servus	Tyneloan, Tarbert, Loch Lomond, Argyll, G83 7DD	01301 702819	★★★	Bed & Breakfast	
Ballyhennan Old Toll House	Arrochar, Tarbert, Dumbartonshire, G83 7DA	01301 702203	★★★	Bed & Breakfast	
Lochview	Arrochar, Tarbert, Dunbartonshire, G83 7DD	01301 702200	★★	Bed & Breakfast	

Unassisted wheelchair access — Assisted wheelchair access — Access for visitors with mobility difficulties
Bronze Green Tourism Award — Silver Green Tourism Award — Gold Green Tourism Award
For further information on our Green Tourism Business Scheme please see page 9.

Stewart House	Bemersyde, Tarbert, Dunbartonshire, G83 7DE	01301 702230	★★★	Bed & Breakfast
Bon-Etive	Arrochar, Tarbert, Dunbartonshire, G83 7DF	01301 702219	★★★	Bed & Breakfast

Taynuilt

Cruailinn	Glenlonan Road, Taynuilt, Argyll, PA35 1HY	01866 822351	★★★	Bed & Breakfast
Tanglewood Lodge Bed and Breakfast	Tanglewood, Otter Creek, Taynuilt, Argyll, PA35 1HP	01866 822114	★★★★	Bed & Breakfast
Taynuilt Hotel	Main Road, Taynuilt, Argyll, PA35 1JN	01866 822437	★★★	Inn

by Taynuilt

Roineabhal Country House	Kilchrenan, by Taynuilt, Argyll, PA35 1HD	01866 833207	★★★★	Bed & Breakfast

Tayport

Forgan B&B	23 Castle Street, Tayport, Fife, DD6 9AE	01382 552682	★★★	Bed & Breakfast
Kirkton Barns	Tayport, Fife, DD6 9PD	01382 554402	★★★★	Bed & Breakfast
Tayport B&B	27A Queen Street, Tayport, Fife, DD6 9JZ	01382 552272	★★★	Bed & Breakfast

The Oa, Isle of Islay

Samhchair	The Oa, Isle of Islay, Argyll, PA42 7AX	01496 302596	★★★★	Bed & Breakfast

Thornhill, Dumfriesshire

Buccleuch & Queensberry Hotel	112 Drumlanrig Street, Thornhill, Dumfriesshire, DG3 5LU	01848 330215	★★★	Inn
The Thornhill Inn	103-106 Drumlanrig Street, Thornhill, Dumfriesshire, DG3 5LU	01848 330326	★★★	Inn
The Old Shop	Carsethorn, Thornhill, Dumfriesshire, DG2 8DS	01387 880799	★★★	Bed & Breakfast

Thornhill, Stirling

Easter Tarr Farmhouse	Thornhill, Stirling, Stirlingshire, FK8 3LD	01786 850225	★★★	Bed & Breakfast
The Granary	West Moss-side, Thornhill, Stirling, Stirlingshire, FK8 3QJ	01786 850310	★★★★	Bed & Breakfast

Thurso

1 Granville Crescent	Thurso, Caithness, KW14 7NP	01847 892993	★★★★	Bed & Breakfast
9 Couper Street	Thurso, Caithness, KW14 8AR	01847 894529	★★★	Bed & Breakfast
Annandale	2 Rendel Govan Road, Thurso, Caithness, KW14 7EP	01847 893942	★★★★	Bed & Breakfast
Holborn Hotel	Princess Street, Thurso, Caithness, KW14 7JA	01847 892771	★★	Inn
Lau-ren House	Barrock, Thurso, Caithness, KW14 8SY	01847 851717	★★★	Bed & Breakfast
Murray House	1 Campbell Street, Thurso, Caithness, KW14 7HD	01847 895759	★★★	Bed & Breakfast
Pentland Lodge House	Granville Street, Thurso, Caithness, KW14 7JN	01847 895103	★★★★	Guest House
Sheigra	6 Macdonald Green, Thurso, Caithness, KW14 7EL	01847 892559	★★★	Bed & Breakfast
Skara	Dixonfield, Thurso, Caithness, KW14 8YN	01847 890062	★★★	Bed & Breakfast

Unassisted wheelchair access · Assisted wheelchair access · Access for visitors with mobility difficulties
Bronze Green Tourism Award · Silver Green Tourism Award · Gold Green Tourism Award
For further information on our Green Tourism Business Scheme please see page 9.

Straven	Haimer, Thurso, Caithness, KW14 8YN	01847 893850	★★★	Bed & Breakfast	
The Old Inn	Reay, Thurso, Caithness, KW14 7RE	01847 811554	★★★	Bed & Breakfast	

by Thurso

Creag-Na-Mara	East Mey, by Thurso, Caithness, KW14 8XL	01847 851850	AWAITING GRADING		Bronze Green Tourism Award
Sharvedda	Strathy Point, by Thurso, Caithness, KW14 7RY	01641 541311	★★★★	Bed & Breakfast	
The Ferry Inn	Scrabster, Nr Thurso, Caithness, KW14 7UJ	01847 892814	★★★	Inn	

Tighnabruaich

Kames Hotel	Kames, Tighnabruaich, Argyll, PA21 2AF	01700 811489	★★★	Inn	
Tregortha	Tighnabruaich, Argyll, PA21 2BD	01700 811132	★★★	Bed & Breakfast	

Tillicoultry

Bramble Cottage	22 Marchglen, Tillicoultry, Clackmannanshire, FK13 6BU	01259 751341	★★★	Bed & Breakfast	
Westbourne	10 Dollar Road, Tillicoultry, Clackmannanshire, FK13 6PA	01259 750314	★★★	Bed & Breakfast	
Wyvis	70 Stirling Street, Tillicoultry, Clackmannanshire, FK13 6EA	01259 751513	★★★★	Bed & Breakfast	Bronze Green Tourism Award

Timsgarry, Isle of Lewis

Baile-Na-Cille	Timsgarry, Timsgarry, Isle of Lewis HS2 9SD	01851 672242	★★	Guest House	

Tingwall

Herrislea House	Veensgarth, Tingwall, Shetland, ZE2 9SB	01595 840208	★★★★	Restaurant with Rooms	Gold Green Tourism Award

Tobermory, Isle of Mull

Ach Na Circe Bed & Breakfast	Strongarbh, Tobermory, Isle of Mull, Argyll, PA75 6PR	01688 302527	★★	Bed & Breakfast	
Baliscate Guest House	Salen Road, Tobermory, Isle of Mull, Argyll, PA75 6QA	01688 302048	★★★	Guest House	
Brockville	Raeric Road, Tobermory, Isle of Mull, Argyll, PA75 6RS	01688 302741	★★★★	Bed & Breakfast	
Buel-na-Atha	11 West Street, Tobermory, Isle of Mull, Argyll, PA75 6QZ	01688 302560	★★★	Bed & Breakfast	
Carnaburg	55 Main Street, Tobermory, Isle of Mull, Argyll, PA75 6NT	01688 302479	★★	Guest House	
Copeland House	Viewmount Drive, Tobermory, Isle of Mull, Argyll, PA75 6PZ	01688 302049	★★★	Bed & Breakfast	
Cuidhe Leathain	Breadalbane Street , Tobermory, Isle of Mull, Argyll, PA75 6PD	01688 305204	★★★	Bed & Breakfast	
Failte Guest House	Main Street, Tobermory, Isle of Mull, Argyll, PA75 6NU	01688 302495	★★★	Guest House	
Fairways Lodge	Erray Road, Tobermory, Isle of Mull, Argyll, PA75 6PS	01688 302792	★★★	Guest House	
Fuaran	Raeric Road, Tobermory, Isle of Mull, Argyll, PA75 6PY	01688 302888	★★★	Bed & Breakfast	
Gramercy	Tobermory, Isle of Mull, Argyll, PA75 6QA	01688 302150	★★★	Bed & Breakfast	
Killoran House	Dervaig, Tobermory, Isle of Mull, Argyll, PA75 6QR	01688 400362	★★★★	Guest House	
Little Erray	Raeric Road, Tobermory, Isle of Mull, Argyll, PA75 6PU	01688 302363	★★★	Bed & Breakfast	

Unassisted wheelchair access · Assisted wheelchair access · Access for visitors with mobility difficulties
Bronze Green Tourism Award · Silver Green Tourism Award · Gold Green Tourism Award
For further information on our Green Tourism Business Scheme please see page 9.

Lonan	Western Road, Tobermory, Isle of Mull, Argyll, PA75 6RA	01688 302082	★★★	Bed & Breakfast
Oaklee	Erray Road, Tobermory, Isle of Mull, Argyll, PA75 6PS	01688 302520	★★★★	Bed & Breakfast
Ptarmigan House	The Fairways, Tobermory, Isle of Mull, Argyll, PA75 6PS	01688 302863	★★★★★	Bed & Breakfast
Staffa Cottages Bed & Breakfast	Breadalbane Lane, Tobermory, Isle of Mull, Argyll, PA75 6PL	01688 302464	★★	Bed & Breakfast
Strongarbh House	Strongarbh, Tobermory, Isle of Mull, Argyll, PA75 6PR	01688 302319	★★★★	Bed & Breakfast
Sunart View Guest House	Eas Brae, Tobermory, Isle of Mull, Argyll, PA75 6QA	01688 302439	★★★	Guest House

By Tobermory, Isle of Mull

Achnadrish House	Achnadrish Estate, By Tobermory, Isle of Mull, Argyll, PA75 6QF	01688 400388	★★★★	Bed & Breakfast
Glengorm Castle	By Tobermory, Isle of Mull, Argyll, PA75 6QE	01688 302321	★★★★	Bed & Breakfast
Ardbeg House	Dervaig, By Tobermory, Isle of Mull, Argyll, PA75 6QJ	01688 400254	★★★	Bed & Breakfast

Tolsta Chaolais, Isle of Lewis

Ten Tolsta Chaolais	10 Tolsta Chaolais, Tolsta Chaolais Isle of Lewis, Western Isles, HS2 9DW	01851 621722	★★★★	Bed & Breakfast

Tomintoul, Ballindalloch

Glen Avon Hotel	The Square, Tomintoul,Ballindalloch, Morayshire, AB37 9ET	01807 580218	★★	Inn
Findron Farmhouse	Braemar Road, Tomintoul,Ballindalloch, Morayshire, AB37 9ER	01807 580382	★★★	Bed & Breakfast

Tong, Isle of Lewis

Kearnaval	10 Tong, Tong Isle of Lewis, Western Isles, HS2 0HS	01851 702853	★★	Bed & Breakfast

Tongue

Rhian Cottage	Tongue, Sutherland, IV27 4FX	01847 611257	★★★	Guest House	Silver Green Tourism Award
	Tigh-Nan-Ubhal Guest House, Tongue, Sutherland, IV27 4XF	01847 611281	★★★	Bed & Breakfast	

Torloisk, Isle of Mull

The Old Mill	Achleck, Torloisk, Isle of Mull, Argyll, PA74 6NH	01688 500259	★★★	Bed & Breakfast

Torlundy, Fort William

Ferndale	Tomacharich, Torlundy, Fort William, Inverness-shire, PH33 6SP	01397 703593	★★★	Bed & Breakfast
Mayfield	Happy Valley, Torlundy, Fort William, Inverness-shire, PH33 6SN	01397 703 320	★★★★	Bed & Breakfast

Town Yetholm

Plough Hotel	Main Street, Town Yetholm, Roxburghshire, TD5 8RF	01573 420215	★	Inn

Tranent

47 Carlaverock Avenue	Tranent, East Lothian, EH33 2PW	01875 614008	★★	Bed & Breakfast
Rosebank Guest House	161 High Street, Tranent, East Lothian, EH33 1LP	01875 610967	★★★	Guest House
Schiehallion	1 Edinburgh Road, Tranent, East Lothian, EH33 1BA	01875 611224	★★★★	Bed & Breakfast

Unassisted wheelchair access · Assisted wheelchair access · Access for visitors with mobility difficulties
Bronze Green Tourism Award · Silver Green Tourism Award · Gold Green Tourism Award

For further information on our Green Tourism Business Scheme please see page 9.

Troon

Copper Beech	116 Bentinck Drive, Troon, Ayrshire, KA10 6JB	01292 314100	★★★★	Bed & Breakfast		
Fordell	43 Beach Road, Troon, Ayrshire, KA10 6SU	01292 313224	★★★	Bed & Breakfast		
No 54	Spey Road, Troon, Ayrshire, KA10 7DP	01292 314134	★	Bed & Breakfast		
Sandhill House	Southwood Road, Troon, Ayrshire, KA10 7EL	01292 311801	★★★★	Bed & Breakfast		
Tigh Dearg	31 Victoria Drive, Troon, Ayrshire, KA10 6JF	01292 311552	★★★	Bed & Breakfast		

By Troon

No 2 Troon Road	2 Troon Road, Loans, By Troon, Ayrshire, KA10 7EY	01292 679927	★★★★	Bed & Breakfast		

Turnberry

Links Lodge	9 Maidens Road, Turnberry, Ayrshire, KA26 9LS	01655 331546	★★★★	Bed & Breakfast		

Turriff

Deveron Lodge B&B Guesthouse	Bridgend Terrace, Turriff, Aberdeenshire, AB53 4ES	01888 563613	★★★★	Guest House	♿	Gold Green Tourism Award
Monydeen Enterprises	Monydeen, Meikle Whiterashes, Turriff, Aberdeenshire, AB53 5RA	07967 249223	★★★★	Bed & Breakfast		
The Gables	Station Road, Turriff, Aberdeen-shire, AB53 4ER	01888 568715	★★★	Bed & Breakfast		

Twynholm

Linthorpe	14 Arden Road, Twynholm, Dumfries and Galloway, DG6 4PB	01557 860662	AWAITING GRADING			

Tyndrum

Dalkell Cottages	Lower Station Road, Tyndrum, Perthshire, FK20 8RY	01838 400285	★★★	Guest House		
Glengarry House	Tyndrum, Perthshire, FK20 8RY	01838 400224	★★★	Guest House		
The Old Church	Dalrigh, Tyndrum, Perthshire, FK20 8RX	01838 400286	★★★	Bed & Breakfast		

Uddingston

Redstones Bar, Grill and Rooms	8-10 Glasgow Road, Uddingston, Lanarkshire, G71 7AS	01698 813774	★★★★	Restaurant with Rooms		

Uig, Isle of Skye

Braigh-Uige	Uig, Isle of Skye, Inverness-shire, IV51 9YB	01470 542228	★★★★	Bed & Breakfast		
Cuil Lodge	Cuil, Uig, Isle of Skye, Inverness-shire, IV51 9YB	01470 542216	★★★★	Bed & Breakfast		
Ferry Inn Hotel	Uig, Isle of Skye, Inverness-shire, IV51 9XP	01478 611216	★★★	Inn		
Suainaval	3 Cradhlastadh, Uig, Isle of Lewis HS2 9JF	01851 672386	★★★★	Bed & Breakfast		

Ullapool

3 Castle Terrace	Ullapool, Wester Ross, IV26 2XD	01854 612409	★★★	Bed & Breakfast		
3 Vyner Place	Morefield, Ullapool, Ross-shire, IV26 2XR	01854 612023	★★★★	Bed & Breakfast		

♿ Unassisted wheelchair access ♿ Assisted wheelchair access 🚶 Access for visitors with mobility difficulties
Bronze Green Tourism Award Silver Green Tourism Award Gold Green Tourism Award
For further information on our Green Tourism Business Scheme please see page 9.

Ardvreck Guest House	Morefield Brae, Ullapool, Ross-shire, IV26 2TH	01854 612028	★★★★	Guest House	
Broombank	4 Castle Terrace, Ullapool, Ross-shire, IV26 2XD	01854 612247	★★★	Bed & Breakfast	
Broomvale	26 Market Street, Ullapool, Ross-shire, IV26 2XE	01854 612559	★★★	Bed & Breakfast	
Chenoweth Bed and Breakfast	66 Strathkanaird, Ullapool, Ross-Shire, IV26 2TP	01854 666331	★★★	Bed & Breakfast	
Dromnan Guest House	Garve Road, Ullapool, Ross-shire, IV26 2SX	01854 612333	★★★★	Guest House	🚶
Eilean Donan Guest House	14 Market Street, Ullapool, Ross-shire, IV26 2XE	01854 612524	★★★	Guest House	
Essex Cottage	West Terrace, Ullapool, Ross-shire, IV26 2UU	01854 612663	★★	Bed & Breakfast	
Oakworth	Riverside Terrace, Ullapool, Ross-shire, IV26 2TE	01854 612290	★★★	Bed & Breakfast	
Point Cottage	22 West Shore Street, Ullapool, Ross-shire, IV26 2UR	01854 612494	★★★★	Guest House	
Riverside	Quay Street, Ullapool, Ross-shire, IV26 2UE	01854 612239	★★★	Guest House	
Riverview	2 Castle Terrace, Ullapool, Wester Ross, IV26 2XD	01854 612019	★★★	Bed & Breakfast	
Strathmore Guest House	Morefield, Ullapool, Ross-shire, IV26 2TH	01854 612423	★★★	Guest House	
Tamarin	9 Braes, Ullapool, Ross=shire, IV26 2SZ	01854 612667	★★★★	Bed & Breakfast	
The Ferry Boat Inn	Shore Street, Ullapool, Ross-Shire, IV26 2UJ	01854 612366	AWAITING GRADING		
Westlea Guest House	2 Market Street, Ullapool, Ross-shire, IV26 2XE	01854 612594	★★★★	Guest House	

Ulva Ferry, Isle of Mull

Torr Buan House	Ulva Ferry Isle of Mull, Argyll, PA73 6LY	01688 500121	★★★★	Bed & Breakfast	Gold Green Tourism Award

Unst

Buness House	Balta Sound, Unst, Shetland, ZE2 9DS	01957 711315	★★★★	Guest House
Gerratoun	Haroldswick, Unst, Shetland, ZE2 9EF	01957 711323	★★	Bed & Breakfast

Uphall, Broxburn

Oatridge Hotel	2-4 Main Street, Uphall, Broxburn, West Lothian, EH52 5DA	01506 856 465	★★	Inn

Upper Largo, Leven

Balhousie Farm	Upper Largo, Leven, Fife, KY8 5QN	01333 360680	★★★	Bed & Breakfast	
Bayview	Drumeldrie, Upper Largo, Fife, KY8 6JD	01333 360454	★★★★	Bed & Breakfast	🚶
Monturpie Guest House	Monturpie, Upper Largo, Fife, KY8 5QS	01333 360254	★★★	Guest House	

Uyeasound, Unst

Prestegaard	Uyeasound, Unst, Shetland, ZE2 9DL	01957 755234	★★★	Bed & Breakfast

Vidlin

Boatsroom B&B	Hamnavoe, Lunnaness, Vidlin, Shetland, ZE2 9QF	01806 577328	★★	Bed & Breakfast
Lunna House	Lunna, Vidlin, Shetland, ZE2 9QF	01806 577311	★★★	Bed & Breakfast

♿ Unassisted wheelchair access   Assisted wheelchair access   🚶 Access for visitors with mobility difficulties
Bronze Green Tourism Award   Silver Green Tourism Award   Gold Green Tourism Award
For further information on our Green Tourism Business Scheme please see page 9.

Walkerburn

The George Hotel	29 Galashiels Road, Walkerburn, Peebleshire, EH43 6AF	01896 870336	★★	Inn	
Windlestraw Lodge	Tweed Valley, Walkerburn, Peeblesshire, EH43 6AA	01896 870636	AWAITING GRADING		

Walls

Burrastow House	Walls, Shetland, ZE2 9PD	01595 809307	★★★★	Guest House	♿
Skeoverick	Bruna-Twatt, Walls, Shetland, ZE2 9PJ	01595 809349	★★★	Bed & Breakfast	

Weem, by Aberfeldy

Ailean Chraggan Hotel	Weem, by Aberfeldy , Perthshire, PH15 2LD	01887 820346	★★★	Inn	

West Calder

Limefield House	West Calder, West Lothian, EH55 8QL	01506 871237	★★★	Guest Accommodation	

West Kilbride

Millstonford House Bed & Breakfast	Millstonford House, West Kilbride, Ayrshire, KA23 9PS	01294 823430	★★★	Bed & Breakfast	

West Linton

Drochil Castle Farm	West Linton, Peeblesshire, EH46 7DD	01721 752249	★★★★	Bed & Breakfast	Assisted wheelchair access; Bronze Green Tourism Award
Ingraston Farm B&B	Ingraston Farm, West Linton, Peebleshire, EH46 7AA	01968 682219	★★★	Farmhouse	Access for visitors with mobility difficulties
Jerviswood	Linton Bank Drive, West Linton, Peeblesshire, EH46 7DT	01968 660429	★★	Bed & Breakfast	
Millburn House Bed & Breakfast	Dolphinton, West Linton, Peebleshire, EH46 7AF	01968 682252	★★★★	Bed & Breakfast	
The Meadows	4 Robinsland Drive, West Linton, Peeblesshire, EH46 7JD	01968 661798	★★★	Bed & Breakfast	

Westray

No1 Broughton	1 Broughton, Westray, Orkney, KW17 2DA	01857 677726	★★★★	Bed & Breakfast	

Whitebridge

Kinbrylie	Whitebridge, Inverness-shire, IV2 6UN	01456 486658	★★★★	Bed & Breakfast	Access for visitors with mobility difficulties

Whiting Bay, Isle of Arran

Eden Lodge	Whiting Bay, Isle of Arran, North Ayrshire, KA27 8QH	01770 700357	★★	Inn	
Ellangowan	Middle Road, Whiting Bay, Isle of Arran, North Ayrshire, KA27 8QH	01770 700784	★★★	Bed & Breakfast	
Invermay	Shore Road, Whiting Bay, Isle of Arran, North Ayrshire, KA27 8PZ	01770 700431	★★	Guest House	
Kindiarmid Bed & Breakfast	Kindiarmid, Whiting Bay, Isle of Arran, North Ayrshire, KA27 8QR	01770 700762	★★★★	Bed & Breakfast	
Mingulay	Middle Road, Whiting Bay, Isle of Arran, North Ayrshire, KA27 8QH	01770 700346	★★★	Bed & Breakfast	
The Burlington	Shore Road, Whiting Bay, Isle of Arran, North Ayrshire, KA27 8PZ	01770 700255	★★★	Guest House	
Viewbank House	Golf Course Road, Whiting Bay, Isle of Arran, North Ayrshire, KA27 8QT	01770 700326	★★★	Guest House	

♿ Unassisted wheelchair access   Assisted wheelchair access   Access for visitors with mobility difficulties
Bronze Green Tourism Award   Silver Green Tourism Award   Gold Green Tourism Award

For further information on our Green Tourism Business Scheme please see page 9.

By Whithorn

The Steam Packet Inn	Harbour Row, Isle of Whithorn, By Whithorn, Wigtownshire, DG8 8LL	01988 500334	★★	Inn
Craiglemine Cottage B&B	Glasserton, By Whithorn, Wigtownshire, DG8 8NE	01988 500594	★★	Bed & Breakfast

Wick

Bank House Bed & Breakfast	28 Bridge Street, Wick, Caithness, KW1 4NG	07721 656307	AWAITING GRADING	
Bayview	14 Port Dunbar, Wick, Caithness, KW1 4JJ	01955 604054	★★★	Bed & Breakfast
Belhaven	13 Portdunbar, Wick, Caithness, KW1 4JJ	01955 603411	★★★	Bed & Breakfast
Seaview Guest House	14 Scalesburn, Wick, Caithness, KW1 4JH	01955 602735	★★★	Bed & Breakfast
The Clachan	13 Randolph Place, South Road, Wick, Caithness, KW1 5NJ	01955 605384	★★★★	Bed & Breakfast

Wigtown

Craigenlee	8 Bank Street, Wigtown, Wigtownshire, DG8 9HP	01988 402498	★★	Bed & Breakfast
Hillcrest House	Maidland Place, Station Road, Wigtown, Wigtownshire, DG8 9EU	01988 402018	★★★	Guest House
Wigtown House	19 Bank Street, Wigtown, Wigtownshire, DG8 9HR	01988 402391	★★	Guest House

By Wigtown

The Old Coach House	34 Bladnoch, Bladnoch, By Wigtown, Wigtownshire, DG8 9AB	01988 402316	★★★	Bed & Breakfast
Bladnoch Inn	Main Street, Bladnoch, By Wigtown, Wigtownshire, DG8 9AB	01988 402200	★★	Inn

♿ Unassisted wheelchair access ♿ Assisted wheelchair access Access for visitors with mobility difficulties
Bronze Green Tourism Award Silver Green Tourism Award Gold Green Tourism Award
For further information on our Green Tourism Business Scheme please see page 9.